101 Best
BUSINESSES TO START

THIRD EDITION

The Philip Lief Group, Inc., and Russell Roberts

BROADWAY BOOKS

NEW YORK

101 BEST BUSINESSES TO START: THIRD EDITION Copyright © 2000 by
The Philip Lief Group. All rights reserved. Printed in the United States
of America. No part of this book may be reproduced or transmitted
in any form or by any means, electronic or mechanical, including
photocopying, recording, or by any information storage and
retrieval system, without written permission from the publisher.
For information, address: Broadway Books, 1540 Broadway,
New York, NY 10036.

Broadway Books titles may be purchased for business or
promotional use or for special sales. For information, please write to:
Special Markets Department, Random House, Inc.,
1540 Broadway, New York, NY 10036.

BROADWAY BOOKS and its logo, a letter B bisected on the diagonal, are
trademarks of Broadway Books, a division of Random House, Inc.

Designed by Chris Welch

Library of Congress Cataloging-in-Publication Data
The Philip Lief Group, Inc.
101 best businesses to start / The Philip Lief Group, Inc., and
Russell Roberts—3rd ed.
p.   cm.
Rev. ed. of: 101 best businesses to start / Sharon Kahn. Rev. ed. 1992.
1. Small business—Handbooks, manuals, etc.   2. New business
enterprises—Handbooks, manuals, etc.   3. Success in business—
Handbooks, manuals, etc.   I. Title: One hundred one best businesses to
start.   II. Philip Lief Group.   III. Roberts, Russell. 101 best businesses to
start.   IV. Title.
HD2341.K28 2000
658.1'141—dc21   99-058567

ISBN 0-7679-0659-4

00   01   02   03   04   10   9   8   7   6   5   4   3   2   1

Contents

Contents

Contents

Contents

HOUSEHOLD SERVICES

PERSONAL SERVICES

Contents

REAL ESTATE

RETAILING

Introduction to the Third Edition

One Hundred and One Best Businesses to Start will help you come up with the right idea for a business to meet your personal needs. To prosper, your start-up must fill a gap amid all those goods and services that bombard customers, and it must fill that gap for years to come. Some ideas for new businesses are tried and tested, and if competition is spare—or if you can offer an appealing twist on a theme—a business idea does not have to be completely original to fly. For example, while cooking and running errands have been around since time began, resourceful entrepreneurs have turned these activities into burgeoning business enterprises. Thanks to the ever-increasing demands on everyone's time, it is becoming commonplace to hire a personal chef to cook and a personal assistant to run errands.

Keep in mind that in choosing a business, it is essential to evaluate the needs of the community you hope to serve. Look at the local demographics and trends. The heightened public interest in preserving the environment is growing stronger and will be a vital concern in the 21st century. Entrepreneurial efforts tied to the national—and worldwide—commitment to preserve our environment have tremendous potential to grow and prosper in the coming years.

The third edition of *101 Best Businesses to Start* reflects the truth that change is the only constant. Even fields that already have experienced a major boom are now expanding in new directions. Due to the emergence of the Internet, the section on computers now has new entries on web page design and Internet consulting.

This book was designed to help you explore a wide range of opportunities and learn from the experience of seasoned entrepreneurs of the potential for success—as well as the challenges—you will face when you decide to launch your own business.

What It Takes to Succeed as an Independent Entrepreneur

Every business is nourished by a specific set of skills, of course, and our profiles detail the training and personality traits that each industry requires. However, in general, an entrepreneur needs the following traits:

- Self-confidence and assertiveness
- Boldness, courage, optimism, and the willingness to take controlled risks
- A capacity for hard work: discipline, diligence, and perfectionism
- Ambition, persistence, determination, and commitment to a goal

- Leadership ability, decisiveness, efficiency, and the ability to delegate authority
- Team spirit and concern for others
- An ability to solve problems: resourcefulness, inventiveness, and organizational aptitude
- Flexibility and adaptability
- Honesty, integrity, and a commitment to high standards of quality
- Street smarts, intelligence, and good judgment

Perhaps most important, you also must love your company. Can you picture yourself in the driver's seat for sixty to eighty hours a week? Will your family and others in your support system back you 100 percent of the time? "To succeed, pick something you love and are gifted at," suggests Jeannie Gehring, president of Slender Center diet service in Madison, Wisconsin. She, for one, remains "an adolescent in love. I love the advertising, accounting, nutrition, speaking, and counseling aspects of the business. I've never had a day I wasn't roaring to get to work."

CAPITAL

Virtually every entry in *101 Best Businesses to Start* provides an estimate of start-up costs. Some home-based businesses can begin with just a few thousand dollars, while others require hundreds of thousands to launch. Of course, the better capitalized businesses reach profitability faster (and are therefore more fun) than those that squeak by from day to day. When capital is scarce, entrepreneurs use a variety of ploys to hold down initial costs. "Learn to improvise and improve," says Erika

Zimmerman, whose Erika's Hair-U-M Inc. beauty shop operates from Darien, Illinois. For example, Dennis Sheaks bought
used equipment to outfit Joe Peep's New York Pizza. Donna
Porter says some of her best advertising at Playful Parenting of
Lancaster (Pennsylvania), a children's gym, comes from en-
rolling her tots in charity Olympics events. Personal assistant
Laura Cribbs made up small candy bouquets to pass out along
with her business card. Innumerable sole proprietorships operate from home until it's time to hire a second person. And many
businesses hire part-time or commission workers who receive
pay only when the work comes in the door.

To be on the safe side, overestimate your expenses and time
until breakeven and underestimate your profits. Don't forget to
factor in living costs. Most experts suggest socking away
enough savings to support your family for a full year, or securing another source of income, such as a working spouse might
provide, that can pay the household bills.

An accountant can help you project your business's expenses,
revenues, and cash flow. When calculating start-up and operating costs, make sure to include the following: the cost of leasing, buying, renovating, and building your place of business;
furniture, equipment, and supplies; gas, electric, water, and telephone utilities; garbage collection, janitorial, maintenance, and
extermination; inventory; payroll, professional dues, and continuing education; promotion and advertising; credit card fees;
licenses and permits; bad debt; taxes; and insurance.

Funding comes in as many guises as there are businesses. The
first place to look, of course, is your own savings. If you can
cover only part of your expenses from cashing in your pension
plan and raiding your bank book, approach friends and family.
Charles Grove, who designs $300,000 to $1 million miniature
golf courses, says it's not unusual for a young couple with

$42,000 to get into the business. "They get their in-laws involved, and a couple of neighbors put up money, which creates a viable financial base to approach the banks. Then the couple sets up a corporate structure with the provision that they can buy the others out."

Small-business owners rarely go beyond family and friends for financing. Commercial banks won't risk lending money to start-ups, although sometimes entrepreneurs can secure personal loans. The Small Business Administration once represented a ready lending source, although its kitty has dwindled in recent years.

Very large (and very promising) start-ups can sometimes approach venture capitalists and limited partners. Occasionally start-ups with massive potential convince investment bankers to float an initial public offering of their stock, enabling them to sell shares to public investors. However, even these funding sources expect the principals to pour substantial home-grown capital into the new business.

TO BUY OR START

Once you determine what sort of business you want, consider whether to buy a company or start from scratch. Both options have advantages and disadvantages: For better or worse, an ongoing business will have all its operating systems in place. You inherit either adept or incompetent employees along with either a ready-made clientele or customers who never seem to pay their bills. If you do your homework well, however, an ongoing business's operating history should give you an idea of future risks and profits.

Ironically, while buying an existing company may be more

costly than starting from your own base, you may need less cash initially. Most small-business purchases are leveraged buyouts, meaning the seller accepts a down payment and the buyer pays the remainder of the cost from the business's cash flow over three to five years. Thus, a $100,000 buyout may require just $33,000 in cash.

If you buy a reputable franchise, you eliminate even more of the risk since the parent company guides your every step. Some franchisors offer financing, and sometimes banks will loan against a franchise purchase. However, you not only sacrifice a percentage of your future profits, you also lose a degree of independence when signing on as a franchisee.

Starting from scratch is the scariest option. Those individuals who succeed with their own idea, however, shape every aspect of the business from store decor to corporate structure. Start-up costs are not as high since you pay neither a seller nor a franchisor.

CORPORATE STRUCTURE

For tax and legal purposes, you can set up a business in a number of ways. To limit your personal liability, you can incorporate. While the owner of an unincorporated business accepts complete personal responsibility for all of the business debts and contractual promises, incorporation limits the extent to which creditors can attach a business owner's personal wealth.

Successful businesses pay greater taxes through the incorporation route, however. The corporation is taxed on the business's profits before it pays shareholders the portion of profits (dividends) due them. Shareholders then owe taxes on their personal profits as well.

To avoid the double whammy of paying corporate and personal taxes, ask your advisers about a subchapter S corporation, which is available to certain smaller operations. In such a structure, the corporation channels all profits directly to the shareholders and pays no taxes. Instead, its owners declare their share of the corporation's income on their personal tax returns. Subchapter S corporations thus offer the advantages of limited liability while avoiding the disadvantages of double taxation on corporate profits.

Single-investor operations often opt for a sole proprietorship structure, which cedes the entrepreneur complete control over every aspect of the business. The business pays no corporate tax since all profits are considered personal income. However, sole proprietors also assume complete responsibility for the business's obligations.

In a similar manner, partnerships distribute all the rights and responsibilities of ownership among the shareholders. Each partner reports his or her share of the business's profits as personal income and shares the liability for losses incurred by the business. Limited partnerships provide a variation on the theme; one shareholder (the general partner) assumes unlimited liability for all business obligations as well as the greater portion of control over operations. The investing, or limited, partners share a smaller amount of responsibility, determined by the size of their investment in the business.

CALL ON THE BEST

Erika Zimmerman doesn't try to operate Erika's Hair-U-M alone. In addition to top stylists, she hires the best bankers, bookkeepers, and attorneys she can find. "If you try to do your book work on your own, you'll end up a nervous wreck," she says. "Your mind's not on what it should be: running your business."

An experienced lawyer and accountant can advise you on which business structure best meets your needs. They can help you file the necessary documents within the required deadlines and also help you make your way through the paper blizzards precipitated by your trying to obtain licenses, permits, insurance, workers' compensation and sales tax registration, and a federal employer identification number. Professionals can help in tax planning and setting up the best possible accounting systems. The right accountant can show you how, by determining inventory and plant depreciation properly, you can greatly reduce your taxes. But most important, your lawyer and accountant can help you structure a business plan.

The recent rise in PEOs (professional employer organizations) has given paperwork-dreading entrepreneurs another option. PEOs act as human resource departments for small and medium-size businesses, taking over the hassle of personnel, payroll, and so on.

THE BUSINESS PLAN

Brian Ford, audit partner in the Philadelphia office of Arthur Young and coauthor of *The Arthur Young Business Plan Guide* (Eric Siegel, Loren Schultz, and Brian Ford, John Wiley & Sons, New York, 1987, $22.95), admits that many entrepreneurs tackle business-plan writing only to impress financiers. "That's a big mistake," he says, pointing out that a business plan serves as a blueprint for operating a company profitably. "If I had independent means to start my own company, the first thing I'd still do would be to write a business plan." Business plans allow the writer to focus thinking on each aspect of the company's operations, from distribution to competition to marketing. Often entrepreneurs recognize mistakes they've made on paper in time to correct them in practice.

Don't skimp in putting together the business plan. Many plans for even small businesses run 30 to 60 pages or more. The experts say a business plan should contain the following elements:

- A clear, concise statement of your business—its name, address, age, product, goals, financial condition, and prospects.
- A description of the products or services you offer—how they are manufactured or supplied, how they compare to competitors' offerings, and what patents, copyrights, or other protection against competitors you hold.
- An overview of your market—conditions in the industry, the economy, and your region; your competition and future competition; your target customers.
- Your marketing strategy—your pricing, sales, distribution, and customer services; your advertising and promotion plans and how they will increase sales.
- An outline of your company's management—personnel structure, management expertise of yourself and other key employees, business organization, and staffing.
- A statement of your business's sources of financing and plans for repayment of loans.
- A review of your company's financial condition and a preview of its future financial state: start-up costs and breakeven date; past statements (for purchase of an ongoing concern) and projected statements, including balance sheets, profit-and-loss statements, cash-flow charts. Experts recommend

monthly or quarterly breakdowns for the first one to two years and quarterly or annual projections through five years.

In addition, if you intend to use the business plan as a document with which to secure financing, your lenders or investors will want to see a two to three-page executive summary at the very top of the business plan. The summary condenses all the information you include in the rest of the plan into a quick-to-read abstract. It concludes with the amount of financing you're seeking and a brief statement of what it will be used for. If this all sounds like too much, then hire a professional business plan writer. Business plan writing has become such a hot profession that this third edition lists it for the first time.

HOME

Unless you are a sole proprietor who conducts business from a spare bedroom at home or at the client's premises (for example, a computer trainer or personal chef), you'll need to find an appropriate location and arrange to lease or buy it and to build or renovate the premises. Like all the other aspects of starting a business, construction always takes longer and costs more than projected, so cushion your opening date with a delay in mind. When selecting a site, evaluate the traffic volume and customer accessibility. Check out your neighbors within a several-block radius. While retailers might be hurt by a direct competitor, many storekeepers say complementary businesses build traffic flow.

Ask yourself what your customers expect of you and pick a site with that in mind. Jennifer Kahnweiler, a Cincinnati, Ohio, career counselor, felt the Fortune 500 clients she wanted to land would respond to an upscale image, so she went for premium space. "In the beginning, I took shared offices in an executive suite to cut overhead and tap into clerical services," she says.

While you won't want to pay for surplus space, be sure to find a location that allows for the growth you project. When renting, negotiate to pay only for usable space. (Landlords often charge for square footage under columns and other such nonusable space.) Ask for the right to sublet or sell your lease. Protect yourself against unreasonable rent hikes, and make sure that the lease gives you enough time to establish your business in its location. As a rule, don't commit more than 10 percent of your projected sales volume to your rental expense.

HELP WANTED

When recruiting employees, as when searching for investors, many small companies rely on family. When family members display talent, drive, and desire, merging home and business represents the best of all worlds since you keep profits and goals within the family.

Beware, however. Although your spouse and children might represent a convenient source of help, make sure that each contributes to the business. Countless small businesses have disappeared because they made do with subpar help when they should have hired the best. Businesses that choose professional, loyal, responsible, competent, hardworking, creative employees stand a much greater chance of prospering. Treat your staff with fairness, pay employees well, and reward individual contributions to the business.

Especially in the beginning, absentee management usually

proves a disaster, so expect to put your time in on the floor. "You can't hire a manager and expect them to do things like you would," says Dorothy McNish, whose Elecia Michelle Inc. children's clothing boutique operates out of Little Rock, Arkansas. "No employee is as interested in your shop as you are."

On the other hand, if you don't want to spend your entire life locked inside your business, train competent people to handle any emergency and all day-to-day operations. At some point, the owner's best contribution should be managing the big picture. Business schools stress that any entrepreneur who can't leave for six weeks and come back never had a business in the first place.

THE CUSTOMER SEARCH

Like it or not, every entrepreneur is a salesperson. Starting before you open your doors and continuing throughout the life of your business, you will need to devote a great deal of energy to attracting customers. Each industry requires a different approach. Retailers buy advertising and places of entertainment invite the local media to review their services. Caterers and party planners throw grand-opening galas and invite local businesses that might use their service. Consultants and financial planners cold-call on individuals who would benefit from their expertise. "You can't sit waiting for the touch of Midas," says Erika Zimmerman. "Make things happen. Send brochures. Talk to your local paper and explain that you're just starting out."

No seasoned entrepreneur downplays the importance of ongoing marketing and sales efforts. You may want to hire outside or internal professionals to help in this area. Experienced advertising agencies, public relations firms, and marketing consultants can contribute the extra visibility that will give your business an edge on competition.

Even those small companies that rely on word-of-mouth advertising say it pays to help pass the word along. Some place ads in the Yellow Pages or classifieds in pennysaver newspapers. You might also consider telemarketing and distributing flyers.

The proliferation of the Internet gives entrepreneurs another way to find customers. Daily Soup does 1,000 "Web deliveries" each day. Mailing list broker Mia Glover credits her company's Internet presence with generating 75 percent of the business contacts for the commercial division. As more and more people jump onto the information superhighway, it's soon going to be de rigeur for a business to have an Internet site.

CALL FOR HELP

101 Best Businesses to Start will help you consider what some of the most promising businesses offer in the realms of wealth, excitement, and lifestyle. This book will give you glimpses of what people like and don't like about their chosen fields so that you might envision yourself in a similar company. But don't stop here. Bear in mind the statistics on failure and tap the wealth of help that is available for the asking. Some aid costs money, of course, while other assistance is inexpensive or even free. The libraries are full of information on the specifics of starting a business. Books cover every aspect from writing a business plan to marketing. The larger and smaller accounting firms offer advice in the form of brochures and personal guidance. Don't neglect distributors, suppliers, and others who have a stake in your success. You can also call on the Small Business

Administration, local chambers of commerce, industry trade associations and publications, and universities and colleges for help both on starting and running a venture.

Those who start their own business risk failure, of course. On the other hand, if you do succeed, you'll be in control of what management consultant Howard Shenson calls your "destiny." Whatever else you experience in the course of running your own business, you'll have the satisfaction of knowing you tried. "Don't be a shoulda, a woulda, a coulda," says Frank Contaldo, who operates Bantam Investment Group, an Elk Grove Village, Illinois, business brokerage firm. "The difference between making a career change to IBM and buying or starting your own business is you're investing in yourself. You'll make the money if you're good at what you do. The glory," he concludes, "goes to the one in the arena."

Why These 101 Are the Best Businesses

To be in the Running as a "best" business in *101 Best Businesses to Start*, a start-up had to promise one of the following products or byproducts (and many promised several):

- Wealth, at least more than an individual with an appropriate background to start a company in a particular field could make working for someone else
- Independence, or the freedom from workplace restrictions
- Fun (or glamour or stimulation or creativity)
- Ease of entry and operations

WHO WANTS TO BE WEALTHY?

Everyone fantasizes about making millions, and we've included some individuals whose businesses surpassed their own expectations. However, many businesses provide healthy salaries but don't generate real wealth until they are large enough to sell or to take public. Gary Penrod, who grew Building Services Industries into a $12-million-annual-sales janitorial service, enticed a British buyer to spend more than $3 million for his company.

However, while most entrepreneurs expect to make more money than they ever could earn working for a boss, true wealth rarely is the overriding motive for launching a business. For most venturers, starting a company involves creating a job—a dream job.

I DO IT MY WAY

In the course of over three hundred interviews for *101 Best Businesses to Start*, we heard the recurring theme that independence is the real prize of starting a company. Instead of the nine-to-five drudgery of working for someone else, a business of your own presents a way to control your hours, your environment, and the tasks you perform. We interviewed individuals who said entrepreneurship means never having to say "I'm sorry" to a boss, or never asking for time off in the middle of the week to go skiing or to stay home with a sick child. Founders talked about the joy of making their own decisions: experimenting with a creative merchandising technique, turning down work from unruly clients, working in Palm Springs in the winter and Maine in the summer. "I'm free to make my own mistakes," said one business broker. "I probably make half a dozen bloopers a day—and some are big enough to have gotten me fired if I made them working for someone else. But the creative freedom I have lets me try a lot of unorthodox approaches that work, too. That's why I've about tripled the salary I made before I started my firm."

IT'S GOTTA BE FUN

Founders typically bemoan the long hours, the sacrifices and hard work that goes into turning their start-up into a profitable concern. Then, whether we were interviewing someone in the entertainment field ("Whodunit" producer) or in a business where the fun potential is less obvious (temporary-help agencies), entrepreneurs went on to tell us of special compensations: "No two days are ever the same. I'm always doing something new. When I'm at my lowest, something goes right and I experience a real high." Some people were even less restrained in their enthusiasm: "I'm having a ball! I love the reaction of my customers, my family, my friends." Most of all, they love knowing that they went for it, whether they succeed modestly or spectacularly. "Now, when I'm ninety years old looking back over my life, I'll never have to regret that I didn't try to create my own destiny," said one woman.

Fun, of course, means different things to different people. But realize you'll spend more time with your business (particularly in the start-up years) than with your family, your leisure activities, or your other passions. The experts have good reason to warn against transforming a hobby into a business unless you also have the managerial and organizational expertise to carry it off. However, nobody can make a hateful business successful, at least not in the long run. You've got to love what you do to make it worthwhile.

IT'S SO EASY

Finally, many individuals confine their businesses to just one part of their lives, rather than making them the domineering, overpowering force. These more "holistically" minded people chose operations in which they could either minimize their hours (as, say, artisans or management consultants) or could hire outside managers to run them in their absence. Some entrepreneurs forgo profits to spend more time with family or to pursue hobbies. Others see the company's smoothly meshing gears as an opportunity to turn their energies to other start-ups. "This business is simple enough, once I get it rolling, to call in a competent manager," said one entrepreneur. "Sure, I'll check everything closely once a week, but I can use the rest of my time to start the second unit in the chain."

BUT WHAT BUSINESS WILL I START?

Many individuals aren't really sure what business to start—but they know they're in love with the concept of entrepreneurship. In fact, as the post–World War II baby boomers age, and as women increasingly enter the workforce, this description will fit more and more people as they come to see in entrepreneurship the alternative to scaling the corporate ladder. The higher a person climbs in a corporation, the more heated grows the competition, simply because there are few positions at that level. In 1975, every midcareer vacancy in corporate America had an average of 10 candidates. By 1985, 20 people vied for the same spot, and by 1995, 40 to 60 candidates competed for that vacancy. The answer for increasing numbers of Americans who see their top-management dreams blocked by too many competitors? Instead of slugging it out in a corporation, they're starting their own businesses.

If you aren't positive which business you want to start, don't apologize: As long as you pour the same enthusiasm into a venture once you pick your star, you can be as successful as the individual who always knew which field to enter. However, you may be faced with your own lack of expertise, so you'll probably look for a business that's easy to enter and provides minimum risk. If possible, try on a career before you plunge into entrepreneurship: If you'd like to become a tour operator, take a job with an existing operation for a few months at least. If producing seminars attract you, line up a gig while you're still drawing a paycheck.

THE BOX SCORE

A note on the numbers that accompany each chapter: Each figure represents a comfortable average. Just as some start-ups may squeeze by on less initial capitalization and others may require more, revenues, profits, and breakeven time will also vary. "Staffers needed for start-up" represents the minimum to open shop, and entrepreneurs may want to employ more help.

The concept of profits varies from industry to industry as well as geographically. Some companies pay their founders handsome paychecks, leaving practically nothing for profits, while other entrepreneurs forgo salaries almost entirely. We've tried to follow industry norms where possible. For example, most retailers pay themselves $20,000 to $40,000 a year, leaving profits of just 1 to 2 percent of revenues. On the other hand, particularly in the beginning, sole proprietorships in service businesses typically dispense with salaries and regard everything left after expenses as profit.

Business
Services

Business Broker

Job Description: *A business broker matches buyers and sellers of small and medium-size businesses.*

- *Start-up cost as low as $7,500*
- *Potential first-year earnings: $100,000*
- *Breakeven time from initial investment: rapid (one year)*
- *Excellent home-based business*
- *No staffing required*

Frank J. Covich, who consults for individuals who want to become business brokers, under the name Business Activity Alliance, quotes firsthand evidence that his clients have chosen the best of all fields: "Brokers continually see what's for sale in all sorts of industries. It's an amazing thing, but none of the people we've helped get into brokerage leave to enter any of these other businesses." The secret attraction, according to Covich, is that "You can make a lot of money as a business transfer consultant, and, unlike a hardware store or manufacturing business, you don't pay a million dollars for inventory and equipment. However, large fees are earned when it's sold."

According to the Department of Commerce, fast-track Americans are an antsy lot: One out of every four U.S. businesses changes hands every five years. Enter a new breed of expeditor to match buyers and sellers of small and, increasingly, medium-size business, ranging from card shops to used car dealerships. As a field, business brokerage has been around since the mid-1970s and is still tiny in comparison to its related sibling, real estate, which boasts 150,000 offices nationwide. Tom West, former president of International Business Brokers Association, estimates fewer than 3,400 full-time brokers hang their shingles across the country.

But the money that changes hands in business sales is enormous. Compared with real estate, which counts $250 billion in annual sales, all business transfers (including those not sold through brokers) generate $300 billion. Estimates on the number of brokered businesses vary widely, but Tom West guesses between 25 and 50 percent of company sales are handled by brokers. And another thing: Business brokers command 10 to 12 percent commissions, compared to 6 to 7 percent real estate agent fees. They still occupy a relatively new niche, however. "One of the biggest negatives we face is people not knowing what business brokerage is," says Leonard Ostroff, who opened The Ostroff Group in Cherry Hill, New Jersey. "I'm looking forward to more competition to help get the word out."

AN OPPORTUNITY FOR PROFESSIONALS

Len Ostroff talked with numerous brokers while shopping for a business he planned to finance with severance pay from a chemical engineering position. He found a wide range of ability among brokers, some of whom he deemed unprofessional. "I had all that money on the line," he says with a grimace, "and no confidence in the brokers I dealt with. There was a real need for somebody to do it right." Ostroff believed he understood how to structure deals that would please both buyer and seller. So, instead of plowing his cash into a buyout of his own, he opened a small office and began brokering.

While they don't necessarily recommend such a seat-of-the-pants approach, Frank and Robert Contaldo managed to get their start without even an office. After selling their chain of three restaurants themselves when they became disillusioned with the brokers they contacted, the brothers launched a franchise they call Bantam Investments Group. With their cars doubling as offices and a part-time employee to answer their home phones, they pounded pavements in search of sellers. They knocked on doors of pizza shops and clothing stores, asking entrepreneurs if they might consider selling. Once they lined up sellers, they advertised those businesses in newspapers.

Half a dozen years later, with eight salespeople ensconced in comfortable digs in the tiny Chicago suburb of Elk Grove, Bantam now sells more dry cleaners and pet shops than any broker in the (Venture Resources) network.

HALF A MILLION

On the upside, the top solo brokerages draw annual commissions in the $250,000 to $500,000 ballpark, says Tom West, who founded United Business Investments a generation ago and served as president of VR. That top-of-the-line brokerage might split commissions fifty-fifty with salespeople and deduct overhead of about $5,000 a month. That leaves the boss $190,000 as profit—more if he or she brokers some sales personally. For instance, Len Ostroff himself generated two-thirds of the $300,000 The Ostroff Group achieved in gross commissions in 1986.

While the majority of brokerages are two- or three-people shops, there is a trend toward multiple offices. Regardless of the number of storefronts, the owner collects half of all fees, so expansion is a nice plan for those who can manage from afar. For example, Ian MacLachlan opened Business Team Inc. in San Jose and added two more California offices within five years, for total gross sales of $12 million and $1 million in commissions, making his company, according to Ian, one of the largest in the country.

THE BIG ONE

Tom West calls the business brokerage field seductive. Even when prospects seem low, brokers stay in business for the same reason people fish: There's always the possibility they'll hook the big one . . . the deal just around the corner with a $400,000 commission. Allowing that such deals occur, Tom advises firms that don't break into the black within a year or so to reassess.

"This is not a business where persistence always pays off," he says.

Nevertheless, don't give up on the challenges. Len Ostroff reports he sees some pretty weird business. "You listen to 20 buyers and think it will never sell," he says. "Then somebody comes in and says, 'I'd love to have that business.' "

YOUR RÉSUMÉ

Those in the business have a hard time delineating exactly what prepares a person for brokerage. Many states require real estate licenses, but a several-month-long course takes care of that stumbling block. A couple of organizations provide training and support services. The Business Activity Alliance, Frank Covich's outfit, specializes in making business transfer consultants out of professional people, who Frank says are already comfortable with the skills necessary to communicate with business owners. Frank's organization now offers a step-by-step approach to establishing a business transfer consulting practice in association with the Business Activity Alliance. While franchises have no product to sell other than a few weeks of training, some forms, and referral networks, Ian MacLachlan advises those truly unfamiliar with brokerage to buy a franchise. "Some training is better than none at all," he says. He also argues that, since some franchise names carry credibility, you could attract commission-paying customers more quickly than with a sign that reads "John Smith Brokerage." But franchising gets to be expensive if you get too successful. "You don't want to give away another 6 to 8 percent of your commissions as a franchise fee," says Ian.

Len Ostroff offers would-be brokers the same advice he

gives buyers who ask him to find a business in any other field: Go work for an established brokerage before flying solo.

CHARACTER

Good brokers generally share certain character traits. Chief among them:

- They understand numbers and the law as they apply to business sales. "You have to be able to read a P&L statement—and know that it stands for 'Pretend & Lie,' not 'Profit and Loss,' " says Frank Contaldo.
- They are good salespeople. Much of a broker's time revolves around selling buyers on the merits of particular businesses—and convincing owners to sell.
- Brokers are good negotiators. "You have to deal forcefully with attorneys, accountants, buyers, and sellers," says Tom West.
- They are empathetic. "Somebody wrote a list of the ten most traumatic events in life, and retirement ranked second," says Len Ostroff. "Consider you represent an entrepreneur who built a business over 15 years. He doesn't want the wrong person to take over his baby, and, if you can't justify divesting, he'll never, ever sell."

Finding all these requisites in an employee may rank on the probability scale with finding oil in your backyard, especially considering just a handful of schools offer courses in business brokerage. "Because it's a growth industry, we don't have a large pool of experienced people to draw from," explains Ian MacLachlan. His solution includes ex-CPAs, ex-bankers, and

ex-business owners whom he trains in-house. Following the industry norm, all forty of Ian's people operate on a strictly commission basis, which holds down operating costs since you
don't have to budget salaries. "We operate more on a partnership basis than as employer/employee," says Ian.

IT COMES DOWN TO SELLING

Clients fall into two groups: buyers and sellers. Referrals from
attorneys and accountants make up sizable portions of both,
but you'll spend a great deal of effort coming up with prospects.
To track down sellers, "walk, talk, knock, and sell," counsels
Frank Contaldo. Although he sees a trend toward telemarketing, Tom West agrees "there's nothing like going to talk to the
small-business community. When it's snowing outside, that
business owner remembers you when he thinks about chucking
it all and moving to Florida."

Lure buyers aboard the easy way: Simply advertise the properties you have to sell. If the particular convenience store they
targeted doesn't work out, chances are you have another
prospect that might. If not, you can subscribe to business-list-
ing services to come up with likely properties. For a fee, listing
networks provide names of franchise and private companies for
sale all over the country. In less formal arrangements, brokers
who provide leads to colleagues generally split fees.

Most brokers charge 10 to 12 percent commissions, payable
by the seller, with $4,000 to $10,000 minimums for smaller
transactions. Tom West says the average sale involves a
$200,000 business. Additionally, many brokers handle deals
worth millions. "We call them mergers and acquisitions, but it's
really the same thing," says Ian MacLachlan. Like many of his

colleagues, he is shopping more large deals. "There's truth to the old argument. 'There's no more work in putting together a big deal than a small one,' " says West. And a solid, larger business with better records may be an easier sale. But the best part: The commissions are higher.

MAKING MATCHES

Ian MacLachlan finds that about four months elapse between getting a listing and closing the sale. But that's an average. Some listings stay on your files for 18 months, while others sell before you complete the paperwork, particularly if you have a ready stable of buyers. Although MacLachlan concentrates on California sellers, Business Team works buyers all over the country, spending $5,000 a month to advertise in the *Wall Street Journal* as well as local newspapers. For large sales, some brokers contact competitors in a given industry who might buy the particular business they have on the block as a way to expand.

THE PERFECT FIT

According to Tom West, 90 percent of buyers who use brokers are first-time owners with zero idea of what particular business they want. The broker becomes an analyst who delves into a buyer's personality in order to find the perfect fit. "People make decisions emotionally," says West, based on the type of lifestyle and environment they want rather than on how much money they can make. For example, because you like gardening you might prefer a flower shop even though you could make more money in a computer-repair business. West recalls the client who answered an ad for a liquor store. "The salesperson found he had six dogs and sold him two pet stores instead."

Frank Contaldo profiles buyers using interview forms made up of fifteen to twenty questions. "We ask why they want to buy a business, who will run it, what are their interests." How much money buyers have in hand ranks close to the bottom of Contaldo's list. "The only way we handle sales is through seller financing," he insists. The buyer puts 25 to 40 percent down, and the seller takes the rest in monthly installments that the buyer meets through his new business's cash flow. Buyers like seller financing because they can afford better deals. "The seller makes a lot of money, because he is paid interest," says Contaldo.

TRENDS

Business brokers predict some fine-tuning of their industry as it matures. The larger acquisitions that brokers now target are attracting large, established real estate and financial specialists. Len Ostroff, for one, happily anticipates this particular trend. "When I'm ready to sell, they'll be ready to buy me out," he grins.

In addition, brokers are becoming both more specialized and more diverse. For example, some are signing up to represent particular franchisors. Others are narrowing their scope to unique niches, such as country inns or professional practices, but aiming for buyers and sellers across the country.

Most of all, business brokerage is becoming more professional. "Five years ago, there was more of a used-car atmosphere," says Ian MacLachlan. "A more professional breed of people are coming in, systematizing the business."

SOURCES

Industry Associations

Institute of Certified Business Counselors, P.O. Box 70326, Eugene, OR 97401, (541) 345-8064

International Business Brokers Association, Inc., 11250 Roger Bacon Drive, Suite 8, Reston, VA 20190, (703) 437-7464

The Business Activity Alliance, P.O. Box 993535, Redding, CA 96099, (530) 241-1600

Business Plan Writer

Job Description: *A business plan writer develops an overall "blueprint" for a new or existing business that includes a five or ten year plan and strategies for such issues as market positioning, competition, reaching target audiences, management structure, start-up capital, and short- and long-term goals.*

- *Start-up cost as low as $5,000*
- *Potential first-year earnings: $50,000*
- *Breakeven time from initial investment: rapid (as little as two months)*
- *Excellent business for people with physical disabilities*
- *No staffing required*

One thing that's certain about entrepreneurs: They burn with a passion for their business. Scratch the surface of any number of businesses and underneath you'll find people linked by the common bond of turning their dreams of self-employment into reality. It takes a lot of courage for people to shed the comfortable cocoon of corporate

America and reach into the unknown for that gold ring, not knowing if they'll drop it or hold on. It's this blood-quickening sense of risk, the feeling that they're boldly challenging the unknown and winning, that makes entrepreneurs so fervent about their business.

However, this same passion sometimes can make people blind to the nuts-and-bolts needs of their creation. Consumed by the "big-picture" desire to keep their business thriving, entrepreneurs often neglect the "little picture"—the need for vital but necessary tasks such as researching the competition, studying the marketplace, and planning for the future.

That's why a business plan is so important—and why talented business plan writers are in demand.

WHO NEEDS A MAP? I KNOW WHERE I'M GOING

Picture this. You're driving down an unfamiliar road. Finally you see a small sign that identifies the road as county highway 537. But when you reach in the glove compartment for your trusty map, it's gone—and you're still hopelessly lost.

That, in essence, is what a company is doing if it's operating without a business plan. Just like a map, a plan guides the way, enabling the company to stay on the main road and not take any detours or ill-advised shortcuts that could lead to disaster.

"A business plan is a written presentation that very carefully explains everything," says business plan writer Donna Barson, founder of Barson Marketing in Manalapan, New Jersey. "It explains the firm, the management team, the products, the services, and the goals. It also has strategies on how to reach those goals."

Business plans have long been fixtures of larger corporations, where they used to be called strategic plans. However, their popularity soared after corporate belt-tightening in the 1980s, when hundreds of thousands of people were "downsized," given early retirement, or simply fired. Too young to retire but too old to start over at an entry-level position in another company, many laid-off workers struck out on their own and established their own businesses. Coming from the corporate world, the concept of a business plan was familiar and logical to them. Thus, as entrepreneurial start-ups bloomed all across the United States, so did the popularity of business plans.

SHOW ME THE MONEY

Business plans have many uses. One, as mentioned above, is to provide a blueprint for a business to follow. Another is to assist the owner/entrepreneur in finding the money to turn dreams into reality. Depending on how elaborate the business/idea is, the amount of money required can range from a small investment to the average salary of a professional athlete. Either way, a sound business plan is vital to an entrepreneur's ability to attract start-up capital.

"In most cases, when you go for financing, you need to have some kind of business plan," says Donna Barson. It doesn't matter whether the seed money is coming from a bank, a venture capitalist, or rich Aunt Minnie; most financiers want to see a business plan. It assures them that they're not sinking money into a hare-brained venture but rather something that has been logically planned. Think about it: If you wanted to start a business, do you think you'd have better luck in borrowing money if you enthusiastically talked about your idea to a financier or if you presented a carefully written plan explaining why your idea will succeed?

Business plans are also useful in other areas, such as recruitment. If a company is actively trying to bring in outside talent to reach the next level, a business plan is a pivotal document that details the company's operations and defines long-term goals. Not many talented executives are going to risk joining a company in which everything seems to be accomplished by the seat of the pants. Barson noted that some public companies are *required* to have business plans, so that they can show their stockholders and prospective stockholders where the company is heading.

BUSINESS PLAN BASICS

What's in a business plan? That depends on the business. The one constant is that all business plans are not created equal.

A summary business plan (one that essentially summarizes the business's activities and goals) can be as short as 20 to 25 pages. A more advanced plan can exceed 100 pages, not including supporting documentation.

To write a business plan you must be part reporter, part detective, and part psychic. Here's why:

Because some of the data for the business plan comes from interviewing company officers and outside principals such as accountants, you need the information-gathering skills of a reporter. The abilities of a detective come in handy when you dig through public records, financial statements, and other documents to obtain the rest of the information for the plan. A psychic's ability to peer into the future is helpful for one of the most critical parts of the plan—trying to analyze the competition and the marketplace in which the business is competing, and determining what the competitive environment will be like for the company and its products in the upcoming years. "A business plan is composed of three major parts," says Donna Barson. "Marketing and sales, operations/manufacturing, and financial. A business plan writer should have either a marketing, management, or financial background."

GIVING YOURSELF THE BUSINESS

Start-up costs for a business plan writer are low. A computer and printer are necessities, as are a fax machine and cellular phone. Your computer should have a fast modem for Internet research.

It is recommended that you spend whatever is necessary to obtain a top-quality tape recorder, so that you don't return to your office after interviewing the company CEO only to find that your machine malfunctioned, leaving you with nothing but the depressing hiss of blank tape.

Other start-up expenses include one or more of the books available that provide assistance and guidance for fledgling business plan writers. Business plan software programs also are available.

Another potential initial expense is professional liability insurance. Since a business plan writer is expected to point out future directions and markets for the business to explore, insurance comes in handy if your crystal ball is fuzzy and the business suffers as a result of your recommendations.

Overall, start-up costs can be as low as $5,000 to become a business plan writer (although the cost of professional liability insurance can raise that figure by several thousand dollars). As for salary, most writers negotiate a fee on a per-project basis. Some charge by the hour, but most business owners reject this method, because it leaves their cost open-ended.

Like other businesses, how much you charge depends on location. If you live in or near a large metropolitan area, you can charge more than if you live in a rural area. It's best to discover through networking or inquiring of other business plan writers what the standard rate is, both per hour and per project, for a business plan in your area, and set your rates accordingly. However, $5,000 is a typical per-project figure. Thus, if start-up costs are kept to a minimum, it is conceivable that you can break even after finding your first few clients.

How do you find them? By networking, networking, and more networking. As with many other businesses, referrals and word-of-mouth are the best advertisements for a business plan writer. Donna Barson, for instance, joined numerous professional organizations, such as chambers of commerce and economic development groups, from which ultimately came several clients.

"Most chamber of commerce meetings have a 'resource table,'" she said. "It's where members are allowed to display literature about their business."

As with all new businesses, getting that first client is the hardest. However, if all goes well, before long you might be doing a business plan for a growing, dynamic young business—your own.

Career Counselor

Job Description: *A career counselor assists clients in defining and understanding career directions and goals.*

- *Start-up cost as low as $2,000*
- *Potential first-year earnings: $60,000*
- *Breakeven time from initial investment: rapid (six weeks to two years)*
- *Ideal home-based business*
- *Excellent opportunity for the disabled*
- *No staffing required*

According to the American Counseling Association, it has become as common for people to seek counseling and advisement for career concerns as it has for them to seek medical help for physical concerns. Betsy Harrison, president of Career Development Corporation, Rochester, New York, observes, "our generation places more value on self-worth and challenge—which means we change jobs relatively frequently. Meanwhile, the corporation no longer can guarantee lifetime jobs. These two forces have absolutely turned society upside down." And, in the process, created a whole new field: career counseling.

Effective career counseling is a three-step process:

1. Self-evaluation, in which the counselor helps a client evaluate skills, aptitudes, and interests through tests and discussion.
2. Research into occupations and careers.
3. Preparation for job hunting, including framing the résumé and honing interview skills.

In addition, some centers steer clients to industry contacts and even provide access to job listings.

But don't confuse career counseling with employment agencies. "We don't promise a job, even though we have a 98 percent success ratio," says Susanne Parente, president of the firm bearing her name in Westfield, New Jersey. "We're here to help identify goals and directions."

WHO NEEDS YOU?

Two types of clients pay your bills: individuals and corporations. "Individuals are primarily professionals making a midlife career switch, people entering retirement, students right out of college, and women returning to the work force," says Jennifer Kahnweiler, of Kahnweiler Associates, a Cincinnati firm. For individuals considering plunging into a new career, Jennifer combines counseling with aptitude tests to help the client decide which avenues to pursue. Then her staff researches the industry to give clients answers to questions they need to get started. What is a typical day like? What skills do you need? What money can you expect? Whom can you contact to tell you more? Who are the prospective employers in this part of the country?

Career counselors command anywhere from $50 to $100 an hour to point individuals in the right direction. Unless the situation teems with some special problems, figure on spending four to eight hour-long sessions with each client. If you charge by the session, a fee of $350 is typical throughout the industry.

Corporations provide bigger bucks than individuals because they buy $1,000 to $2,000 seminars for a group of employees, or they put you on retainer to help a more-or-less steady stream of employees. In a seminar setting, you might talk with employees when layoffs are inevitable. Topics include how to write résumés or deal with the depression that typically accompanies the pink slip. The corporation also may pay you to tackle career problems for individuals, particularly in two areas: outplacement (or helping laid-off employees adjust and find a new job) and spouse relocation (or helping the spouse of a new employee find work in the area). In spouse relocation, you may still be paid by the hour, but many outplacement counselors ask for 15 percent of the employee's last annual salary.

OUTPLACEMENT

Fired or laid-off employees typically have suffered emotional wear-and-tear that counselors address before launching a job search. "People need to understand their anger or frustration," says Kanhweiler, who counts a psychologist among the associates at Kahnweiler Associates. "People who lose jobs often feel a loss of identity," Sue Parente agrees. "We help them put things in perspective. We help them realize they're performing a function—they are not their job."

Such delicate advising explains why the industry's professional societies and those states that require a license say you need a master's degree in counseling psychology in order to call yourself a career counselor.

After you've made what Sue Parente calls "the warm and fuzzy" psychological approaches, you counsel former employees the same way you do others who question their careers. Take spouses, for instance.

TRAILING SPOUSES

According to a recent survey by Atlas Van Lines, while U.S. companies are transferring more employees, they are cutting back on relocation assistance. The survey found that in 1997, 55.1 percent of the companies queried reported an increase in relocations for the previous year, while 75 percent said they expected more relocations during the next five years.

However, despite these figures, 87.5 percent of the companies surveyed offered no assistance in helping an employee's spouse find work in the new location, up from 79 percent the previous year. Ironically, the survey also revealed that nearly 20 percent of relocations fail because of a spouse's lack of adaptability. That last number screams "opportunity" for career counselors in the "relocated spouses" market.

To attract corporate clients, call on those employers in town that are branches of large corporations that tend to transfer employees. Jennifer Kahnweiler watches the newspaper to see which firms are relocating to Cincinnati. Then she sends the personnel department letters along with a brochure explaining her company, recommendations from other clients, and even articles about the career counseling industry. "The field is so new, we still have to do a lot of education on what career counselors actually do," she explains.

The career counselor helps the spouse of the transferred employee with résumé writing, interview skills, and the task of identifying contacts in the new town. Some get involved in relocation counseling. (See "Relocation Consultant," page 529.) Career counselors place a high value on networking. "We put clients in touch with individuals who know a lot about a field," explains Kahnweiler. "The president of Women in Communications might know which Cincinnati companies are good to work for in the journalism field, for example." She says most people are surprisingly willing to take time away from busy schedules to chat about their areas of expertise. They're flattered that you value their experience enough to ask their advice.

In addition, counseling firms introduce clients directly to employers. Kahnweiler Associates maintains a database that lists area employers and the skills each looks for. Susanne Parente establishes formal working relationships with particular employers and employment agencies who expect to see résumés she prescreens. "They're happy to get résumés from me because we don't charge them a fee."

BUILD AN IMAGE

Some career counselors start from a home office, particularly if they conduct seminars at many corporations' sites. But you'll probably want to move into an office as soon as you can afford one so you can see individuals more comfortably. Jennifer

Kahnweiler rented an executive suite where she had access to clerical help who type client résumés. "We felt we needed premium space to project a professional image, particularly to corporate clients," says Kahnweiler. She hired an artist to design a logo, letterhead, and brochures.

As you grow, you'll need additional counselors. Kahnweiler subcontracts with five independents rather than putting them on salary. That way, she pays them only when she needs them to handle the client load.

Income for solo practitioners generally tops out around $60,000, because fees for the most part are hourly. While that's certainly not bad, you can make more by running some group sessions, which pay more than one-on-one counseling. But career counselors expect even more opportunity in the future. "Within five years, anyone who's starting now will have a booming business," predicts Sue Parente. "This is particularly true because we're seeing a market increase in the number of men who relocate when their wives take transfers. They're increasingly asking for spouse location as a legitimate demand. It's a sad comment on society, but maybe because they're men, they get it."

SOURCE

Industry Association

American Counseling Association, 5999 Stevenson Avenue, Alexandria, VA 22304-3300, (703) 823-9800

Janitorial Service

Job Description: *A janitorial service cleans commercial buildings. In addition, the company may offer other services such as drapery cleaning and parking lot maintenance.*

- *Start-up cost as low as $5,000*
- *Potential first-year earnings: $40,000*
- *Breakeven time from initial investment: rapid (one month to two years)*
- *Excellent home-based business opportunity*
- *No staffing required (initially)*

A large interstate chemical conglomerate asked Gary Penrod, a former high school English teacher, to figure out why turnover was so high and the results so inadequate in the company's in-house cleaning department. We're talking hundreds of thousands of square feet of office and industrial space that a couple hundred employees cleaned every night, so the stakes were high. That assignment changed Penrod's life. "I went in with the crews at night. I found people with a second-grade education who were illiterate and knew they had no chance of advancement. There was no upward mobility for these people." It was hardly shocking they couldn't work up enthusiasm for pushing a broom the rest of their lives.

Penrod made two recommendations: Bring in educational consultants to teach the cleaners how to read or disband the in-house janitorial crews in favor of outside contractors whose business involves dealing with constant turnover and low motivation.

THE MILLIONAIRE JANITOR

A few years after making those recommendations, Gary Penrod borrowed $3,700 for equipment and payroll and "listened to my own advice. I started a contract cleaning company." Although it took him a few years to hook his former employer as a client, Penrod offered office cleaning services in two states within the first year. After 14 years, his Building Service Industries, Wilmington, Delaware, grossed $12 million and employed 1,600 in eight states as far-flung as New York and Texas. Penrod sold the company to a British group for a figure "in excess of $3 million." He also stayed on to help the new owners acquire similar contract cleaning services throughout the United States.

While your business may not burst out of the starting gate quite that fast, there is still real moneymaking potential here. The Building Service Contractors Association International (BSCAI) says that the most significant growth in the U.S. economy between now and the next couple of years will be in service industries, and janitorial service is anticipated to grow faster than virtually every other service category.

Indeed, the commercial cleaning industry has been mopping up in the growth category for years; the number of commercial cleaning franchises rose 38 percent from 1991 to 1993. (This is on top of 14 percent average yearly increases from 1984 to 1989.) Industry revenues soared as well, leaping from approximately $37 billion in 1990 to about $58 billion in 1996.

A SLUSH FUND

If you plan to start with several contracts, you'll need equipment, marketing, an office, and payroll. (Traditionally, contractors bill on the last day of the month, so plan on meeting weekly payrolls before you ever see a dime of reimbursement.) To do it right, industry experts recommend $50,000 in seed capital and a similar line of credit to help you grow. Most of that goes for buying heavy-duty equipment. You can also buy existing contractors for about 40 to 50 percent of their annual revenues.

But you can start for less if you're willing to grow slowly; namely, do all the cleaning and marketing yourself, using a home-based office. Some individuals even start part time, hanging on to daytime jobs and cleaning at night. "I wouldn't rule out what I and hundreds of others did—start with virtually no cash and hang on to make a company work," says Gary Penrod. Franchises start at a few thousand dollars, and many franchisors provide financing. Several even throw in a few contracts to get you started.

In fact, profits are best in those early days because your only expenses involve lining up contracts and buying the supplies and equipment you need to clean. Some franchisees claim one-person outfits net 70 percent of sales (not counting the owner's salary). But you're limited to the few jobs one person can do, so annual revenues may hover around the $50,000 mark. To expand, add another cleaner, which immediately cuts profits in half. Put on a few staffers and you'll need supervisors, office space, possibly a warehouse, and a sales force to sustain the whole bunch, which explains why the bigger companies are thrilled to pocket $1 out of every $10.

A CLEAN SWEEP

To boost those margins, many contractors add other services, ranging from carpet dyeing to parking lot maintenance. Not only will the additional services improve your bottom line, but many clients like "one-stop shopping." If you clean draperies twice a year, they won't have to hire an outside service.

While you can certainly advertise in the "Business Services" listings of newspaper want ads and in the Yellow Pages, the spoils usually go to the aggressive. "I used to take Sunday afternoon rides looking for real estate signs announcing new buildings, then call on the landlords," recalls Gary Penrod. In other words, dig up potential clients and ask to bid on their cleaning contract.

Make the proposal professional. You might call a building's contractor to learn what materials it contains. Then contact the chemical manufacturer to find the best way to maintain that particular llama-wool–blend carpeting. Show off your expertise by stating how you plan to care for a client's computer room. If you run across a company that does its own cleaning, point out that you may be able to polish floors and dust word processors for less than an in-house cleaner because you have trained personnel and buy supplies in bulk.

Once you quit vacuuming yourself, expect labor to eat up about 55 cents of every dollar you bring in. Really efficient firms in nonunion areas usually bid around 60 cents a square foot per year. But before bidding, check out all the variables. "It takes longer to clean 10,000 square feet where 500 people work than the same space with 200 people," says Gary Penrod. "Also, determine if the space is carpeted, how old it is, and how it's heated and air conditioned. Are you dealing with an insurance office where you'll have to pick lots of staples off the floor or an executive suite that's basically clean?"

REVOLVING DOOR SYNDROME

Expect your biggest headache to be employee turnover—200 to 300 percent a year isn't unusual. Cleaning personnel often are transients—students or their parents who quit as soon as school is paid for. Few people see janitorial work as a career, so they lose nothing by quitting when another opportunity arises. "Nobody aspires to be a cleaner," Gary Penrod recognizes. "That's not so much a problem as a fact." The turnover is the reason corporations gave up in-house cleaning in the first place, remember?

You may hold on to people longer if you pay above minimum wage and train for advancement. Recruit employees by offering to transport crews to outlying corporate parks that are far from most employees' homes. Some companies praise the loyalty of disabled and older workers.

High technology may eventually change the way we clean

our businesses. Robots already sweep a few Japanese factories. The steam jets that hospitals use to sterilize operating rooms could be adapted for scouring bathrooms. But those solutions are probably years away from large-scale implementation. Meanwhile, there's still time for entrepreneurs to apply some elbow grease.

SOURCE

Industry Association

Building Service Contractors Association International, 10201 Lee Highway, Suite 225, Fairfax, VA 22030, (800) 368–3414

Mailing List Broker

Job Description: *A mailing list broker performs numerous functions with mailing lists for clients, including researching to find the proper list and maintaining lists.*

- *Low start-up costs (if home-based)*
- *Breakeven time from initial investment: rapid (if home-based)*
- *Home-based business possibility*
- *No staffing required (initially)*

Direct mail. Junk mail.

Call it what you will (and direct marketers *hate* it when you call it "junk" mail), direct mail is one of the most remarkable marketing phenomena of the 20th century. In 1997, Americans spent $244 billion responding to direct mail pitches. That's a lot of cash for something that nobody asked for and that arrived in their mailbox unannounced.

Whether you love it or loathe it, direct mail doesn't appear in your mailbox without an assist from something just as important as the solicitation itself—the mailing list. From the mailing list come the names of people selected to receive the direct mail—names that are geared toward a very specifically targeted solicitation.

The mailing list is often the difference between a successful direct mail campaign and an unsuccessful one. For instance, how many responses would a company that markets rock-and-roll memorabilia get if its catalog was sent only to members of symphonic societies? The obvious answer: not many. As the *Capital Times* of Madison, Wisconsin, says: "The most important element of a successful direct mail campaign is a good target or potential customer list." This is why mailing list companies are in demand—and possibly why you could be too if you started your own mailing list broker service.

MAILBOX MANIA

Each year, Americans receive an average of 553 pieces of direct mail—a total of 4.5 million tons. It is estimated that every mailbox in the United States is stuffed with 34 pounds of direct mail annually.

Although people moan and groan about receiving junk mail, it's not disappearing anytime soon. Direct mail is popular because it offers several advantages: It's inexpensive compared to other forms of advertising; it allows concentration on targeted markets; it provides for personalized sales pitches; and it has a sense of immediacy about it that prods customers to respond.

Of course, without mailing lists, direct mail is like a racing car without gasoline—a powerful machine standing idle. Mailing lists are the fuel that make direct mail go. Companies that locate mailing lists are called mailing list brokers. It is their job to find the list that best matches the target audience for the solicitation.

In general, there are two mailing list categories: compiled lists (telephone books, associations, or directories) and direct response lists. The direct response list contains people who order through the mail and who past experience shows will respond to direct mail pitches.

DESTINATION DIRECT

In 1986, R. Mia Glover took a secretarial job with a mailing list company in Crofton, Maryland. It was her first entry into the workforce, and it seemed like a good opportunity to make some money until she got married someday.

"I thought I was going to be a housewife," she says.

Ten years later, believing that the company could be modernized and more aggressive in its pursuit of business, she bought it. Glover changed the name to Destination Direct and revitalized the company with new computer equipment as well as a new outlook. Since its inception Destination Direct skyrocketed from 3 clients to 300, moved from a 900-square-foot facility to a 2,500-square-foot facility, and became one of the leading mailing list brokers on the East Coast.

Destination Direct determines the best target audience for a customer's direct mail campaign and then researches to determine which mailing list(s) are available to fit the targeted criteria. According to Glover, all lists are not created equal; some are outdated or contain errors. Thanks to experience, Destination Direct knows which lists are called the "cleanest" and will meet their client's needs. After they obtain the list, the client either uses it to implement the direct mail campaign or else turns the entire campaign over to Glover, for her company to fulfill (mail out). The company also manages numerous mailing lists, making sure that the data are up to date and organized.

When Glover took over the business, she added an in-house graphic design department as well as copywriters and marketing campaign strategy planners. Her goal was to turn Destination Direct into a one-stop shop for all direct mail needs.

"We wanted to establish a turnkey operation," Glover says, "so that whether clients had never been in the industry before or were long-time industry veterans, we could work for them using a turnkey approach. It's so much easier if you don't have 16 people touching it [the direct mail solicitation]."

To market the company's new image and services, Glover issued press releases, established a website, and used e-mail to alert direct mail marketers about Destination Direct's new services and outlook.

It took about six months for business to begin picking up. However, once it started it didn't stop. Today business has increased at least 50 percent over what it was when Glover took over. She attributes the rise in business to the Internet. Destination Direct is listed on the top 50 search engines, so that someone looking for a mailing list broker via the Internet almost can't help but find the business. Every time the company's website is updated, Glover has her technical team verify that the business still pops up on those search engines.

"We've developed relationships with three very large public relations agencies," she said. "The only way they could have found us is on the Internet. They contact us all the time for [mailing] lists for their customers."

The Internet has helped the company in other respects, such

as regional theaters and charitable organizations. Prior to Glover's takeover, the company's client base had been completely nonprofit. Glover began a commercial division and again used the Internet to get the word out. Today the commercial division is thriving, with 75 percent of its business resulting from Internet contacts.

Because of the great success she's had promoting her business over the Internet, Glover only advertises with a small Yellow Pages ad.

MASTER OF THE LISTS

If you want to establish your own mailing list broker business, a prerequisite that won't cost anything but is invaluable is industry experience.

"You just can't open a shop," said Glover. "It requires a lot of research. You have to develop a reputation within the industry."

If you've got the experience (or just simply the desire), however, there are two methods worth exploring to establish your business.

The first is to run it as a home-based business in which you primarily obtain, maintain, and sell lists. The only equipment required is computers, fax machines, and so on. Mailing software (at a cost of about $2,000) that complies with ever-changing postal regulations is also a requirement. Don't forget about up-front capital, in case you have to prepay for lists before the money starts rolling in. Total start-up costs for this method shouldn't exceed $10,000, and it's possible to recoup your initial investment within one year.

The second method is to establish a turnkey operation. Computers, of course, are still necessary, not only to perform

routine office functions but also to direct the printers that produce the actual solicitation materials (letters, forms, and so on).
You'll also need a direct addresser (cost approximately $15,000
to $20,000), which pre–bar codes every piece of mail, and a
tabber machine (cost about $5,000), which tabs direct mail in
accordance with postal regulations so that it can receive automated rates. If you decide to add graphic design capability, as
Glover did, then you need top-of-the-line computers as well,
which will add additional equipment expense.

Glover estimates that overall it would take about $100,000
of start-up capital to launch a mailing list broker business.
"That, and a lot of blood, sweat, and tears." She laughed.

As far as earnings, list fees are given in terms of cost per
1,000 names. The cost per 1,000 for consumer lists (reaching
people at their homes) typically ranges between $50 and $200.
For business lists (reaching people at their workplace), the rates
tend to be higher.

Is E-Mail the Future?

One concern within the direct mail industry is that "direct mail
e-mail" might have a negative impact. Glover, however, doesn't
buy this.

"A lot of junk mailers have decided e-mail is the better source
for their solicitations, but the direct mailers understand that in
order to hit a specific market, they really have to use the mail.
It's the best medium available. Everyone's got a mailbox,"
Glover says.

"I think that [direct mail e-mail] is going to separate the true
marketers from the fly-by-night marketers. A true marketer

knows that they've got to integrate their marketing strategy—
the Internet, direct mail, and customer service all have to play a
part."

Quite possibly, you might play a part, too—as a mailing list
broker. We'll look for your handiwork in our mailboxes.

Meeting Planner

Job Description: *A meeting planner arranges meetings for companies, associations, and other large organizations, handling everything from reserving hotel rooms to picking out dinner menus and entertainment.*

- *Start-up cost as low as $6,000*
- *Potential first-year earnings: $37,000*
- *Breakeven time from initial investment: rapid (three months to one year)*
- *Ideal home-based business*
- *No staffing required*

Meeting Planner Scene 1

You've just breakfasted on the balcony of the resort hotel where you booked your client's Caribbean meeting. Soft breezes stir the notes you've made detailing which seminar speakers agreed to attend. You reach for the phone; the skipper of the schooner that you're considering for an evening cruise during the three-day conference invites you to come to the harbor after your appointment with the caterer. Speaking of the caterer, you decide to switch that clams casino order to shrimp cocktail for the opening cocktail party.

Meeting Planner Scene 2

Another hotel room, another city. This time it's Chicago in February, and you're on the phone negotiating with a limo service to pick up conventioneers stranded at the airport by the taxi strike. Of course, if the blizzard arrives, ground transportation won't matter since O'Hare will close anyway. That may be just as well, since the convention hall says your booking begins Thursday—not tomorrow as you told attendees.

Is the life of a meeting planner glamorous? You bet. You stay in the best hotels and eat at fancy restaurants. All the vendors pamper you with VIP treatment because they want your clients' business.

It's no wonder that you're popular. According to a 1995 study, direct spending by the convention, meeting, and incentive travel industry for 1994 equaled $82.82 billion. Considered as a single industry, the convention, exposition, meeting, and incentive travel industry would rank 22nd among all U.S. private sector industries. According to the U.S. Department of Commerce, in 1993 the travel and tourism industry (encompassing meetings, conventions, expositions, and incentives) generated an estimated $322.5 billion in revenues. Is it any wonder that the meeting planner is the hotel owner's best friend?

Is the life of a meeting planner stressful? To say the least. You're at the mercy of catastrophes you can't control, like weather and personalities. That doesn't count those glitches that are worth worrying over because human error can creep in—like making sure 2,000, attendees' name tags are spelled correctly.

"Meeting planning is a lot more complicated than planning a wedding or party," warns Carl E. Mischka, who runs CEM Enterprises from his Newport Beach, California, home. "A meeting planner is like the conductor of an orchestra who also composed the piece." And that's just one symphony. Meeting planners typically work on several projects simultaneously. Respondents to the Meeting Professionals International (MPI) survey planned an average of 46 meetings a year. Some larger firms coped with 2,000.

JOB DESCRIPTION

What does a meeting planner actually do? Everything depends on the clients' needs and your own specialties. But here's a sampling from a much longer laundry list of meeting-planner functions compiled by The Convention Liaison Council:

- Establish meeting design and objectives.
- Select and negotiate with site and facilities.
- Budget.
- Handle housing and transportation.
- Plan the program.
- Establish registration procedures.
- Manage exhibits.
- Manage food and beverage.
- Select speakers.
- Schedule promotion and publicity.
- Produce and print meeting materials.

You might plan everything from educational seminars for 500 to a 20-member board meeting to an international junket for a franchise group. Carl Mischka offers a number of planning services at CEM (an abbreviation that, coincidentally, works equally well for "Conferences/Events/Meetings" as it does for Mischka's initials). "Sometimes we do everything including program design, or sometimes just site selection," says Mischka, who started CEM after stints planning numerous meetings for a textbook publisher he worked for and then publishing a now-defunct magazine. In addition to managing client events that attract from 25 people to 2,500, he also produces his own trade show—for meeting planners, no less. Typically, the client pays a planner to manage an event, but Mischka puts up his own capital for the meeting-planner trade show, which he recovers from exhibit fees. (For an in-depth look at trade show producers, see "Trade Show Organizer," page 638.)

Some planners specialize in particular functions, such as registration or publicity, while others concentrate on specific industries or a particular region. One Nashville-based planner, for example, offers convention services to meetings booked in her city. After all, what out-of-towner knows the area sights and services better than a native? She collects referrals from the chamber of commerce, convention bureau, and hotels.

Those planners who tackle just one particular industry usually branch out over time as a contact in one field recommends them to a colleague in another area. For example, planners who started organizing computer company events because they know the industry's arcane jargon might soon offer their services to the artificial intelligence community. If you manage three large meetings for $25,000 each every year, you've got a good living wage. Add on special services, like audio/visual presentations and market-research projects for your industry niche, and income moves into six figures.

CLIENT HUNTING

There are two paths to signing up meetings to plan: through others in the industry or directly through your own clients. Most planners are one- to five-person firms and often subcontract when they're overloaded or a job requires some special skills. So let competitors and in-house meeting planners know your areas of expertise. Also, talk with convention and hotel managers and ask for referrals. In the beginning, you might offer to handle limited functions—just junkets for spouses whose partners are attending the trade show, for example.

But once you have a track record, you'll probably want the income that comes from developing your own major accounts. Telemarketing and direct mail set the stage for in-person interviews, followed by formal proposals. Call on groups that mount their own meetings and try to interest them in farming out duties. Some presentations require elaborate audio/visual or slide shows and four-color brochures, so you might want to set aside some capital for marketing.

If both you and the client remain interested after the get-acquainted session, next comes the formal proposal. Depending on the complexity of the meeting, the number of functions you'll take on, and the budget at stake, proposals range from a couple of pages to a 20-page report. Here you detail your plans, including exactly what you'll do for the client and what duties the client will keep in-house.

Meeting planners ideally like 12 months to pull together a large meeting. Like everything else, a meeting is easier the second time around because you learn the personalities and industry. If you pitch an annual event, write a renewal clause into your contract that gives you a shot at producing the event next year.

The client will expect you to bring in the meeting on budget, which means you negotiate down such items as hotel space and transportation. Some planners take commissions from airlines, hotels, and ground transport, which allows them to hold down their own fees to the client. Other planners argue that the practice creates a conflict of interest and take fees only from the client. At any rate, "After the negotiations, you need a good working relationship with vendors," says Carl Mischka. "Then everybody has the same client and goal: to make the meeting work."

According to the MPI, the typical U.S. meeting planner earns $37,340. Certification by the Convention Liaison Council is worth approximately $4,000 more per year in earnings.

OUTSIDERS WITH CLOUT

You can still get paid while you train by handling meetings on staff at a large corporation. But meeting planning is evolving from an in-house function to a field dominated by entrepreneurs. Increasingly, big business, trade groups, and professional societies are turning to outside professional meeting planners, which creates a lot of opportunities for you to hang your own shingle.

The switch away from in-house meeting planning partially involves economics. In addition to fees to hotels, convention centers, transportation companies, and like, which the client fronts, a typical New York planner may charge $30,000 (sometimes paid in installments during the planning process) to set up a three-day convention. Others take a percentage of the gate, if we're talking about a for-profit trade show, on top of a flat fee.

Even so, those groups that once carried a planner on staff say it's cheaper to contract with a planner once or twice a year than to pay a staffer's full-time salary and benefits.

But corporations are jumping out of the meeting planning business for another reason. Executives are recognizing that meeting planning requires a whole stable full of skills that professionals handle better than someone who doesn't plan meetings for a living. As meeting planning moves from a field of part-time dabblers to full-time professionals, and as more meetings are called every year, opportunities look bright—if you don't mind taking Chicago in February along with Caribbean breezes.

SOURCES

Industry Associations

Convention Liaison Council, 10200 West 44th Avenue, Suite 304, Wheat Ridge, CO 80033-2840, (303) 422-8522

Meeting Professionals International, 4455 LBJ Freeway, Suite 1200, Dallas, TX 75244-5903, (972) 702-3000

Professional Employer Organization

Job Description: *Professional employer organizations (formerly known as staff/employee leasing) contractually assume the responsibilities of human resources, benefits consulting, government compliance, and other administrative services primarily for small businesses, enabling the owner to concentrate on the revenue-producing side of the company.*

- *Start-up cost between $50,000 and $100,000*
- *Breakeven time from initial investment: as little as one year*
- *Future growth potential: high*
- *Dynamic, fast-growing industry*
- *Excellent business for people with physical disabilities*
- *No staffing required (initially)*

In 1997, according to the Small Business Administration, the average owner of a small or medium-size business spent between 20 and 40 percent of his or her time on payroll, benefits, government compliance, and other human resources functions instead of focusing on how to make the business a success.

That one statistic alone should explain the explosive growth in the field of professional employer organizations (PEOs) in recent years. But just in case you're still uncertain if this industry has a dynamic future, here's another eye-opening number—experts say the PEO industry is growing at an annual rate of 30 percent.

It was statistics like these that led *Entrepreneur Magazine* to cite PEOs as one of 1998's "hottest" businesses and the *Denver Business Journal* to predict that "outsourcing human resources . . . is just now on the verge of explosive growth."

Still not convinced? Then maybe this will do the trick: Experts also assert that PEOs have penetrated only 3 percent of their potential client market. You don't have to be a math whiz to understand it means there is a vast, untapped market out there for this service.

THE NEW AMERICAN MOUSETRAP

Milan P. Yager, head of the National Association of PEOs, uses a simple yet effective example to describe the future for the PEO industry.

"In 1974, computer makers said that in 25 years, everyone would have a lightweight computer," he says, referring to a time when giant mainframe computers were prevalent. "That same analogy can be used now, for PEOs—in 25 years [a vast majority of businesses] will be using PEOs."

According to Yager, the late 1980s fueled the growth of the PEO industry. A host of comprehensive government laws and regulations came into effect during this time, such as the Americans with Disabilities Act (ADA), the Consolidated Omnibus Budget Reconciliation Act (COBRA), and the Family Medical Leave Act. At the same time, people became more dependent on the workplace to provide healthcare and other benefits. This combination greatly increased the amount of time and effort companies spent on human resource issues such as payroll, regulation compliance, and healthcare.

For a large company, it means more work for the human resources department. But for a small or medium-size business, it causes the owners/operators to take precious time away from the core business to deal with these tedious and time-consuming matters. The end result is that the business often suffers.

"It's crazy for an entrepreneur to focus on product plus non–revenue generating functions of their business," says Yager.

"We felt that the business of being an employer was just far more [time-consuming] than the small and medium-size business owners could deal with effectively," says Paul Sarvadi, who cofounded PEO industry giant Administaff in 1986. "We set out to create Administaff as a human resource department for small businesses."

Since PEOs act as employers with many staff on their payroll from the various client companies, they often obtain deep discounts on medical and dental insurance and worker's compensation costs at rates that small business owners typically cannot obtain on their own.

For instance, a small construction business that needs excellent workers' compensation coverage can pay between $20 to $30 for this coverage for every $100 paid to employees. But a PEO can save a firm 5 to 30 percent on those rates, depending on company size, industry experience, and risk level.

"PEOs are a one-stop shop for solving payroll, benefits, and employee problems," says Yager. "We're the new American mousetrap."

WHAT YOU NEED

If reading, studying, and comprehending government regulations, financial statistics, and insurance information is your idea of an insomnia cure, then starting a PEO is not the business for you. You must be a numbers-cruncher of the highest order to deal with the reams of statistics, facts, and figures that running a PEO involves.

Before beginning Staff.Net, Inc., in 1992, Michael D. La-Mancuso was a certified public accountant, already familiar with the business of numbers. Seeking a career change, and aware of employee leasing from previous experience with clients, he launched his own company as a home-based business in Williamsville, New York (near Buffalo).

LaMancuso's start-up costs were only a few thousand dollars. He began with a computer, telephone, and several software packages on payroll processing. He also purchased books that provided templates on how to prepare contracts and employee handbooks.

"I had all these pieces in place before I stepped out the door the first time," he says. "I had the full gamut [of materials] before heading out. I think that it helps a lot."

Since technology is so sophisticated today, your needs for starting a PEO will be more elaborate. Among the office equipment you need are: a computer with a high-speed modem for accessing data off the Internet, a fax machine, a high-speed copier, an envelope-stuffing machine for checks, and a postage meter. In

Business Services

the beginning, even if you buy used office equipment, the outlay is significant. (LaMancuso says that most of the capital he's obtained for his business has been used to buy office equipment.) Depending on whether you rent an office or work out of your home, figure on start-up costs between $50,000 and $100,000.

Determining a fee for services depends on numerous factors. LaMancuso likens it to applying for a life insurance policy; health, risk factors, and so on determine your rate. PEOs operate in a similar manner; they try to estimate the "risk factors," so to speak, before determining a client's fee. How many, and which type, of services does the PEO have to perform? Are these services straightforward, or are there going to be unusual circumstances or exceptions? Thus, depending on the number of clients you obtain and the number and type of services you perform, breakeven time on your initial investment can stretch anywhere from a few months to a few years.

One of the best ways to generate clients for a new PEO is by networking, as LaMancuso did. Thanks to his previous employment experience, he knew which businesses might be amenable to hiring a PEO. "It was fortunate for me that I had type of experience, because I had the ability to know where to go to talk to people."

Advertising is also a possible way to build your business. Administaff places a series of radio spots to promote the company and services when it expands into new markets.

WHAT'S THAT AGAIN?

If you start your own PEO, chances are that you're going to have to educate potential clients on its concept. This is still a largely unknown field; in fact, one of the reasons

Administaff went public in 1997 was to raise awareness of the PEO field.

"The only inhibitor to growth in the business, in the broad context, is awareness and education," says Paul Sarvadi.

During the early days of his business, Michael LaMancuso joined over 12 chambers of commerce, so he could meet and educate potential clients on how a PEO could benefit them. The way he sold the concept was as paperwork alleviation for the small business owner. Indeed, one of a PEO's main functions remains lightening the paperwork load from business owners.

Another way to market your PEO to future clients is to explain the risks of noncompliance. Many small businesses have informal policies on issues such as harassment, drug use, and discrimination. But it they're ever brought to court over one of these issues, they could lose their business.

"Ninety percent of businesses out there have big compliance issues that aren't even dealt with," LaMancuso notes.

LaMancuso was extremely successful at promoting the PEO concept. Within one year his business had grown so much he moved out of his home and into an office. By 1997, his company had landed on *Inc.* magazine's list of the 500 fastest-growing companies in the United States, thanks to an average annual growth rate of 1,600 percent.

As far as becoming a success in the field, LaMancuso advises new PEOs not to "promise more than you can deliver. We always deliver ten times more than we promise." Since most clients in this field come via word of mouth and referrals, it's important to establish a good reputation and customer loyalty.

As human resources issues become more and more complex, the future for PEOs seems bright indeed. "Small businesses have always needed a human resources department," says Paul Sarvadi. "The need for it is stronger than ever."

Although the PEO industry has been consolidating lately, there should always be room for the smaller firms. "If we [the smaller PEOs] do it right, we should be able to beat the big firms on service and attention," says LaMancuso.

SOURCE

Industry Association

National Association of Professional Employer Organizations, 901 N. Pitt Street, Suite 150, Alexandria, VA 22314, (703) 836-0466, www.info@napeo.org

Public Relations

Job Description: *Public relations means promoting a client, company, product, event, and so on, to the media in a variety of ways, including press releases, special events, and press conferences.*

- *Start-up cost as low as $5,000*
- *Potential first-year earnings: $35,000*
- *Breakeven time from initial investment: rapid (within one year)*
- *Ideal home-based business*
- *Excellent opportunity for people with physical disabilities*
- *No staffing required*

When Carol Cone wanted to snare the prestigious McDonald's Restaurant of New England account, she spent almost $40,000 in time and expenses to prove her Boston-based firm had the enthusiasm to sprinkle new glitter on the account that another public relations agency had gripped for 20 years. One of her ploys: a skywriting plane that played off McDonald's advertising theme to splash across

the sky: "It's a great time for a great PR agency—Cone & Co."
Carol Cone got the job.

Public relations is part showbiz, all right, at least the type of PR
that Cone practices. Your job involves carrying a client's message
to the media or directly to the public. Sometimes you use quiet
press releases and gentle persuasion. Other times you set up special
events or other eye-catchers as part of an overall program meant to
develop an image or theme that will stick in consumers' minds.
One of Cone's more visible programs helped push the Rockport
Company from an obscure maker of walking shoes to the acknowl-
edged leader in this burgeoning new field. The program, which in-
cluded securing an endorsement of its walking shoe by the
American Podiatric Medical Association and hiring a medical
spokesperson, culminated with one man's walk across America.
Rob Sweetgall's 11,208-mile hike grabbed coverage on ABC's *Good
Morning America*, in the *Wall Street Journal* and *Parade* magazine, as
well as in lots of local spots. Of course, Carol tipped them all off to
what a great story an interview with Rob would make.

INVESTOR RELATIONS

On the other end of the PR spectrum sits Robert Amen, of
Robert Amen & Associates, Greenwich, Connecticut. His idea
of razzle-dazzle is a coffee-and-croissant buffet for security analysts at New York's Pierre Hotel. "I consider myself a corporate
and investor relations consulting firm," explains Amen. Instead
of promoting new consumer products, he reaches institutional
investors to talk about a client's stock.

Investor relations is possibly the fastest-growing niche
within the swiftly expanding public relations field. The

membership of The National Investor Relations Institute has grown over the past seven years and now has more than 2,000 members. The reason: Corporations, skittish over the mass of corporate takeover attempts in the 1980s, are paying more attention to their shareholders, particularly the large shareholders.

Before he set up shop, Bob Amen already had an investor relations background, having worked in that capacity for several corporations as well as with a Wall Street firm that specialized in proxy solicitations. If you enter this PR niche, come equipped with a legal or financial background. "You need contacts in the financial field and financial knowledge," explains Amen, who adds that journalism expertise is handy in other areas of public relations. In addition, if you understand a particular field well and know which publications like which stories, you can turn that experience into PR for your industry. As you grow, increase your knowledge of other industries.

THE ACCOUNTS

PR agencies generally have two types of clients:

- Project accounts that need to get across a particular message. These relationships last anywhere from a few weeks if all you do is distribute a press release and arrange any follow-up with reporters, to several months if you promote a product roll-out that might involve luncheons and media coverage in several cities. Of course, agencies generally hope the project will lead to the second type of client.
- Retainer accounts that pay a set fee over a longer period. You handle a client's ongoing public relations, which include keeping the media appraised of newsworthy events, and

might develop into writing annual reports and employee brochures. "Retainer clients are crucial so you can plan ahead," says Bob Amen. "They provide cash flow, the continuity that allows you to hire a staff or budget for the future." Robert Amen & Associates' ten retainers provide the bulk of its $750,000 in billings.

To attract those retainers, call on corporations in your areas of expertise and ask to pitch a campaign. Even firms with an in-house PR department may need to farm out particular functions, like developing the West Coast image for a New England–based company.

Don't neglect your company's own PR. Some firms send press releases on new accounts or staff promotions to advertising and industry publications. Success breeds success, so don't be shy about letting others know you landed a big account. You can also host a cocktail party to launch your firm or to celebrate your first anniversary. Invite the press as well as current and potential clients. Also, don't hesitate to network: Meet potential clients through trade organizations or host a seminar on the value of PR. Without being too pushy, let clients know you can perform similar services for their corporate friends. "Some firms in investor relations link with bankers or lawyers," says Amen. "If you handle their PR, they recommend you to their clients."

MAKING TALENT PAY

If you secure enough clients, you can make a good living in PR. Overhead is low: Once you start hiring associates, your biggest expense is for salaries. A solo practitioner can expect to keep the bulk of billings for profit and salary; the owner of a larger firm with many account executives and a lavish office can still earn 10 percent of the gross as profits in addition to a salary that easily moves into six figures.

In the beginning, many general public relations agencies start at home with a word processor and a telephone. But if image is particularly important, you might need a classy office address. Bob Amen felt he needed an office to attract Fortune 500 clients who might balk at paying high fees to a home-based business. Even so, Amen spent only about $1,000 to set up shop and hire a part-time secretary. You also must pay for your clients' mailings, for phone calls and travel to meet with out-of-town media, and for expenses (such as research) incurred on special projects. But usually you can bill those expenses on top of your fee.

The bigger PR firms gravitate toward larger cities because traditionally that's where the clients are. If you specialize in investor relations, you gain a big edge by locating near New York, since at least 60 percent of the assets managed by institutional investors congregate on the eastern seaboard. But more general boutiques can round up clients any place businesses need public relations. "If a company deals with press releases that have to be cleared every week or two, it makes sense to be close to the client," says Amen. "You may even have an advantage if you know the local culture and can also deal with the national press in New York and the trade press in Chicago and the entertainment media in Los Angeles."

Most observers expect PR agencies to flourish in the future for two reasons. Corporations increasingly see the value of public relations, even to the point of switching dollars once allocated for advertising to PR. Seventy percent of Fortune 500 companies surveyed spent over $1 million on public relations in

1997, and 65 percent increased their public relations budgets during the past five years.

Meanwhile, as contradictory as it seems, those same corporations that can't live without PR are paring their in-house staffs as part of the overall cost-cutting climate. That move leads to the second reason why agencies will flourish. Instead of staffing a PR department, corporations increasingly contract with outsiders to handle their media contacts. According to the U.S. Department of Labor, employment of public relations specialists is expected to increase faster than the average for all occupations through 2006.

SOURCES

Industry Associations

National Investor Relations Institute, 8045 Leesburg Pike, Suite 600, Vienna, VA 22182, (703) 506-3570

The Public Relations Society of America Inc., 33 Irving Place, New York, NY 10003, (212) 995-2230

Seminar Producer

Job Description: *A seminar producer arranges, and often hosts, seminars for corporations, associations, businesses, and others.*
- *Start-up cost as low as $5,000*
- *Potential first-year earnings: $65,000*
- *Breakeven time from initial investment: rapid (one year)*
- *Ideal home-based business*
- *No staffing needed.*

Case Study: When Jimmy Calano was fired from his job producing seminars, he was indignant. The then 24-year-old had produced seminars since his college days and had no intention of letting some employer knock him out of the business he knew best. Undaunted, Calano hooked up with a partner, 27-year-old Jeff Salzman, who owned a Boulder, Colorado, advertising agency. They then hired their first instructor to do a three-city tour. The seminar was called "Image and Self Projection for Professional Women."

The pair posted "Sold Out" notices on two of those first three seminars and grossed $220,000 during their first year. But such success is nothing compared to what's happened since. After four years, Boulder-based CareerTrack grossed over $26 million, primarily on seminars costing clients $48 a shot. Calano and Salzman were soon projecting $32.5 million in revenues while lining up participants as far away as Australia. In addition to advising young executives on "Stress Management" and "Business Writing," their 60 trainers wax profound on consumer topics such as "How to Find and Keep a Mate."

Okay, class, what lessons do we learn from Jimmy Calano's true-life experience?

A. The seminar business can be cutthroat.
B. The seminar business offers easy entry.
C. The seminar business has a huge and ready market of students.
D. The seminar business can be hugely profitable.
E. All of the above.

If you answered E, take a gold star and enter the wonderful world of seminars.

THIRST

Jimmy Calano knew by instinct what Jack Tumminello, president of The 1st Seminar Service, a Lowell, Massachusetts, seminar broker, confirms through experience: "The thirst for knowledge and know-how is enormous," says Tumminello. "The number of seminars is going to grow."

The 1st Seminar Service makes a living by matching its list of seminar providers with individuals and corporations craving instruction on particular topics. The service estimates some 4,000 "seminarians" discoursed on about 25,000 topics during a typical one-year period. Counting those courses that enjoyed multiple runs, Americans attend 100,000 seminar sessions each year. Counting all forms of in-house training, John Naisbitt writes in *Reinventing the Corporation* that "corporations spend nearly $60 billion a year on education and training . . . about the same amount spent on education in the nation's four-year colleges and universities." That's a lot of seminars.

Because the audience is there, and because seminar production is a relatively cheap business to get into, there seems no end to the types of people entering the seminar business: Nonprofit trade associations, such as The American Institute of Electrical Engineers, sponsor curriculums for particular industries; universities experiencing declining student enrollments give courses not only on campus but in cities far from home; and corporations disguise sales calls as seminars, using desktop-publishing workshops to hustle computer software or tax-planning sessions to push municipal bonds.

Even entrepreneurs profess more than one motive: Seminars often generate substantial income, and, if you're a consultant or other professional selling your expertise, they also introduce you to potential clients. Entrepreneurs interviewed for other chapters of this book praised seminars as reputation builders in such varied fields as garden-center retailing and financial planning.

FILLING THE CLASSROOM

Getting started in the seminar business is dead simple—if you have a course that someone agrees to pay for. Just show up with whatever teaching materials you use, which may be no more than your notes and a gallon of water to keep the vocal cords in working order. Assuming you're a dynamite educator with a hot topic, word-of-mouth can carry you a long way. You may eventually hire an assistant or a whole staff to give similar seminars. Or you may branch out with audio- or videotapes.

But chances are, clients won't drop out of the sky like raindrops. "We find the biggest problem is not finding people to teach but putting people into their sessions," says Jack Tumminello. "The average marketing cost for producing a seminar is 30 percent to 60 percent of sales." The 1st Seminar Service offers one aid. It serves as a clearinghouse for anyone who wants a particular seminar. The service earns a fee from the producer by putting the customer in touch with the right producer.

Depending on your topic and your audience, you have several choices on how to market. Newspaper ads and even flyers handed out on the street attract consumers interested in "How to Achieve Happiness in Ten Minutes a Day." You can also try posting notices on the Internet. If you have a very specific but useful topic, cold calls to corporation training managers might be best. You might try direct mail for seminars meant for more general but still targeted groups, such as medical doctors who want to learn the latest malpractice news. But direct mail costs can be stiff—figure $25,000 for a 50,000-piece campaign. Expect to attract no more than 1 percent of that mailing (500 people), which means each student has to fork over $50 just to pay for the marketing. If you want to pay for the meeting facilities, the instructor, and make a profit, better plan on charging a lot more than that!

THOSE WHO CAN'T MARKET, TEACH

Or you don't have to market at all. Instead, sign on with seminar producers such as CareerTrack or the American Management Association that contract with instructors. According to Jack Tumminello, depending on which course and how often you teach, an independent instructor can earn $25,000 to $100,000 a year.

The flip side of this suggestion calls for marketeers who don't have specific expertise to sell rather than teach a seminar. The instructor doesn't put up a cent but contributes expertise. The marketeer, or producer, must find the audience and facilities. But, since the instructor is an independent contractor, producers don't worry about payrolls; instead, they just pay the instructor from the proceeds of the seminar. "Usually the organization taking the risk—whoever's doing the marketing—gets the larger percentage of the proceeds," says Tumminello.

The typical provider conducts 8 to 12 programs a year, all focused on an area of expertise. "You can have half a dozen topics that apply to data-processing people, but don't try to address finance people, because then you have to market to a whole new group," advises Jack. But if you build a curriculum for one group, it is hoped that they'll come back for additional seminars over the years.

Of course, CareerTrack provides the exception to that rule, since it markets to everybody in cities of 50,000 or more. Recently it scheduled over 3,000 seminars for a half-million people. Although the courses often enjoy free publicity in newspaper "What's Going On" columns, CareerTrack relies almost exclusively on brochures sent through direct mail to line up participants. "It's not that advertising doesn't work," explains

Gillian Goodman, corporate communications specialist. "It's just that direct mail works so well for us."

CareerTrack seminars attract 200 to 500 people per session, often held at a hotel conference room. "The average class is not a workshop," admits Goodman. The company needs the volume to reach breakeven because it charges only $48 per participant.

If your topic is general, such as "Basic Supervision Skills," you may be limited to a gate price of less than $200. But if you have a special expertise in high demand, such as "Robotic Engineering," you can charge $600 to $1,200 for a similar-length program. In this case, the generic seminar needs to draw 50 participants to produce the same revenues as a 10-participant robotics program.

Overhead for a seminar producer can be minimal—an office staff, marketing, a registrar at the course site, and the cost of staging each seminar, including the instructor and renting meeting facilities. Some producers cut deals with hotels and line up accommodations as well. For a busy producer who counts on repeat business, profits can approach 65 percent of revenues.

In addition to live-instructor courses, technology offers new outlets to the seminar business. CareerTrack sells each of its seminars as four-hour, $39.95 audiotapes meant to turn a commuter's car into a university on wheels. And other companies have gone the step further to videos, which teach everything from "Assertiveness Training" to "Auto Mechanics." Computer-aided instruction teaches children about algebra and professionals about new surgical techniques. The latest—but undoubtedly not the last—frontier: laser videos that allow a student to interact with a taped instructor.

SOURCE

Industry Association

American Society for Training and Development, 1640 King
Street, Box 1443, Alexandria, VA 22313-2043, (703) 683-
8100

Soft Skills Employee Trainer

Job Description: *A "soft skills" employee trainer specializes in teaching businesspeople skills related to human interaction, including stress management, conflict resolution, and team building.*
- *Start-up cost as low as $3,000*
- *Potential first-year earnings: $25,000*
- *Breakeven time from initial investment: six months to one year*
- *Ideal home-based business*
- *Excellent opportunity for people with physical disabilities*
- *No staffing required*

I t wasn't too long ago that training employees in so-called soft skills—such as how to get along with coworkers and other "people-to-people skills"—was dismissed as too touchy-feely by most of corporate America. Why waste money telling employees to like each other? the business world thought; it didn't matter if employees like each other or not, as long as they do their jobs.

Considered as little more than cogs in a giant machine, employees were left to their own devices in dealing with workplace stress. Ironically, it took the mass corporate downsizings of the late 1980s to awaken companies to the value of their workers. In the aftermath, many of these businesses suffered, as their depleted and exhausted workforce struggled to pick up the slack while being resentful, angry, and contentious. After seeing the negative effects of the layoffs, businesses realized the impact of their workers' "soft skills" on the companies' overall success.

"Employers began to realize [at that time] that employees are part of the productivity chain," says Mark Van Buren, director of Research for the American Society of Training and Development (ASTD). Employees went from being considered a necessary evil to "human capital"—something that no company could afford to squander.

When acts of workplace violence became newspaper headlines, such as the killing of a supervisor by an angry worker who was passed up for promotion, the value of this type of thinking became terribly clear. Suddenly the light bulb is going on: Companies are waking up to the fact that their employees are people, not machines, with all of the problems, worries, and anxieties of human beings everywhere. In this context, spending money on soft skills training seems not foolish but prudent—an insurance policy that may prevent a sudden and terrifying explosion of violence by a distraught employee.

But in order to offer these services to companies, you need trainers. Good trainers became hard to find, as demand for their services skyrocketed. Today numerous sources, including the National Association of the Self-Employed, list "employee trainer" as one of the top-ten high-income businesses that have the best prospects for growth.

Human Capital

Today soft skills training is considered not a frivolous luxury but a benefit, a way for companies to keep employees by offering them classes in such topics as leadership, diversity awareness, and time management. Workers, for their part, realize that they are receiving training that not only helps them in their current positions but also makes them more attractive candidates if they ever decide to test the job market. Thus both sides have their own reasons for embracing training.

The result, as Mark Van Buren points out, is that training is up "across all sizes of companies." And because the ASTD expects training demand to continue to increase, trainers should find themselves with a wide-open market.

Low Barriers

One of the factors that makes employee training such a wise business to start is that it's an inexpensive field to enter. "There are very low barriers to entry," Van Buren notes. Start-up costs are low (typically between $3,000 and $9,000), with most of that going toward standard office equipment: personal computer, software, printer, fax machine, cellular phone, and so on. While a professional office site is useful, it's not necessary; many successful trainers get their start working out of their homes.

For such a small start-up cost, the rewards can be tremendous. The top 2 percent of personal trainers earn approximately $300,000 annually.

But while money purchases equipment to get you started as an

employee trainer, there is one thing that it cannot buy: life experience or, more specifically, how to relate to people and an understanding of how to communicate with them. That, as employee
trainer Dee Clarke knows, is something that is earned over time.

EXPERIENCE IS THE BEST TEACHER

Dee Clarke has headed her own employee training company,
the Clarke Training Group, since 1984. She is recognized as
one of the best in her profession. Her client list includes some
of America's leading companies, including Intel, Chrysler,
General Motors, and The Money Store.

Clarke was working as a recruiter in the Minneapolis area
when she began teaching a course about sales training ethics at
the University of Minnesota. At the same time a company that
was familiar with her work needed an employee trainer and
asked her to take the position.

This was Clarke's entry into the training world, and she
quickly found that she enjoyed it. For a while she kept her recruiting and teaching jobs as well, but thanks to extensive networking, she developed a list of potential employee training
clients. In 1984 she entered the field full time.

To grow her business, Clarke avoided spending money on
advertising, choosing to focus on networking instead. "People
are hiring *you*," she says, "and they want to get to know you as a
person. [When I first started out] I did a lot of networking—
finding out which were the most powerful associations in town,
such as the chamber of commerce, [and then attending meetings and forming personal relationships with the other members.]"

Another way in which Clarke increased her business was by making cold calls—unsolicited telephone calls to human resource managers at companies, during which she explained her services and inquired if they outsource training.

Her methods paid off. Clarke's business grew at a rate of between 20 and 30 percent for the first five years, before she cut back on growth to avoid being overwhelmed with work.

Clarke credits her choice of training topics as another big reason for her firm's success. "I chose topics to which I could bring some life experience," she said. "I had been in commission sales, so when I was teaching sales training it was obvious that I was talking about something I had done, not something I just researched and wrote about. People could identify with what I was saying."

Now based in Las Vegas, Clarke says that over the years, companies increasingly come to see the value of soft skills. Just as a business is made up of processes and systems that must mesh seamlessly in order to produce goods and services, it is also composed of people who must work together. With the increasing diversity of today's workforce, such skills as good communications, leadership, and conflict resolution are even more important in smoothing over differences between employees. Workers come from a variety of religious and ethnic backgrounds; an atmosphere of suspicion and anger among employees breeds intolerance, which can easily lead to violence. Soft skills are the way to wipe out that illness before it gets started and affects a business.

"Our tag line is 'If your employees are the engine that drives your business, we have the tools to tune up your workforce,'" says Clarke.

A Fee a Day Is What Clients Pay

Traditionally, soft skills training lasts no more than a full day (as compared to hard skills training, such as how to work a new computer system, that may require much more time). If more time is required, it stretches out over a few weeks.

While lecture plays a part in Dee Clarke's training methods, she notes that years of public school taught most of us how to tune out a teacher. Thus, she relies on hands-on training, such as role-playing, simulations, or a game, that teaches the skills she wants to impart. She also says that people usually make judgments early in the class as to whether the session is worthwhile, so that first impressions are very important.

"It's really critical that in those first few minutes they see that you're credible, that you have an upbeat approach, and that you're going to offer them skills that they can actually use," she says.

Usually Clarke charges a daily fee; any external training materials that are required are extra. Fees for employee trainers vary widely, from $1,000 per day (or even less) up to $10,000 per day. You should structure your fees according to how you want your career in this industry to proceed. If it's your desire to establish long-term relationships with numerous clients, it's best to charge less, so that clients believe they're getting value for your services and will not hesitate to call you back.

Another factor in how much to charge is the employee level that you're going to be training. "Companies will pay more to send their executives to training than they will their administrative assistants," notes Clarke.

For beginners, Clarke recommends deciding if you're going to specialize in one particular field (such as the healthcare

profession) or be a generalist. Obviously, if you have specialized knowledge of a particular industry, it's best to start out offering soft skills training in that area, because that's where your
credibility and experience count the most.

"Credibility is an important thing, because there's a lot of
competition in this business, especially at the starting level,"
she says.

BRIGHT FUTURE

All the indicators point to the fact that soft skills training is going to continue to be a hot profession over the next decade.
Even though technology, such as video conferencing, may impact and change the format of such training, the interpersonal
skills that trainers teach still need to be delivered in a "hands-
on" setting. People need to work together; this simple truth is
the key to the what the future holds for the training profession.

SOURCE

Industry Association

The American Society for Training and Development, 1640
King Street, Box 1443, Alexandria, VA 22313-2043, (703)
683-8100, (800) 628-2783

Temporary Help Service—Professional

Job Description: *A temporary staffing service agency specializes in providing professional employment, such as lawyers, physicians, and so on.*

- *Start-up cost as low as $50,000*
- *Potential first-year earnings:$250,000 to $400,000*
- *Breakeven time from initial investment: rapid (one year)*
- *Excellent opportunity for people with physical disabilities*

Like many great ideas, The Lawsmiths struck Eric Walker when he was least expecting it. The engineer was visiting an attorney friend, Robert Webster, when Bob's sister stopped by. "She mentioned she was a lawyer who freelances," recalls Walker. "I asked about temporary agencies, and she said there were none in the legal field.

"If we were doing this story as a comic strip," he continues, "that's where the light bulb would go on." Walker knew temporary-employment services existed not only for clerical workers but also for engineers, nurses, and accountants. After Webster's sister left, the two old friends kept talking, a discussion that led to the formation of The Lawsmiths, a San Francisco–based temporary employment service for lawyers.

A ROSE IS A ROSE

According to the National Association of Temporary and Staffing Services (NATSS), the technical/professional and medical fields contribute more than 25 percent of the 2.8 million individuals employed daily in temporary jobs. Niches for accountants, marketing specialists, draftspeople, and other professionals—which barely existed a few years ago—represent the fastest-growing segments of the burgeoning temporary-services industry.

NATSS statistics also reveal more good news for entrepreneurs in this industry. In 1998, staffing companies helped create about 300,000 new jobs in the United States. The entire temporary-help industry has grown at a healthy rate of 9 percent annually.

Rather than "temp," doctors and clergy prefer the term *locum tenens*, which the dictionary indeed defines as "a substitute physician or clergyman." But, just like a word processor, professional temporaries want to work only three days a week or only during the summer. Most employers won't hire a nuclear plant designer for a day when their own happens to call in sick, but that's part of the beauty of the professional side of the temporary-service industry: Instead of rotating your employees daily, as do clerical agencies, a doctor or lawyer or chief executive stays on the job for weeks at a time. Dr. Alan Kronhaus, an internist who founded Kron Medical Corporation in Chapel Hill, North Carolina, estimates his temps average four weeks on a job, although rare

assignments last two and a half years. Longevity on the job elimi-
nates much of a temporary service's expense of employee placement. Another plus to running an agency for professionals is that
instead of collecting fees from a hodgepodge of clients, professional services take aim at very specific employers, such as hospitals or financial departments within Fortune 500 firms.

NEW MATH

Like their clerical cousins, most temporary professionals are on
the temp service's payroll; the service pays its employees
directly and bills clients for work performed by the temp. A
difference at this juncture involves basic arithmetic. A top-of-
the-line word processor might command $600 a week. Kron
Medical charges between $2,000 and $3,900 a week for its doctors, depending on their specialties, which include pediatrics,
internal medicine, radiology, and pathology. In turn, the company pays salaries competitive with doctors starting out in
group practice, which range from about $60,000 for a family
doctor to $135,000 for an anesthesiologist, if he or she works
full time—or $1,150 to $2,600 for a 40-hour week.

Okay, you may provide far more aid to professional employees than a clerical firm does, which cuts into profits. For example, Kron Medical covers medical malpractice insurance and
pays for air transportation and lodging on assignments, since it
places M.D.s all over the country. It even helps them apply for
licenses in various states. Nevertheless, Kron's high price tags
allow much higher pretax profits than the clerical temp agencies achieve.

Kron Medical, with revenues of $12 million, now bases its
45 full-time staffers in a $4-million building that bears the

company's name. But Alan Kronhaus launched the company from a spare bedroom. Despite modest beginnings, start-up cost $30,000, primarily for payroll until clients reimbursed Kron Medical for the doctors' salaries.

A START-UP SHORTCUT

Eric Walker and his partner detoured around the costly start-up phase with two ingenious maneuvers. The Lawsmiths kept overhead to nil and, more important, signed its lawyers as independent contractors rather than employees. In effect, The Lawsmiths acts as an agent, negotiating an hourly rate with clients and billing for the lawyers. The attorneys wait for payment until The Lawsmiths is paid, and the firm bypasses the cumbersome task of withholding taxes. "This arrangement means we don't have to have a slush fund to pay people before we are paid," says Walker. The entrepreneur warns that establishing your temps as independent contractors is a complicated legal procedure. Some states forbid the arrangement, and the IRS studies the contractor–temp firm relationship closely. "Check with a CPA or attorney who is familiar with recent tax law changes to make sure you meet the federal and state requirements," Walker emphasizes. "Penalties are harrowing— you can end up liable for all the taxes not withheld, even if you can prove the employee paid taxes."

The Lawsmiths' attorneys take home approximately $30 an hour. The firm tacks another $10 to $15 on top of that fee as its cut. Says Eric: "It doesn't take many people working to make a decent income if we get $10 to $15 an hour."

Indeed. At any one hour, about 20 Lawsmiths' lawyers render services to legal departments of large corporations or help sole practitioners whose workloads got out of hand. If 20 people work 40 hours a week, 50 weeks a year, The Lawsmiths accumulates fees of $400,000 to $624,000—after paying the lawyers.

To make things even more attractive, The Lawsmiths claims that expenses total near zero. "Be visible to the rest of the world, but start with as low overhead as possible," counsels Eric Walker. To cut costs, he and his partner work from their homes. In the beginning, a call-forwarding telephone service, costing only $18 a month, gave The Lawsmiths a business phone listing in the Yellow Pages. The partners spent $500 on stationery, business cards, and mailings, plus a similar amount to print a brochure. "Pay a design firm to do your brochure layout right," says Walker. "Don't reek of rinky-dink."

The principals do their own billing and correspondence with a personal computer and use a laser printer. Other expenses include lunches to entertain clients and rent on a conference room several times a month. "Clients never see your place of business since you call on them at their offices," explains Walker. "But you need a place to interview the temps." The half-hour interviews help weed out perfectly capable lawyers who make lousy temporary attorneys. Experience, top-notch schools, and letters of recommendation can't answer the gut question of who makes a good temporary. "The personality type has to be 'street smart,' " he says. "If an employer asks for a quick summary, the temp can't spend days on a long legal treatise." To interview attorneys, The Lawsmiths schedules a dozen interviews in a single day and spends $80 to rent a conference room from a turnkey office concern.

Some states require at least one partner to have a degree in the service you provide. Alan Kronhaus, who still practices one half-day a week, says his medical background helped convince clients he understood the type of doctor they needed. He stresses that dealing with payrolls, billings, and interviewing both clients and professionals requires some business knowledge as well. "If you don't have a business background, team up with someone who does," he advises.

FINDING THE CLIENTS

Kron Medical mails about 250,000 letters a year to nudge hospitals and group practices to hire its doctors. The company suggests clients might need a fill-in physician until they hire a surgeon or pediatrician full time, or until their own employee recuperates from an illness or injury. Other practices just can't afford a year-round associate when the bulk of their business comes during beach weather or ski season.

Rather than Kron's national focus, The Lawsmiths court a local base of corporations and small legal practices that hire temporaries to ease their workloads. To alert clients to their service, Eric Walker and Bob Webster spend hours calling heads of corporate legal departments. Walker figures he has 30 to 60 seconds to make his initial pitch, merely explaining how the temporary concept works.

"You have to have explanations at your fingertips," he warns. "People say: '$40 an hour amounts to annual salaries of $80,000—I don't pay my full-time employees that.' You have to jump in and invalidate that method of comparison right away. Explain the overhead factor—benefits, vacations, taxes usually amounts to 33 percent on top of wages. That's a hidden cost that they don't pay temporaries."

TRACKING DOWN THE TEMPS

Temporary services advertise for employees in professional publications. The Lawsmiths averages one résumé a day from a one-inch classified ad in the *San Francisco Law Journal*. Walker says many of his firm's regular attorneys have families and don't want to commit to long hours on a continuing basis. Others are sole practitioners who need supplemental income. Kron Medical runs ads in key national medical journals. Many of its temps have just completed medical training and aren't sure where they want to settle or even what specialty they want to practice. Kron offers them an opportunity to sample. Some are part-time physicians, such as the missionary who works in Third World countries half the year.

As temporary help becomes more accepted in the professions, service firms see lots of room for expansion, geographical and otherwise. The Lawsmiths plans offices for Los Angeles and New York, and Alan Kronhaus has far-reaching, if somewhat mysteriously phrased, plans for Kron Medical Corporation: "I'd like to conceive and implement other innovations in the organization and delivery of medical services."

SOURCE

Industry Association

National Association of Temporary and Staffing Services, 277 South Washington Street, Suite 200, Alexandria, VA 22314-3646, (703) 549-6287

Trade Association

Job Description: *A trade association is a collection of groups, individuals, and companies in a particular field that belong to a single association for the purpose of lobbying, advocacy, member education, and awareness.*

- *Start-up cost as low as $10,000*
- *Potential first-year earnings: $50,000*
- *Breakeven time from initial investment: six months to three years*
- *No staffing needed*

Aerobics instructor Kathie Davis was complaining to her husband Peter that professional conferences she attended frustrated rather than informed her. "The trade associations were for coaches or club owners, but nothing for instructors. We needed safe, new information on how to teach classes and services such as insurance. We needed a way to share ideas."

When the aerobics industry was still new, its members were scattered; some owned salons while others worked part time in health clubs or in a Y. And nobody, but nobody, talked to competitors. The Davises realized if they waited for aerobics instructors to band together to form a trade association in the usual way—where a number of leaders call a conference and everybody chips in money for lobbyists or research—they might never see one.

For Kathie and Peter Davis, the proverbial light bulb flashed on with thousand-volt strength. That night, "we figured out we should start the trade organization ourselves, and the next morning we got our business license," explains Kathie. A couple of weeks later, Peter resigned as a tennis coach at the University of California, San Diego. "We just never doubted it would work," says Kathie.

Five years after start-up, the International Dance-Exercise Association Inc. (IDEA) boasted 12,000 members and 35 full-time employees. While Kathie Davis declines to talk about revenues or profits, dues alone would bring in well over a half-million dollars a year.

"PROFIT" IS NOT A DIRTY WORD

Virtually every established business group has at least one trade association. Meeting-prone industries, or those that need lots of representation in Washington, have many splinter groups. While the majority still operate as not-for-profit representative bodies, an increasing number of founders say they intend to make a bundle. "I was afraid that many people would object to our designation as a for-profit group," admits Jane Booras, former executive director of the Executive Suite Network (ESN), the association that represents turnkey offices. (Today this group is called the Executive Suite Association and is member-owned.) "But what better incentive do we have to do a good job? We have to renew the members' confidence every year before they sign on with us again." Not only do members accept that reasoning, "I think many relate to us better because they're small business people and so are we," says Booras.

Most established trades already have an association, although you can buy one just as you can any other business: Booras purchased ESN nine months after it was founded by the National Association of Secretarial Services, itself a for-profit group. However, the opportunities lie not with entrenched industries but in start-up fields. In the course of researching this book, we found numerous brand-spanking-new trade groups (most operating in a for-profit mode). On the other hand, many fields are still stranded, waiting for an enterprising entrepreneur to take control of the situation and help unify the industry.

Unless lobbying represents a major part of your raison d'être, you can start a trade association as easily in Podunk as you can in Washington, D.C. We contacted organizations for this book in places as diverse as Moline, Illinois (The American Rental Association) and Albuquerque, New Mexico (The United States Personal Chefs Association). Until you need staff, an executive director can operate from home—and even part time if you don't mind starting slow. Your initial costs will involve marketing: identifying potential members and giving them a reason to join. That reason might be a newsletter or an upcoming convention.

WHO NEEDS YOU?

Before quitting your job to start a trade association, conduct some market research to see if industry members are numerous and interested enough to support you. Kathie and Peter Davis researched aerobics—sort of. They invested $10,000 in a 20,000-name mailing list of health clubs and hired an editor to put together an eight-page newsletter with tips on dos-and-don'ts, nutrition, and injury prevention. "Then we sent a flyer asking people who were interested to send us $1" to cover the mailing costs, says Kathie. The 500 replies, representing 2.5 percent of the mailing, amounted to an overwhelming endorsement since similar solicitations mostly garner less than a 1-percent response rate. With the first newsletter, the Davises offered annual newsletter subscriptions for $20 or membership in the new IDEA for $32. Those who joined the association got the newsletter for free.

The Davises didn't realize how lucky they were that their industry even *had* a mailing list. Many fledgling fields aren't so readily identifiable, and the trade organization has to build a data base from scratch. In fact, one profit-making activity most trade associations eventually spin off involves renting the member list to manufacturers or publications interested in addressing their targeted audience.

Jane Booras still copes with how to reach her industry. "No list exists of executive suites," she complains. "You can't even find them listed that way in the Yellow Pages." Within eight months of taking over ESN, Booras had identified 2,300 turnkey offices across the country. "In some cases, we found them listed under 'Secretarial' or 'Office Space' in the Yellow Pages. Also, we asked members to tell other suites about us."

SPIN-OFF $$$

Many trade associations are lucky to break even on membership dues. But your membership roster provides a group of people with very specific focus, people who have already proved how keen their interest in what you have to offer is by forking over dues. Once you build a membership, you can sell that captive audience all manner of services, often beginning with a convention.

Conventions serve two functions. They provide a much-needed forum where members network, meet suppliers, and hear experts; and, eventually, they can make lots of money for the trade association. (See "Trade Show Organizer," page 638.)

Most new associations start with newsletters or some form of communication to members. Early in its history, IDEA changed its newsletter into a full-fledged magazine called *Dance Exercise Today*. Not only did the magazine format provide more space to inform readers, it also found support in revenues from advertisers ranging from Reebok shoes to Lincoln-Mercury cars. Most trade organizations also sell reference and marketing material, including audio- and videotapes.

Once you let members know you're available on a continuing basis, decide what service is most crucial to your particular industry. If you decide to include the service as a member benefit, it can act as a powerful enticement to join the association; if you charge extra for the service, it can add money to your coffers.

What the aerobics industry most needed was liability insurance. An IDEA member could purchase $100,000 worth of insurance through the association for yearly premiums of just $150. Kathie Davis estimates similar coverage would cost an independent anywhere from $500 to $1,000.

The turnkey office group, on the other hand, sorely needed a referral network. When a new suite joins ESN, its name immediately goes into the continually updated directory that the association sends to anyone interested in renting turnkey offices. If a corporation needs satellite offices in a half-dozen sites, it calls ESN for referrals. Although the network is free both to the corporation and to the turnkey office, it is an expensive undertaking since ESN must print directories and maintain a toll-free number. But because it is a valuable service, ESN can charge relatively hefty dues of nearly $300 a year.

Jane Booras, who ran an executive suite herself for 15 years, also consults. Not only does consulting provide extra income, "It also keeps me in touch with the day-to-day concerns of the industry. It helps what I do on a national basis," she says.

SUGGESTION BOXES

How do you know what your members most need? Ask them, and ask other people who follow your industry. Set up an advisory panel of industry leaders early on to get feedback and to associate opinion makers with your association. They often consider the publicity as payment enough.

IDEA created an advisory board of medical experts. "We found ten professionals from various fields—a nutritionist, cardiologist, and exercise physiologist, a doctor in sports medicine," Kathie Davis recalls. "That was one of the smartest things we did, because we had no track record. People didn't know who we were, but these professionals added credibility."

It is absolutely possible to run a trade association without ever stepping foot in the field it represents, if you're willing to invest in lots of quick industry education. But outsiders will battle uphill. Former operators empathize with their members because they've been there. And vice versa. Members, particularly in new fields, like to know the president of this new club they're joining has earned the right to the crown.

SOURCE

Industry Association

The American Society of Association Executives, 1575 I Street, N.W., Washington, DC 20005-1168, (202) 626-2723

Turnkey Office

Job Description: *Turnkey offices, also known as executive suites or business centers, are small furnished offices with shared amenities (conference room, receptionist, and so on) for one or two people that a client rents from you.*

- *Start-up cost as low as $18,000*
- *Potential first-year earnings: $75,000*
- *Breakeven time from initial investment: six months to two years*
- *No staffing needed*

When Barbara Hildenbrand's boss quit to start his own marketing company, he asked his former secretary to do his typing from her home. "I was out of a job anyway, so I said why not?" she recalls. Soon the boss took office space in an executive suite and began to sell word processing, "which was mainly me typing twelve letters an hour from home."

I CAN DO THIS

Barbara Hildenbrand decided that barely making a living wage for typing day and night made little sense. But her boss had taught her some valuable lessons. As the former secretary helped cope with his start-up details, "I saw the mystique go out of starting a company," she recalls. "I felt this isn't hard, I can do this." He also introduced her to the concept of turnkey offices, also known as executive suites or business centers.

Executive suites are small one-or two-person offices that a tenant rents, complete with receptionist, furniture, common areas such as conference rooms, and optional extras such as world processing services. According to Jane Booras, former executive director of the Executive Suite Network (now the Executive Suite Association), an industry trade association, each of the 2,000 to 3,000 such turnkey offices across the country "generates a generic office environment." One-person proprietorships or branch offices "need space, but not the 1,000 square feet a developer wants to sell."

Intrigued by the concept, Hildenbrand called the real estate offices at Las Colinas, an office-and-residential development under construction near her Irving, Texas, home. "I signed the standard lease for 5,200 square feet at $6,000 a month. I didn't know enough to negotiate. I met with their space planners, and we put in 18 offices."

Hildenbrand had a $72,000 annual commitment—and nobody to pay the rent. It was then she realized she had bought herself not just a typing job but also a sales job. As the building's construction dragged on, she met with prospective tenants in coffee shops and pointed to the hole in the ground that was going to be their office.

A real estate broker saw a tag line on the bottom of the construction sign that advertised executive suites and became her first tenant. The development's real estate office also referred some tenants, and Hildenbrand got another referral from the local chamber of commerce soon after she had joined. But lining up tenants was only one of many challenges. Income also depended on selling her typing and telephone answering services to outside clients. A Yellow Pages ad brought in some business for the answering services, and notices pinned to university bulletin boards generated some typing.

By August, 9 of her 18 offices were rented. Hildenbrand, wearing hats of office manager, receptionist, typist, and space salesperson, had gone through $3,000 in savings, $4,000 from a bank loan against her car, and $4,000 from her parents. "I was so scared I broke out in hives," she recalled, until, somehow, during the last two weeks in August, she rented seven more offices. By year-end, she had hired a receptionist/typist and rented an additional 800 square feet. This time, however, Hildenbrand's real estate client negotiated the lease and got her better terms.

Today, Hildenbrand Associates Inc. operates 47 offices from 11,000 square feet. Rent has escalated to $17,000 a month, and Hildenbrand's payroll covers one part-time and three full-time employees. Revenues topped $380,000 with expenses—including Hildenbrand's own salary—of about $360,000.

THE DEVELOPER CONNECTION

Barbara Hildenbrand's success story is being duplicated in turnkey offices across the country. "You see basically three scenarios," says Jane Booras. "An entrepreneur takes a lease on anything from 2,000 square feet to a whole floor, then subleases to tenants.

Or developers see executive suites as a way to incubate tenants and bounce them to larger space, so they divide a floor and hire somebody to run them. Or finally, developers contract with secretarial services who run the space on a joint venture basis."

Jane Booras says five offices in a low-rent industrial space might cost as little as $15,000, assuming the telephone system is already in place. You can rent furniture, or even have tenants rent their own if you're on a shoestring. However, larger space in a high-rent district can go for many times that amount. Lease commitments usually run five years, so make sure you have either tenants lined up or a cushion to pay the rent.

Some landlords like the idea of executive suites, gambling that small business tenants will grow and buy larger space in their buildings. Barbara Hildenbrand estimates that former tenants now occupy 35,000 square feet in and around her building. With such trading-up potential in mind, you might talk some developers into favorable rent terms or ask landlords to throw in an extra, such as maintenance.

WHOM WILL YOU RENT TO?

Once you have the space, you have to fill it. In addition to tapping real estate and civic contacts, Jane Booras recommends targeted direct mail. "Decide who the best clients are according to your location and expertise," she advises. For example, a downtown executive suite may appeal to financial types or attorneys. Or you might have a word processing system that allows you to write press releases quickly, which might appeal to public relations firms.

Another client source is the Executive Suite Association, which lists members in a directory and provides a toll-free telephone service to companies wishing to locate turnkey office space in distant cities.

Selling turnkey office space differs from selling commercial space, because you're selling your services as well as an address. Point out the benefits. Tenants make no capital investment in furniture or secretarial and reception personnel. Clients can be in business overnight since everything is already in place. They don't have to make long-term commitments. While many executive suites ask for six-month or one-year leases, Barbara Hildenbrand leases month to month and requires no contract. "I found even those companies that sign a lease leave when they're ready." She shrugs. "Also, it's a selling point to say you just have to pay me a month's rent." Those tenants who are branch offices of out-of-town corporations also have to pass leases through legal departments, a procedure that can take as long as the duration of the lease.

SERVICE MENU

When you sell space in an executive suite, you sell convenience. A large menu of services provides two advantages: First, it attracts clients, and, second, it adds profit centers. Barbara Hildenbrand, for example, gets about half her revenues from rent. She prices office space high enough to cover rent on common areas, such as conference rooms, hallways, and the reception area. Secretarial and answering service income, both from tenants and off-premise clients, provides about 12 percent of revenues. A similar amount comes from Telex and facsimile services. The rest comes from what she calls "miscellaneous": markups on photocopies, postage, and office supplies.

Keep in mind that your biggest expense beyond rent is personnel. Typing is a necessity for your tenants, but you may barely cover a typist's salary from what you can charge. However, you can get better markups on telephone answering services since a receptionist can answer calls for dozens of clients. If you buy a software package to handle your billing, you might offer to do client billings as well.

By offering a number of special services, your client base encompasses more than your tenants, although they represent your captive audience. Barbara Hildenbrand also offers an incoming mail service for $20 a month to entrepreneurs who want a snazzy business address but operate out of their homes. "One client is an interior designer who needs a place to receive fabric samples and the image our address gives her."

While offering services other than office space boosts income, it also adds an unknown element to your business. You always know how much rent to expect, but you never know how much typing you'll have from week to week. The period between Thanksgiving and New Year's may be dead, for example. One solution is to keep your staff lean and hire temporaries for busy periods.

You also sell a tangible ambiance. Hildenbrand points out that clients are typically one-person shops who would miss the social interaction of an office if they didn't talk with other tenants and her staff. "I tell the phone room crew to talk with the tenants. If you're not on the phone, talk about the game last night or your vacation. It's not goofing off, it's PR. The tenants don't realize it, but we baby-sit a lot."

Because you "incubate" start-up entrepreneurs until they leave for larger quarters, executive suite managers say they see all sorts of interesting new businesses. Hildenbrand's former boss—the one who introduced her to turnkey offices in the first place—actually took space in her complex. "First he leased my smallest office, then he ended up with two of my largest spaces," she says. "He finally moved out because he needed more space. Then he signed on with my answering services."

SOURCE

Industry Association

Executive Suite Association, 438 East Wilson Bridge Road, Suite 200, Columbus, OH 43085, (614) 431-8295

Child Care and Education

Daycare Center

Job Description: *A daycare center provides child care during the day, primarily for children of working parents.*

- *Start-up cost as low as $30,000*
- *Potential first-year earnings: $200,000*
- *Breakeven time from initial investment: several years*
- *Future growth potential: high*

Society has not experienced such high numbers of mothers in the workforce since Rosie the Riveter went home at the end of World War II. As more women enter the workforce and two-income families become the norm, the dilemma of what to do with children during the day grows more acute. In 1995 the U.S. Census Bureau estimated that 14.6 million preschool children had mothers who were not full-time home-makers. For these parents, daycare is the only acceptable care alternative.

Daycare operators in most parts of the country simply don't worry about advertising to sign up enrollees; many for-profit

centers have waiting lists of children clamoring to get in at tuitions ranging from $50 to as much as $200 a week. *Venture
Magazine* reported that licensed centers cared for just half of all
children needing such supervision. Demand simply outstrips
supply. "Some children are signed up months before they are
born," reports Jamie MacIntyre-Southworth, whose five
Learning Tree schools in Pittsburgh generated revenues of
$800,000 in 1986. Her schools were so successful, she opened
another two facilities.

THE GOOD-CAUSE SYNDROME

If you're successful, you can expect easily to garner 10 percent
pretax profits. Given that norm and the country's demographics, the industry's reputation for lousy profits is downright con-
fusing. Roger Neugebauer, editor of a child care publication
aimed at daycare directors, suspects that "the profit motive is
not as strong for a daycare operator as someone who is in the
business of selling knickknacks." Because "daycare operators
may enter the business with a good-cause syndrome," perhaps
many fail to stress cost-savings and to pursue opportunities that
could add substantially to the bottom line.

Many observers claim anyone who doesn't make a comfortable living from daycare suffers from a lack of business sense. "A
lot of elementary school teachers are really dissatisfied with
their jobs and think they can just open a daycare center,"
observes Jamie MacIntyre-Southworth, who taught early-
childhood education on the university level before launching
the first of her schools.

Although teachers may start the majority of daycare centers,
many team with partners who have some business expertise.

Teacher Kay Koulouras, director of Perry Kay Nursery School and Kindergarten in Southfield, Michigan, concentrates on managing her center's 14-person staff and curriculum but turns over business chores to her husband, Perry, who has a management background. This division of labor is one reason Kay says her school has been successful. "My husband takes on most of the bookwork responsibilities," such as filling out federal tax forms, she explains.

FAMILY AFFAIR

Daycare, more than many other businesses, often assumes a family flavor. During various stages in Perry Kay's 25-year history, Kay Koulouras's mother cooked, her mother-in-law watched the grandchildren, her father-in-law did the gardening, and her sons earned allowances for cleaning the facilities. "It's a nice human story," says Koulouras. "But it also helped us cut costs."

The enormous 316-child Council Oaks Learning Campus in the Tulsa suburb of Broken Arrow, Oklahoma, goes a step further in its division of responsibilities by installing a business manager to run each facility. "The education people are free to concentrate on education," says President Jim Seawright, an architect who opted to build the school after a client backed out of the project. Of the narrower range of responsibilities, he says, "The teachers love it. They don't like to worry with the payroll, accounting, scheduling."

The $1.5 million that Jim Seawright's limited partnership raised to open his first school brushes the highest costs of entering daycare. With seed money of $20,000 to $50,000, you can rent and furnish a church basement or renovate a house to accommodate 50 children, which Jamie MacIntyre-Southworth suggests as a threshold for breaking even. To build your own facility, at least quadruple that figure. "A good number of kids is 60 to 80" she says. "Too many facilities with more children are just warehousing." Some operators gain reputation and experience by first offering family care out of their homes.

A START-UP QUIZ

With no national guidelines to follow, you'll run across different requirements for licensing, building codes, and certification depending on your state. Local social or human services divisions of state government can provide legal guidelines for starting a daycare center. In addition, check with one of the 350 early-childhood associations across the country affiliated with the National Association for the Education of Young Children (NAEYC) for more tips on starting a center.

Beyond legal requirements, the entry decisions you face come in great big clumps. In taking the following "test," recognize that not all answers are clear cut. What's right for one neighborhood and one operation may receive failing marks in a different situation. Nevertheless, questions to consider include these:

- Should you apply for government funding? A time-consuming, laborious process, some warn, but government funding can help you break even faster, particularly if you locate in a disadvantaged area.
- Should you accept babies? Parents of infants literally scurry to find facilities, and you can charge more for little ones than for their older siblings. The downside: Infants suffer higher

health risks, and you need a greater staff-to-child ratio to care for non–toilet-trained babies.

- Will purchasing a facility rather than renting pay off in the long run?
- Will serving lunch be worth the extra personnel and insurance costs involved in running a kitchen?
- Should you offer transportation? Many parents view transportation as a big enticement, but keeping vehicles on the road is expensive. Kay Koulouras recalls the emotional relief she felt when Perry Kay dropped its bus service: "I was not comfortable till the last bus came back every day."

THE PERSONNEL DILEMMA

As with any service company, personnel remains the most costly part of doing business in a daycare center. Kay Koulouras reserves 65 percent to 70 percent of her facility's annual budget to meet the payroll costs of her professionals, all trained in early childhood education. No one expects personnel costs to shrink. But operators say daycare has barely explored ways to cut costs and make money through implementing procedures that other industries take for granted. Consider computerizing some administrative functions, for example, or join a central commissary kitchen that services several schools. One dietitian can prepare meals for several schools and scout out discounts for buying in bulk.

In addition, utilize your assets—namely your building and teachers—for longer hours. Offer services beyond baby-sitting. For example, Council Oaks' offerings range from music, dancing, and karate instruction, to scuba diving lessons in the school's indoor-outdoor pool. Parents pay for these ancillary services on top of tuition fees. "If both parents work, their time is limited," explains Jim Seawright. "They just don't have time to take a child for ballet lessons after they come home from daycare. Our job is to cut down on the taxicab effect."

Council Oaks, which accepts kids aged 6 weeks to 12 years, also rents out its gymnasium to neighborhood groups a couple of nights a week. Some operations increase revenue by staying open late for parents who work night shifts. Latchkey of University Place in Tacoma, Washington, attracts some 25 students to a "kids' night out" once every three months. For $10 each, the children attend a Friday night slumber party, complete with popcorn, video cassettes, and dance marathons; the parents get the night off; and the center averages a $150 profit.

Jamie MacIntyre-Southworth looks for her edge by attaching her centers to hospitals, an affiliation that provides many advantages. For one thing, the facilities furnish a ready pool of enrollees: Some 90 percent of the 400 kids enrolled in Learning Tree schools are offspring of hospital staffers. Perhaps more important, the hospitals help foot the bills in various ways. In addition to outright subsidies or deductions from paychecks of parents who wish to participate, one hospital provides rent-free space and maintenance. "In that center," says Jamie, "we charge parents just $50 a week."

CASHING IN ON EMPLOYER CARE

Learning Tree's hospital connection acts as a variation on the theme of employer child care. Once touted as an enlightened employee benefit, daycare programs operated by the boss have not materialized to any serious degree. The Conference Board of New York City recently reported that out of 6 million U.S.

businesses, "only 3,000 gave support to employee child-care needs." Working parents should not lose hope, however. The Employee Benefits Research Institute forecasts child care as the benefit of the 21st century.

Instead of operating a business they know nothing about however, many employers turn to people like Jamie MacIntyre-Southworth. These corporations subsidize for-profit centers rather than open their own. Barbara Willer, director of information services at NAEYC, calls on-premise employer care just one of many options favored by employers. "In one common situation, various employers form a consortium and contract out child care to a central center," she says.

START AND SELL

In daycare, bigger often means better—or at least more profitable (as long as you don't sacrifice quality for quantity). If you cater to masses of children either in one location or in separate centers, you can buy bulk quantities of everything from crayons to apples to cleaning services. When you employ dozens and collect tuition from hundreds, you need—and can afford—tools like computers for bookkeeping. Economies of scale lead many operators to expand before their first center hits profitability. Jim Seawright says that even before Council Oaks opened, he lined up investors for the second of the 15 to 20 centers he plans to build. With eager investors waiting, "Financing is just not a problem," he insists.

Despite the advantages of size, daycare remains an industry of small operations. The five existing national chains manage fewer than 15 percent of all for-profit centers. However, the National Association for Child Care Management singled out an entire midsized segment of new companies, each of which has plans to open anywhere from 75 centers to 2,000. While many of those new facilities will start from the ground up, adding one new center at a time, "there are now a number of entrepreneurs whose game plan is to build up their child care companies to a certain size, then sell," the association reports. In fact, a number of brokers specialize in finding daycare buyers and sellers, a resource you might tap to get in quickly or when it comes time to sell.

LICENSING AND THE FUTURE

Most entrepreneurs expect stricter government guidelines in the future. And, at least publicly, most say that professional operators have nothing to fear. Guidelines are minimums, after all, and many centers set far higher standards than does the government. "We exceed guidelines so far that we won't be affected at all by increased licensing," says Jim Seawright. Jamie MacIntyre-Southworth is more vocal in her support of licensing: "I can take you to five places where people keep half a dozen children in the basement and tell fire department inspectors they are all grandchildren or nephews," she fumes. "Children lose their lives and are damaged emotionally by programs run by individuals who have no understanding of the business."

The national demand for child care seems poised to grow. The Market Compilation and Research Bureau reports that within six months of the birth of their babies, 63 percent of new mothers currently return to work. As with any other start-up, check out the competition before moving in. If advertising to attract enrollees appears heavy, or if tuitions seem uniformly low, you might want to locate elsewhere.

Barbara Willer at NAEYC has no doubt that in the future greater percentages of parents will choose licensed daycare over other options, such as one parent remaining at home or leaving a child with a relative or neighbor. "The decrease in numbers of babies will be offset by a larger percent of children in group programs," she predicts. "Economic conditions dictate that both parents work." And, as daycare becomes more commonplace, she suspects parents increasingly value the social experiences daycare provides to their children.

Even the financial community appears impressed with daycare and its potential. *Money* magazine named Kinder-Care Learning Centers, which operates more than 1,000 facilities across the country, as one of the "12 stocks that should stand the test of time."

SOURCES

Industry Associations

National Association for the Education of Young Children, 1509 16th Street, N.W., Washington, DC 20036, (202) 232-8777, (800) 424-2460

National Child Care Association, 1016 Rosser Street, Conyers, GA 30012, (800) 543-7161

Playgym

Job Description: *A playgym combines play, exercise, and learning with physical activities designed not only to help young children stay in shape but also to help them be more stimulated and aware of the world around them.*

- *Start-up cost as low as $18,000*
- *Potential first-year earnings: $35,000*
- *Breakeven time from initial investment: six months to several years*

If parachute play doesn't delight you, then the silly pool surely will. These are a couple of favorite activities that Playful Parenting, a Sinking Spring, Pennsylvania, franchise, devised for parents and their six-week- to six-year-old kids.

In Parachute Play, a half-dozen four-year-olds pile into the multicolored parachute while their moms and dads hold the edges high. Giggles turn to uncontrollable, down-in-the-tummy laughter as the parents circle, lifting the parachute to create bubbles that the children scramble to break. Each time a kid tries to climb out, she tumbles back and the laughter reaches higher. (This event teaches concepts of space and volume.)

The Silly Pool: Sometimes bright red Jell-o cubes fill the wading pool. Sometimes it's rice, tortilla flour, or cooked spaghetti. Turn a bunch of one-year-olds loose in the silly pool with plastic utensils to scoop up the "yuk." Then take bets on who has more fun: the babies or their parents. (This event teaches tactile and sensory awareness.)

TYKE-SIZED PHYS ED

Playful Parenting is part of a new phenomenon of businesses that offer improved physical fitness for very young children. There have always been Little League and Girl Scouts for boys and girls of grade-school age. But these new programs start with massaging activities for children as young as six weeks. Parents today are open to the idea of child fitness programs because they're worried about warnings that our children spend too much time in front of the tube and because physical education has withered in budget-strapped schools.

Some programs are full-fledged children's gyms, with equipment, activities, and instruction. Sportastiks, a program franchised out of Champaign, Illinois, that takes children age 18 months to 18 years, estimates that 5 percent of its children are "serious gymnasts," some bound for the Olympics, according to Bev Hayasaki, president of the company and wife of vice president Yoshi Hayasaki—who just happens to be 20-time U.S. national champion in gymnastics.

But rather than train superbabies, most gyms (including Sportastiks) emphasize the fun and learning of physical education. Explains Bill Caplin, proprietor of My Gym Children's

Fitness Center, a five-unit chain headquartered in Santa Monica, California: "There's a need for competition, but not in the ages we work with. We lay the foundation for physical education with cooperative sports and games—for instance, two children hold a ball between their tummies in a relay race. They have to learn sharing and working together to make the game work."

Some programs involve parents as equal participants and aim to strengthen the parent-child relationship along with the little one's biceps. This is particularly appealing to working professionals who crave quality time with their children but are a little inhibited about where to start. Gary Siebert, president of Playful Parenting, often recites statistics indicating "the average American mother spends less than four minutes a day playing with her child, and the average American father spends less than thirty seconds a day playing with his child."

All the fitness programs emphasize social and cognitive skills along with the physical ones. "We change the room decor with each five-week session," says Donna Porter, who operates Playful Parenting of Lancaster from the top floor of a Landisville, Pennsylvania, firehouse. "This session, the emphasis is on letters, so we have alphabet designs throughout. When we do the letter 'E,' we pretend we're elephants and swing our 'trunks' during the 'Make Believe' session."

BEVERLY HILLS OR CHURCH BASEMENTS

Start-up costs depend on the type of facility. Franchises of Gymboree, Burlingame, California, sometimes set up in churches or Ys where rent is almost negligible. The company's franchise literature says $20,000 will buy you play equipment, insurance, and rights to two franchise locations. Playful Parenting centers range from mall locations, where the rent alone might run $60,000 a year, to franchises in existing daycare centers, where the primary expense is equipment, such as tumbling mats and hoola hoops. Its brochure says to expect to pay $25,000 for equipment and setup and have access to another $10,000 to $20,000 for advertising, insurance, and working capital.

Bill Caplin chose a Beverly Hills site for his second My Gym. "For us, exposure is important. We're the Cadillac of the children's fitness industry and need to look the part." My Gym spends a lot of money on equipment, as well, ranging from a ceiling mechanism to lower swings and rings to a custom-designed, crawl-through castle. Keep in mind that above all, the exercises have to be safe and fun.

Charging $80 for eight one-hour classes, My Gym targets the higher end of the income spectrum. Says Bill: "We're getting more nannies these days. Both parents are working, and the nannies bring the children for social interaction with other kids."

Operators of less expensive programs agree that the better educated the parents, the more likely they are to enroll their children. "A lot of my parents are doctors or schoolteachers, who recognize the value of what we do," says Donna Porter, who charges $30 for a five-week session. The lesson: Look for neighborhoods with professional parents.

BE AGGRESSIVE

The big challenge is spreading the message that organized fitness programs that combine social and mental games beat taking the kids to the park. If you can't afford advertising, let local reporters know about your program. You may get great publicity through articles describing toddlers who slide, bounce, climb, and crawl. "You have to be pretty aggressive about getting out in the community and making yourself known," says Donna Porter. She calls several families every night, picking numbers from the phone book, to let them know about her center. She also rounds up some of her toddlers and their parents to participate under the Playful Parenting banner in charity events, like the Baby Olympics benefit for the March of Dimes.

Bill Caplin sends mailers to schools and invites parents into My Gym for open houses. "You can also send an instructor to a school with portable equipment," he suggests. Daycare centers looking for ways to entertain their charges might welcome you with open arms.

Such an outreach program also can provide a few extra bucks. You can arrange to visit a daycare facility once a week and give classes all day long to different age groups. Give the center a percentage of the customer fees, and the school director likely will welcome you aboard. You'll probably convert some of those children into regular members at your facility, too.

While classes will provide the bulk of your revenues, use your facilities for such extras as birthday parties and even summer camp. "Business is a little slower in the summer because some people take their children to the pool instead of coming to us," says Porter. On the other hand, "Kids in nursery school come to us only during the summer." Her camps run three hours a day, and parents can sign up for one to four weeks.

For entrepreneurs who really think big, consider what happened with Gymboree. The company generated $10 million through 350 franchise centers. In addition to exercise classes, Gymboree keeps the fun—and revenues—rolling with such extras as videos, books, dolls, clothing, and toys. Twelve years after setting up the first Gymboree class in a San Raphael, California, community center, *Fortune* magazine put founder Joan Barnes's personal net worth at over $2 million.

But before you think big time, you must build a name—and an income—with your gym. Recognize you're dealing with little people who have yet to learn the fine points of walking, much less tumbling, somersaults, or more advanced techniques. Make sure you staff accordingly. Bill Caplin limits My Gym's classes to 15 children and puts 3 teachers on the floor. Donna Porter needs only 1 teacher for about 10 kids since parents participate, spotting for their own children. "But you can't just hire teachers off the street. Both my part-time instructors have degrees in education and experience with handicapped and preschool-age children."

YOU GOTTA LOVE 'EM

Bill Caplin loves playing with the children. "I was a camp counselor and taught phys ed at a Catholic school. But teachers are underpaid and not appreciated. So, wanting to combine my love of sports and children, I went to work at a children's gym." After running somebody else's gym for a while, he decided to open his own. Now he owns two My Gym Children's Fitness Centers, a partner owns two, and his brother-in-law runs another—and Bill talks of franchising.

Like so many people who deal with children, Donna Porter acknowledges her satisfaction with her work goes far beyond the $40,000 or so she expects to make in her first year after buying the business from another Playful Parenting franchisee for $30,000. A bookkeeper by training, Donna once ran a daycare program from her home and wanted to work with children again. "But I wanted something people chose to come to, rather than felt they were forced into."

Porter finds a personal fulfillment working with her families. "From the time I was four years old, I always wanted lots of children," she says.

Playful Parenting's franchise brochure quotes President Gary Siebert: "A hundred years from now it will not matter what my bank account was, the sort of house I lived in, or the kind of car I drove—but the world may be different because I was important in the life of a child."

Supplementary Education and Coaching

Job Description: *Supplementary education and coaching involves helping students with their studies in a private, non-classroom environment as well as expanding their educational focus and broadening their academic horizons.*

- *Start-up cost as low as $20,000*
- *Potential first-year earnings: $25,000*
- *Breakeven time from initial investment: six months to several years*
- *No staffing required*

As the quality of education in the United States continues to lag, parents are seeking ways to augment and expand the educational opportunities available to their children. For some parents, that means locating a summer science camp or finding an art appreciation class for kids at the local Y.

Others are focused on goals such as extra coaching in one subject or improving test scores on aptitude tests. Whatever the specific concern, parents looking for extracurricular learning opportunities for their children are creating a new market for teachers and education professionals involved in the educational development of children.

Joan Lamport, founder and co-owner of The Teacher's Room stores, is one teacher-turned-entrepreneur who has brought her considerable skills to that market. In 1979, Lamport and a colleague—both of whom hold master's degrees in the teaching of reading—had grown weary of the layers of bureaucracy in the school system. Since Lamport's work in the schools always had involved making recommendations to teachers about materials to use with students, she was well aware of the suppliers for children's books, music, games, and educational toys. Lamport had also written a textbook called *Teaching Reading* for Macmillan Publishing Company and had designed and sold games and even songs for children prior to deciding to start her own business.

What Lamport had in mind was opening a store where teachers could purchase the books, games, educational toys, and other items that would help them to work more creatively and effectively with their students. After about a year of what she calls "very informal research," she and her first partner put up about $7,500 each, rented approximately 700 square feet of space in a commercially zoned house and opened The Teacher's Room. They were able to furnish the store with adapted home furniture: A butcher-block kitchen table served as a display area and Lamport's children's old desks took their place in the store too. The bulk of the initial $15,000 investment that she and her partner had put up went into buying stock for the store.

The two kept track of their inventory on index cards stored

in two file boxes—entering each item as it arrived and then subtracting each item sold every night after the close of business. "Pretty soon," says Lamport, "I was spending two hours every night on inventory!" Word of mouth from their former colleagues and occasional ads in local papers kept business coming their way.

Moving Up

Lamport and her partner were forced to move when their landlord decided to sell the property that housed The Teacher's Room. The two found a storefront space just five blocks away. "My son rented a van and we just packed up and moved," recalls Lamport, who was not thrilled with being forced to move so quickly that they had no time to fix up the new space.

The new move augured well for the success of The Teacher's Room; not only did they retain their former clientele, but their new storefront location drew in street traffic—a new market of parents and children. Lamport, who set up shop without even knowing "what business plans and marketing plans were," welcomed the widening of her market and began to add more games and other items to the stock that she had originally tailored almost exclusively for teachers.

"It was about that time that we decided to turn our informal partnership into a subchapter S corporation."

Growing the Business

The volume of stock in inventory grew steadily in the five years that they stayed in their first storefront location. Though the business broke even almost from the start, Lamport reports that she was doing about $400,000 a year when they left that location to move to an even larger space. The cash box and bulging file card inventory were beginning to take up more and more of her time—begging a better solution. "One day, a young man I'd taught in school came around selling cash registers. Initially," says Lamport, laughing, "I bought it because I liked him." The purchase did make doing business easier, however, and then one day her son pointed to her inventory system and said, "Hey, Ma, there's something called a computer for things like that." Lamport's son offered to enter all the data on easy-to-use off-the-shelf software, and The Teacher's Room went high-tech.

When Lamport's partner decided to return to teaching, Lamport ran her store in White Plains, New York, with part-time help for a year and a half before she found another teacher interested in buying into the business. Since then, Lamport and her partner, Linda Stern Levine, have opened a second location in Stamford, Connecticut, and installed an entire computer network as they've grown. Today, the White Plains store serves as the central order and receiving station and the two shuttle inventory to Stamford by themselves. Billing, bookkeeping, and inventory run from their computerized point-of-sale terminals. "Now I go home at night and my computers talk to each other!" says Lamport with obvious delight. Both she and her partner make heavy use of fax machines to handle inventory and orders. The store publishes its own catalog of materials for school programs for gifted children—a longtime interest of Lamport's. Levine is about to launch a newsletter of her own, as well.

Well beyond the simple cash box, The Teacher's Room accepts major credit cards and does a substantial catalog business.

Just four months after the opening of their second location, Lamport and Levine realized their first million-dollar-sales year.

Today, Lamport sees quite a few stores like hers supported by college and university towns in other parts of the United States. "The two go hand in hand." Teachers and education students as well as the local population support the store, says Lamport. Soon Lamport intends to branch into computer software for children. "If I'd had a business plan," says Joan Lamport as she considers the success of her two stores, "I couldn't have made it turn out better than it has."

TAKING THE CLASSROOM ON THE ROAD

Richard Zoffness and Janet Rogow's Prep Course, Inc., offers an interesting look at how teachers can have their cake and eat it too. Zoffness, a math teacher, and Rogow, an English teacher, both continue to teach full time and love it. They've channeled their considerable entrepreneurial energy into a business that specializes in preparing students to take their SAT exams.

Serious about their business from the start, the two hired a lawyer and formed a subchapter S corporation at the beginning. Later, they hired an accountant to do their books. Zoffness found the inspiration to open the business while teaching an SAT preparation course at a local college. The "inspiration" came when Zoffness took a hard look at how much of the fee for his course went to the college rather than to compensate him. "I thought, 'Anyone can rent classroom space,'" says Zoffness, and after talking over his plan with colleague Janet Rogow and enlisting her as a full partner, the two set out

in search of space. Fees for classroom rentals can range anywhere from $600 to $1,400 per semester, depending on the location. They started out renting space in a local high school at
night, where they taught two-hour SAT prep classes. Two problems arose in the early days of the business that Zoffness and
Rogow have since solved: The rent they paid to the high school
was still too high, and the fact that they held only late-
afternoon classes kept the two from drawing students who
played team sports in the late afternoon and early evening.

Rogow and Zoffness are both adamant that they are in business because they are teachers first, and both were also concerned by the fact that late-afternoon classes were not well
timed for students tired from a long day in school. Since their
business was new, Zoffness wisely decided to stay in the same
market when they moved. "Our reputations as teachers are
good in our school community and we didn't want to venture
too far outside so early in the game." Eventually they moved
their classes to a local community center that offered cheaper
rental space and more time. Now The Prep Course, Inc., offers
Saturday classes for students involved in sports during the week
as well as early-evening courses. The classes, which are limited
to 20 students in order to ensure quality education, meet for
two and a half hours each, and students improve their SAT
scores by an average of 140 points. The fee for each course is
$550 for 12 weeks. Despite postal costs for the direct mail cam-
paign Zoffness and Rogow send out twice a year, they've been
operating at a nice profit almost from the start, doubling their
business in just two years' time.

Communications

Book Packager

Job Description: *A book packager collects all the necessary elements for a book (idea, writer, designers, and so on) and presents them to a publisher for possible publication.*

- *Start-up cost as low as $1,500*
- *Potential first-year earnings: $50,000*
- *Breakeven time from initial investment: six months to several years*
- *Excellent opportunity for people with physical disabilities*
- *No staffing required*

Quick, what do the following books have in common? *The Joy of Sex, The Way Things Work,* and *Items from Our Catalog.* Number one, each was a bestseller. Number two, each and every one was created by a book packager.

Book packagers perform many functions, depending on the project, so the definition is still somewhat hazy. But the several hundred independent producers of books (compared with maybe 50 a decade ago) do for books what movie producers do for films: Just as independent Hollywood producers hire script writers, actors, and put up part of the capital to entice a major studio to take a film under its wing, book packagers hire writers, contract with designers and editors, and sometimes line up printers to deliver bound books to publishers. In other words, they take an idea for a book and nurture it into something a publisher wants to buy. Packagers deliver to publishers anything from edited manuscripts to camera-ready copy and artwork to finished books. The big difference between packaging and publishing is that packaging leaves distribution to the publishers' massive networks.

FROM OBSCURITY TO RESPECTABILITY

Years ago publishers often distrusted packagers as purveyors of slapdash balderdash; today they increasingly welcome book packagers aboard, almost as respected copublishers. The reason for the 180-degree turn? Unencumbered with bureaucracy, packagers often turn out books faster and cheaper than traditional publishers. The average packager has 5 to 15 books in the works at any one time, while a single editor at a publishing house is responsible for more titles than that. As a packager, you can devote more attention to a project, generally producing books more efficiently and for less than a publisher could.

Packagers are becoming even more important to the book industry as mergers continue to change the face of publishing. Every merger means less staff to handle an increasing load of existing titles, and consequently, fewer people to do the all-important work of securing new titles. Thus publishers are counting on book packagers more than ever today to supply them with fresh ideas, new writers, and potential bestsellers.

Your edge comes by being better equipped to tackle particular projects than anyone else. A number of book packagers specialize in particular areas—and their books on do-it-yourself woodworking or financial management show their expertise. Or you can specialize in books that require sophisticated design and production techniques. If publishers produced such four-color, illustrated books, they likely would need to price the book out of the market just to cover their costs.

Think you might like to enter the world of book packaging? A publishing background makes life a lot easier since, according to a *Publishers Weekly* article, packagers wield "knowledge of almost all facets of publishing: contracts, selling, rights, editing, production, design, finance, etc. The packager completes about 80 percent of the publishing functions, whereas the in-house editor handles 15 to 20 percent."

Sue Katz, who launched Sue Katz & Associates Inc. from her New York City home, had worked on both the sales and editorial end with such publishers as Holt, Rinehart & Winston, Bantam, and Scholastic. She also had a master's from Columbia University in business, which proved invaluable in putting together such titles as *Forecasting Revenues and Planning Profits*. "My original idea was to do marketing consulting for publishers, but I had a portfolio of ideas for books that I kept coming back to," Katz recalls. In the past, if her employer vetoed an idea, her only route was to drop it. "Now I had a chance to influence those ideas—but I had to get them sold."

BOOK PACKAGING FOR NONPUBLISHERS

Even if you haven't spent years in publishing, you might consider entering the field if you have an organized mind, can write a quality book proposal, and have expertise in an area where publishers are clamoring for books. While you provide the specific industry expertise, you'll probably want to enlist a partner who can play all the right notes in the publishing world. And don't restrict your expertise to a single book. "Look at the broad market," advises Sue Katz. "Not just books, but newsletters and audio/visual. For example, a retailer might say, 'Retailing is a very "today" business. Maybe I could generate a newsletter on hot store designs.' Or, 'I know retailing is taught in schools. What books do they need?' "

Also, take a few courses on publishing procedures and read such industry publications as *Publishers Weekly*. Every publisher treats packagers differently, but boning up on the publishing world at least helps you learn the lingo. Once you can convince publishers you have the know-how, you'll have an easier time selling your wares.

MAKE AN OFFER

The first step in selling a book is putting together a proposal. Proposals run 25 to 100 pages or more and include a chapter-by-chapter outline, a sample chapter or two, and a biography of the author. Include any data that will sell the book, initially to the publisher and ultimately at the bookstore. Figures on the success of similar books or on the public's growing interest in a subject help convince a publisher that your project will sell. While too many books on a similar subject suggests a glutted market, beware of the project that has *no* competition: Perhaps publishers just don't think a book on the subject will sell.

Above all, make your proposal look professional. "Book

packagers might spend more money on slicking up the proposal than a writer would," says Sue Katz. "You should have more marketing information. We fuss a fair amount with the presentation."

Katz warns that for every proposal you sell, several others never see a publisher's imprint. Especially in the beginning as you develop a reputation, "you have to be very agile and know the moment to let go." On the other hand, you also have to know when to push an idea. Katz recalls the origins of the *Rock Video Book,* which she ultimately presented in camera-ready form. "The idea was born when I was watching MTV. Soon after, I met a writer who would be perfect: She was rock music critic of *Stereo Music Magazine.*" Katz bounced the idea of a book on the new music video phenomenon off an editor she knew at Bantam. Although he expressed interest, he had moved to Simon & Schuster by the time the proposal was ready. Katz had faith, however, that he'd still be interested, and sent him a mock-up of the book (meaning a cover and page layout design) along with the proposal. Simon & Schuster bit—and eventually published the book.

"If you include art, a mock-up could cost $250 to $750," says Katz. If the proposal is never sold, the designer accepts that as a kill fee. However, the designer usually bets that a publisher will buy the book. Then the mock-up fee acts as a down payment on the larger project.

Writers are a different story. In some cases, packagers write the sample chapters themselves. Or you can contract with a freelance author to supply the sample chapters in return for expenses, usually phone bills and possibly travel fees. Like the designers, the writers hope to land a larger contract when a publisher buys the book. Knowing that many proposals never result in contracts, Sue Katz usually pays a writer a flat fee to produce sample chapters. "Sometimes it's embarrassing how small," she admits.

Once you sell the proposal, writers either sign on for a flat fee or receive a percentage of the advance and royalties. (A 50-50 split between packager and author is common.) You either subcontract other functions, such as editing and proofreading, or perform them in-house.

ROYALTIES

Publishers pay packagers in three stages. First comes the advance—or rather half the advance, since the second installment comes only after you deliver the completed project. The third stage occurs after the book is in the bookstores, when the royalties start rolling in.

Here's how it works: Let's assume you receive a $20,000 advance against royalties, which means you won't receive any further royalties until your advance is earned out. If the book sells for $20 in the bookstore and you've negotiated a 10 percent royalty fee, then 10,000 copies must be sold before your royalty payments kick in. In addition to the advance and royalties, many packagers also negotiate a flat production fee, pays for producing mechanicals.

In a variation on the theme, packagers who specialize in books that require production expertise often charge publishers a per unit production cost, much as a printer charges a publisher for books. Say a packager can deliver a full-color book for $3 per unit, using an overseas printer. The packager charges a flat rate of $3.50 per book. To offset these relatively slim profit margins, some packagers retain the right to sell the book in foreign markets. Since they've already paid the expenses for color separations, producing the foreign edition costs far less than what a U.S. version costs, assuring higher overseas profits.

How Long Is a Piece of String?

Packagers try to cover their expenses with the advance and production fee and make their profits on royalties. How much can a packager make? "Remember everything you've heard about what writers get paid?" says Sue Katz. "Some books get minuscule advances, others get millions. There's just no rule of thumb."

Some packagers expand their base of acting as the middleman between writers and publishers. To increase profits and keep the creative juices flowing, Katz coauthored (as well as packaged) *Having a Love Affair with Your Own Husband (Before Someone Else Does)*. Others coventure projects with other book packagers. The approach gains them expertise and valuable publishing contacts while multiplying their projects and visibility. "I did a coventure on *Sports Widow's Revenge*, an event book for wives of sports fanatics," says Sue. "My coproducer was familiar with sports, so I didn't have to research that aspect of the book."

While publishers, with their vast distribution networks, remain the most common source of packagers' income, lucrative contracts are to be found elsewhere. You can produce premium editions—a giveaway pamphlet, for example—for a corporation or association related to a particular book. Or you can package books for nonpublishing companies such as industry trade associations. Philip Lief, packager of *101 Best Businesses to Start*, finds that packaging books for an association requires just as much work as packaging for a publisher. But, he says, "You're guaranteed the sale of a certain quantity, which takes some of the risk out of the business."

Whether you package books for publishers or private organizations, industry analysts predict that packagers will play an increasingly important role as publishers merge into huge conglomerates. Publishers suffer from pared-down staffs while their marketing departments demand more "big" books. "Packagers have the opportunity to produce books that are financially successful because we don't have to worry about the financial and editorial constraints that are normally found in a publishing house," explains Philip Lief. Given book packaging's 150 percent growth rate in the past ten years, chances are there's room for creative entrepreneurs to carve out a niche.

SOURCE

Industry Association

American Book Producers Association, 160 Fifth Avenue, Suite 625, New York, NY 10010, (212) 645-2368, (800) 209-4575

Desktop Publisher

Job Description: *A desktop publisher produces a variety of printed material for clients, including newsletters, reports, flyers, and even books, using a personal computer, color printer, and special software.*

- *Start-up cost as low as $10,000*
- *Potential first-year earnings: $20,000*
- *Breakeven time from initial investment: rapid (one year or less)*
- *Excellent home-based business*
- *Excellent opportunity for people with physical disabilities*
- *No staffing required*

Malcolm Ross dumped a 20-year career in chemical research to become a desktop publisher. He traded in a monthly paycheck for freelance jobs wherever he could find them. Instead of having the swanky offices and staff backups of a large corporation, he works from his Gaithersburg, Maryland, home and doubles as his own receptionist and typist.

He gave up security to enter a field so green most potential clients don't even know they need him.

Although the desktop publishing industry is now booming, when Malcolm Ross began he was a pioneer in the industry by producing brochures, advertising, and other company correspondence for corporate clients. Additionally, he also started his own newsletter devoted to desktop publishing, *The Electric Page*. Did he make the right choice? "Oh Lord, yes. I don't want to be a manager again, but I'm growing so fast I'm now looking at premises outside my home." Acknowledging the inevitability of his success, he sighs. "Sooner or later, I guess I'll have to hire some help."

DEFINITION, PLEASE

Desktop publishers are no more than personal computer users who employ very "friendly" technology to compose designs on-screen rather than through paste-up, typesetting, art creation, or the like. Then desktop publishers go one step further by reproducing typeset-quality printouts of what they've envisioned on the screen. While some entrepreneurs use laser printers hooked up to their computers to produce a final copy, others hire a printer to deliver the final step of printing.

Just as you don't have to understand the mechanics of a car to drive one, you don't have to know the first thing about Silicon Valley to stage a desktop operation. But Malcolm Ross explains the process clearly in a monthly newsletter he sends to 1,400 clients or potential clients: "The laser in the printer is made to 'paint' a picture of your computer file on the drum of what is really a photocopying machine, by scanning back and forth at high speed while the drum rotates. Toner, similar to that used in photocopiers, is attracted to or repelled from the image ('painted') or un-imaged areas of the drum. From there the toner is transferred to a piece of paper as it is fed past the rotating drum." To make copies, you take the "camera-ready" image to a printer who runs off duplicates.

Suffice it to say the pseudotypography you produce on $10,000 worth of equipment contained on the top of your desk is professional enough to satisfy most major magazine and book publishers. Unless you scrutinize the type with a jeweler's eye, you probably wouldn't guess that it wasn't typeset.

A TOOL OR AN END IN ITSELF?

Desktop publishing is fast finding favor with advertising firms and large corporations to produce everything from company newsletters to menus to advertising flyers. Malcolm Ross pockets two sets of clients: corporations such as Holiday Inn and the World Bank, which hire him as a consultant to guide them through the rudiments of a desktop operation so they can publish in-house; and small businesses, which ask him to design and print brochures, flyers, letterhead, and other material, and for whom he acts as the publisher. "Basically, we're talking about designing direct mail," he explains. "Clients? Drycleaners, church associations, or anyone who needs to get the word out on meetings and services."

Sharon Bobbitt, whose Publications Plus performs similar services from her Evanston, Illinois, home, knows of a dozen desktop publishers in the Chicago area. Six months into her venture, she had matched the salary she made as AT&T's Chicago manager of public relations. Bobbitt's plans include branching into magazine publishing on her Apple Macintosh. "The machine makes up for my lack of eye-hand coordination," she explains. "Previously, I didn't have the freehand ability to create my own layouts and designs."

Whether you see desktop publishing as a means to another end, such as newsletter publishing, or as the basis of a business, such as designing brochures for local businesses, you probably can get started for less than we indicate here, simply because hardware and software prices continually fall. In addition, the computers simultaneously get easier to use and offer more sophisticated options. You may want to rent an IBM-compatible or Apple PC from a computer-leasing store to see which you like best. Also, you may want to update your equipment in a year or two as manufacturers spring glitzy surprises on the market.

You'll gain expertise daily, so don't let a little thing like computer illiteracy slow you down. A short course on the subject given at a community college might help, but the best thing to do is get in there and practice. Fluency comes within a month or two. "The Macintosh seemed to take my gloves off," says Malcolm Ross. In addition to using it to design flyers for the Main Street florist, he uses his Mac for writing his newsletter, for facsimile transmission, forecasting and spreadsheet analysis, data management, and other aspects of running his own business.

KNOCK-KNOCK

If you work from the spare bedroom in your house, how do you let customers know they need you? Ross joined two Maryland chambers of commerce where he "hit people over the head with a two-by-four—anything to let them know I was here." He sends his monthly newsletter to those small and large company contacts he made. *The Electric Page* contains a hodgepodge of desktop publishing news and information on Electro Graphic Services. Ross says on any given issue, anywhere from 0.5 to 5 percent of newsletter recipients call to ask about his services. Of course, the Internet affords another excellent opportunity for promotion and marketing for your business. Putting up your own web page enables clients to discover you and also to evaluate your work, services, and prices.

Sharon Bobbitt relies on contacts and references. In one coup, she took AT&T work with her when she left her job. "Large companies are downsizing their public relations departments and don't have the staff to take on new chores," she explains. Another early client was the Women's Business Development Center, a nonprofit group that advises small business. "It was invaluable to have a real client while I was learning," says Bobbitt. "I didn't charge them much, but I got a lot of referrals through them."

You also might ask printers and office supply stores to refer you to their patrons. Some might prove hostile, particularly small printers that offer similar services. But many may recommend you to clients as a less expensive alternative to typesetting shops.

If you decide to specialize, you may want to advertise

directly to businesses in a particular industry. Direct mail or trade publications can alert all the lawyers in North America that you can design their legal forms, for example.

Most desktop publishers begin with a variety of income sources. But Malcolm Ross, who consults as well as publishes, suspects aggressive promoters can take the desktop publishing business in any direction they want. As we said before, the field is growing and changing and it's up to the participants to create the rules—and the opportunities.

Computers

Computer Consultant

Job Description: *A computer consultant advises clients on computer topics, including what type of system to buy, how to integrate it into the business, and what type of hardware and software to buy.*
- *Start-up cost as low as $3,000*
- *Potential first-year earnings: $40,000*
- *Breakeven time from initial investment: very rapid (immediate to one year)*
- *Ideal home-based business*
- *Excellent opportunity for people with physical disabilities*
- *No staffing required*

Peggy Morgan is an entrepreneur with a unique product: gray matter, the unique knowledge she'd accumulated about computers. She'd learned "information systems"— a/k/a computers— on the corporate fast track at Sun Oil and in academia, teaching at Temple University. "I could not have considered starting this business five years earlier because computers were just becoming accessible to smaller businesses. The vast majority of my clients are under $20 million [in sales] and the vaster majority are under $10 million. They just could not have afforded computerization before."

COMPUTERS FOR EVERYONE

Well, now everyone sees benefits in owning a computer. As the cost of processing vast amounts of data falls and the use of computers as a standard tool of competition rises, far smaller companies than Peggy Morgan's clients latch onto PCs. The most prevalent problem: They often don't know which system best serves their needs or what to do with it once they bring it aboard. Enter the likes of Peggy Morgan and a growing cast of computer specialists. "If a company spends $35,000 or $50,000 for a computer, they might need to spend that much for a professional to develop strategies to use it," Morgan explains. "Many companies can afford that as a one-time fee but can't afford that salary every year."

Computer consultants serve two basic functions:

- They select the appropriate computer system, including which peripherals, networks, and software to buy (a one-time project for a consultant).
- They integrate the computer into day-to-day management (a situation the client may call you back for).

"Essentially," says Morgan, "a computer should make a business so much more productive that it pays for itself. We help people realize the profit potential in computers."

LOW OVERHEAD

As a consultant, you don't build any inventory, so you can start inexpensively. Unlike your clients who need more sophisticated hardware, you can start with a personal computer, which you probably already have since you must be a computer expert to consider this sort of business. Since clients expect you to visit their job sites, a spare bedroom or den can provide your office. Your biggest costs will involve marketing. However, the Internet provides a low-cost marketing opportunity.

You have to target appropriate corporate customers and let them know you exist. Like Peggy Morgan, who started Morgan Systems Inc., from her Cherry Hill, New Jersey, home, you'll identify your best prospects as midsize companies. Fortune 500 companies probably will hire an on-staff expert, and start-ups and mom-and-pop businesses can't afford you.

Decide if your expertise cuts across industries: Can you recommend a system as easily for a school as a chemical distributor, or are you more comfortable dealing with a specialty, such as accounting packages for financial departments? Geography must play a role in identifying clients. For example, if your specialty involves robotics, your factory customers may be scattered across the country. However, generalists may have all the business they can handle within commuting distance. Keep in mind that you don't want to eat up your start-up capital with travel expenses.

While your job as a consultant is to complete a specific project, many computer experts forge ongoing relationships with corporations. Many clients find it far cheaper to pay a consulting retainer, good for the few hours a month worth of questions or programing, than to hire a staff person. Set up flexible fee schedules and let clients know how you can help them in day-to-day management.

What computer expertise you don't possess, you can usually buy. Get to know other computer experts around the country and in your area. Many college professors, for example, free-lance as consultants. Depending on how much input you provide, either subcontract, by putting the freelancer on your payroll, or simply locate the right specialist for your client and fade into the background. Even though you may not receive any remuneration for recommending a specialist, keep in touch with the client. This approach builds goodwill both with clients and with other consultants who may bring you in on cases where *your* experience can shed light.

Those first contracts will be the hardest, because clients want references. However, even after you're consulting to capacity, never forget that new business represents next month's paycheck. "When you start, you market like crazy," recalls Peggy Morgan. "Then you get so busy with one or two clients that you forget that consulting is cyclical. When those jobs come to an end, you're in the hole with nothing. Gradually you learn to say, 'Dumbo, all this comes to an end without bringing in new jobs.'"

Morgan figures she fills only half her week with "billable hours," consulting for clients. She spends up to 15 percent of her time in administrative functions, such as billing. About the same number of hours is devoted to "practice development"—for example, keeping up with products and researching and lining up seminars that she gives for university classes or for chambers of commerce. Practice development also can provide revenues. You can make your reputation by writing articles for computer magazines or publications geared to your field of expertise. And if you have a better way to explain, say, a particular software package, consider writing a book. In addition to the royalties or fees, these projects provide dividends when a reader or audience member calls.

Peggy Morgan devotes the other 20 percent of her time to marketing. "At my strung-out busiest, I still need to court clients," she explains. "If my billable hours fall off, I devote more time to marketing." Morgan stocks a file drawer with folders on prospects she gets from talking to clients or even from the telephone book. She sends brochures and personal notes to the decision maker in charge of computers at each corporation, and follows up with phone calls.

TO GROW OR NOT TO GROW

Many computer consultants choose to stay one-person operations. The whole attraction of consulting, they say, is going solo, leaving the hassles of corporate life. However, an individual consultant is limited to the number of billable hours in a day. The owner of a large computer-consulting firm gets a hefty percentage of the fee generated by each associate. Despite the "user-friendly" movement and the help large computer manufacturers provide, business's growing dependence on number-crunching and computer productivity translates into an increasing demand for computer consultants.

SOURCE

Industry Association

Independent Computer Consultants Association, 11131 South
Towne Square, Suite F, St. Louis, MO 63123, (800) 774-
4222, (314) 892-1675

Computer Repair

Job Description: *A computer repair technician fixes all makes and models of personal computers.*

- *Start-up cost as low as $12,000*
- *Breakeven time from initial investment: rapid (six months to one year)*
- *Ideal home-based business*
- *No staffing required*

Two kinds of people get into the computer repair field: manufacturers and so-called third-party service companies. The biggies like IBM still control the lion's share of the business, but independents are marching away with a larger piece of the growing computer pie every year. The reason is simple enough: The corporations that sign the multimillion-dollar maintenance contracts would rather pay less money for better service—a package entrepreneurs can offer.

YOU DON'T HAVE TO KNOW COMPUTERS

Two other kinds of people get into the third-party computer repair field: technicians and everybody else.

"Say you're an IBM service representative," says Joseph O'Donnell, who once was one, before he began running the Mt. Laurel, New Jersey, Office of Service Inc. "If you can offer your clients a better deal [either a less expensive contract or better, quicker service—or both], they may guarantee you won't go out of business." For example, clients who know your work may pay their first six-month contract in advance. Or they may stockpile their own parts so you don't have to buy inventory. Meanwhile, concentrate on signing on more clients until you generate enough contract revenues to support yourself. In any event, you can probably hold start-up below $12,000 by stocking the most necessary parts and operating out of your home.

In addition to the technicians, there is everybody else. "More important than technical knowledge is personality and an orientation to a high level of service," says Joe O'Donnell. Sales types who line up the accounts contribute as much to a computer maintenance business as the repair whizzes, and many entrepreneurs have built fortunes by managing the operating while hiring their technicians.

Besides, computers are increasingly easy to repair, thanks to manufacturer safeguards and software that tells you exactly what's wrong when you insert it in a particular machine. "Instead of diagnostic knowledge, you need logic—if I pop out this board, this will happen," says O'Donnell. "Then you send the old board back to the manufacturer. With a little education, a good businessperson could be a fairly good technician."

BUILD AND SELL

Most newcomers specialize in a particular type of machine and its peripherals and try to saturate a geographic area. Service Inc., which focuses on IBM machines within a 50-mile radius, develops new accounts through referrals from computer consultants, telemarketing and direct mail (to executives of companies that use computers), and personal contacts gleaned from joining chambers of commerce and computer-user groups.

While several national repair companies exist (including some big enough to go public), as well as companies that tackle most any brand computer on the market, the more common scenario depicts a company growing to local capacity on one manufacturer's computer, then selling. "When you have to subcontract with independents in other areas, you've probably reached $15 million to $20 million in sales," calculates Alan Andrus, a computer consultant. At that point, a company has employees and office expenses that allow pretax profits of 20 percent of revenues—up to $4 million on $20 million gross. "Those companies at the upper end usually sell for one times annual revenues," Andrus suggests. In other words, if your company grows to $20 million in sales without partners or substantial debt, you might walk away in ten years with $20 million.

THE RETAINER

Many computer-repair firms service home computers—usually if the customer brings the PC to the shop and leaves it for technicians to work on. Many also charge by the hour for customers who don't want a contract. But the lifeblood of a third-party repair company is the steady cash flow that business contracts bring.

While competition from other independents isn't yet a concern for most entrepreneurs, you still have to give clients reasons to spend $200 to $2,000 every month with "Moe's Computer Repair" instead of with Hewlett-Packard. "You have to know which hot buttons to push," says Joe O'Donnell. Price is one button, as is the immediate and quick service many start-ups promise. Service Inc. trains its telephone operators as troubleshooters. "Thirty percent of problems can be fixed over the phone by knowing how to operate the machines," says O'Donnell. "The client has the machine operating immediately."

PRESSURE FROM ABOVE?

As computer sales leveled off, many manufacturers began stepping up their maintenance efforts to bring in revenues. Some third-party firms filed suits against the manufacturers, alleging that the big guys refused to sell them parts and told falsehoods intended to drive them out of business. However, most observers see this adversarial posture as temporary. "If the computer market grows again, the manufacturers will concentrate on pumping out products," says Alan Andrus. In down cycles, customers look for the most inexpensive contract they can find to maintain their products. "The third-party side of the business is almost a recession-proof business," says Andrus.

Computer Trainer

Job Description: *A computer trainer teaches clients how to use both computer hardware and software.*
- *Start-up cost as low as $4,200*
- *Potential first-year earnings: $40,000*
- *Breakeven time from initial investment: extremely rapid (one month to one year)*
- *Ideal home-based business*
- *No staffing required*

In the dinosaur age of computers (circa 1960), virtually every penny that corporate America spent on computers bought hardware and some rudimentary software. Today industry experts estimate that 95 percent of the money U.S. companies budget for computers goes for salaries. What happened? Over the period of swift evolution, the price of hardware fell drastically, placing computers in almost every company. Compared with yesterday's elite circle of computer eggheads who understood the working of every last silicon chip, today's computer users range from secretaries to lawyers.

Despite the proliferation, many nascent computer users would as soon sleep on a bed of nails as sit down at a PC terminal. Enter computer trainers: a growing number of educators who teach everything from basic word processing to intricate maneuvers around databases. And technology still changes so rapidly that even skilled technicians need constant brush-up courses. "We protect that investment in salaries," explains Lawrence K. Grodman, president of QED Information Sciences Inc., a Wellesley, Massachusetts, firm that trains intermediate and advanced computer users.

The Ways to Go

QED uses the seminar or workshop format, in which an instructor explains computer dos-and-don'ts firsthand to a department of employees. Other trainers range from solo practitioners who teach executives one on one, to video producers with tapes explaining spreadsheet analysis, to software houses distributing disks for operators who use the computer to learn about computing. "We estimate roughly 5 percent of the amount a company spends on computing should go for training," says Larry Grodman. "For professionals, that works out to about ten days a year."

Don't Byte off More Than You Can Chew

Manufacturers offer some training, and some larger trade schools have entered the business. But there's still plenty of room for the newcomer, especially if you carve out a specialty, such as how to write software or how best to get computers to communicate with each other. "If you try to teach too many things, the cost of marketing and sales can drive you out of business before you ever get started," warns Larry Grodman.

His point is well taken: You must isolate your market and let potential customers know you're in business. You may be lucky enough to line up clients through industry contacts and thereby restrict advertising to word of mouth. If that's the case, you probably can get into business for the pocket money required to set up a home-based office.

However, drumming up clients (a/k/a marketing) costs money. In addition to sending a sales staff on cold calls to corporations, QED mails brochures that resemble university catalogs—and cost as much to produce. (Smaller educators can print an inexpensive flyer that fits in a business-size envelope.) Because QED addresses employees who are already well versed in computing, it advertises in computer trade magazines. However, if you target a more general audience, opt for more general business magazine.

If your scope is more regional, check out the host of local business publications that now blanket large cities. You also can hook up with a community college or seminar producer. In addition to income from tuitions, you make invaluable contacts by teaching classes. If one of your students also works for a corporation, you may find yourself invited to teach the rest of the staff in-house.

HOW MUCH DOES IT COST?

Start-up costs also depend on the type of teaching you envision. Shooting and duplicating a video training guide will run at least $10,000, not counting the cost of placing it with users. QED conducts about half its training at "learning centers," or permanent classrooms it operates in a half-dozen cities across the country. "Our people conduct courses for corporate clients on a subscription basis," explains Larry Grodman. "The 165-member companies pay an annual fee that entitles them to blocks of student-days." Tuition varies with how many hours a corporation signs up for, but open enrollment runs about $300 a day. QED charges $2,000 a day to send an instructor to teach in-house, regardless of the number of employees who sign on.

If you instruct at the client's address, overhead is truly minimal. Most of QED's training takes place in the eastern United States because that's where the company concentrates its marketing. But Grodman doesn't think twice if he gets a request to train in Trinidad or Ireland. "We don't open an office, we send a person for a week or two, so it's very inexpensive. We've trained all over the world. How else is a staff in Lagos, Nigeria, going to get training except to contract with a company like ours?"

ACCORDION-STYLE CURRICULA

Once you create a rapport with a client, why not expand your curriculum? If you're competent in data processing, point out that employees could use instruction. If you're weak in an area where a client needs help, offer the course anyway; call in a "guest" lecturer and split the fee. "About two-thirds of our staff are independent contractors," explains Larry Grodman. "Most are private computer consultants who see their relationship with QED as a steady source of income." The flip side of this lesson: Let other training firms know you're available for courses in your specialty.

QED also offers management courses to heads of computer departments. These nontechnical seminars have little to do with IBMs. But remember the lesson of the railroad firms that failed to realize they were transportation companies and missed the opportunities in air travel? In other words, once you are big enough to diversify, recognize you are an educator, not just a computer trainer.

But chances are you will have your hands full teaching just computer courses. As computers continue to filter to increasing numbers of staffers who never touched a keyboard, and as manufacturers dream up one innovation after another for even experienced users, the computer education field presents lifelong opportunity. "It's a dynamic, technical environment that offers no end to growth," says Grodman. "This company I founded can go on long after I'm dead."

SOURCE

Industry Association

Independent Computer Consultants Association, 11131 South Towne Square, Suite F, St. Louis, MO 63123, (314) 892-1675, (800) 774-4222

Database Consultant

Job Description: *A database consultant advises clients on how to manage, update, and maintain their databases.*

- *Start-up cost as low as $9,000*
- *Potential first-year earnings: $45,000*
- *Breakeven time from initial investment: extremely rapid (one to six months)*
- *Excellent home-based business*
- *Excellent opportunity for people with physical disabilities*
- *No staffing required*

With corporate offices and small businesses relying on computers for their businesses needs, the market for people with the ability to write custom databases that speed the flow of information continues to expand. While many people are mystified by the thought of learning to write in the various computer languages used to create databases, entrepreneurs with a knack for computers are stepping in to fill the gap.

When Jane Kelly, a 50 year-old former schoolteacher, brought a $500 Radio Shack computer, she had no prior experience in computing. When she began to experiment with it, she discovered she had an aptitude for computers and began to teach herself how to program in BASIC—just one of the many computer languages available. Shortly thereafter, she struck a deal with an employer to hire her and train her on the job. She attended computer courses and continued to learn on the job until she started to investigate becoming an independent contractor. Kelly sent her résumé around while setting up her business as a corporation: JSK Programming Service, Inc. In the interim she worked for Banker's Trust and another client in New York City although her goal was to work from home. Two years later she landed a client big enough to make the move to a home-based business. Kelly continued to learn new computer languages—running through "X-base" family languages and then D-BASE III and IV before settling on a language called CLIPPER, which she has come to use almost exclusively in her work for clients.

Janice Pauly, founder of JTP Software Service in Ridgefield, Connecticut, was able to pick up computer training through her job at Xerox Corporation. A trainer in the Xerox Fitness Center, Pauly worked with the computer consultants assigned to help her create a database that would track workout periods and employee participation in the fitness center. One day she bought herself a book on programming, and six months later she bought her first Xerox PC for the work she was bringing home at night. Mastering BASIC and then the D-BASE languages, Pauly also settled in with CLIPPER when it came on the market. In 1986, she went out on her own as a sole proprietor in a home-based business.

FINDING CLIENTS

Jim Ragsdale, founder of Noteworthy Software, Inc., another successful database entrepreneur, suggests that one way to keep up a steady flow of clients in this business is to work through an agent. He estimates that in his nine years as an independent database consultant, he has discovered between 175 and 180 agencies that place database consultants on temporary assignments in major corporations. In fact, he worked on assignments for Pepsico, American Can, and IBM, among others, before moving his office to his home when he found a client big enough to support his start-up. According to Ragsdale, the one drawback of agencies is that they typically take a third of a database consultant's hourly rates—which usually are around $100 per hour. Today, in addition to working for major corporations, Ragsdale has found a nice niche among smaller businesses in his hometown—among them plumbers and electricians who use his services to create databases for inventory, clients, and billing.

Jane Kelly's clients come to her largely through referrals from her present clients. Currently she's trying to confine her networking to lunches and dinners, leaving her days free for work, thereby raising the number of her billable hours.

EQUIPPING YOUR BUSINESS

All three entrepreneurs agree that the beginning entrepreneur needs a powerful computer, a laser printer, and, if possible, a backup printer as well. A modem is essential for working on-line with a client's computers whenever a visit to the client's office isn't necessary. In addition, a basic home office setup that includes a computer desk, printer stands, an answering machine, and a good chair for long hours of work are the bare essentials. Some may wish to have more than one computer to work with. Jane Kelly prizes her portable computer and a portable printer for working in client's offices, and the many available laptop computers can easily fill the bill when portability is required. Kelly also highly recommends investing in a media safe to store all the backup disks that contain valuable client data. Kelly says her media safe has saved her many a sleepless night. "I know that those disks are protected from fire and humidity."

There's no need to maintain an outside office at the beginning. However, since computers, printers, and other office equipment can encroach on your living space, an outside office is worth considering. Since most database consultants must work on-site in their clients' offices, it's rarely necessary to maintain an outside office for the sake of clients.

EDUCATION FOR THE ENTREPRENEUR

Although many entrepreneurs are largely self-taught, Kelly, Pauly, and Ragsdale strongly recommend joining computer users' groups as you study each new language. There are users' groups all over the country for every language and software package on the market, and they offer newcomers valuable networking experience and contacts. On-line bulletin boards—where computer users can write back and forth to each other with questions and solutions—are also a major source of education and information. They are available through most on-line networks. On-line users' groups dedicated to particular languages and software programs are also available. The process of learning to program in new languages in continuous. As new and better software packages come to market, languages draw their own loyal database professionals. For the entrepreneur just starting out, the constant development of new languages and software programs is good news. The personal computer is here to stay. The constant demand for faster ways to process information assures room to grow for database consultants.

SOURCE

Industry Association

Independent Computer Consultants Association, 11131 South Towne Square, Suite F, St. Louis, MO 63123, (314) 892-1675, (800) 774-4222

Internet Marketing Consultant

Job Description: *An Internet marketing consultant advises clients on how to successfully market their business and its products and services on the World Wide Web.*

- *Low start-up cost*
- *Breakeven time from initial investment: rapid (one year)*
- *Future growth potential: high*
- *Excellent home-based business*
- *Ideal opportunity for people with physical disabilities*
- *No staffing required*

For years, marketing consultants have used their expertise to help businesses improve their bottom line by navigating the often-complex waters of the consumer marketplace.

Today, however, the proliferation of personal computers in homes and businesses across America gives rise to another new marketing opportunity—the Internet. As more people go on-line, the tremendous commercial opportunities of the Internet sound a clarion call to American business. Companies are jump-ing onto the so-called information superhighway as fast as possible, but often they need help understanding this new and often-confusing sales tool. That's when they call on the services of an Internet marketing consultant.

CHANGING RULES

If the Internet were an animal, it would be a rabbit . . . on steroids. That's because it hops around so much, and in such an unpredictable manner, that even the experts don't know which way it's going next.

Although the conventional marketplace is also in a state of constant flux, it tends to change at a more measured and under-standable pace. Tried and true methods of selling may have to be altered in the conventional marketplace to fit with modern times, but the point is that they can be altered and will often work.

The Internet, however, throws all rules out the window by constantly reinventing itself. What worked sales-wise on the Internet last month may not work tomorrow or, worse yet, it may be considered tired and stodgy. No one wants her Internet presence to be greeted by yawns and groans, like parents' sto-ries about how tough they had it when they were children. Instead, a company wants its Internet site to have "buzz," to be considered cool and trendy. Unfortunately, since the Internet constantly changes, today's cool site is tomorrow's snoozer. For instance, whereas static informational pages were once accept-able for a company's website, today's sites must be interactive, attention-grabbing, and updated constantly. A company that does not stay current with these developments risks not only falling behind but getting left in the dust by its more Internet-savvy competitors.

The Internet's perpetual evolution wreaks havoc on the old ways of doing business. For businesses raised on the "old ways," the Internet is a baffling beast—yet one that they dare not ignore. Revenue generated by the Internet is expected to exceed $1.2 trillion by 2002; confusion or not, for most businesses, that figure means it's damn the electronic torpedoes and full speed ahead into the world of e-commerce. Thus businesses leap onto the Internet, often smacking their lips in anticipation of the big bucks, only to watch in dismay as their big new sales venture goes bust. Hits to their site can be measured in the single digits, resulting orders are even lower, and even those people who return usually do so by accident.

What's going wrong? That's for an Internet marketing consultant to discover and fix.

THE WRITE STUFF

Early in 1989, Debra Jason opened her own copywriting business in Boulder, Colorado, specializing in direct marketing. After launching her own website in 1995, Jason added "Internet marketing consultant" to the list of services that she offers. For her, it seemed a logical move.

"I was specializing in direct marketing. The best and most effect websites are direct marketing oriented in terms of style and technique," says Jason. "So it was a natural progression for me to begin writing creative content for websites."

To promote this new aspect of her business, Jason wrote

articles about web marketing for trade publications. This circulated her name throughout the industry and earned her a reputation as an Internet marketing expert.

"Inevitably, almost every time an article was published, I got an inquiry through my website," she says.

Along with "electronic networking," Jason gave presentations about Internet marketing to various groups and organizations, such as the Boulder chamber of commerce. She also taught classes about marketing (on-line and off) and the Internet at several area colleges.

Her efforts paid off. Today, acting as an Internet marketing consultant constitutes approximately 30 percent of her business, and she anticipates that it will continue to increase.

Although she is quick to note that she is not a computer expert, her success as a consultant comes from her marketing background. Thanks to her experience, Jason can study a client's website and usually find ways to improve its performance.

"The mistake a lot of people make about having a website is that they don't realize that you have to market it like you market your business," she says. "You don't just put up a website and hope that people will find you."

Jason is extremely knowledgeable about search engines (the services, such as Yahoo, that initially look for user information). Each has its own criteria for determining a site's relevancy and therefore its positioning in the search results. Jason knows how to optimize a site's contents so it is consistent with keywords and phrases in the HTML code and, therefore, shows up early whenever a search engine looks for that particular subject or topic. This is a self-taught skill, and Jason continues to educate herself about the vast and sometimes bewildering world of the Internet.

"I have the basics for what I need to know," says Jason, "and I'm always learning more [by reading books and trade publications and taking classes]."

ELECTRONIC EXPERT?

To be an Internet marketing consultant, you must know marketing. While this doesn't mean that you have to spout marketing theories with every breath, you must know how the complex world of American commerce operates. Why have some products and/or campaigns succeeded and others have failed? What makes a good marketing campaign? What have some companies done to sell their products? At its core, Internet marketing is still marketing.

You also need to know the Internet. While the Internet is too vast and changeable for anyone to really *know* it, you must keep up with the latest trends and developments. What companies are having great success with their websites? What sites are bombing? You also need to keep tabs on new technology and trends, so that you can steer your clients in the appropriate direction. Remember, you are being paid for your expertise.

As Jason has proven, one thing you do *not* need to have is technical expertise in computing. You should have some basic understanding of HTML code, search engines, and web design, but most often your job will entail simply telling computer experts employed by your clients what to fix, change, or delete. In other circumstances, you can use the services of an independent contractor/computer expert to perform technical services for you.

The main piece of equipment that you need to start an Internet consulting business is a computer with a modem. It must be powerful enough to search the Internet quickly and efficiently and able to download large files and client websites effectively. You'll also need a high-quality color printer to print out this material. To create image files from existing photos, a scanner is also required. Altogether, the total equipment cost for starting a business shouldn't exceed $5,000.

As far as advertising your new business, the best advice is probably to do what Jason did and establish a reputation within the industry. Not only will this prevent large and possibly futile expenditures on advertising, but it will also help you network and make contacts.

Fees for Internet marketing consultants range between $75 and $150 per hour. Since start-up costs are minimal, once you get your business off the ground it should be possible to recoup your starting costs within a year.

IS THE INTERNET IN YOUR FUTURE?

Although there is much debate about the future of Internet sales, businesses are expected to continue trying to understand how to best use the Internet and their website for marketing purposes. That's why the future for Internet marketing consultants looks extremely bright.

"I think that we're at a point where [Internet marketing] is still growing at a rapid speed," says Jason.

Maybe those two words—"rapid speed"—can also describe your career as an Internet marketing consultant.

Systems Integrator

Job Description: *A systems integrator builds custom personal computers for clients.*

- *Start-up cost as low as $5,000*
- *Potential first-year revenues: $60,000*
- *Breakeven time from initial investment: six months to several years*
- *Ideal home-based business*
- *No staffing required*

A systems integrator assembles computer systems custom-tailored to suit an individual client's needs. He or she can build a computer to meet the precise needs of a business. At the beginning of the personal computer explosion, Edward Heere was vice president of marketing for Berkey Corporation. He was charged with the mission of finding a new product that would raise the profit margin of the ailing photo-equipment company. Heere, who had taken up computing as a hobby with a Radio Shack TRS-80, decided that the product that would make that profit was an IBM-compatible computer.

Heere searched offshore markets—primarily in Asia—for inexpensive computer components from which he could piece together that first IBM clone. The computer he produced equaled the IBM in quality and could be offered at a far lower price to a world newly enthralled with personal computing. The dispiriting opinion of Berkey's board of directors, however, was that without a brand name like IBM on it, that first IBM clone would never sell. Since that time, the world has witnessed the successful launching of scores of IBM clones, and the Berkey Corporation was in Chapter 11 bankruptcy three years after the board meeting in which Ed Heere had presented his model.

When Heere left the Berkey Corporation, he had just purchased a new home on four acres in Redding, Connecticut. "I had a huge mortgage, no income, very little in savings, and what amounted to a tin umbrella instead of a golden parachute from Berkey." It was then that Heere launched Absolute Computers—a corporation that builds and sells personal computers at a price point well below IBM's.

GETTING STARTED

Working from a home office, Heere ran a classified ad in a local paper offering IBM-compatible computers at mail order prices with local support. The ad listed the price and Heere's phone number. "I am the only person who runs an ad in a local paper every day," says Heere. "Even in the beginning, people called and said, 'I've seen your ad for several months now and . . . ' It's very important, I think, to let people know that you're there every day. They know I'm in this market to stay."

Heere aimed his business at the home-based consultants in his bedroom community of Redding, Connecticut, meeting the needs of people "who had already worked with PCs and knew exactly what they wanted out of their computer." Heere builds custom computers that give his clients exactly what they need while demystifying the process of putting the precise components together. "Everyone wants a computer and everyone's afraid of buying one," says Heere. "What you have to do is find out what the customer wants, supply the product, and do it in a way that allays the customer's fears."

For the first two months that Heere was in business, he and his family lived off savings. He already owned the PC he used to run the business, and the ad he ran every day in the local paper (and that still constitutes the only advertising he does) cost $150 a month. Apart from that, his only other overhead was for letterhead, business cards, and the components he used to assemble his custom computers. Initially, Heere also sold smaller items (such as modems and monitors) because they were needed by clients and they helped increase his profits. Markups range from 40 to 45 percent for computers with his company's name on them. If he sells a brand-name product to a customer, his markup is about 10 percent, while the markup for a product requiring support services can command a 10 to 15 percent markup. His business broke even in its first month—paying for the ad and his phone bill. Six months later, it afforded him the same lifestyle he had enjoyed on his $100,000 salary at Berkey Corporation.

Heere grew his business without ever taking a loan from the bank. He financed his own inventory and receivables and took building credit for his business very seriously. "Even if you have to starve for the first few months, you pay your bills. Eventually, someone gives you net 14, then someone else gives you net 30, and so on. After you establish good credit in a couple of places, lenders start coming to you." Heere, who still doesn't borrow money to grow his business, received a BB1 credit rating from Dun & Bradstreet—the highest rating in his industry.

While Heere came into his business with a great deal of technical expertise, he says that a sophisticated background is not essential for the beginning entrepreneur. "You need to bring a basic knowledge of the PC to this business. You must know the basic components and how to assemble them and you need good marketing skills. You'll find out soon enough from your customers what problems you'll run into. That's when you call up everyone you know who understands PCs and brainstorm to solve the problem." Ed Heere has, in fact, never taken a computer course, although he has served as an instructor. The beginning entrepreneur also can take advantage, as Heere himself does today, of offshore companies that build "bare-bones" systems (complete with hard drive and video card) for a fee, and then add the custom features each client requires.

As for other equipment required for a start-up, Heere advises that, at minimum, an entrepreneur must own a fast, powerful computer with a VGA color monitor and a large hard drive as a demonstrator. Heere estimates that with a low start-up investment similar to his own, an entrepreneur can expect to sell eight systems a month.

SOURCE

Industry Association

Independent Computer Consultants Association, 11131 South Towne Square, Suite F, St. Louis, MO 63123, (314) 892-1675, (800) 774-4222

Web Services

Job Description: *Web services involve the Internet and the World Wide Web, such as designing web pages, building websites, and providing Internet database interactivity.*

- *Extremely low start-up costs*
- *Breakeven time from initial investment: rapid*
- *Future growth potential: high*
- *Ideal home-based business*
- *No staffing required*

What do you think of when you hear the phrase "on the web"?

If you immediately think of being stuck on a giant spiderweb, then skip this section and take a deep breath. You've got a lot of catching up to do with the modern world, and you might as well be rested before you start. The Internet has so pervasively invaded the lives of virtually every American over the last decade that it's hard to imagine a time when it didn't exist.

American business has been profoundly affected by the arrival of the Internet age. Suddenly the old rules of commerce have gone out the window, replaced by a brave new world in which the rules seem as ephemeral as the electronic images whizzing through cyberspace. Many businesses require or want a presence on the World Wide Web (WWW). Anyone who performs web services is in extremely high demand—a fact that probably will not change in the foreseeable future.

Hyperlinks Make It Happen

As the Internet evolves, it's become clear that the World Wide Web is the place to be for business. Nicknamed the "web" because it encompasses many sites linked together, the web is the user-friendly part of the Internet. Users travel to various sites without having to know or understand how to operate the complicated software that runs the Internet. Instead, by clicking on simply worded hyperlinks, users happily zip from one site to the other while all of the computer wizardry that makes the trip possible speeds by unnoticed in the background.

Like any new technological innovation, it took awhile for the Internet to become part of American life. However, as more and more people went "on-line" and began using the Web for everything from researching a term paper to planning a vacation, American businesses realized it's where they need to be. After all, the web seemed like a businessperson's dream: a sales tool available for consumers 24 hours a day, 7 days a week. But who was going to put these businesses on the web? That's where webmasters and web designers come in. People skilled in the art of building websites, placing them onto the Internet, and maintaining them suddenly are in demand.

Initially, the functions of a webmaster and web designer often were split. A web designer builds the site, while the webmaster maintains it. However, nothing stays the same in the computer world for long. Today it is common to combine both functions.

As the Internet grows and matures, it is evolving into more of an interactive medium; instead of being content just to have a page or site filled with information, businesses want their consumers to interact with their site. They want their clients to have the ability to order merchandise and material from it, they want to know which areas of their site people visit, they want to recognize return customers, and so on. To get these results, they turn to a web services business—such as DataDrive.

MASTER OF THE WEB

It was 1991 when graduate student Alan D. Thornhill began noticing the embryonic Internet.

"I started paying attention to what was going on with hypertext and data exchange," he says. Faced with a need to send large amounts of data to colleagues, Thornhill began experimenting with early servers such as Gopher. In 1993 he launched his first web server using bits and pieces of software he pieced together, since there wasn't an easy way to get onto the still-developing Internet at the time. Still, he saw the potential that the Internet held.

"I was waiting tables at the time to survive, and I realized that I could make a lot more money consulting on the Internet than I could waiting tables," he says.

Thornhill began consulting with companies and individuals that wanted to put themselves onto the Internet. In 1996 he moved to Houston, took an academic position at Rice University, and launched DataDrive as a Web services company. Today DataDrive (www.datadrive.com) supports the WWW presence of approximately 120 clients.

Although Thornhill started out as primarily a designer of websites, the advent of more powerful and easy-to-understand software meant that anyone could build a site. Thus he positioned DataDrive as a company that provides a variety of web services. Among the company's services are web page construction, web-optimized image and graphics creation, and securing/establishing a presence on a web server.

DataDrive's specialty is providing database interactivity, which means building websites that actually can deal with and react to a client's needs, rather than just being a static document. Thornhill feels that this is the future of the Internet.

"This is where the Internet must go if it's going to survive," he says. "It has to interact with the user, because people get bored with static pages that don't change. A website has to adapt to a user, and those are the type [of sites] that we build."

Although his company is located on the Internet, one of the most pervasive advertising/marketing vehicles ever devised in the modern age, Thornhill says old-fashioned referrals and word of mouth caused DataDrive's client list to swell. Today his company is so successful that it serves clients all over the world.

"It's all I can do to keep [the client roster] reigned in," says Thornhill.

SPINNING YOUR OWN WEB

Thanks to the dramatic drop in the cost of computer hardware, starting your own web services business is extremely inexpensive. For under $3,000 you can buy a sufficiently powerful computer and software to begin designing web pages. Even better, some web software is available for free directly off the Internet, or else as shareware, which means that you pay just a small fee if you utilize it.

Since this is an ideal home-based business, the expense of finding and renting a commercial location is eliminated. In addition, any computer that's powerful enough to design websites certainly is going to be sufficient to serve your other business needs such as bookkeeping, which excludes the need to buy a separate system just for those purposes.

"The real expense is in having a machine connected to the Internet 24 hours per day, 7 days per week," says Thornhill. "You have to have a server connected to the Internet." One way to cut that cost is to buy the services from a company that specializes in maintaining continuous contact with the Internet.

Even with these costs, however, it is possible to begin a web services business for under $7,500. Your start-up cost can be recouped rapidly once you obtain paying clients. If you consult, the standard fee ranges from $100 to $150. As for project fees, DataDrive uses a three-tiered rate schedule that is representative of the industry in general: $2,000 to $4,000 for basic services, such as setting up a "no-frills" website; $8,000 to $15,000 for establishing a more sophisticated site with some interactivity; and $20,000 to $40,000 for having a completely interactive site. The majority of DataDrive's projects fall within the $8,000 to $15,000 range.

ARE YOU "WEB" WORTHY?

Obviously, in order to start a web services business, you must understand computers and the Internet right down to the last byte. Since you will be interacting with clients and trying to understand their needs, as well, you also must be adept at dealing with a diverse group of businesspeople. Often they come to you not knowing what they want, and need you to guide them.

"You have to understand your client's needs, even if they don't," says Thornhill.

As with all businesses, the more you put into a Web services firm, the more you earn. Since credibility is important in this field, Thornhill advises anyone starting out to do a few nonpaying jobs in order to build a reputation.

"That's what DataDrive did early on," he says. "They [the clients] couldn't afford much, but I saw a real opportunity to make a big splash on the Internet with their project. Thus I was able to build my portfolio and able to sell myself to others and find paying clients."

Once you have paying clients, however, it's possible to make a six-figure income if you want to invest the time and effort. The Internet has become an integral part of American commerce. Businesses are searching for those who know how to make it speak their language, as well.

Environment-Related Businesses

Ecotourism

Job Description: *Ecotourism involves arranging environmentally themed tourist expeditions all over the world, such as to Africa to look at elephants or to Alaska to observe wildlife.*

- *Start-up cost as low as $5,000*
- *Potential first-year earnings: $40,000*
- *Breakeven time from initial investment: six months to several years*

When baby boomers take a vacation these days, they want more than a sojourn in a new country or a chance to immerse themselves in a new culture—they want their travels to stimulate them intellectually and help them to return home fitter and healthier than when they took off. And in a world where both national parks and Brazilian rain forests have been threatened by environmental hazards and less-than-considerate tourists, they want their vacations to be environmentally correct. Enter the relatively new industry of "ecotourism," which offers travelers a chance to better the condition of the planet while improving their own health and fitness.

According to the World Tourism Organization, in 1996 there were 592 million tourists, who spent $423 billion. It is estimated that ecotourism accounted for one-third of these travelers. A 1997 article in the *Economist* called ecotourism "hot." Some companies in the industry go even further in their commitment to the ecosystem by donating a portion of the proceeds received for a tour to a conservation group in the area. In fact, at Sobek Expeditions, a leader in the field of ecotourism, founder and president Richard Bangs has an Environmental Desk with a full-time employee dedicated to seeking out the conservation groups and sites most in need of contributions in each country where his company offers tours.

Opportunities for entrepreneurs in the ecotourism industry abound. Those who operate small tours by gathering interested vacationers from advertisements taken out in the back of industry magazines are known as "outfitters." An ecotourism venture has the potential to grow into a multimillion-dollar corporation that can take environmentally minded tourists virtually anywhere in the world. Among the countries that are leaders in ecotourism are Australia, Kenya, and Costa Rica; the latter two estimate that eight out of ten visitors come to observe the wildlife.

The entrepreneurial adventures of Richard Bangs offer an inspiring profile of someone who has become a pioneer in the industry. A longtime outdoors enthusiast who had spent his college summers as a guide on the Colorado River, Bangs decided to take a year off after graduating from Northwestern University for what he calls "a last yahoo before getting serious about life." Bangs immediately set his sights on going to Africa to try "running" a river similar to the Colorado. He spent hours researching the trip in libraries, gathered some friends to join him, and eventually found some sponsors to augment his meager $150 of capital. Soon they were where they wanted to be— running rivers in Ethiopia and offering small tours for expatriates. Bangs said his African sojourn inspired them: "We said 'Wow! Why don't we try to start a little company?' " Bangs and his friends placed two ads in major newspapers announcing their first commercial trip. They placed a one-shot ad in the *Wall Street Journal's* Thursday edition and a small ad in the Sunday *New York Times*. Those two ads generated enough responses to launch their first commercial trip. They had ten clients and six guides. The group continued to offer trips to Africa for about a year before they "got ambitious," says Bangs. They started offering more exotic trips to South America and New Guinea as their horizons expanded.

Bangs and two of his original partners incorporated in 1973. Prior to that, they had been able to run a far more "loose-knit operation," according to Bangs. "This is not a very capital-intensive business even now," explains Bangs, since the entrepreneur collects the fees for the trip from clients in advance and therefore does not need to front a lot of money to get a trip off the ground. "To survive in the business is very difficult," cautions Bangs. "We had a very rough time for the first five years." Among the difficulties that he and his partners encountered during those early years was the struggle to get travel agents to recognize and sell their product. Bangs notes, "We were pariahs in the travel industry." But as they offered more trips and produced more satisfied customers, word of mouth and good press coverage combined to give their company the legitimacy it needed. Business really took off as the partners recognized and tapped into the demand for vacations that catered to the generation that had grown up in the 1960s and wanted more rigorous travel and an experience that would stimulate tourists physically and intellectually. There is also the general appeal of escape from stress to continue to fuel the market for ecotourism.

At first, Bangs and his partners did not directly market their tours to people interested in the environment. But, he says, creating an understanding of our goals "was something that was just of de facto importance to us. Each group that we took received an extensive lecture before departure on such matters as environmental and cultural sensitivity. We didn't go into this for the almighty buck," says Bangs. "We really believed that this was a worthwhile endeavor." There is, however, a very sound business reason for their environmental concern. "We're traveling to places with very fragile ecosystems, and if we contribute to their demise, we're out of business. No one wants to travel through litter-covered, pillaged countries."

Despite the tough early years of growing their business, Richard Bangs reports that Sobek Expeditions now does $15 million of business a year with an annual growth rate between 10 and 15 percent. The partners employ 45 people in their main office—among them sales agents and trip processors, who plan each trip and prepare the clients for the experience, a process that covers everything from getting the right equipment to making sure that the clients are mentally prepared for the expedition. "These days travelers expect a lot of professionalism from an outfit like ours," says Bangs. "We're no longer living in those innocent times when a basically 'ragtag' outfit can take out an ad and put together a trip on little more than a good concept."

Today, Sobek Expeditions offers boat trips in the Galapagos Islands and tours on their leased cruise ship, *The Illyria*—which boasts spacious cabins and daily lectures by scientists and naturalists on board. They even plan tours to the North Pole. With each new tour they offer, responsibility and liability increase, and liability insurance is a major expense for the operation. The company has to abide by limits placed by foreign governments on the maximum number of tourists allowed into a protected area at any given time and book their trips accordingly. The rapidly changing geopolitical map continually opens up new areas for travel, too, but creates occasional headaches when a trip has to be canceled owing to unrest or even a coup in the area chosen for a tour. Providing equipment in each country also requires meticulous planning—and in this business, equipment includes everything from rafts and cooking supplies to first-aid kits.

It is possible to get into the ecotourism business on a smaller scale on very little capital, and even a small operator can gross $50,000 a year and up. "The sky's the limit!" says Richard Bangs when asked about the potential earnings for an entrepreneur, and he ought to know as he now has planes in those skies, boats on the Nile, and is opening new territory to environmentally conscious tourists every day.

Recycler

Job Description: *A recycler collects paper, glass, aluminum, and other waste materials and recycles them for profit.*

- *Start-up cost as low as $2,000*
- *Potential first-year earnings: $10,000*
- *Breakeven time from initial investment: rapid (as little as six months)*
- *Ideal home-based business*
- *No staffing required*

Looking for a venture in a relatively new field, with low start-up costs and an infinite supply of raw materials? As added incentives, throw in the documented support of the American public and the knowledge that your involvement in this enterprise will contribute to an ever-growing global battle against pollution. If your interest is piqued, then recycling may be the business for you.

According to the Council for Solid Waste Solutions, each American now discards over four pounds of waste each day—as a country, we throw away about 180 million tons of solid waste each year. We used to thoughtlessly toss out empty jars and cans. But as landfill space has become alarmingly scarce, and increased public awareness has led many communities to disavow noxious methods of waste disposal such as incineration, the search for disposal alternatives has set the stage for the emergence of the environment-friendly recycling industry.

"Recycling," as we have come to know it, is an umbrella term for a set of procedures and techniques that bestow new life on used manufactured products such as glass, paper, and cans. This broad perception of the field underscores the vast range of opportunities that are available to entrepreneurs on all levels. While the beginning businessperson probably will discover that industrial aluminum recycling is not viable as a low-cost start-up, the more rudimentary phases of recycling, consisting of collection and redemption, offer a solid and accessible starting point from which to form a company.

REDEEMING ACTIVITIES

As a result of losing a bet, Guy Polhemus spent four weekends working in a New York City soup kitchen in 1984. With a B.A. in mass communications from Emerson College in Boston and a background in film production and media consulting, Polhemus was not exactly primed for a transformative experience. However, his direct confrontation with the profound daily problems of the homeless affected him deeply. During those weekends, he saw thousands of homeless people benefiting from New York State's "bottle law," which requires consumers to pay a five-cent deposit on purchased containers, to be refunded by the bottler upon return. Polhemus observed that consumers and collectors who hauled their containers to local supermarkets faced long hostile waits before they received their refunds. Prompted by his desire to exploit the inadequacy of these existing structures, Polhemus decided that a redemption center catering to homeless collectors would comply with the "bottle bill," aid the environment, and provide job opportunities for the homeless as well. Within three years, Polhemus set up WE CAN, a not-for-profit organization based in midtown Manhattan.

Polhemus's story is flecked with small miracles, such as his stumbling upon a rent-free 10,000-square-foot vacant lot when he searched for start-up space, and the initial foundation support he captured, thanks to a healthy dose of publicity. Yet, while his company is philanthropically oriented, its growth and success are due to the type of savvy management to which any organization should aspire. Polhemus started collecting containers with $7,000, a staff consisting of 3 homeless people, and incorporation papers drawn up on a pro bono basis by the law firm of Milbank, Tweed, Hadley & McCloy. Today WE CAN has four redemption centers, employs 100 people, and has paid out over $5 million in nickel deposits.

The redemption centers work on a very simple basis. WE CAN pays collectors a nickel for each container they bring in. The returned containers are accumulated on the grounds of the redemption center, where employees separate them by brand. No distinctions are made according to color or size, nor are labels removed. Then trucks from various bottling companies arrive regularly to cart off the latest stockpiles of the city's plastic, glass, and aluminum containers. Bottlers are required by state law to buy back used containers and to pay an additional handling fee of one and a half cents per container to the redemption center. As the Glass Packaging Institute notes, approximately 30 percent of all glass containers now contain recycled material (known as "cullet"), so it is clear that bottlers are responding to both government mandate and the public's mounting concern.

COLLECTION BOXES

In addition to the redemption centers, WE CAN operates the Collection Network, which places collection boxes in offices throughout the city, enabling organizations that participate to "comply with local recycling laws while helping poor and homeless New Yorkers." Companies fill the three-feet-tall boxes with nonbreakable "empties," and WE CAN picks up the discarded material on a scheduled basis. The proceeds from the "donated" containers offset the operating costs of the redemption centers and pay the salaries of the formerly homeless employees. Simply put, diversification has allowed Guy Polhemus's dream of recycling to become a triumphant reality.

While WE CAN operates on a not-for-profit basis, there is certainly money to be made in the collection and redemption of beverage containers. The key to succeeding in this business is to find an area that has yet to be tapped by collectors or redemption centers and to get the word out once you open up shop. Although it would seem as if recyclers would fare best in densely populated areas, the Aluminum Recycling Association notes that the abundance of storage space enjoyed by the rural entrepreneur results in higher rates of recycling away from the cities.

WE CAN's Collection Network gets its goods for free, as participating businesses reap benefits such as a lower volume of garbage to be taken away by private carters, tax deductions, and a reputation for environmental and social concern. On the entrepreneurial side, private collectors usually pay a flat fee, such as $20 per ton of glass bottles, for the right to place a receptacle on the property of a participating establishment, and then arrange for regular pickup. Profit emerges from the sale of collected containers to recycling companies. In the case of glass, collectors can sell their amassed goods to recycling companies for as much as $90 per ton. If you consider the volume of glass waiting to be harvested from universities, restaurants, and hotels, the potential for success is clear. According to the Glass Packaging Institute, just 35 percent of all glass bottles and jars sold in the United States were recycled in 1997. Glass is easiest to sell; aluminum cans pose more of a problem, mostly because of the intense competition generated by a preponderance of existing redemption centers.

Diversity is another key to cracking this business. As the field has grown, many entrepreneurs have developed multi-material recycling operations, centers where consumers can bring all of their recyclable plastic, glass, and aluminum materials; receive refunds when appropriate; and rid themselves of unwanted, space-consuming trash without filling up another landfill. With persistence and a smart marketing approach, a collector of discarded Coke cans can become an emperor of trash.

PAPER: REAMS OF POSSIBILITY

According to research by Franklin Associates, Ltd., 33.9 percent of the garbage filling up our nation's landfills is composed of glass, metal, and plastic materials, while paper waste products rest in 34.1 percent of the available space. This incredible volume of discarded paper pours out of businesses, which daily generate enough paper to circle Earth 20 times, says the National Recycling Coalition, Inc., a Washington-based alliance of businesses, individuals, and recycling and environmental organizations. While the recycling of paper causes the quality of its components to deteriorate slightly, it is important to note that one ton of recycled paper (whose composition meets the EPA's standard of at least 50 percent waste material) saves 17 trees. Clearly, paper recycling makes good sense and good business. If paper is your material of choice, the best prospects for profit lie in collecting high-quality papers from businesses and selling products made from recycled paper.

The United States is the largest consumer of paper in the world. Unfortunately, paper recycling is proceeding very slowly. In 1985, about 20 percent of all paper products were recycled. By 1995, that figure had increased to only 27 percent. This paper has to get to the companies that will turn it into pulp, filter it of its contaminants, de-ink it, mix it with virgin material, refine it, and press it into usable form. Collecting newspapers is not often a viable possibility for the low-level entrepreneur, as large refuse companies have pounced on collection opportunities that evolved from the enactment of curbside recycling laws in many states. The best way to start out in paper is to look away from the sidewalks and focus on your area's office buildings.

BE CREATIVE

In soliciting clients, use common sense. Look for businesses that probably have a high volume of waste, such as print or copy shops, or offices where many computers are in use. Corporate settings will demand that you be extremely persuasive, because a contract with you requires the initiation of an officewide recycling program. According to the San Francisco Recycling Program, collectors of office-generated paper usually require 500 to 1,000 pounds of paper for a pickup, so clients will need to know that you can be relied on to facilitate the flow of waste products from desktop to truck. Some collectors, such as Vangel Paper Co. in Baltimore, pay clients as much as $50 per ton for high-grade paper, while others, such as Newhallville Recycling, Inc., in New Haven, Connecticut, get it for free—it all depends on the level of competition in your area. As the price of paper can waiver dramatically, you'll have to convince your clients that the quality of your service will not be affected by market fluctuations.

Use a little ingenuity—produce desktop boxes for all of your clients' employees and central storage bins to be placed next to computer clusters and photocopying machines. Another possibility is to rent large storage receptacles to your clients, to be situated in an outdoor spot easily accessed by your trucks. Again, this centralizes the collection process and offers another opportunity for your start-up to generate revenue.

At the most basic level, you will need a truck, a telephone, a method of promoting your business, and boxes in which your clients can accumulate paper. A somewhat more sophisticated start-up might involve the purchase of scales, shredding equipment and a baler, warehouse space, and even facilities for expansion into nonpaper materials. Above all, explore the rates at which paper mills are willing to purchase discarded high-grade paper—you should always be able to get more for this than for waste paper or newsprint.

The recycling of paper can be justified commercially only if goods made from recycled paper are marketable. Bountiful opportunities await the paper recycler with a proclivity for retailing. Gift bags, greeting cards, envelopes, and animal bedding are just some of the examples of items in demand. Whether sold out of a mail-order catalog or a storefront operation, products made of recycled paper often are expensive to produce, so it is imperative that you choose merchandise whose cost is not prohibitive.

Americans finally have begun to recognize the damage inflicted by a century of unchecked pollution. If we are to make a serious commitment to repair the environment over the coming decades, then surely recyclers will lead the way. An understanding of the opportunities combined with an entrepreneurial spirit will yield results in this growing field. As Guy Polhemus puts it, a recycler is on the right track if he or she "sees a need, addresses that need, and still manages to survive!"

SOURCES

Industry Associations

American Paper Institute, 260 Madison Avenue, New York, NY 10016, (212) 340-0699

The Glass Packaging Institute, 627 K Street, N.W., Washington, DC 20006, (202) 887-4850

National Recycling Coalition, Inc., 1101 30th Street, N.W., Suite 305, Washington, DC 20007, (202) 625-6406

Recycling Consultant

Job Description: *A recycling consultant advises public and private agencies on all aspects of overseeing a recycling program.*
- *Start-up cost as low as $5,000*
- *Breakeven time from initial investment: rapid (six months)*
- *Future growth potential: high*
- *Excellent home-based business*
- *No staffing required*

Just about all of us are doing it—separating our trash into cans, bottles, plastics, newspapers, and cardboard, in order for it to be recycled rather than sent to the landfill. Recycling programs have swept across the nation as the United States tries to reduce the amount of garbage it produces.

Helping the public and private sector figure out how to organize, implement, and manage recycling programs offers excellent opportunities as a career choice. *Entrepreneur Magazine* picked "recycling consulting" as one of the "hottest" businesses of 1998, saying: "Talking trash is big business for recycling entrepreneurs." The magazine pegged 1996 revenues for the resource recovery industry at $14.3 billion, stating: "Industry growth has been largely centered in the post-consumer-waste sector, fueled by concern for the environment and limited landfills."

EVERYTHING OLD IS NEW AGAIN

Although it may seem as if we've been recycling all our lives, in reality it has only been within the past 10 to 15 years that most of us have been trying to turn our trash into something useful again.

Interestingly, despite the great strides the United States has made in recycling, we still lag behind other nations. Recycling statistics from European trade associations indicate that the majority of European countries recycled at least 50 percent of their glass containers in 1996, while the United States recycled just 32 percent. Our neighbors across the Atlantic also surpassed us in waste paper recycling, reusing nearly 50 percent to America's 44 percent. However, the United States does recycle about the same amount of plastics (9 percent) as most European countries.

The point of all these numbers is that there's still a lot of work to do in the recycling industry, for those with the knowledge and dedication. Although markets for recycled materials such as paper fluctuate, the nation as a whole still supports recycling. Late in 1998, for instance, a national campaign was launched in 44 states, the District of Columbia, and 2 U.S. territories for consumers to pledge to buy recycled products. First prize was a $200,000 home built primarily with recycled-content products. In the summer of 1999, aluminum can manufacturers were running television commercials promoting the recycling of aluminum drink cans.

Patricia Moore knows trash—and how to recycle it.

Since forming her own company, Moore Recycling Associates Inc., in 1989, Moore has been one of the leading consultants in the recycling industry. Her firm, based in Sonoma, California, helps primarily private-sector industry and associations implement recycling programs.

Moore's recycling career began in 1983, when she started working at a recycling center in Wilton, New Hampshire. She enjoyed working at the facility and in 1985 became the manager. Prior to that she had an eclectic background, working in professions as diverse as apple picking and sail making.

The Wilton facility was part of an aggressive regional recycling program, and Moore tracked the program's progress via computer. This was a new concept in the early days of computing and recycling, and Moore found herself constantly receiving telephone calls from outside environmental consultants requesting her data to help them design and create reports for their own clients.

After rising to director of the Wilton Solid Waste District, Moore decided to strike out on her own in 1989, with two partners. "I decided that there was a lot of opportunities for someone who had my hands-on knowledge," she says.

To get her business off the ground, Moore took out a second mortgage on her house to buy computers, printers, and telephones. Her total start-up costs were approximately $5,000.

Networking was important to the growth of her business. By the time she was ready to go out on her own, she had already made many contacts in the industry. Writing articles and speaking at conferences just added to her credentials, while at the same time increasing her circle of contacts.

"I made a conscious effort to get myself on the agenda of regional and national conferences so that I could learn what was going on, and also so that people would recognize me," Moore says. "It was all networking."

Having seen the work of other recycling consulting firms suffer because they grew too big too fast, Moore consciously keeps growth at her firm under control.

"I don't have any desire to head up a huge company," says Moore. "Then [my work] would be all administrative, and that doesn't interest me."

In 1993 Moore moved the firm to California. Today Moore Recycling Associates has a steady client base and a respected reputation in the recycling industry. One of the company's major projects is managing the daily business operations of the Plastic Recycling Corporation of California (PRCC). PRCC was formed as a nonprofit organization in 1987 by California's soft drink companies and PET (polyethylene terephthalate) bottle manufacturers to provide a stable market for all PET beverage containers collected in the state.

RECYCLING YOURSELF

If you want to recycle a previous career into becoming a consultant for this industry, or even if you are entering it for the first time, there are guidelines to follow to avoid winding up in the refuse heap.

It's important to understand that the days when a consultant could easily find work by helping a community put together a glass, plastic, or paper recycling program are over. Most towns have those in operation.

"Curbside recycling geared up, and communities, counties, and states implemented their recycling plans, [so now] that kind of work doesn't exist anymore," says Patricia Moore.

The opportunities in this field are in what Moore calls the "niches"—devising and implementing recycling programs for areas such as food waste, building materials, wood waste, and medical waste. If you are involved in one of these fields now in another capacity, you could parlay your specialized knowledge into a recycling consulting career.

And make no mistake, opportunities abound. Moore says that there's "no question" that the figure of $14.3 billion quoted as industry revenues by *Entrepreneur* have risen over the past few years, as recycling evolved from being supported by the private sector to being promoted and subsidized by government.

"As material has become available and needed to be recovered [recycled], the industry has grown to accommodate that," says Moore.

The bottom line is you must have a thorough interest in and knowledge of recycling before jumping into the field. Although no specialized equipment is needed to launch a recycling consultant business besides the basic home office needs (computer, printer, high-speed modem, fax machine, and cellular phone— total cost between $3,000 and $5,000), in effect knowledge of the industry is your "specialized equipment."

"You're selling your knowledge," says Moore. "You have to have a special skill that you're selling."

Where can you get this knowledge? Obviously, the best way to work in the industry itself. Another method is to work for an engineering firm, a large recycling consulting firm, or a government agency that deals with recycling. Of course, it goes without saying that you should also read as many industry publications as you can and attend recycling conferences. Since these cost money, you should allot funds for them in your start-up costs.

As far as annual revenues, keep in mind Moore's advice: "You're never going to get rich consulting—but you will make a decent living." Hourly fees range between $40 and $150. Since it's likely that you'll have just a few clients in the beginning, annual revenues of $40,000 to $50,000 are possible. Thus, an initial investment of $10,000 ($5,000 for office equipment, the remainder for miscellaneous expenses such as industry publications, conferences, and so on) could be recovered in as little as one year.

It's also easier to get a recycling consulting business off the ground in a high-density population area, since that's where trash problems are the most acute. "[In these areas] the cost of disposal is high, which makes it cost-effective to recycle," Moore noted.

RECYCLE FOR TOMORROW

Although the recycling industry itself has undergone boom-and-bust cycles, and undoubtedly will continue to do so, the future for recycling seems secure. Landfill space, already at a premium now in many areas, will continue to shrink. Barring the invention of any miraculous solution, recycling still seems to be the best method to solve the problem of what to do with waste materials.

"Like most industries, recycling will have its ups and downs," says Moore. "On the whole, however, it's growing."

Food and Drink

Caterer

Job Description: *A caterer provides food for corporate occasions, private parties, weddings, and other large gatherings.*

- *Start-up costs as low as $15,000*
- *Potential first-year earnings: $30,000*
- *Breakeven time from initial investment: one year or longer*
- *No staffing required*

Ginger Swallow's Creative Cuisine catered three parties in the Houston area in every week during her second year of operation, but she'd rather do just five events a year. In fact, "One bash a year would be fine—as long as it's the right bash." Her definition of the "right bash" owes more to economies of scale than snobbery. "I want to feed parties of 30,000 . . . 40,000 . . . 50,000 people." At $50 a head, revenues mount quickly. Ginger's single-person shop hasn't reached those heights yet, but the effervescent hostess has catered some Texas-size shindigs. For example, she has done six parties for between 1,500 and 2,500 people, and booked two more affairs at $110,000 and $140,000.

The best part of it all, Ginger admits in an undertone, "I usually keep two-thirds of the revenues as profits. That's what's left after I pay for food, help, and transportation."

THE SWEETNESS OF THE BOTTOM LINE

Two-thirds?? That's pretax profits of $66,666 on a $100,000 dinner! These figures aren't so hard to believe when you realize that Ginger Swallow employs tactics that keep her overhead to zip, which gives her a richer bottom line than the average caterer. For example, her house serves as an office and she hires employees and even a kitchen in a nearby bankrupt restaurant only on days she actually caters events. But even operators who invest in $50,000 kitchens and full-time chefs, even those who spend heavily to promote their service to corporate clientele, allow that catering profits are the best in the $354 billion restaurant industry. "Once you deal with enough masses, your profits can be 25 percent of revenues. In some cases, you'll do 50 percent," says Frank Spinarski. With those figures in mind, he left a swank hotel chain where he was director of catering to launch The Aristocrats catering outfit in Huntington Beach, California.

Those figures, however, may grossly underrepresent the industry since many home-based caterers don't even list in the phone book. Ginger Swallow shuns a phone listing, reasoning that anybody hosting hundreds of people will hire by reputation, not by Yellow Pages. "I don't want the kind of occasional business that such advertising would bring," she insists. "I want to be known as *the* caterer in the Dallas area to come to for large bashes."

SANDWICHES BY CONTRACT

But extravaganzas are certainly not the only route to the catering hall of fame. If you can carve out a reputation in any one area, you can do quite nicely. For example, anyone connected with the wedding business in the Washington area knows Love at First Bite. Consultant Jay Treadwell recommends lining up six-month contracts with corporations, a move that brings in continual business from executives who don't have time to go out to lunch.

Despite the one-shot profit potential in $800 filet mignon birthday dinners for six people, which the Aristocrats occasionally cater in an individual's home, Frank Spinarski says, "Corporate is where the bread and butter is." Not only do they throw bigger and more expensive parties, corporations party more often.

To tap that corporate sector, Frank Spinarski took along a client list of 8,000 area corporations when he left his former position at the hotel chain. (You also can find corporate names through chambers of commerce and on the Internet.) "We called everyone on that list to see if their company used caterers," he recalls. "Probably 1,000 people in the county consistently use caterers. We call every one of them regularly, asking 'When will you use us?'" Such cold calls bring in meager business at first, but once the corporations hear of the other fantastic parties you host, they start responding positively. Frank says that now of the 30 contacts he makes during a typical week, 6 or 7 book parties.

Make Them Talk About You

Word of mouth is undoubtedly worth more to caterers than to restaurateurs. Anxious brides or corporations throwing parties for new product send-offs "are not going to risk embarrassment by trying an unknown caterer," says Jay Treadwell. "They ask for recommendations." Your reputation as a fabulous restaurant chef may be recommendation enough. Ginger Swallow worked as corporate chef for a wealthy Texas real estate couple famous for their flamboyant soirées. All the banks and real estate brokers and corporate execs knew Swallow because they'd attended her parties.

But those entering the field with less visible credentials say there are as many ways to create reputation as there are parties to throw. "Build a party into your start-up costs," recommends Jay Treadwell, who was formerly the general manager of Ridgewell Caterers, the Washington giant that regularly feeds the White House along with the rest of the Capitol Hill society. Make that give-away party an impressive showcase for your talents. Beef Wellington and baked Alaska for 100 guests may be prohibitively expensive, but you might do something special with cocktails and canapés. Spend the money for an ice carving or a baked Brie that your guests will remember. And rent the local museum garden or another enticing locale to lure influential people. "If you plan to specialize in weddings, invite florists, department store heads, musicians, people in charge of places that book weddings," explains Treadwell. "The bride will ask those people to recommend a caterer. The answer might be 'I went to

a fabulous party this caterer gave last month.' That's all the recommendation you need."

Especially while building a following, don't cut corners.
"Compensation comes in all ways, not just dollars and cents,
but sometimes in reputation," says Swallow, who adds, "I give
stuff away. It may not be worth 10 cents of my time to add edi-
ble flowers, but it's a way to sell my company." If you can't get a
client to pay for the frills but enough influential guests are attending, you may wish to add carved pineapples anyway. Look
at it this way: Such extra attention is cheaper and more effective than advertising.

TO BUY OR RENT

Unlike many other businesses, you can start as big or as small in
catering as your pocketbook allows, because you can buy your
own elaborate facilities or rent just about anything you need.
Jay Treadwell figures $100 per square foot will outfit an institu-
tional kitchen. (Caterers do most actual cooking on-site, either
with equipment they bring or facilities supplied by the clients.
But you need a kitchen for "prep work," such as cutting vegetables.) Heavy-volume jobs require a truck and temperature-con-
trolled holding cabinets. You either rent china, linens, and
other staples, or buy them outright and keep the cut that otherwise would go to the rental agency.

Anticipating monthly revenues of $50,000 (after nine
months in business, they are halfway there), Frank Spinarski
and his partners invested $50,000 in their kitchen and hired a
full-time chef and secretary. But you can get by with far less.
Ginger Swallow catered her first $22,000 party using her own
pots and pans and rented kitchen space. She invested $5,000 of

her $15,000 profits from that first affair in equipment meant to enhance her signature. For example, "I hired carpenters to make a huge, fancy cheese board shaped like a cowboy boot" to serve 40-pound blocks of cheddar at Tex-Mex barbecues.

While you can certainly administrate from a spare bedroom, consider Health Department regulations before actually cooking from home. You're legally considered a restaurant when you cater. But many places rent their kitchens. Some large city restaurants advertise their facilities for caterer use. In addition, don't forget church or school kitchens. "If you offer something special, like cooking a treat for the kids, you might get a good deal on using the school kitchen after hours," says Jay Treadwell.

As for personnel, a freelance legion makes its living by working for caterers. Ask party planners or banquet managers to recommend servers or ice carvers. Says Ginger Swallow: "If I go to a restaurant and see somebody I like, I approach them—the chef, the bartender. . . ."

WHO DOES IT

Restaurateurs are the most obvious converts to catering, but marketing types who hire culinary experts are sprinkled throughout the field. Jay Treadwell warns against underestimating the business aspects of catering. "The restaurant business is 70 percent food-oriented, with the rest going for service, organization, etc. Those figures flip-flop in catering; 30 percent food and the rest delivery, transporting the food, lining up rental equipment, juggling personnel." In catering, organization counts.

Another handy trait is a smooth manner. On one hand, you

must deal professionally with corporate clients and party planners who expect a receipt for every shrimp. But you also must assure parents of the bride that you'll be on time and everything will be beautiful for the special day.

You don't have to limit your business to gastronomy. Ridgewell Caterers, with expected annual revenues of between $15 million and $17 million, was begun in 1928 by the cook of the French Embassy and the butler of the British Embassy to supply all the accoutrements, such as china. Party rentals are still a big part of the business. Ridgewell's, now headed by identical twin brothers Jeff and Bruce Ellis (grandsons of the founders, who fell in love and were married), did not build its kitchen until 1970. "People like one-stop shopping," says Jay Treadwell. "You can rent items from a rental store, but act as a coordinator on flowers, tents, whatever. In all likelihood, it's a profit center for the caterer and a relief for the client."

Never lose sight of the fact that people come to a caterer for the unusual. If they want the restrictions of a set menu, they would go to a restaurant. "Outline menu possibilities, but leave the impression that you can do anything," advises Jay.

And make suggestions. Ginger Swallow recalls an aviation company that requested a Tex-Mex picnic for 1,200. Instead, "I suggested an international theme, and we ended up with cuisine from six countries, including a luau with a huge pig in honey sauce and steaks branded with the company's logo. My fee went from $5,000 to $35,000." The meeting planner moved the party into an airplane hangar and added a band, Vegas tables, and a limousine containing a Joan Collins look-alike; his fee leaped from $3,500 to $10,000. The client? "They were ecstatic," says Ginger. "They threw a party everybody remembers."

SOURCES

Industry Associations

National Association of Catering Executives, 5565 Sterrett Place, Suite 328, Columbia, MD 21044, (410) 997-9055.

National Restaurant Association, 1200 17th St., N.W., Washington, DC 20036-3097, (202) 331-5900

Gourmet Food Products Producer

Job Description: *A gourmet good products producer develops speciality food items for the consumer market.*

- *Start-up cost as low as $5,000*
- *Potential first-year earnings: $30,000*
- *Breakeven time from initial investment: rapid (six months to one year)*
- *Ideal home-based business*
- *Excellent opportunity for people with physical disabilities*
- *No staffing required*

Duggan and Robert Peak were setting up their booth at the San Francisco Food & Wine Show when the enormity of what they were doing hit Duggan, a former restaurant manager and the creator of Duggan's Own products, which range from a Poppy Perfect salad dressing to a cucumber dill vinegar. "Robert had just left this prosperous advertising agency and we had moved to Oregon, hundreds of miles away from my restaurant contacts in southern California." She looked over at their baby, whom they had smuggled into the show, hoping the officials wouldn't notice and throw them out. "It felt like opening night, and I was scared. I looked at Robert and said, 'My God, look what we've done.'"

As the doors opened at 9:00 A.M., throngs of wholesale buyers from department and specialty stores clogged the aisles, leaving Duggan Peak no more time to worry. The couple had transformed their booth into a pastel kitchen. The look, unusual in contrast to the sterility of most booths, attracted crowds right away. Robert had created progressive packaging in airy grays and pinks, a memorable departure from the homespun clichés of most specialty foods—the burgundy bonnet topping the jar of marmalade. And Duggan had tasted every oil, vinegar, and salad dressing in California when concocting an all-natural, really different taste. By 10:30, Robert was discussing terms with the buyer from Nieman-Marcus when Duggan felt someone grab her hand. "You don't want to go exclusive with Nieman-Marcus," he said. "I'm from Macy's."

"We thought we'd be okay if we sold 2,000 cases during our first year," recalls Robert. "We sold that many our first show." During their start-up year, the couple hit sales of $1 million—and profits of $420,000. Within two years, sales had tripled as Duggan's Own grew from 14 products to 59.

YOU'VE GOTTA BE SPECIAL

First the bad news: For every Robert and Duggan Peak success story, failures in the specialty food business abound. Your family recipe has got to be really special to compete with giant conglomerates that unleash entire research and development (R&D) departments on $4 mustards. "Individuality is really important," says Robert. "Do some research to come up with something unique either in the packaging or product." Adds Morris Kushner, a consultant who has introduced to America more than 600 items during his career, including the first cappuccino mix and the first crouton: "If you can get the customer to pick up and read your label, you're half way home."

A tip on the label: In addition to conveying a quality image, many food manufacturers add a recipe either on the packaging or tied around the bottle's neck. After all, the more customers use your marinade, the sooner they will be back for more.

LANDING ON THE SHELVES

The first customer you must sell is the merchant. In the old days, food entrepreneurs sold to local clientele and watched their distribution expand as their fame slowly grew. "We used to take new products to the corner grocery to get an idea of how they would sell," says Morris Kushner. That approach is increasingly difficult as supermarket chains muscle corner groceries out of existence. Some specialty food stores still take samples on consignment, but many supermarket chains now charge a "slotting fee" of several thousand dollars to introduce new products. In the United States, the specialty food market is estimated at $13 billion.

Now for the good news: Kushner adds to that picture: "When I first started, specialty products looked at 5 percent of the population. Now we can target 18 to 20 percent—that's the number of families with gross incomes of $35,000 or more. The first thing they can afford is good food."

SUPPORTING CAST

This new interest in top-of-the-line consumables has catalyzed an entire industry to help entrepreneurs introduce the latest in shiitake mushrooms and coriander marinades. Perhaps the most important new aid is the growth of trade shows: These allow mom-and-pop operations to go national (or international) immediately by attracting the attention of department and specialty stores that buy in bulk. Although specialty food shows have been around for a generation, recently their popularity has exploded. The International Fancy Food & Confection shows, sponsored by the National Association for the Specialty Food Trade, attract from 15,000 to 30,000 attendees from specialty food, wine, gift, and department stores as well as restaurants, mail order, and other related businesses. The Peaks attended nine shows in one year, including jaunts to Tokyo, Paris, and West Germany. "Shows literally showcase your products," explains Morris Kushner. "Brokers and distributors will see your products and latch on to you."

Food brokers do not take title to your herbal cheese sticks but merely act as your sales representative with accounts all over the country. For enticing retailers to buy your products, brokers receive 2.5 to 5 percent commissions. You handle the shipping and accounts receivable. Food distributors go a couple of steps further for their 25 to 30 percent fees. They act as middlemen by actually buying your product and shipping it to retailers they sign up.

SOMEONE'S IN THE KITCHEN

Two avenues exist to produce the products: You can do it your-self or hire a copacker. Duggan and Robert Peak chose the ini-tially more expensive route of operating their own factory. "To hold our overhead low, we moved from Los Angeles to Oregon," says Robert. The manufacturing plant they rented in-cluded acreage where they grow basil, tarragon, thyme, and marjoram to supplement herbs grown by local farmers. The couple's first $5,000 went for show fees and labels for their sam-ple jars in the San Francisco show. Then they proceeded to in-vest $75,000 from savings to meet those increasing orders. "During our first six months, every time we got a check from a client, we would rush to the bank and get cash for more inven-tory," recalls Robert.

The Peaks chose to manufacture their products so they could control quality. More commonly, entrepreneurs manufacture through copackers who agree to maintain high standards by ad-hering strictly to recipes supplied by the food's creators. "You take the recipe to someone who produces it under your label," explains Morris Kushner. "A copacker buys vinegar and oils in tankfuls for all their customers, so volume provides savings."

As a rule of thumb, expect to "keystone" your products—double the cost of producing the item to wholesalers, who then tack on another 50 percent at the shelf. For example, if your overhead, including food and packaging, labor, rent, and deliv-ery, amounts to $1 per jar of wild mushroom pâté, charge wholesalers $2 and consumers $3. "That strategy should cover all the essentials and leave a few pennies for advertising and new-product development," says Kushner. Costs should fall as your volume increases; some overhead items, such as rent, remain stable no matter how many cases you churn out a day, and bulk buying actually lessens per-unit food costs. "Volume production will bring the $1 cost down to maybe 87 cents, which allows you to give a product a shot with a coupon or a ribbon on the top of the jar after a few months," says Kushner.

KEEP THOSE PRODUCTS COMING

Savings also frees up cash for new-product R&D. "Nowadays, you don't stand a chance with one item," warns Kushner. "You have to build an image with pizza, onion, avocado—all the salad dressing flavors under one label."

Specialty food retailers and suppliers deal regularly with cottage manufacturers, so don't try to pretend you have General Food's resources. Buyers want assurances you can deliver as promised and suppliers want to know you can pay on time—so don't make promises you can't keep. Possibly because they projected a professional image in their packaging and with their factory, Robert and Duggan Peak had no trouble lining up suppliers. "People gave us credit—vinegar and olive oil companies put us on net days," says Duggan, still amazed. "Some shipped their first order COD, then established a line of credit."

Retailers likewise were helpful. "Our first orders were all prepaid or COD," says Robert. "Some larger orders can't do that, but department-store buyers said they knew we were just starting and offered to pay us the day after they got the goods."

Today Duggan laughs recalling her anxiety at the first show. "But you know, this was supposed to be a kind of early retirement for us," she says. (Duggan is in her early 30s, Robert is in his mid-30s.) "Everything happened so fast. We were bitten by success."

SOURCE

Industry Association

National Association for The Specialty Food Trade Inc., 8 West 40th Street, 4th Floor, New York, NY 10018-3901, (212) 482-6440

Gourmet Food Store Provider

Job Description: *A gourmet food store locates and sells specialty, hard-to-find, and unusual/exotic food items.*

- *Start-up cost as low as $5,000*
- *Potential first-year earnings: $2,000 to $5,000 per month*
- *Breakeven time from initial investment: six months to several years*
- *Ideal home-based business*
- *Excellent opportunity for people with physical disabilities*
- *No staffing required (initially)*

Walking through the big burgundy barn that houses Expression unltd. offers quite a sensory experience. More than 100 varieties of crackers line its shelves, as well as 126 jams, 45 mustards, and spices from unpronounceable regions. The bright colors of 38 flavors of jelly beans vie with the warm earth tones of 23 whole-bean coffees in burlap sacks. The take-out food section sends odors wafting through the aisles. Generous samples of goat cheese and Swiss vegetable pâté mean nobody leaves Expression hungry. Located on a remote country road in the Wachung Mountains of Warren, New Jersey, 40 miles from New York City, the store sells one ton of cheese every three days.

"Six or eight years ago, specialty food stores didn't exist," says Elaine Yannuzzi, who owns what many consider the ultimate in specialty food stores. "Meats were available in old-fashioned German delis, and you could get a dozen of the more pedestrian cheeses at the supermarket. But nothing like this existed."

EXPRESSION THROUGH FOOD

In fact, Expression unltd. began without a single food item in sight. "Things were different in 1970; a woman expressed herself through her children and her home," explains Elaine Yannuzzi, who stocked the original Expression with a stitchery department, children's toy area, decorating section, and gourmet cookware corner. In the mid-1970s, she added cheese to complement the cookware, and soon inserted other gourmet items. Today, all the old departments except cookware are gone, and cheese represents 30 percent of the store's sales. Revenues now amount to millions, and, with the addition of take-out foods, sales jumped by at least one-third. (See "Take-out Restaurateur," page 262.)

Nobody knows the true size of the gourmet or specialty food market, because an exact definition of specialty foods doesn't exist. Is the Brie that you could buy only in specialty cheese shops a decade ago still considered a specialty food even though you now can choose from a half-dozen Brie brands at the supermarket? But, as an indication of the industry's growth, the National Association for the Specialty Food Trade

(NASFT) estimates that the specialty food market is at least $13 billion in the United States.

WHY WE EXPERIMENT

The reasons for Americans' new taste for gourmet foods include

- Increasing popularity of home entertaining
- Less time for food preparation coupled with higher incomes (well over half of all homemakers also work)
- Improved refrigeration and transportation that provides fresh, exotic fruits and vegetables year round
- Increased preference for "all-natural" foods made without preservatives, salt, or sugar
- Availability of hundreds of new products that are expanding Americans' diet to include salmon pâté and radicchio

However, along with this heightened receptivity to specialty foods comes new competition. In addition to increasing numbers of specialty food boutiques, every supermarket in the country now has its gourmet food selection. To bring customers through your doors, you must create an experience they just can't get in a fluorescent-lit supermarket that stocks dogfood and detergent along with the arugula and extra virgin olive oil.

If your start-up budget is skinny, you can open a 1,000-square-foot true specialty store: just teas or cheeses. Carry only a handful of companion items, such as biscuits or balsamic-flavored vinegar. By addressing such a narrow market, you become known to the area's aficionados. You may eventually send out a catalog to attract mail-order customers for your chocolate truffles or whole-fruit jellies.

A GENERALIST IN
SPECIALTY FOODS

Rather than creating a niche in a particular food category, Expression unltd. goes to the opposite extreme by providing the last word in specialty food shopping. Although Elaine Yannuzzi earns 80 percent of her sales from just 20 percent of her products, she carries thousands of items to create an atmosphere that brings customers from a 100-square-mile radius. "We carry a line of Indonesian spices that maybe 50 people travel from around the area to get at Expression. We do special orders on really odd items," she says.

To choose which items to stock, Yannuzzi shops the massive Fancy Food & Confection Shows twice annually. The show's 2,200 booths "overwhelm a person just starting out," she warns, "but I assure you [choosing a product mix] really does become manageable after a few years." Her first criterion in deciding whether to stock a particular item involves taste. "A specialty mustard sells for $3.50 to $5.00, compared with 79 cents in the supermarket. The taste has to say 'Oh, wow!' "

She continues, "If price is very much out of line, we'll still stock a superb product, but in lesser quantity till we see how it sells."

365 TURNS A YEAR

Because specialty foods retailers look for fast inventory turnover, you don't have to pile up debt to stock your store. "You don't bring in a spring line of sportswear that takes three months to turn," points out Elaine. "Try for weekly or biweekly turns on jarred foods and daily turns on prepared foods." Use proceeds from this month's sales to buy next month's. Stash additional funds for prime buying times, such as before Christmas.

Of course, to get such fast turnover, location is crucial. A specialty food store's 40 percent margins, while vastly superior to the 10 percent margins a supermarket copes with, just don't support mall locations. But try to get the most visible spot your pocketbook allows. Expression unltd. broke this cardinal rule; Elaine Yannuzzi located her shop in a building she already owned because it needed a tenant—even though she was miles from nowhere. After struggling a few years, she overcame the disadvantage of her remote site; now, during Christmas season, Expression needs a police officer to direct traffic out of its back-roads parking lot. "But 'location, location, location' is a good rule," she admits. "Rules make life easier."

To combat its isolation, Expression advertises weekly in New Jersey's largest newspaper as well as in other papers less frequently. In addition, the store employs a full-time public relations manager to call on caterers, corporate customers, restaurants, and other clients who get discounts for buying in bulk.

SAMPLING BOARDS

Once you get customers into the store, you still have to sell the foods. Because many of your items are unusual, they can be intimidating. (Question: Does blackberry sauce go over ice cream or lamb? Answer: Both.) The 35 year-round and 60 holidaytime Expression employees taste each new item and learn about its origins so they can answer customer questions. To provide customers with a firsthand experience, the store gives away 350 pounds of cheese, chicken salad with water chestnuts, and chutney a week in samples. On weekends, one employee does nothing but refurbish the sampling boards. Elaine Yannuzzi asks manufacturers to provide as many free samples as possible, arguing that a smear of basil mustard on a pretzel can sell a whole jar. Even with help from food packagers, she still spends $150,000 a year on freebies.

Specialty food stores walk a thin line between offering the foods that customers know they want and exposing them to an ever-increasing number of new treats. A specialty food customer is almost by definition, adventurous: Your job is to create an atmosphere conducive to experimenting. "Even though an item may be unknown to a customer, they are secure because they know we select with care and feeling," says Yannuzzi. "Specialty food stores sell confidence. We sell a spiritual thing lingering behind the products."

SOURCE

Industry Association

National Association for The Specialty Food Trade Inc., 8 West 40th Street, 4th Floor, New York, NY 10018-3901, (212) 482-6440

Juice and Smoothie
Bars Owner

Job Description: *Juice/smoothie bars owner serves freshly squeezed concoctions made with fruits and vegetables as well as smoothies, which are fruit-based drinks comprised of fruit, ice cream and/or yogurt, and other ingredients.*

- *Start-up cost: $100,000 minimum*
- *Potential first-year earnings: $100,000*
- *Breakeven time from initial investment: rapid (as little as one year)*
- *Future growth potential: high*
- *Health-oriented business that appeals to consumer's desires for nutritious meals*

What's the latest, hippest trend in beverages?
If you said "coffee bars," go to the rear of the class and repeat "What's In/What's Out 101." Coffee bars are yesterday's news. Today the juice/smoothie bar is America's choice for liquid refreshment. The exploding popularity of juice/smoothie bars led *Entrepreneur Magazine* to label

them one of the "hottest businesses" of 1998. "Juice bars continue to pack a hefty punch in the beverage world," said the magazine.

But *Entrepreneur* wasn't alone in pointing out the juice/smoothie trend. "All Hollywood seems to be juicing now," proclaimed *Los Angeles Magazine* in January 1998, summing up Tinseltown's fondness for juice drinks and juice bars. But it isn't only celebrities who are wetting their palates this way. According to one source, the American juice market rang up approximately $2.8 billion in annual sales by the close of the 1990s. Clearly, this is an excellent field to "squeeze" into.

HEALTHY HABIT

What are the reasons behind the explosion in juice/smoothie bars?

A primary force driving this market is health. No matter how you foam it, top it, or flavor it, coffee is never going to be as healthful as juice. Heightened awareness about the health danger of caffeine has also led to concern about coffee drinking.

Health-conscious consumers, however, consider juice drinks nutritious. Besieged by news reports touting the advantages of consuming more fruits and vegetables, people are searching for fast ways to get their "five a day" servings of both. Knocking back several juice drinks daily seems to be the perfect solution. As an article in the *Toronto Star* said: "Most Canadians have trouble consuming the five to ten servings of fruit and vegetables that [a Canadian health agency] recommends we eat every day. [But] drinking just one cup of juice a day counts as two servings of vegetables and fruit."

Many people head to their local juice bar to get the nutrients they need instead of relying only on regular meals. Fruit juices, for instance, are a great source of vitamin C. Vegetable juices such as carrot juice are rich in antioxidants such as beta-carotene. Purple grape juice contains flavonoids that produce an anticlotting effect and are good for your heart. It also contains resveratrol, which helps lower LDL, or "bad," cholesterol.

It's not only the United States that has embraced the juice bar concept. In October 1998 the British newspaper *The Daily Telegraph* reported that "a whole host of juice bars has recently opened on this side of the pond."

REAL SMOOTH

Smoothies—blend juice concoctions of fruit, nonfat frozen yogurt, sorbet, and juice—are popular offerings of many juice bars. In fact, some juice bars feature smoothies over standard juice drinks.

It isn't hard to guess where the emphasis lies at a retail establishment called Smoothieville. Located in Chapel Hill, North Carolina, Smoothieville opened in October 1996 by brothers Jim and Robert Millican.

"We were both in sales," says Robert, "and we had a hard time finding healthy ways to eat in a hurry."

Realizing that a lot of other people were in the same situation, the brothers—who had always wanted to be in business together—searched for a field that was in the early stages of development but yet still offered long-term growth potential. The two looked at many different businesses; the one that kept popping up was juice/smoothie bars.

"We saw how popular smoothie and juice bars are on the West Coast," says Jim. "Comparisons were being drawn with the smoothie business now to where [frozen] yogurt was 20 years ago."

Aware that the juice/smoothie bar concept was beginning to migrate east, the brothers decided to open their own business. Besides being native North Carolinians, they chose Chapel Hill because of its progressive outlook. (It's the home of the University of North Carolina.) They knew a contemporary mind-set was essential to their chance of succeeding with such a new, innovative food product.

Without downplaying the healthy aspects of smoothies, the Millicans positioned the product as a tasty meal replacement. In advertisements on local AM radio as well as in personal appearances before civic and professional groups, the brothers sought to educate the public about the great taste and health benefits of smoothies, and why they are a preferable meal alternative.

Their target efforts paid off. Business boomed from the start, even though they opened in crisp weather October with essentially a cold beverage product. Sales were so strong, increasing at an annual rate of approximately 25 percent, that the brothers opened a second location in Durham, North Carolina, in 1998.

One factor the Millicans believe has contributed to their success is using whole fruit, pure juices, natural sweeteners, and nonfat dairy products rather than sherbets or yogurts that may contain sugar. When customers see their smoothie being made, they know they're getting a unique-tasting product that is also extremely healthy. If customers don't want any of the 15 varieties that are on the Smoothieville menu (all with unusual, fun names such as "Hairy Dog" and "Bluezilla"), they can order their own combination of ingredients.

"We get a big crowd for breakfast; people take it on their commute to work," says Jim. "The same for lunch." This illustrates that the Millicans' strategy of positioning smoothies as meal replacements has made an impact.

Prices at Smoothieville range from $2.80 to $3.85. The cost depends on the ingredients in each drink. It takes ten employees to run a store effectively, with two or three working each shift.

BLENDING YOUR WAY TO SUCCESS

As you might expect, it takes more than a blender and a handful of fruits and vegetables to begin a juice/smoothie bar business.

Since this obviously isn't a home-based business, you need a retail location. Add that cost to an equipment investment that can easily reach (and even surpass) $50,000 due to the large amount of specialized equipment that must be purchased (refrigeration units, countertops, blenders, and so on). Other expenses include staff salaries, an advertising budget, and supplies (cups, spoons, napkins, and the like). Overall, the minimum investment to begin operating a juice/smoothie bar is approximately $100,000.

Annual income for this type of business depends on numerous factors, including location, competition, and expenses. However, it is possible to make $100,000 in your first year, which means you could recoup your initial investment in 12 months.

A variable expense with this business is food. Obviously, a juice/smoothie bar is particularly vulnerable to sudden fluctuations in the cost of fruits and vegetables due to weather, insects, and other causes. While Smoothieville has managed to hold the line and not raise prices in response to unexpected increases in the cost of fruit, the Millican brothers constantly study the market and are kept aware of any possible shortages/price increases from their suppliers.

One way to help keep profits smooth is to diversify your menu. Some juice/smoothie bars offer sandwiches, healthful snacks, and other items. On the menu at Smoothieville is coffee, mainly because the Millicans wanted to be able to offer a hot drink during cold-weather months. Eventually, the brothers anticipate offering sandwiches as well.

One important factor the Millicans believe has helped them become successful is that they keep the experience at Smoothieville fun. The Millicans maintain a good relationship with their customers, even to the point of posting pictures of "frequent smoothers" on the Smoothieville website.

Frivolous Fad or Favorite Food?

The $64,000 question for juice/smoothie bars is whether they have the staying power to survive in the highly competitive food industry. After all, the retail food establishment is littered with the bones of concepts such as frozen yogurt that seemed so sturdy at the beginning, only to wilt when consumers moved on to the next big thing.

Experts think that juice/smoothie bars will escape that fate, mainly because of their healthful reputation. As people seek ways to eat and drink more nutritiously yet still retain their busy lifestyle, they seem likely to turn to a glass of "liquid fruit or vegetables" as a perfect alternative to fast food.

Another factor that may help juice/smoothie bars prosper is

that the market is still largely untapped. The Millicans estimate that only 25 to 30 percent of their potential customer base knows what smoothies are; that means that nearly 75 percent of their potential customers have yet to learn about their product.

"For that reason it [the market] is still on the upswing. It's still growing," says Jim Millican.

Pizza Parlor Owner

Job Description: *A pizza parlor owner cooks and serves pizza and other Italian-style foods.*

- *Start-up cost as low as $60,000*
- *Potential first-year earnings: $150,000*
- *Breakeven time from initial investment: one to four years*

Here's a statistic bound to please pepperoni producers everywhere: Approximately 10 percent of all U.S. restaurants serve pizza. Americans were estimated to have gobbled up $22.5 billion worth of these tasty, round, tomato and cheese creations in 1998. To put it another way, people in the United States consume about 100 acres of pizza each day—and we show no signs of stopping. According to Technomic Inc., a Chicago restaurant consulting and research firm, pizza sales are estimated to grow at a yearly rate of 4.5 percent between 1998 and 2003. With approximately one out of four belonging to a franchise, the rest range from elaborate shops (such as the one topped by a Leaning Tower of Pisa emblazoned with "PIZZA" in two-foot-high letters, which grossed an astounding $2.25 million in one year) to tiny take-outs that provide 40 percent profits to moms and pops.

A SLICE OF AMERICANA

The credit for the insatiable pizza hunger lies both with a better product and with today's lifestyles. "Fifteen years ago, pizza was greasy kids' stuff," says Paula Werne of *Pizza Today*. "High school kids liked it, but their mothers didn't. Today we're rid of the grease and have turned pizza into a healthy food with the four different food groups—milk (cheese), bread (crust), vegetables (toppings like spinach and tomato sauce), and protein (sausage and pepperoni)."

Product improvements made pizza acceptable; product convenience made pizza flourish. Unlike other fast-food customers, pizza eaters call ahead for take-out, or have Domino's deliver it to the door in less time than it takes to bake a pizza at home. "Families are converting that one night a week they used to go to McDonald's into a night at home with take-out and the VCR," says Dennis Sheaks, who attributes 46 percent of Joe Peep's N.Y. Pizza's orders—and 57 percent of its dollar sales—to delivery. And never mind what Burger King says, pizza operators invented "have-it-your-way" fast food. Want a slice instead of a 17-inch pie? No problem. Hold the anchovies, add extra cheese? Sure thing.

NOT A LOT OF DOUGH

Pizza restaurants are like a raw canvas: You can create anything you want on the basic concept, ranging from an inexpensive take-out to an elaborate chain. If you want to start small, you can set up a two-oven take-out operation in a reasonable location for $50,000 or less, compared with ten times that figure for most fast food franchises or a sit-down restaurant. The difference boils down to the degree of difficulty involved in the operations. Pizzerias sell simple products (even those that add antipastos and sandwiches) that require little expertise, equipment, or décor.

Dennis and Diane Sheaks bought used equipment when they moved Joe Peep's N.Y. Pizza into larger quarters in North Hollywood, California, ten months after buying the restaurant for $70,000. "Toasters or automobiles have lots of moving parts to wear out," says Dennis, "but an oven is just a big insulated box with gas controls. Ovens are like wrenches—they never wear out."

The functional, unassuming look the Sheaks chose for Joe Peep's not only kept opening costs to $80,000 (including renovation to add plumbing) but also created a "fun atmosphere" that involves customers, says Dennis. "The kitchen is separated from the order area only by a low-level counter. The customers watch their pizza being made."

As for ambiance, you can install Tiffany-like lamps and stained glass or go for a minimal look. Dennis Sheaks invites customers to scribble graffiti on the walls—anything that has to do with Joe Peep's or pizza—during the 20-minute wait while their order cooks. "People stand on each other's shoulders or bring in a friend who's never been here before to show what they wrote in the past. It's a form of entertainment."

Because they require little space, pizzerias sometimes can afford expensive mall locations or retrofit buildings other restaurants would shun. For example, some gas stations abandoned during the oil crisis of the 1970s were reborn as pizzerias.

Delivery doesn't have to be expensive, either. If you don't want to spring for your own vans, hire drivers with their own cars and insurance and reimburse them on a per-mile basis.

STAND OUT

Despite the presence of national chains, independents do quite well in the pizza business. However, if you choose to go it alone, recognize you'll never match Pizza Hut's advertising budget. Therefore, you have to have something going for you: location, product, price, or atmosphere. Dennis Sheaks offers a top-notch pizza at a premium price. "Domino's large pizza costs just 75 percent of Joe Peep's biggest size," says Dennis. "But Joe Peep's is twice as big. If you don't give value, gear for low-income people who only have $4 to spend anyway, or very high-end customers, looking for an avant-garde style."

Let's assume you and your spouse run your pizzeria with two employees and operate with a 30 percent food cost and average strip-shopping-center rents. If you gross $200,000 a year, $80,000 or so will find its way into your pockets.

In a different scenario, you might shoot for the heights. As Dennis Sheaks sees it, if you don't mind plowing hours and profits back into operations, there's plenty of room for expansion. For himself, he envisions a ten-unit Joe Peep's chain, possibly followed by franchising. His first step is to perfect a pilot restaurant. And the Sheaks are well on their way to that goal: Joe Peep's grossed $750,000 in its second year under the couple's management, compared with just $200,000 when they bought the restaurant. Joe Peep's still sells the same secret-recipe pizza that had already earned the restaurant a loyal customer base. The difference, says Sheaks, boils down to marketing.

"The first thing we did was capture on our computer the name and address of everyone who came into the restaurant," he explains. "Then we created a VIPeeper Club." (To join, all you have to do is sign up.) Each month, Joe Peep's sends discount coupons or announcements of "members-only" parties to 16,000 members. While the mailings cost $2,500 a month, that's far below the thousands more it would cost to reach those people by television or even newspaper.

Joe Peep's also proclaims it will deliver "anywhere in the world, except South Africa." Dennis warns this is an expensive strategy, because for every driver he sends on a 15-mile journey, additional employees must handle local deliveries. But he's thinking ahead. "We've already got customers 10 miles away from this store. I'll open my second store on the periphery of my customer base. Those existing customers will establish the new store through word-of-mouth advertising."

That second store is the second step in a pizza empire, says Sheaks, who holds an MBA and ran his own management consulting firm before buying Joe Peep's. As he points out, "I figure I'm more qualified than Ray Kroc was when he started McDonald's."

SOURCES

Industry Associations

National Association of Pizza Operators, P.O. Box 1347, New Albany, IN 47151, (812) 949-0909

National Restaurant Association, 1200 17th Street, N.W., Washington, DC 20036-3097, (202) 331-5900, (800) 424-5156

Sandwich Shop Owner

Job Description: *A sandwich shop prepares and serves a variety of sandwiches.*

- *Start-up cost as low as $40,000*
- *Potential first-year earnings: $100,000*
- *Breakeven time from initial investment: six months to one year*

Just ask Fred DeLuca about the American Dream. As a high school senior he worried about how he'd pay for college. He mentioned the dilemma to Peter Buck, a nuclear physicist and family friend, hoping Peter would reach into his pocket. Instead, Peter remembered how good submarine sandwiches were when he was a kid and offered to back Fred in a business venture. If Fred ran the shop well, the income would pay for his tuition.

A couple of decades later, Frederick A. DeLuca has his bachelor's in psychology, all right. He's also president of the largest sandwich chain in the country, with 13,500 Subway Sandwiches & Salads franchises in business as of mid-1999.

HERO WORSHIP

Right now, the entire sandwich industry isn't as big as what Fred DeLuca has in mind. But he's not the only sandwich shop—keeper poised for growth. In addition to several franchises, independents are doing better than ever. According to one estimate, over the last several years the sandwich segment was the fastest growing among all QSR (quick service restaurants) categories, increasing more than 40 percent during that span.

Bob Seneff had a hunch hero sales were on the upswing. But market share was only part of the attraction when he opened the Sub-Station in the Milwaukee suburb of New Berlin, Wisconsin. "I had no restaurant background whatever. And I figured this was a part of the restaurant business I could get into with the least amount of knowledge. Start-up costs were a factor, too. Because I owned the building, I opened the doors for about $25,000." If you don't own valuable real estate you'll have to buy or rent, which will push entry costs higher. Figure on another $7,500 to $15,000 if you buy a franchise. Nevertheless, sandwich shops are to restaurants what garage sales are to Saks Fifth Avenue: cheap to start and easy to operate.

One reason start-up costs are thinner than a cold cut is because you don't have to outfit an expensive kitchen. The Sub-Station heats up prepared chili and soups during the Wisconsin winter, and Subways bake their own bread from frozen loaves. You might want to throw in a microwave oven to create a hot roast beef. Otherwise, you don't have to know the first thing about cooking.

You also keep food inventory to a minimum. Subway

prepares its salads with the same ingredients it uses to dress its sandwiches. Operators swear by freshness, however. Nothing discourages repeat business faster than stale bread.

Bob Seneff developed the Sub-Station menu with some detective work and willing test subjects. "I did a lot of snooping in the sandwich business," he recalls. He would eat late lunches at competitors' shops when employees weren't so busy. "I'd ask how they cut their onions, that sort of thing." Then he tapped a friend in the food distribution business for some free passes to food shows. "That gave me ideas of what products are on the market." Most important were the "scientific" taste tests with the help of employees of a construction company Seneff owns with his father. "I brought lots of meats, cheeses, and breads and had the construction crew tell me which they liked best."

SANDWICHES PLUS

Bob Seneff says his product is superior—and also larger than anybody else's he knows. But he attributes most of his success to location. The Sub-Station is the only eatery within walking distance of 800 businesses in the industrial park his father owns. The site generated great weekday business, but weekends were slow with no residences or commerce in the area. The Sub-Station still closes on Sunday, but Saturday picked up with two new additions to the restaurant: video rentals and really great ice cream in 32 flavors that brings those who know off the highway. "I can't make a living on video alone, but it's nice extra money," says Seneff. Also, video renters are likely to buy sandwiches to go with their movie.

The Sub-Station also added delivery service to the nearby

industrial park during its second winter. "Maybe it's because we live in Wisconsin, where it gets really cold and snowstorms keep people indoors," says Seneff. "But there was a fall-off in business during the first winter." If the customer won't come to you, is there any reason on earth you can't go to the customer? Seneff delivers up to 10 percent of his winter sales.

In its second year in business, Sub-Station garnered $30,000 in pretax profits on about $180,000 in sales. "I'm only here for an hour at lunch time," says Seneff, who leaves running the store to a dozen employees during less busy periods. "It's not bad for an hour's work, don't you think?"

Soup Restaurateur

Job Description: *A soup restaurateur owns and operates an eatery offering a variety of mouth-watering soups from exotic to traditional.*

- *Low overhead*
- *Breakeven time from initial investment: rapid (as little as one year)*
- *Future growth potential: high*
- *Nutritious food business that appeals to health-conscious consumers*

Soup's on!

That's the cry entrepreneurs across the United States have been yelling during the past few years, thanks to the phenomenal growth of the soup restaurant industry.

What used to be a rather mundane and simple side dish has suddenly become one of the hottest trends in food. According to the National Restaurant Association (NRA), soup's popularity is on the rise not only at restaurants but in other venues, as well. In a 1997 study by the NRA citing trends in the industry,

21 percent of respondents reported buying more soup than they did in the previous two years.

So if you're looking to start a business in the food industry, grab a ladle and pour yourself a hot, steaming bowl of success as a soup restaurateur.

JERRY AND THE SOUP NAZI

Those who don't follow the food industry might believe the entire soup craze sprang up overnight, following the television airing in the fall of 1995 of a soup-related episode on the popular sitcom *Seinfeld*. In the show, a tyrannical restaurateur nicknamed "the Soup Nazi" made delicious bowls of soup, but made his customers follow a very strict procedure concerning how to order and when to pay before they could get their food. If they violated this procedure, the owner snapped "No soup for you," and they were sent away empty-handed and ordered not to return.

At the core of the episode was the fact that the soup was so good that Jerry and his friends, as well as hundreds of others, didn't mind subjecting themselves to the Soup Nazi's abuse. But while this episode was extremely popular, it did not start the soup trend. In reality, New Yorkers had been lining up for years to visit a popular soup restaurant on the city's West Side (which provided some of the inspiration for the *Seinfeld* episode).

From there it was a short leap into full-fledged soup mania. In 1998 the NRA reported that more than a dozen soup take-out restaurants had opened in Manhattan since 1995. Growing numbers of soup restaurants were also ladling out their delectable offerings in Washington, D.C., and Boston.

Some soup restaurants added to their allure by adopting

distinctive names. In New York City alone there is the Soup Nutsy, Daily Soup, and Souperman. Boston boasts the New England Soup Factory, while Washington, D.C., is home to Natural Jack's Mineral River Soup Co.

Existing restaurants are fueling the soup trend by adding soup onto their menus. The NRA found that 92 percent of restaurant menus offered a soup selection in 1997, compared to 87 percent of menus in 1992.

Spooning Up a Meal

Soups that are packing in the customers aren't just any run-of-the-mill varieties, such as chicken noodle or vegetable. Rather, these are rich, full-bodied soups such as spicy Moroccan chicken and Thai chilled melon bursting with delicious and exotic ingredients.

Today's soups are meant to be a meal rather than just a side dish. When *Entrepreneur Magazine* listed soup restaurants as one of the hottest businesses of 1998, they quoted Carla Ruben, cofounder of New York City's Daily Soup chain of soup restaurants, on how the company views its product: "We're making it more of a meal," she says. "We try to imagine the customer taking the soup and putting it on a piece of bread and making a sandwich."

Reasonable prices—between $4 to $9 per serving—help attract customers. Many restaurants change their menu often, thus enabling customers to frequently try new selections. Some offer as many as ten soups per day. Given the option of a healthful, nutritious meal at a reasonable price, it's little wonder that consumers are choosing soup over fast food.

For the entrepreneur, opening a soup restaurant has several advantages over other types of eateries. Primarily, soup restaurants can achieve high-volume sales in a relatively small amount of space and with a minimum staff. Many soup restaurants offer limited or no seating (take-out only) and have a shorter operating period (typically 11:00 A.M. to 7:00 P.M.) than standard restaurants.

Low overhead can mean high revenues. The NRA pegged 1997 revenues at one Soup Nutsy location in New York City at $1 million. That's a lot of ladling!

DAILY SOUP

Daily Soup is emblematic of the rapid success soup restaurants can obtain. The first Daily Soup restaurant opened in November 1995 on 41st Street in New York City. By the summer of 1999, with ten locations, Daily Soup has become one of the Big Apple's leading soup restaurants in under four years.

Bob Spiegel, CEO of Daily Soup and one of three partners who started the business, is a former chef. The trio started Daily Soup because, in true entrepreneurial fashion, they were responding to what they perceived to be an obvious consumer need.

"We thought that the lunch crowd in midtown needed something of quality, something that was more health conscious, and we saw a lack of soup," Spiegel says.

They thought right. Three days after it opened, Daily Soup had lines down the street. All of this occurred without advertising. (The company still hasn't advertised.) Word of mouth (and of course great-tasting soups) grew the business into a spectacular success; Daily Soup posted a 400 percent growth rate in its first year of operation.

Initially Daily Soup offered an unusual selection of soups, such as pea parmesan and chicken with coconut. In response to customer requests for more traditional fare, the company adjusted its menu to offer a selection of both types. Today the company boasts a repertoire of 400 soups. Each soup is sold with fruit, bread, and a cookie.

Since its inception Daily Soup has marketed their thick, hearty soups as a meal. The menu, which changes daily, contains such unusual selections as poblano corn chowder with chicken, along with standards such as chicken barley. Prices range from $3.95 for a 12-ounce container to $8.95 for a 16-ounce serving.

Spiegel feels that the burgeoning popularity of soup restaurants is both logical and overdue. "People probably laughed when the first bagel shop or donut shop opened too," he says.

Of course, any time one gets involved in a nonmainstream food business, the $64,000 question is whether the category has staying power or is just another fad. Spiegel says that soup restaurants are here to stay.

"Soup was probably one of the first meals ever cooked, so it's not a new type of food," he says. "Everybody likes soup of one kind or another, so it's not a fad. There's no question that soup is going to be sweeping the nation."

Because of soup's nearly universal appeal, Spiegel believes the entire soup business will grow in the coming years. However, he added that he felt that the competition within the industry will become intense and that the high-quality soups will emerge victorious.

So You Want to Be in the Soup Business

If being a soup restaurateur sounds right up your alley, then prepare to spoon up some serious cash. Like any food service business, opening a soup restaurant requires special equipment, a commercial location, staff, and, of course, ingredients with which to make the soup. Anticipate spending a minimum of $250,000 to get everything up and running. The majority of your business will be at lunch. (The lunch trade is 80 percent of Daily Soup's business.) In addition, expect some decline in business during hot weather.

The rise and fall of business activity also will affect staffing needs. At Daily Soup, for instance, it takes 7 people to run a shift during the slow time (prior to and after the lunch rush) and 22 during the busy time. Of those 22, 9 are delivery people.

Even though Daily Soup made it big without marketing, the growing competition within the category means you must advertise in order to survive. Along with marketing, another additional avenue you might consider is getting a web page up and running on the Internet. The Daily Soup's page, for instance, is packed with information, such as career opportunities and company news. Most important, it allows customers to access the daily menu from any store and order soups on-line. Spiegel says that 1,000 customers per day, per store, receive the Daily Soup menu and that each store averages 100 "web deliveries" per day.

But even with start-up costs that can approach $400,000 or more, the revenues can be significant. Thus it may be possible to recoup start-up costs for an individual store in as little as one year, if your business is structured for profit rather than growth.

So if you've been taking "stock" of the restaurant industry, then you might just want to try soup!

S O U R C E

Industry Association

The National Restaurant Association, 1200 17th Street, N.W., Washington, DC 20036-3097, (202) 331-5900, (800) 424-5156

Take-out Restaurateur

Job Description: *A take-out restaurateur prepares and sells a wide variety of food that customers usually take home to eat.*

- *Start-up cost as low as $60,000*
- *Potential first-year earnings: $250,000*
- *Breakeven time from initial investment: six months to two years*

- Item: A National Restaurant Association (NRA) study once asked how often Americans purchased take-out foods. Eight out of ten people said they purchased a take-out meal or snack at least once a year, and seven out of ten respondents from households where the female head worked full time said they bought take-out more than twice a month.
- Item: A Louis Harris poll found Americans' leisure time declined by eight hours over a recent ten-year period. "Juggling careers and families means little time is left for leisure activities," observes an NRA publication. "Consequently, many consumers look for ways to 'expand' their time" with such tricks as buying prepared meals.

- Item: With the introduction of such fascinating toys as videocassette recorders and compact discs, the home has evolved into the prime entertainment center of the 1990s. And many homes also have microwave ovens that heat up prepared foods in seconds. If you want to stay home but don't want to cook, one attractive alternative is to purchase delivered or take-out food.

SUZANNE'S

When she was starting out, Suzanne Reifers didn't consider those market indicators. "Instead of doing market research," says the former speechwriter, "I did research on myself. I lived in this Washington, D.C., neighborhood near Dupont Circle, and there wasn't much there at that time. I wanted a place to buy cheeses and pâtés." Since Reifers knew *she* would frequent a gourmet take-out shop, she figured other apartment dwellers would, too.

Evidently she was right. The ground-floor take-out shop at Suzanne's, which also includes an upstairs restaurant and a catering operation, contributed $400,000 of her $1.7 million in revenues. "The average ticket is low—around $5—because people pick up two cookies on their way home from work," says the proprietor. "But we do volume." In addition to homemade pastries and salads, Suzanne's boasts some justly renowned specialties: Torta Rustica, a double-crusted quichelike pie stuffed with salmon, cheese, and herbs; and Indian Somosa, "which sounds yucky but is really delicious," according to Suzanne, who adds that the cream cheese–stuffed pastry contains a vegetable purée topped by a yogurt-and-poppy-seed sauce.

Suzanne Reifers opened Suzanne's with "you're going to

laugh—$130,000," when she came into a small inheritance. That is incredibly low considering the capital went for a sit-down restaurant as well as the take-out boutique. Reifers says she kept costs down by doing her own massive renovations to turn a dilapidated, turn-of-the-century townhouse that housed a jewelry and watch-repair shop into an attractive restaurant and retail food shop.

A Food Service Bargain

Anything under $200,000 is indeed paltry for a restaurant. However, one major attraction a take-out operation holds for entrepreneurs is its relatively low opening cost. You can open a gourmet carry-home shop for $100,000, compared with a total start-up cost of $500,000 to $1.5 million for a full-service restaurant. With no seating to worry about, you need just half the space of a typical restaurant—say 1,000 square feet—to ac-commodate a take-out operation. A well-stocked display case full of mouth-watering delicacies serves as your best decora-tion. Kitchen and clean-up facilities are smaller. And if you spe-cialize in just one or two foods, start-up costs are even lower.

A take-out operator also doesn't suffer the crazy hours that a restaurateur puts in. People who want to run a food service op-eration and still spend time with their families score this advan-tage high. Depending on your neighborhood, you might open in time to catch residents who buy a croissant and royal Dutch chocolate coffee on their way to work. But you surely dish out the last yellowtail tuna by 7:00 or 8:00 P.M., when the restaurant next door still has hours to go before taps.

Take-out counters need an abundance of help, because

customers consider convenience of supreme importance and don't relish waiting in long lines. But you can pinpoint the heavy traffic crunches fairly easily: when workers stream home from work, or, if you're in a commercial area, at lunchtime. So part-timers can make up the bulk of your staff.

NOT WHO YOU ARE BUT WHERE YOU ARE

Where you hang your take-out sign is probably even more important than what you serve, unless, of course, your customers expect delivery. If 75 percent of your gross comes from deliveries, opt for the lower-rent district. Suzanne's tacks on a $10 delivery charge, which admittedly is pretty steep for customers who spend just $8.99 to stock a picnic basket. But her intent is to accommodate those few customers who really want deliveries and encourage most people to stop by the shop.

Today, however, say "delivery" and most consumers still think pizza. That reputation stems in large part from Tom Monaghan, who, in 1961, traded in his Volkswagen for controlling interest in a Ypsilanti, Michigan, pizzeria. Since then his creation, Domino's Pizza, has revolutionized the entire food delivery industry with its promise of hot pizza in 30 minutes. Domino's has grown to more than 6,000 corporate and franchise stores, with worldwide sales of over $3.1 billion.

According to David Smith, a Domino's vice president, "The job of getting the product out in 30 minutes is accomplished in the store, not on the delivery route." A fairly open secret is Domino's insistence on a simple menu, consisting of several varieties of pizza and only one beverage. "That way," continues

Smith, "we focus on one concept: delivering our product within 30 minutes. We've got it down to 60 seconds from order to oven, and we're always looking for ways to shave seconds off the process."

But if customers come to you rather than the other way around, look for accessibility. Take-out only works on a well-traveled street in a densely populated area, which rules out most smaller towns altogether. Also, make sure you have the right population within a few blocks of your store. Shoppers won't do you much good, since they need a place to sit in order to eat. On the other hand, a railroad station could be perfect as tired commuters pick up your moo goo gai pan on their way home. "My partner and I spent a lot of money getting a good lease in Georgetown," says Geoff Elliott, who opened Take Me Home in the affluent Washington neighborhood ten years ago. "But our customers didn't match what we wanted to do. Georgetown is populated by tourists [who eat in restaurants rather than order take-out foods] and older residents [who are not from the 18 to 44 age group the NRA says is most likely to order take-out]." Thanks to a busy lunchtime trade from area office workers, the carry-out menu still contributes about 20 percent of Take Me Home's $375,000 in annual sales. But Elliott survives on the catering service he added when he realized the strategic location mistake he had made.

A COMBINATION PLATTER

Like Geoff Elliott and Suzanne Reifers, many entrepreneurs combine take-out with other types of food service. You can use a kitchen and chefs for dual purposes. Indeed, your kitchen can prepare take-out foods before the restaurant lunch or dinner crowd arrives. Suzanne's operations complement each other. "The retail shop goes gangbusters at Christmas when the restaurant is dead," she says.

Decide what statement you want to make with your food. Ethnic take-out operations like Mexigo in New York City have proven popular, as have fast-food deliverers. But if you're taking the gourmet route, suggests Suzanne Reifers, "you need a well-rounded place. You can't put in just a little bit of this and a little bit of that." In addition to the quiches and broccoli, red pepper, and corn salads she proffers, Reifers sells shelves full of packaged specialty foods, like virgin olive oil.

Reifers discovered another must is pastry. "When I began, I assumed people in these health-conscious days didn't want desserts," she recalls. "So I hired a chef who would spend half her time preparing desserts and half pâtés. The desserts were so popular we had to hire a full-time pastry chef, assistant pastry chef, and cookie baker." Now 35 percent of all shop sales are sweets. "I guess when people decide to splurge on calories they'd rather get something really delicious than buy a Heath Bar," says Reifers.

Gourmet take-out is still a city phenomenon, since smaller towns and suburbs lack the numbers to support carry-out services. Most suburbanites settle for supermarket-prepared take-outs and drive-through windows at fast-food chains. However, some operators say the gourmands and closet gourmets could get their shot in the future. Thanks to the success of operations like Domino's, more and more Americans consider buying somebody else's cooking to eat in their home as an accepted alternative. What's the next carry-out hot spot? "I might consider opening a gourmet take-out in Topeka," says one operator.

SOURCE

See "Pizza Parlor Owner," page 245.

Wrap Restaurateur

Job description: *A wrap restaurateur owns and operates an eatery offering primarily wraps—typically a tortilla or flatbread filled with ingredients such as chicken, shrimp, beef, vegetables, sauce, and so on.*

- *Start-up cost: approximately $300,000*
- *Breakeven time from initial investment: as little as two years*
- *Future growth potential: high*
- *Nutritious food concept that appeals to health-conscious consumers*
- *Exciting food concept business that allows for flair and creativity*

Wrap me up two wraps to go!"

Even though it's a mouthful, Americans are repeating that phrase, or something very similar, more and more these days. Wraps are sweeping the country, and, along with them, so are wrap restaurants. It's the latest trend in eating that doesn't seem as if it will be "all wrapped up" for many years to come.

RAPPING ABOUT WRAPS

What is a wrap? Strictly speaking, it's a cousin of the burrito and the sandwich, for it shares similarities with both. Basically, a wrap is a tortilla or flatbread filled with a variety of ingredients, such as chicken, beef, fish, and vegetables. Sometimes it also contains a sauce or spread (barbecue sauce, salad dressing, salsa, and so on). The name "wrap" comes from the fact that once all these ingredients are put onto the tortilla, it is folded, or "wrapped," over so that everything remains inside. This makes wraps the king of convenience foods.

The convenience of wraps is one factor that helped spur their popularity. With the ever-busy, ever-mobile lives more and more Americans lead, wraps are the perfect solution for eating on the run: Just grab a couple while on the road and eat them with one hand while holding onto the steering wheel with the other.

Another factor driving the wrap revolution is they're more nutritious than fast food. As people seek healthier but yet still convenient ways of eating, wraps have become more popular.

Of course, none of this would matter if wraps tasted like boiled tarpaper, but fortunately that's not the case. The ingredients inside these tasty treats are limited only by the imagination of the maker. Fish, chicken, beef, seasonings, lettuce, onions, tomatoes, peppers, and bacon are just some of the ingredients found inside wraps.

It is believed wraps originated in California in the mid-1990s and have gradually spread eastward across the United States. Today many cities have wrap restaurants; some have even brought in top-notch chefs to add their own unique flair to the menu. At California-based World Wrapps, such menu selections as Mango Snapper and Caribbean Jerk Pork helped redefine the wrap and move it to a higher culinary level.

Several national restaurant chains have examined the wrap trend and pronounced it viable enough to get in on the action. KFC Corp. added flatbread-wrapped sandwiches called Chicken Twisters to its menu. TGI Friday's introduced rolled sandwiches called Wrappers in its restaurants, while Au Bon Pain added Wraps to their menu. The fact that these national chains adopted wraps is the clearest indication yet that wraps have gone mainstream in a major way.

WRAPPIN' AT THE CAPITAL

Sometimes entrepreneurs just jump into a new field with both feet, with little more than hope and a good idea. Rick D'Alessandro, however, knew exactly what he was doing when he and his brother Ed opened Capital Wrapps in Bethesda, Maryland, in 1996. Not only did Rick have two decades of experience in the full-service restaurant business, but he was also well aware of wraps long before they became one of America's favorite foods.

D'Alessandro knew restaurants in the Hispanic section of San Francisco had long sold Mexican-style food wrapped up in tortillas. He decided to bring that concept East, where his family lived. At the same time, wraps were just starting to emerge on the West Coast, and D'Alessandro realized the wrap concept could be applied to a large variety of foods besides Mexican.

"I said to my brother, 'This is a phenomenon. We should consider doing this here [in the East],' " he says.

D'Alessandro and his brother devised the entire wrap menu

for their store. Thanks to experience, D'Alessandro knew what ingredients would taste good together, while not straying too far from the wrap concept.

Without advertising, Capital Wrapps opened in the winter of 1996, and the restaurant was immediately flooded with so much business that the two could barely keep up with the demand. Word of mouth helped keep business at a fever pitch, and favorable stories in such newspapers as the *Washington Post* and the *Wall Street Journal* continued to send a steady stream of customers through its doors.

Capital Wrapps has 1,600 square feet with 50 seats inside the restaurant and 17 on the patio. Prices range between $5.50 and $6.25, and 25 different wraps are available in small and large sizes. The restaurant also offers salads and smoothies to drink. (By offering smoothies, Capital Wrapps is mirroring a trend of other wrap restaurants around the country that combine smoothies and wraps because of the nutritional value of both. See page 238 for information on juice/smoothie bars.) Capital Wrapps also "unwraps their wraps" and puts the entire thing in a bowl.

D'Alessandro credits the quality of the food at Capital Wrapps with the eatery's success. "I can't tell you how many people come long distances to our place, simply for the quality," he says.

WRAP 'EM UP

Like any food service business, start-up costs are high for a wrap restaurant. Anticipate spending between $250,000 and $300,000 initially to get a 2,000-square-foot restaurant with seating off the ground. This includes acquiring a location, equipment (for both food preparation and business), ingredients, and staffing. During busy times, it takes at least five people to staff a restaurant.

Additional costs come from marketing. (Not everyone can be as fortunate as Capital Wrapps and do a landmark business without spending money on advertising.) If $300,000 sounds like an awful lot of cold hard cash, try finding existing space that once accommodated a restaurant. This will be less expensive than acquiring a brand-new location or refurbishing one that didn't have a restaurant in it initially. As D'Alessandro advises, the location that you choose is a critical factor in whether your restaurant sinks or swims.

"It all depends [success] on the environment that you're going into. That's the key," he says.

As far as recouping your start-up costs, the food service business is more difficult to figure out than most because of the many variables that impact profits: consumer acceptance, cost of ingredients, rental cost, staffing costs, and so on. However, D'Alessandro, who has been a restaurant industry consultant, estimates that on annual sales of $600,000 to $700,000, an owner can realize profits of approximately 20 percent. Thus, it can take a few years to recoup your initial investment. (Again, making a profit in the food service industry sometimes is an uncertain proposition. For example, some wrap restaurants had sales in the seven-figure range yet lost money due to management inexperience.)

As far as location, since wraps are still a relatively unknown food, it's best to find a spot where people are amenable to trying new things as well as where a commuting lifestyle is prevalent.

DO WRAPS HAVE LEGS?

As with all food business trends, the main question about wraps is if the concept has "the legs" to go the distance and become an established part of the American diet, or if they're just a fad that will fade away.

"I don't think that wraps are going to go away," says D'Alessandro. He also added his feeling that a wrap restaurant needs to have other items on the menu in order to survive.

Because wraps do offer many positive benefits, such as portability, nutritional value, taste, and the ability to combine numerous ingredients together to have a different taste experience each visit, they seem to have the potential to become a permanent staple in the American menu.

Healthcare
and Fitness

Adult Day Services Provider

Job Description: *An adult day services provider helps seniors with their daily needs, including nursing care, transportation, meals, social activities, eating, and bathing.*

- *Start-up cost: high (depending on location, facility, and services offered)*
- *Future growth potential: high*
- *Staffing: variable (depending on facility and type of service)*

B orn of a need to provide seniors with health, social and support services, the [adult day services] industry is gaining momentum, fueled by longer life spans and an older population," stated *Entrepreneur Magazine*, naming it one of 1998's "hottest" businesses.

Although the industry is growing rapidly, many people are completely unaware of its existence. In fact, *Entrepreneur* called it "one of the best-kept secrets around." However, with the growing number of aging baby boomers, adult day services are destined not to remain unknown for much longer.

Day Trippers

Although some date the emergence of the industry to the early 1970s, in reality it started in the late 1940s. That's when psychiatric day hospitals began adult day services to assist patients following their release from mental health facilities.

Gradually the idea spread. In 1978 the Health Care Financing Administration of the U.S. Department of Health and Human Services published a directory listing nearly 300 adult daycare centers in the country. In 1979 the National Institute on Adult Daycare (NIAD) was organized as a unit of The National Council on the Aging, Inc. In 1995 NIAD became the National Adult Day Services Association (NADSA).

Care with Dignity

Some people may confuse adult day services with assisted living facilities. (See "Assisted Living Facility Provider," page 298.) The difference, according to NADSA director Mary Brugger Murphy, is that assisted living provides 24-hour care, if necessary, while adult day services cover a preset number of hours.

"Adult day programs are typically six, eight, ten hours per day," she says.

Murphy feels that this type of care for older Americans is catching on because it simply makes sense. "It's such a very logical way of serving increasing numbers of very frail, very old people. As the population shifts, and more people live longer and become more frail, we have to find better ways to serve them."

Logic is indeed one component that drives this industry.

Instead of sending a healthcare professional to the home of a stroke patient, for instance, it makes more sense to take that person to an adult day service center where the professional can work with that person and others at the same time. This also provides clients with much-needed social interaction.

As Shaune Shields, executive director of the Greater Seacoast Adult Day Services Center in Portsmouth, New Hampshire, points out, adult day services are designed to help seniors who don't need 24-hour care while maintaining their dignity and independence.

"The goal is to keep people living in their homes as long as possible," she says.

As is typical in most programs, Greater Seacoast does a nursing assessment of patients when they first enter the program, to see what services they need to provide. This is done in conjunction with information obtained from physicians detailing patients' physical status. Although there is no profile of a "typical" adult day services patient, Seacoast is focusing on the frail elderly and those with Alzheimer's disease. Why? Because that's what the community needs.

COMMUNITY RESEARCH CRITICAL

There are an estimated 4,000 adult day service centers operating in the United States. However, as knowledge of the industry spreads, demand for these centers continues to grow. Mary Brugger Murphy says that anyone interested in getting into the field should start by surveying the local community.

"Human services are not really a build-it-and-they-will-come phenomenon," she says. "You really have to know the community. You have to do a good market analysis of the community and find out what's there, what the competition is, and how many people need to be served."

Murphy warns that the analysis must be thorough. While a freestanding adult day services facility may not exist in a community, prompting someone to believe that the way is clear to open one, an existing nursing home or hospital may already offer those same services. Approximately one-third of the adult day service centers in the United States are freestanding facilities; the remainder are folded in with a hospital or other healthcare provider.

If you're interested in getting into this field and believe you see an opportunity, your next step should be to contact the NADSA. Adult day service regulations differ from state to state; NADSA can direct you to the agency in your state that oversees the industry. The association also has a set of voluntary standards and guidelines that it urges anyone getting into the field to follow. Outside of these, there are no uniform national standards governing either the operation of centers or the qualifications of staff members.

"A very useful contact is with the state association of adult day providers," Murphy says. "In Ohio, for example, the state association provides a two-day training course in how to start an adult day program. This is a very good way of determining if this makes sense for you."

Fees for adult day services vary, depending on the region of the country and the range of services provided. Daily fees range between a few dollars all the way to $185, depending on the services provided and reimbursement levels (where applicable). Greater Seacoast charges a flat rate of $6.50 per hour, with a minimum of $39 per day and a maximum of $45.

Even at that rate, however, Greater Seacoast is losing money on each patient. The primary reason is that government reimbursement to adult day services facilities is extremely low, because the whole concept is so new that traditional government medical payment plans do not recognize its existence.

"Adult day services is the new kid on the block," says Shaune Shields. The major source of funding for adult day services is private pay. However, some programs accept people who are Medicaid eligible.

Another consideration before opening a facility is transportation. Although those seniors who can drive use their own cars to get to the facility, many can't and suffer from conditions (such as Alzheimer's) that rule out public transportation. Thus many centers, such as Greater Seacoast, hire vans to pick up patients at their homes. However, this is often another money-losing situation. Greater Seacoast, for instance, charges riders just 25 cents per ride but is billed for van use at a rate of $25 per hour.

As far as what services to offer, it depends on what exists in the local community. The "average" adult day center offers a wide range of services, including: transportation, social services, meals, nursing care, personal care, counseling, therapeutic activities, and rehabilitation therapies. It is recommended that you focus on providing services that aren't readily available in your area.

Murphy says, "If there's a community where there already is a very strong network of sophisticated and accessible healthcare services, but people with Alzheimer's who are relatively healthy have nowhere to go, then that becomes your target population, at least to start with."

NADSA has defined three different categories of services to use as a general guideline: core (a client needs socialization, some supervision, supportive service, and minimal assistance with activities of daily living); enhanced (a client needs moderate assistance); and intensive (a client needs maximum assistance).

Early in 1999, NADSA unveiled an accreditation program for adult day service centers. Developed through collaboration with CARF, the Rehabilitation Accreditation Commission, the program sets national standards by which the activities at centers are monitored and rated.

Services offered also dictate staffing needs. For example, your staffing needs will be much different if you're going to serve a mobile population as compared to one that is severely impaired.

Another cost consideration is the actual building itself. To build one entirely from scratch costs in the hundreds of thousands of dollars. However, sometimes renovating an existing facility is no bargain, either. Greater Seacoast spent approximately $900,000 to totally overhaul a building that had been built in the 1950s.

"You have to be in this business because it's a mission for you," says Shields, speaking about some of the financial pitfalls. "You have to do it from the heart."

ACTIVE GROWTH

Active Services Corporation exemplifies a successful adult day services company. By mid-1999, after just four years in existence, the Birmingham, Alabama–based company was operating 36 adult day health centers and had become an industry leader.

Active Services was founded by Kenneth W. Oliver in 1995, a veteran with more than 20 years in the healthcare industry. Oliver started the company when he realized that patients often had needs that were not met by visiting facilities that offered just one type of service. Friends or family usually had to ferry the patient around to other facilities to receive the required treatments. At the same time, Oliver's elderly parents became ill and required almost continuous access to the healthcare system. As the child who lived the closest to them, it fell to Oliver to help his parents get the services they required, and he was again reminded of how difficult it was to coordinate everything. Thus was born the idea of creating a company that offered a wide range of services.

"Basically, we created a platform of service that is a comprehensive point of care," says Oliver. "A person recovering from a stroke or cardiac problems who is experiencing difficulties with the activities of daily living can be brought into a congregate setting and have 10 or 11 hours of interaction with other people, while also receiving [necessary] care."

Because of ignorance about adult day services, Oliver says that "the biggest challenge" that Active Services faces whenever it goes into a community is to get the word out about itself and its services. The company advertises and also tries to get the local media to do stories on the company and its services. It also develops a list of 20 to 30 key sources (physician offices, advocacy groups, discharge managers at hospitals, and so on) and contacts them to explain their programs and services.

"It's ongoing," Oliver says of the public relations effort. "We continue doing that, even after we've opened."

In terms of a payment schedule, Active Services normally uses a per-diem system based on the level of care required. The less-intense level of care costs between $45 and $50 per day, while the most extensive care costs approximately $65.

THE FUTURE IS NOW

Adult day services is an industry that's just coming into its own. As with assisted living, demographics—such as the projection that the number of people over 65 is going to double in the next two decades—favor continued growth.

"I think the field is wide open," says Oliver. "It's estimated that today, we're meeting 30 to 40 percent of the need in the country. This need will at least double in the next twenty years. [This industry] has an extremely bright future."

"I think it will expand. It's so logical that it can't help but take off," Murphy adds.

SOURCE

Industry Association

The National Adult Day Services Association, 409 3rd Street, S.W., Washington, DC 20024, (202) 479-1200

Aerobics/Exercise Instructor

Job Description: *An aerobics/exercise instructor teaches fitness through the use of aerobics and other exercise routines.*

- *Start-up cost as low as $2,500*
- *Potential first-year earnings: $10,000*
- *Breakeven time from initial investment: one month to three years*
- *No staffing required*

Karen Shaffer taught French by day, but her passion was the Jazzercize exercise classes she took several times a week. Deciding to combine her love of dance exercise with her love of teaching, she bought a Jazzercize franchise. "I began by teaching at an adult school, then rented church facilities," she recalls.

Like many aerobics students who make the leap to instructor, Karen Shaffer got hooked. "Each routine is a performance and I ham it up. I teach people to make the most of themselves." She points to a svelte woman who was once overweight.

"Before class she talked about her new boyfriend. The students give such positive feedback."

A WAY OF LIFE

Although the national obsession with exercise has already begun to level off, Karen decided a steady core of exercisers would always want to flex and stretch and move to the music. So she and another franchisee went into partnership; instead of continuing to scrounge around for subpar Y and firehouse facilities to rent for their classes, they plowed $60,000 into opening their own Jazzercise salon in a Pennington, New Jersey, shopping center. (Shaffer talks with near reverence about the custom floor they now possess.) Today, except for minimal salaries, they still pour every dime into making the business work, but Shaffer foresees a steady 5 percent growth every year; and she never contemplates returning to the less strenuous drills she once led conjugating French verbs in a classroom.

According to studies by the Sporting Goods Manufacturers of America, women 18 to 34 do aerobics more often than any other group. But these Generation X'ers are not bumping and grinding to those old Jane Fonda videos that were hot in the 1970s. Instead, they sweat and strain to videos put out by MTV and the New York–based Crunch fitness gyms; these are videos with an in-your-face attitude, complete with heaps of sarcasm and funky music. This "new" style of aerobics has become so popular that it's even gotten a name: GenXercise. True, the double-digit numbers of those who discovered aerobics each year in the 1970s may never again occur, but aerobics isn't losing adherents, either. The difference now: Aerobics entrepreneurs can no longer be mere instructors. Today it takes marketing acumen to keep those revenues in shape.

BREAKING IN

IDEA estimates that most of the aerobics industry's instructors work part time. If you wonder whether you can make a living doing sit-ups and jumping jacks, why not hold on to your current job and moonlight?

Three avenues lead to exercise instruction:

- **Independent contracts.** Many instructors freelance at health clubs or studios that pay by the hour. You don't need to worry about marketing since somebody else rounds up students. Bare-bones start-up capital covers leotards and Reeboks, and possibly some tapes and a portable stereo if your club doesn't provide them. If you go the independent route, be sure to carry liability insurance if your employer doesn't.

- **Satellite classes.** Following Karen Shaffer's entry strategy, many instructors lease community facilities, such as a recreation center or school gymnasium. You probably can hold initial costs—for rent, tapes and a stereo system, clothing, and insurance—below $2,500. If you join a franchise, tack on another $500 or so. (Jazzercize, for example, sells franchisees videotapes with its routines and provides training and the use of its name. In return, the franchise takes 30 percent of revenues, after expenses.) Operating with a floating home base, as Karen explains, has its drawbacks—when basketball season begins for a school, or when the church expands Wednesday bingo to Thursdays the landlord grabs back the site. After scrambling to find a new place, invariably you lose members who won't travel with you.

- Opening a studio. One estimate is that converting a 2,400-square-foot empty shell into an aerobics studio would cost $32,600 to $60,200, depending on how much you spend for a ceiling, floor, lights, sprinkler, mirrors, air conditioner, professional sound system, and fans. This figure assumes a studio hosting 30 classes weekly could attract a total attendance of 600. If you charge a fairly typical $3.50 per head and pay instructors $10 an hour, you'll net around $88,000 per year. From that, deduct overhead, advertising, and debt service.

DIVERSIFY

Of course, you can offer other moneymakers beyond those 30 classes. "It's imperative to add things other than aerobic classes to survive," advises Barbara Fisher, who runs Bodies by Fisher in a Victorian brownstone in the Back Bay section of Boston. "You can only offer classes at the times when lots of people want to take them. During the other times, offer individual consultation, rent the space to dance groups, or offer skin care or nutritional counseling." And don't forget clothing and food and drink concessions.

Many studios expand their repertoires beyond challenging workouts. Lead classes for special groups such as pregnant or overweight women or even children. You also can offer less stressful exercises, such as low-impact aerobics or, if you have access to a pool, aquatic routines.

The biggest untapped market is spelled M-E-N. The National Sporting Goods Association has estimated that men

make up less than 15 percent of aerobics' participants, a stat ambitious entrepreneurs regard as an opportunity. (Even though
the Gen X videos are designed to appeal to men as much as
women.) And some observers see hopeful signs. Kathie Davis
of IDEA notes that some high school football teams now emu-
late the pros by including aerobics in their conditioning. Could
be players will continue aerobics after their football glory days
are gone. Davis suggests aerobics instructors make slight
changes to erase the effeminate stigma, such as offering a sports
conditioning class—basically aerobics with dance references
deleted from routines. Instead of incorporating graceful flour-
ishes into the routine, clench those fists.

GET OUT THERE AND SELL

"Try to tap all markets," Barbara Fisher advises. Many corporations pay dues as an employee benefit, so why not call on area
employers and leave a notice on their bulletin boards? Once
you book your own facilities to capacity, add outreach programs. Some schools that have cut back on physical education
classes hire instructors to lead after-school aerobics in the gym
as an extracurricular activity. Ask the recreation director of a senior citizen condo whether residents might like aquatic aerobic
instruction in the pool. Barbara sends instructors to hotels and
corporations for on-site aerobics and goes through the convention bureau to find meeting organizers. "Propose health breaks
instead of coffee breaks. Corporations provide yogurt and juice
instead of coffee and donuts, and you lead 15 minutes of
stretching and breathing to break up the seminars. Low-impact
aerobics won't leave them sweating."

While many aerobics instructors build a loyal following of

students who stay with them for years, count on constantly re-plenishing your exercisers. As many as 6 million of those 23 million aerobics participants are debutantes, and a similar num-ber of exercisers drop out each year. To replace the transients, budget for advertising: newspapers, direct mail and handout flyers, and even radio and TV in some markets. Studios can of-fer open houses and guest passes, while freelance instructors can demonstrate at the local country fair. You can even offer a membership as a prize in a charity-related fund raiser.

SOURCES

Industry Associations

Aerobic & Fitness Association of America, 15250 Ventura Boulevard, Suite 200, Sherman Oaks, CA 91403-3297, (877) 968-7263

International Dance Exercise Association, 6190 Cornerstone Court East, Suite 204, San Diego, CA 92121-3773, (619) 535-8979, (800) 999-4332

National Sporting Goods Association, 1699 Wall Street, Suite 700, Mount Prospect, IL 60056-5780, (847) 439-4000

Ambulatory Care Center Provider

Job Description: *An ambulatory care center provider treats medical patients on a walk-in basis, usually without an appointment.*

- *Start-up cost as low as $250,000*
- *Potential first-year earnings: $250,000*
- *Breakeven time from initial investment: one to two years*

The healthcare industry is changing faster than you can say "freestanding emergency medical centers." On one hand, modern medicine is increasingly able to cure all manner of deadly diseases, allowing us to live longer and healthier lives. On the other hand, we're paying for it. According to a story in *Time* magazine, Americans spend $733 billion a year on medical care, which is nearly twice what they spent just seven years ago.

As insurance companies and Medicare throw up their hands with cries of "We're not going to take it any more," premiums increase and payments to patients fizzle. In response, the medical establishment is scurrying for ways to provide quality healthcare at more affordable rates. Instead of prescribing lengthy hospital stays, physicians recommend home health-care. (See "Home Healthcare Provider," page 309.) Instead of treating heart disease when an attack necessitates surgery, em-ployers are signing on for preventive care with health mainte-nance organizations.

DOC-IN-THE-BOX

In addition to home healthcare, observers report a trend toward ambulatory care centers—patients walk in without an appoint-ment at any hour of the day or night. Because private walk-in centers operate without a hospital emergency room's high over-head, they can charge a small percentage of what a hospital might charge for the same procedure. For example, Jerry Hermanson, president of North Federal Management Group, says the four Minor Emergicenters that his group operates in Pompano Beach and Deerfield, Florida, charge $125 for admin-istering to an arm injury that requires suturing and X rays. "A hospital in my area would charge $225 for the same procedure," says Hermanson, a hospital administrator before he opened the first Emergicenter.

Lured by less costly bills and shorter waits for treatment, pa-tients turn to ambulatory centers in increasing numbers. With every treatment, they learn to trust the care they receive at the centers the media used to call "doc-in-the-boxes." The public's heightened awareness, along with increased visits, result in more centers opening to fulfill the demand. According to an ar-ticle in *Compensation and Benefits Review*, "ambulatory care . . . is growing rapidly . . . due to managed care incentives." The article also stated that experts believed this growth would continue.

WHATEVER AILS YOU

The complexion of the centers is changing. The early clinics treated almost exclusively non–life-threatening emergencies such as sore throats or sprained ankles, as reflected in such trade names as Minor Emergency Center or Urgent Care. In the future, many operators expect that primary-care facilities will provide the biggest boost to the new business. These facilities treat patients for all kinds of illnesses on an ongoing basis, just as general practitioners have always done. A separate trend is toward centers that specialize in such areas as birthing, X rays, and ophthalmology.

You can build a freestanding clinic for about twice the cost of setting up a general practitioner's office (which doesn't require a laboratory or X-ray equipment). While the initial cost is higher, you'll turn profits far faster: Seeing patients in volume means higher revenues. If you rent real estate and lease medical equipment, you can fund an emergency center that operates 80 hours a week for as little as $250,000. That assumes you're doing some advertising and paying only for two doctors, two nurses, two receptionists, and two X-ray technicians for the year or so before breakeven. If you buy your own building and equipment, or staff a larger center, plan on needing more capital. Some of the larger medical equipment companies can provide a list of equipment, pharmaceuticals, and incidentals you need to get started.

You can afford to pay your staff salaries similar to what they would make working in a hospital or doctor's office. Doctors, for the most part, are young and see working in a center as a way to increase their experience.

The medical community splits in about a dozen different directions on whether they like the walk-in centers. "Local primary-care physicians see us as direct competition," says Jerry Hermanson, who consults for hospitals and individuals wanting to set up ambulatory care centers. "Since we refer patients to specialists, the specialists don't object." Hospitals, already feeling the revenue pinch as insurance providers insist on shorter stays and fewer tests, recognize that the emergency centers are stealing their emergency room clientele. Their reaction: If you can't beat 'em, join 'em. Nearly 50 percent of hospitals set up their own freestanding centers, says the National Association for Ambulatory Care. The hospitals operate a center either as a hospital adjunct or as a joint venture in partnership with an entrepreneur.

MARRY A DOCTOR

As often as not, the opening partner isn't even a doctor. In fact, some centers are backed entirely with non-M.D. dollars, although, says consultant Arthur E. Auer of Auer & Associates, "I find centers don't work unless a physician has a billfold on the line. If you work with a partner who has medical expertise, the centers can represent good business opportunities."

They sure can. Once you break even on annual revenues of a half-million or so, you probably can keep 20 percent ($100,000) as pretax profits. Since you commit to low-cost, quality care in order to beat out hospitals, the key to profitability involves volume. Jerry Hermanson says a center needs to treat 30 patients a day at $50 each to break even. That would represent annual revenues in the $525,000 range. An even busier facility with two doctors on board at all times could bring in double or more the annual revenues.

A revolving door waiting room is just as important to the patient as to the medical center. After all, most patients don't worry too much about whether you are cheaper than the competition; they expect their insurance carrier to reimburse the cost of the visit. But who wants to wait all Saturday afternoon in a hospital to get that nasty burn treated when they'd rather return to the barbecue? "We look at a 20-minute turnaround from the time the patients walk in the door until they leave," says Hermanson. "It may take another five minutes if they need a test, or ten minutes for an X ray. But if the visit takes longer than that, it's time to open another center."

Which is just what Hermanson did. When the first Minor Emergicenter grew too busy in Pompano Beach, he and his three partners opened another one five miles away in Deerfield, Florida. Hermanson wanted the second clinic near enough to benefit from shared advertising but distant enough to avoid overtaxing the patient base.

WHERE YOU WANT TO BE

Location is as important to a walk-in clinic as it is to a retail store. In addition to considering what clinics are nearby, check out other medical competition, such as hospitals and primary-care physicians. Competition isn't always bad. If the emergency room in the only hospital in a five-mile radius is overburdened, your center may catch the overflow just by proximity. A dense population is important, but it should be the right kind of population. For example, Jerry Hermanson warns against locating in a retirement area. "The over-65 population has already established a relationship with a doctor, so they are low utilizers of emergency centers."

Hermanson also looks for a good industrial and residential mix, since Minor Emergicenter's employers refer 15 percent of its patients. "We have an active marketing campaign to get work-related patients," he explains. "We provide a group rate for preemployment physicals, for example." While his company doesn't discount worker's compensation treatments, businesses often refer employees for minor injuries because the centers are convenient and swift. In a similar fashion, Minor Emergicenters also contact schools and camps to suggest students stop by for required physicals.

You might also lean toward a location that allows bold signs. If you're too discreet, patients who have passed your clinic a thousand times may not recall you exist as they drive the other direction to take care of that earache.

HEALTH FAIRS

Increasing chunks of health providers' budgets are going for advertising. Even hospitals dole out great gobs of money to bring in "customers" nowadays, and your walk-in service has to compete. Although Jerry Hermanson advertises in the Yellow Pages, the newspaper, and through direct mail, he says the best returns come through community involvement, such as participating in chambers of commerce health fairs.

Minor Emergicenters enjoy about 55 percent repeat business, meaning more than half of its patients have visited the centers before. That's a fairly high statistic, considering most consumers see walk-in clinics as emergency facilities. But Hermanson says the staff physicians court the repeat business. "We make a point of following up visits with next-day phone calls" to see how an infection is healing, he explains. In the minds of entrepreneurs who are opening the ambulatory clinics at an increasing rate, patients are quickly accepting walk-in service as an alternative for ongoing care as well as emergency treatments.

SOURCES

Industry Associations

American Hospital Association, One North Franklin, Chicago, IL 60606, (312) 422-3000

International Federation of Ambulatory Care, 1755 Highland Oaks Way, Lawrenceville, GA 30043-3270, (770) 416-0700

The Society for Ambulatory Care Professionals, One North Franklin, Chicago, IL 60606, (312) 422-3900

Assisted Living Facility Provider

Job description: *An assisted living facility provider designs comfortable living environments that allow older citizens to age with dignity while providing support for daily activities.*
- *Start-up cost: high (depending on location and size of facility)*
- *Booming industry with excellent future growth potential*

Americans are getting older. That simple fact has spurred the phenomenal growth of the assisted living facilities industry in the United States. From ground zero in 1980, assisted living mushroomed to an estimated $13.5 billion in sales in 1998. Even more extraordinary, that figure doubled in 2000.

This amazing growth rate led *Entrepreneur Magazine* to label assisted living one of 1998's "hottest businesses," saying ". . . the growing number of seniors in America is creating a need for healthcare businesses the likes of which we've never seen before. Assisted living facilities mark another segment of this trend."

Although it is a cash-intensive business, potential rewards and seemingly limitless future make it a field every true entrepreneur should investigate.

THE AGING OF AMERICA

If you watch television, go to the movies, read magazines, or listen to the radio, you might believe that young people populate the United States almost exclusively. They appear in many television shows and films, and virtually all of the commercials and ads.

Until 1980 that assumption held some truth, as the country's median age rarely exceeded 30, meaning that half of the U.S. population was younger than 30 and half was older. If that sounds incredible, consider that for most of the 19th century, the median age in the United States was 20 or less!

Beginning in 1980, however, due to a declining birth rate and greater life expectancy, America began aging. By 1997, the country's median age was almost 35. In another three decades, it is projected to approach 39.

One of the most rapidly growing age groups is people over age 80. In 1970 the United States had 1.8 million people over that age; 20 years later that figure swelled to 2.8 million. By 2010 experts estimate 3.8 million Americans will be at least 80 years old. This rapid rise in the over-80 population is one of the keys to the industry's explosive growth.

AGING WITH DIGNITY

According to the Assisted Living Federation of America (ALFA), an assisted living residence is "a special combination of housing, supportive services, personalized assistance and healthcare designed to respond to the individual needs of those who need help with activities of daily living and instrumental activities of daily living."

A typical assisted living resident is 83 years old, female, and either single or widowed. Seniors who use assisted living facilities receive help with everything from taking medication, eating and dressing, to bathing and doing their laundry. Support services are available 24 hours a day, and residents can take advantage of any of these services. This allows them to function on their own as much as possible, which helps them to retain their dignity and quality of life. Adding to their comfort is the fact that assisted living facilities typically resemble homes or apartments instead of an institution.

The resident or family usually pays the cost of residing at a facility. Some states provide reimbursement for assisted living services through programs such as Medicaid waivers. In general, however, the government offers limited payments for assisted living residences. Thus, contrary to many other aspects of healthcare, assisted living is an industry fueled by private pay and customer satisfaction. As Karen A. Wayne, president and CEO of ALFA, points out, people use assisted living facilities out of choice.

"Before assisted living became an option, your choices were very limited," says Wayne. "You could either stay in your home and have a home-health nurse provide some care during the day, or you could go into a nursing home. Assisted living provides a true residential option that meets [seniors'] needs for independence and treats them with the dignity that they feel they deserve."

MAN OF VISION

Although it seems like a logical idea now, in the beginning it took an awful lot of entrepreneurial spirit to get the assisted living facilities industry off the ground. Considering the idea ludicrous, banks refused to lend money for building residences. Determined to succeed, early visionaries scraped together the financing to build their first homes.

Before starting Alterra Healthcare Corporation in 1981, Bill Lasky held management positions in two national nursing home companies. "That gave me the advantage of being in a lot of institutional environments. I had an urge to create an alternative to nursing home care for seniors," says Lasky.

Lasky built his first assisted living residence in Glendale, California, in 1981. He undertook the venture "cold," without any clients, and it took 18 months to fill the residence. But even through his long wait he knew he was on the right track because he saw people were willing to pay out of their own pockets to choose their own home rather than live somewhere dictated by a third-party payer such as an insurance company.

Today Alterra is the largest assisted living provider in the United States. It operates 369 assisted living facilities in 25 states across the country. In 1998 the company posted $250 million in revenues. For Lasky, the beauty of the industry is that it's consumer-oriented; if seniors and their children were not happy with the facilities and lifestyle the industry offers, they wouldn't support it.

"Seniors have a lot of rights and a lot of empowerment," he says. "The idea that you don't need long hallways, fluorescent lights, and tiled floors to take care of older people is such a simple idea, and one that has caught on."

MAKING YOUR WAY

As noted earlier, this is an extremely capital-intensive industry. According to a 1999 ALFA report, the average cost to build a large assisted living facility in 1998 was approximately $8.2 million. This figure includes land cost, architectural fees, land improvements, building cost, marketing, and all other factors involved in building such a facility.

However, before that amount causes you to skip ahead to the next section in this book, it's important to realize that the figure represents a 53,593-square-foot facility with 69 units and 81 beds. There's nothing that says you have to start out building such a large structure.

"There's a wide variety [of types of residences], and the development costs vary according to the prototype you wish to build," says Karen Wayne.

If you're considering getting involved in this industry, the best advice is to contact ALFA first. It has excellent documentation on regulations (government regulations on assisted living vary greatly from state to state) as well as a primer for developing assisted living facilities.

According to ALFA, in 1998 daily basic fees for units ranged from a low of $12.75 to a high of $205, with an average of $73.54. Unlike most other businesses discussed in this book, it is impossible to determine how quickly you can see a return on your start-up costs because of all the variables involved, particularly how much you spend on construction and the size of that facility. The cost of staff and services will also depend on many factors, including facility size.

However, opportunities abound in this industry. Between 2000 and 2010, the age group of those 85 and older is expected to grow 33.2 percent. Few businesses enjoy such a projected increase in their target clientele. In addition, other businesses such as restaurants and retail ventures require a significant capital investment, with no greater guarantee of success. Although it may take a sizable outlay of money to enter the assisted living facilities industry, Wayne points out that the future looks bright.

"If an entrepreneur wants to consider the industry, it certainly is a great opportunity," she says. "The demographics show that there will be a great need in the future, particularly as the baby boomers reach the marketplace. Assisted living is becoming the cornerstone of healthcare in this country."

SOURCE

Industry Association

The Assisted Living Federation of America, 10300 Eaton Place, Suite 400, Fairfax, VA 22030, (703) 691-8100

Diet Clinic Provider

Job Description: *A diet clinic provider helps clients to lose weight through diet and eating strategies.*
- *Start-up cost as low as $75,000*
- *Potential first-year revenues: $45,000*
- *Breakeven time from initial investment: several years*
- *Excellent opportunity for people with physical disabilities*
- *No staffing required*

Behind every successful weight-loss clinic is a former fat person. After years of unsuccessful dieting, the typical entrepreneur found the secret formula to losing 50 pounds . . . 75 pounds . . . 100 pounds. . . . Once the dieter loses all that excess weight, the natural thing to do is to found a diet company or buy a franchise. In fact, knowing that previously overweight individuals understand the rules and can best empathize with their clientele, both Diet Center Inc., Rexburg, Idaho, and Fortune Life Center, Charlottesville, Virginia, sell franchises only to individuals who have completed their programs.

Sybil Ferguson, who founded Diet Center based on a strategy that helped her lop off 58 pounds, offers some clues as to why about 70 million Americans are overweight: "Ten years ago, the average man burned 3,500 calories a day; he now burns only 2,800 calories. Women ten years ago burned 2,400 calories daily; today they burn only 1,800. Based on these figures alone, a person could gain up to five pounds a month if his or her eating habits are basically the same as they were ten years ago."

"I THINK I CAN, I THINK I CAN"

While some diet clinics combine exercise with nutritional advice and others sell diet supplements, the majority stress behavior modification using individual diet counselors. The theory: "If you change your eating habits, you can become thin." Once they've provided hints on how to eat for health, the centers back up that message with loads of positive reinforcement and subtle peer pressure that comes with scheduled weigh-ins.

"We stress 'Breakthrough Thinking,'" explains Jeannie Geurink, who was a client with 100 pounds to lose and then a franchisee before she bought the Slender Center parent company in Madison, Wisconsin. A 256-page manual and individual counseling sessions lead Slender Center clients through FRIA, an acronym that stands for Focus (on how to change your eating behavior), Relaxation (you can't change your behavior if you're uptight), Imagery (imagining that you are thin motivates you to carry through), and Affirmation (think positive, you can do it!).

The dilemma weight-loss centers face is snaring clients who have heard it all before. The typical customer, a woman under age

50, has been through numerous self-help diets in the past. None worked in the long haul, otherwise she wouldn't be 25 to 35 pounds too heavy, which is about average among Slender Center clients. Now you must convince her that your solution really will help her. "Our message tells people not to feel guilty about those times they tried and failed to lose weight," says Geurink. "Don't feel guilty about asking for help. Then we offer a written guarantee that, as long as dieters make no deletions, additions, or substitutions to our diet, they can lose two to three pounds per week."

Plan on spending as much as 25 percent of gross on advertising and marketing when you're first establishing a reputation. Advertise in newspapers and the Yellow Pages, and possibly radio and TV in markets where rates are low or where you can share expenses with other centers. Once you are better known in the community you can downscale your ad budget to 7 to 10 percent of gross, since most clients come through referrals from skinny customers.

Missionary work helps, too. Set up booths in health fairs or ask the local radio or TV talk show host if you might do a spot on nutrition. Also, more corporations are investigating "wellness programs." You can offer a corporate discount to attract employees.

FIND US IF YOU CAN

One reason you have to advertise so heavily involves location. Many diet clinics look for an easily accessible—but not terribly visible—site. This advice could change in the future if the heavy crowd becomes less inhibited about walking through the doors of a diet clinic. But many clients today "don't want to meet their neighbors when they go into a diet clinic," says Jeannie Geurink. "They have a fear of failure until they're about

20 pounds down." Geurink recommends a professional office setting near, but not in, a mall. "Even a back entrance or upstairs is okay," she says. Of course, the benefit of choosing a secondary rather than a prime location involves start-up costs. Depending on what backup materials you offer, even franchisees likely can hold initial capital in the $20,000 ballpark.

Your staff-to-client ratio depends on your market and the approach you take. Slender Centers usually begin with just the entrepreneur and a part-time counselor to handle the 30 to 75 clients that a start-up clinic might schedule per week. The weigh-ins, which range from twice a week to daily, usually last about 15 minutes, during which time the counselor discusses FRIA with the client in conjunction with the particular weight loss and problems encountered. Slender Center's fees differ from location to location. But in the Madison company-owned center, a ten-week program with daily weigh-ins costs around $600. Each client receives four weeks of stabilization counseling after the weight loss is achieved and six months of maintenance supervision at no extra charge.

What type of person makes a good counselor? If you're joining one of at least 15 franchise organizations, you can pick up a knowledge of nutrition and the basics of a particular program from them. Solo entrepreneurs can take nutrition courses at community colleges. Beyond that, "it helps to be outgoing," says Barbara Davies, who runs the Diet Center of Hunterdon in Flemington, New Jersey. Barbara admits she was introverted until she lost 100 pounds in nine months with Diet Center before buying her franchise. "After losing all that weight, I really like myself—and others like me, too," she says. "That gives a person confidence."

Diet clinics have no fear that they'll run out of clients. Despite the growing emphasis on health, more Americans are overweight than ever before. Particularly as the millions of baby boomers age, pounds increasingly become a problem. "I can see acceptance growing every year since I first started," observes Jeannie Geurink. "People still have reservations about joining a weight-loss program, but that reluctance is declining. She also believes that the future trend will be for someone to automatically join a weight-loss center anytime they need to lose five pounds."

Home Healthcare
Provider

Job Description: *Home healthcare providers bring medical treatments and procedures to patients in their homes.*

- *Start-up cost as low as $40,000*
- *Potential first-year earnings: $50,000*
- *Breakeven time from initial investment: several years*
- *Future growth potential: high*

A number of major trends are converging to bolster the home healthcare business. As our population ages, more people need medical care or just assistance in performing their daily routine. Capital-strapped hospitals discharge patients—regardless of age—quickly, often before they are ready to resume their day-to-day activities. And nursing homes hold little attraction for those seniors who want to remain independent. Meanwhile, the largest users of home healthcare—elderly people—have more money than ever before, enough to pay for their own well-being.

These trends promise a growth of home healthcare agencies, companies that bring to clients' homes everything from high-tech respirators and chemotherapy to aides who help bathe aged or ill patients. According to the National Association for Home Care (NAHC), annual expenditures for home care were $40 billion in 1997 and were expected to reach $42 billion in 1998. NAHC estimates that there are approximately $20,000 providers—including over 2,200 hospices—delivering home care services to around 8 million individuals.

PEOPLE WHO NEED PEOPLE

But those are just numbers. What really counts to typical entrepreneurs who enter the home health field is people. Consider

- Ninety-three-year-old Jesse. Although her son Frank cooks for her and cleans her house, a nursing home seemed imminent because neither felt comfortable sharing intimate tasks such as bathing. A home aide visiting three times a week allowed the proud woman to remain at home.
- Stanley, whose active lifestyle screeched to a halt when he suffered a stroke at age 60. Home therapists assisted his wife in returning him to independence.
- Tiny Mary, born prematurely with severe respiratory problems. Instead of months of hospitalization, Mary grew stronger in the warmth of her own home with the help of visiting nurses and a home respirator.

"Home healthcare is a badly needed service, especially for older people," states an empathic Ruth Constant, who holds a Ph.D. in nursing and operates four agencies in Texas. "People ask why I stay in, when I might make more money elsewhere. But it gets under your skin."

YOU'RE BETTING ON THE FUTURE

Despite the obvious benefits of home care (the NAHC estimates that even extensive home care can cost just one-quarter the bill for institutional care), the field still struggles. But nearly everyone sees home healthcare as a top moneymaker of the future for those who can hang on until the federal government loosens Medicare purse strings and insurance companies agree to reimburse more of the costs. "The industry will overcome the crisis because demographics will demand it," says Jennifer Hirshan, a spokesperson for the NAHC. She also points to legislative action and lawsuits that she predicts will force the government to be more generous with home healthcare dollars. Already some large hospital chains are starting home healthcare divisions or buying entrepreneurial companies as they bet on the field's potential.

This attention comes despite the fact that Medicare-based home health companies can barely meet costs—and making a profit on Medicare alone is out of the question. Until the industry's health improves, operators compensate by accepting only non-Medicare/Medicaid patients, or by providing a balance of private-pay and government-reimbursed healthcare.

For example, Ruth Constant, who also does outside consulting with home-health start-ups, bids on state contracts to perform such social services as meal preparation for patients under a physician's care. "The primary- and family-care programs supplement what I lose in Medicare," she explains. When more than one agency competes for state-funded programs, the low bidder wins. "But hopefully you bid $10 to cover something that just costs you $9 to perform so you can make a profit." As a rule, companies providing primary care—meaning nonmedical functions, such as house cleaning for an infirm client—shoot for about 5 percent profits.

You can do a lot better—maybe 15 to 20 percent profits—in private care or providing services paid for by the family—or by the private-insurance carrier. Much of the financial elbow room comes because you don't deal with the sheer bureaucracy of government programs. "I can provide the same services for 50 percent less when I don't have to deal with the Medicare red tape and restrictions," says Constant.

Private services also cost a lot less to set up. Kay and Jim Hollers invested less than $100,000 to launch Wellstream Health Services in Austin, Texas. Most of the capital went to open a small office, secure licensing, and do marketing—which meant a Yellow Pages ad and brochures mailed to zip codes in areas where older and more affluent citizens live. "If you plan on government reimbursements, you can wait six months to a year to get paid—and even then you're not assured you'll get 100 percent," says Kay, who ran a chapter of the nonprofit Visiting Nurses in Lansing, Michigan, before she and her husband decided to move back to their hometown and start their own business. The couple also avoided governmental red tape: "Because we didn't go into Medicare, Jim and I could handle most of the records. We didn't need rooms full of clerks getting records together for the government."

Wellstream's first year was slow. However, after signing on 20 patients (some requiring full-time care, others just four hours a week), the company realized "better than breakeven" on revenues of $200,000.

Kay blames Wellstream's difficult break from the starting gate on undercapitalization. "To grow faster, I would have liked $200,000 to market to bring in patients," she says. A larger marketing budget would have allowed a full-time staffer to call on physicians who in turn might refer patients to them. Also, Wellstream lacked a major source of referral: the government. Because the company shunned the Medicare license, it lost the beneficial side effect of Medicare patients who eventually improve and graduate to private care.

THE START-UP CATCH-22

A home healthcare agency has three challenges the entrepreneur has to work on simultaneously: getting government approval to operate, hiring employees, and lining up patients. Like the song says, you can't have one without the other, or in this case the others.

Whether you go the government or the private route, you still need licensing in most states. In addition, some states have certificate-of-need laws—you must demonstrate there is enough need before you set up a home care agency. (Research your state's requirements with your Department of Health.)

To get a license, some states require a limited track record before they'll even review your policies. Getting patients during that start-up period without the state stamp of approval provides a frustrating Catch-22. To get past it, you might sign on with a franchise that already has similar branches afloat. The recognition factor pacifies both patients and regulators, because they know something about you from the start. The trade-off, of course, is paying the parent company an entry fee and a percentage of profits. Another shortcut to finding those first patients is hooking up with as many physicians as possible. In fact, the federal government requires that a home health agency list a physician and registered nurse on its professional advisory committee before it becomes eligible for Medicare.

Kay Hollers paid some courtesy calls on area doctors but says most referrals came after proving Wellstream's reliability with a specific patient she shares with the physician. "We call about arranging for Mrs. Jones's appointment, for example." Then, next time a cataract patient needs transportation for an exam, the receptionist remembers Wellstream. Or the next time a surgery patient needs companion services after being released from the hospital, the doctor recalls the conscientious attention Wellstream provided in a similar situation.

The moment you open for business, you also need aides or nurses to provide care for your patients. Some states stipulate that aides have some hospital or nursing home experience, and a few require certification, which Medicare programs also demand. In addition, you might think about accreditation through one of the agencies listed at the end of this section. Even in states that don't require it, accreditation adds credibility.

While you can find employees through newspaper ads, unless you can keep them well supplied with jobs, you could lose them to other employers. To keep its employees busy, Wellstream supplements home healthcare by offering sick-child services. "We will care for a seriously ill child over a period of time, but ordinarily our children have chicken pox or the flu and can't go to school," says Kay Hollers. Wellstream lets daycare centers know of its service and advertises in the Yellow Pages. Kay estimates sick-child care contributes just 15 percent of Wellstream's revenues, "but it fills in the gaps for workers who don't have other cases this week."

NOT JUST HEALTHCARE

Kay Hollers suspects that Wellstream will offer even more varied services in the future. Currently its aides perform primarily homemaking chores and personal grooming services for ill or elderly patients. "We get their meals, clean their homes, and help them dress and bathe," she explains. The company also runs errands, such as food shopping, and provides transportation to doctors' offices. "We usually start with people who think they need nursing care, but really need maid services with a healthcare base," explains Kay. Charges range from $7 to $9 an hour, depending on the types of services requested.

However, Kay expects her clients will request nursing care as they age, which Wellstream is prepared to provide. "We will evolve to answer what our clients need." Those needs could extend beyond the medical arena. One possibility is providing legal services through attorneys who make house calls. "We constantly ask: What is home care and how do we do it?" says Hollers. "The fairly traditional answer is professional and paraprofessional healthcare. But there's no reason we have to stop with that."

Jennifer Hirshan of the National Association for Home Care points to other nonmedical services—such as banking and dog grooming—that agencies are placing on their home care menus. "We're moving in two directions," she says. "Especially as the population ages, we'll expand to more nonmedical care. On the other front, as technology grows, we can provide more medical procedures at home." She notes that in Sweden, considered a leader in the home care industry, even minor surgical procedures such as vasectomies are performed at home.

SOURCES

Industry Associations

American Association for Continuity of Care, P.O. Box 7073, North Brunswick, NJ 08902, (800) 816-1575

American Federation of Home Health Agencies Inc., 1320 Fenwick Lane, Suite 100, Silver Spring, MD 20910, (800) 234-4211

American Hospital Association, a division of Ambulatory Care, 840 North Lake Shore Drive, Chicago, IL 60611, (312) 280-6461

National Association for Home Care, 228 Seventh Street, S.E., Washington, DC 20003, (202) 547-7424

National Council on the Aging, 409 3rd Street, S.W., Washington, DC 20024, (202) 479-1200

Accrediting Agencies

- Accreditation Commission for Home Care, Inc.: (919) 872-8609 (currently limited to Alabama, Georgia, Kentucky, Mississippi, North Carolina, South Carolina, Tennessee, Virginia)
- Community Health Accreditation Program: (212) 363-5555 or (800) 669-1656 ext. 242
- Homecare University: (202) 547-3576
- Joint Commission on Accreditation of Healthcare Organizations: (630) 792-5000

Medical Transcriptionist

Job Description: *Using a computer and transcription machine, a medical transcriptionist transcribes the medical records (letters, histories, physicals, progress reports, and chart notes) dictated by a healthcare professional.*

- *Low start-up cost*
- *Breakeven time from initial investment: rapid (one year)*
- *Future growth potential: high*
- *Ideal home-based business*
- *No staffing required*

Get me a medical transcriptionist stat!"

Okay, maybe it's not exactly what the doctors on *ER* say, but it's not too far removed from what thousands of real-life physicians, nurses, and other healthcare professionals *are* saying today and every day. Faced with growing demands on their time, but still required to document all aspects of a patient's history, harried physicians are turning to medical transcriptionists for assistance. They are the unsung heroes of the healthcare industry, producing reams of legible, accurate medical documentation that physicians and others increasingly rely on. This dependence has made medical transcription a burgeoning industry—and, quite possibly, your ticket to establishing a satisfying and rewarding business.

TAKE TWO CCS OF TYPING AND CALL ME IN THE MORNING

In 1986 Linda Jackle, a pianist and music teacher, purchased a word processing company in Montvale, New Jersey, called A Personal Touch. Although her instincts were good, her timing was bad. At the same time, personal computers became widely available, and suddenly all those customers who used A Personal Touch for typing their documents decided to do it themselves with their own PC. Jackle had to find something else for both her and her company to do—and fast.

Noticing repeated classified ads in the newspapers for medical transcriptionists, Jackle set her sights in that direction. At the time, there were no courses available to learn how to become a medical transcriptionist; you either knew how to type and understood the unique language of the medical profession, or you didn't.

Jackle had the typing skills but lacked the medical knowledge. However, with true entrepreneurial elan, she got her first job in the field by claiming to have five years' experience.

"She [the client] sent me a Jiffy bag full of microtapes." Jackle laughs. "After I stopped crying, I bought a bunch of books and learned how to do it."

Getting her first job helped Jackle establish her business in the medical transcription field. Next she approached her family physician, told him that she was doing medical transcription, and was soon working for him as well. The company's biggest break came in 1990, when it successfully bid on a contract to do medical transcription for a local hospital. From this point the company grew steadily.

"A lot of it [growth] was by word of mouth," says Jackle. "Word of mouth happens. Doctors talk to other doctors; they go to the administrator of a hospital and say 'Who do you use [for transcriptions]?' The majority of our calls come in from one doctor who happens to know another doctor who we work for."

Depending primarily on word of mouth, A Personal Touch steadily expanded its customer roster. Today the business services approximately 30 clients, including several hospitals and multipractice medical groups. Jackle estimates her company produces around 7,000 pages of medical transcription a month. She employs numerous medical transcriptionists, all of whom are independent contractors working from their homes.

A BURGEONING FIELD

During the past five years, Linda Jackle estimates her business experienced tremendous growth. Although some of it reflects the company's excellent reputation and high-quality documentation it produces, part of her success is attributable to the explosive growth experienced by the entire medical transcription industry.

One reason it experienced an upswing is that more doctors are utilizing transcriptionists. Insurance companies now demand clearly typed medical records to avoid deciphering a doctor's chicken-scratch handwriting. Hospitals and physicians in their own practice are discovering it's better to outsource their medical transcription rather than paying in-house staff to do it and worrying about staffing changes, illness, and time pressures. The advent of managed care and its voracious appetite for written documentation also has helped increase the need for medical transcription.

As a result, the medical transcription field is scrambling to find enough qualified workers to fill an ever-growing need. According to the American Hospital Association and the American Association of Medical Transcription, there is a significant shortage of medical transcriptionists in *all* settings, not just hospitals.

A Transcription a Day Keeps Bringing in the Pay

If you decide that typing and medical lingo are the perfect combination for success, there are a couple of ways to start a business in the medical transcription profession.

Before you take the plunge, however, you must be skilled at the keyboard and understand the often-arcane language of medicine. You also must be organized, dedicated, and able to work under pressure; doctors frequently wait until the last minute to dictate their material and then need it in a frantic rush—sometimes as little as two hours.

If you decide to set up your own medical transcription company, you'll naturally need a computer. It's not necessary to buy the most powerful, top-of-the-line model, because you're going to use it exclusively for word processing. Most transcriptionists use an IBM-compatible machine, with either WordPerfect or Microsoft Word. You'll also need a top-quality printer.

Along with a computer, you're going to need a transcription machine. Similar to a tape recorder, it has a foot pedal to adjust its speed so the typist can keep both hands on the keyboard. The machine plays the dictation tapes, which are generally micro- or standard size. Quite often it's possible to purchase used transcription machines through newspaper ads. Since you don't need an outside office or employees, your total start-up cost for this venture is around $5,000—all of it on equipment.

Some transcriptionists and transcription services have moved away from tapes and use digital "call-in" systems. Doctors dial into the system via telephone, dictate their notes, then hang up. The transcriptionist then accesses the dictation from the system. These call-in machines, while the latest in dictation technology, are extremely expensive, costing approximately $100,000 new. A preferred method is leasing (which is what Jackle does); a typical lease costs around $2,000 per month. With this method, you also need a special $1,200 telephone for accessing the dictation system.

Another possible expense is taking the certification program offered by the American Association for Medical Transcription, which costs $300.

Even with a leased digital call-in system and special telephone, start-up costs still shouldn't exceed $10,000. It's possible to see a return on your initial costs with either method in as little as one year's time.

Earnings vary in this business. If you get paid by the line, the fee is typically 10 to 12 cents per line. (The average number of lines per page is 45.) If you get paid by the page, the fee ranges anywhere from $1 to $2.35 per page in dense metropolitan areas such as New York or Los Angeles. In less-populated regions, the per-page rate is lower.

Eventually you can earn a good living running a medical transcription business, but Jackle warns that it's going to take time to build up your clientele and your cash flow.

"This is not the kind of business that you open up and immediately start making a ton of money," she said. "You can get there, but it's going to take a lot of hard work. If you do your homework you're going to make money—you're just not going to be rich overnight."

THE PROGNOSIS

While medical transcription appears to have a bright future, the one dark cloud on the horizon is the possible emergence of voice-recognition computers. Individuals in the field worry the industry could witness a severe impact if doctors can sit down and dictate their notes into a computer that will then "type" them.

However, problems with voice-recognition technology make this only a theoretical threat at this time. In addition, the attraction of medical transcription for physicians is they dictate into their telephone or a hand-held tape recorder, almost anywhere, such as their car or while in the elevator. Actually sitting down in front of a computer to dictate notes might take more time than most physicians have. Still, Jackle has a word of caution for future transcriptionists.

"If you're going to do this, get very good at what you do," she says. "With the advent of voice recognition, the mediocre transcriptionists will lose their jobs. We'll only need the ones who are really good, who can understand the doctors, have a good eye and good ear for grammar, and can proofread to make sure things are right."

If that last sentence describes you, then maybe it's time to scrub up and prepare to "operate" your own medical transcription business.

SOURCE

Industry Association

The American Association for Medical Transcription, P.O. Box 576187, Modesto, CA 95357-6187, (209) 551-0883

Personal Coach

Job Description: *A personal coach offers one-on-one assistance, advice, encouragement, and other forms of support to help individuals gain competence and confidence in any number of professional or personal areas, from public speaking, to social skills, to investing.*

- *Start-up investment as low as $7,500*
- *Potential first-year earnings: $40,000*
- *Breakeven time from initial investment: rapid (one year)*
- *Excellent home-based business*
- *Ideal opportunity for people with physical disabilities*
- *No staffing required*

Send me in, Coach. I'm ready.

It used to be that when that phrase was uttered, it always had something to do with sports. But no longer. Today it's just as likely that you will hear those words in the boardroom as on the ball field. Why? Because of the phenomenal growth of the personal coaching profession—a field that has nothing to do with athletics but everything to do with the game of life.

"Personal coaching has come into vogue in the last five years," says Doug White, a veteran personal coach who runs the Success for Life Foundation, a coaching organization based in Los Angeles. The *Christian Science Monitor* called personal coaches "the 21st century's answer to corporate therapy" and referred to the industry itself as "booming."

PEOPLE NEED REPAIRS, TOO

To understand why personal coaching has become so enormously popular, witness the hundreds of self-help books crowding bookstore shelves. Books on how to lose weight, how to be more communicative, how to dress for success, and a host of other topics capitalize on Americans' insatiable hunger to teach themselves new skills and competencies.

Basically, a self-help course is the essence of personal coaching. A person skilled in motivation (the coach) uses his or her knowledge and abilities to encourage clients to achieve something that they might not be able to achieve on their own or to solve a problem that may seem too overwhelming to deal with by themselves. Need help in asserting yourself at work? Have trouble expressing your feelings to your loved ones? Can't lose weight? A personal coach can help you deal with all these situations.

Doug White likens the skyrocketing popularity of personal coaching to calling for technical support when you buy a computer. Although computers can self-diagnose many problems, eventually a problem crops up that requires the advice of a technical expert. A personal coach is like a technical expert, only one who deals in flesh and blood, not machinery. When people cannot self-diagnose a problem or situation that is vexing them, they turn to a personal coach for assistance, guidance, and reassurance.

Teri-E Belf, who runs the Virginia-based coaching organization Success Unlimited Network, feels that coaching is booming because more people are questioning who they are and what their purpose is in life. She also feels that coaching is the next logical step after therapy and that people are seeking to apply the insights they've gleaned from therapy via coaching.

COACHING QUALIFICATIONS

What makes a good coach?

The ability to inspire others, no matter how steep the challenge, helps keep both the coach and the client motivated to achieve their goal. That takes life experience, creativity, and lots of self-confidence.

"A good coach needs to be able to live in the question [understand the problem]," says Teri-E Belf. "That's the inquiry process and is the foundation of all our work. A good coach also should be able to see matters holistically, and not just one particular slice." In order to do this, you must understand the ebb and flow of life, which comes only from experiencing it yourself.

A good coach also must be willing to learn. According to both White and Belf, successful personal coaches use their life experiences for the benefit of others. Every time a coach learns something—such as what seems like an insurmountable problem today can seem much less so after a few days of thought and reflection—it can be taught to a client. Thus a personal coach must be someone who embraces the world and the diverse personalities that inhabit it, viewing everything with an open mind. A personal coach must be a "people person"—someone who can consider situations and obstacles from a number of different perspectives.

A personal coach also must possess excellent listening skills. According to White, "A personal coach has realized that he has two ears and one mouth, so that he can listen twice as much as he talks."

Personal coaching is an extremely adaptable and versatile business. It can be done over the telephone, via e-mail, or in person. It is such a new field that no national certification program exists for the profession.

"Personal coaching is so new that there isn't any specific criteria or credential that you can give to someone that says 'You are capable of being a personal coach,' " says White.

FEES AND SERVICES

Unlike other professions, where a business vendor performs certain clearly defined services, the end result in personal coaching is often determined not by the vendor but by the client. For example, if a personal coach is helping a client become more assertive at work, it's the client who has to make the determination that the goal has been achieved.

Because personal coaching is such an individual profession, coaches structure their fees according to how they organize their program. Doug White charges $295 for a three-hour "intake" session, at which he gathers basic information (personal and professional details, and so on) about his client. This is followed by ten 30-minute sessions per month (three-month minimum), which costs a total of $750. After this, clients can continue receiving personal coaching and pay either weekly or monthly. White's standard hourly fee is $180. For people with less complex or challenging needs that can typically be solved over the telephone, White offers a special fee of $3 per minute.

Belf, who only sees clients in person, has a program of eight two-hour meetings, spaced out over a period of approximately five months. Her program costs $2,000 in advance, or $2,300 on a pay-as-you-go basis.

Like some other professions, the area in which they live dictates the amount that coaches charge. Belf, who certifies coaches around the country, says that the same five-month program she offers for $2,300 in Virginia costs approximately $1,600 in Maine, $2,500 in Atlanta, and $3,000 in California.

START-UP COSTS VARY

Although the start-up investment for a personal coaching business is relatively low, the breakeven point depends on many factors, including what type of certification program the coach takes. Teri-E Belf, for instance, offers a certification process that requires the "coach in training" to first take the actual course and then a certification process program costing a minimum of $5,000. She recommends that coaches first starting out charge $1,600 for their first few five-month programs and slowly increase it to reach their area's level. Belf estimates that a first-year coach can earn between $40,000 and $60,000.

Other expenses associated with setting up a coaching business depend on the individual. Most coaches have an office—Belf's overlooks a lake, and the peaceful vista is one of the attractions for her clients in high-pressure professions. A good computer is also recommended, both for communicating with clients and operating a website, which many personal coaches have up and running. Other communications tools that are helpful to a personal coach include a cellular telephone and a fax machine.

So if you enjoy people and like the challenge of helping them face their personal and professional problems on a one-to-one basis, consider the personal coaching profession—and get ready to play the game of life.

Personal Trainer

Job Description: *A personal trainer works one on one with each client, designing an exercise program to fit each person's unique needs and supervising workouts and other fitness regimens.*

- *Low start-up costs (if working at clients' homes)*
- *Breakeven time from initial investment: rapid (if working at clients' homes)*
- *Fast-growing industry*
- *Excellent future growth potential*
- *No staffing required*

It used to be that only movie stars had personal trainers. Consumed by a hectic filmmaking schedule yet still faced with the need to look great on the silver screen, celebs employ personal trainers to keep in shape, either at home or on location. A personal trainer helps the star stay fit and toned through a specific exercise program designed just for him or her.

Today the use of personal trainers has spread well beyond Hollywood to become part of mainstream America. No longer are personal trainers called on just to get someone ready for their close-up. Now ordinary people use them as part of a personal fitness program. This has created a booming demand for personal trainers and made it one of the hottest industries of the 1990s.

ONE, TWO, THREE, FOUR, ONE, TWO, THREE, FOUR . . .

What's behind the incredible growth in the personal training field? That's an easy question with some surprising answers.

Unless you've been living in a cave, you couldn't have missed the flood of media coverage about the favorable effects of staying fit. Each day brings another report about the benefits of eating right, losing weight, exercising, and staying active, leading to an unparalleled fitness boom in the United States. The emergence of personal trainers for "just plain folks" is an offshoot of a growing desire to stay fit among people everywhere.

However, as much as people want to get into shape, many don't know where or how to start. Plunging blindly into a vigorous exercise program can be as unhealthful as not exercising at all; discomfort and injury can result from exercising improperly. Yet it can be difficult to learn the correct way to start exercising. Few people have the self-confidence to go into a public gym crowded with hardbodies in perfect shape and start fumbling around with exercise machines.

A personal trainer solves these dilemmas. A personal trainer is just like a tutor, only for the body. A personal trainer works at the client's pace, in accordance with the client's specific needs. Every person is different; a personal trainer recognizes these differences and structures a fitness program accordingly. It's this one-on-one attention, as compared to figuring out the maze of equipment in a public gym or taking a class that might make you feel awkward, that has sent the personal training industry soaring.

"The personal trainer field is huge right now, and it's getting even bigger," says Kurt Murray, provider program director at the Aerobics and Fitness Association of America (AFAA). "People are learning that being fit is beneficial to their health."

AFAA was founded in 1983. The world's largest fitness educator, it promotes, teaches, and researches safe and proper ways of achieving fitness through aerobic exercise. AFAA offers a national certification program and training curriculum for aerobic exercise instructors and personal trainers. So far, the association has certified more than 135,000 fitness instructors in the United States and abroad. Nine thousand of these are personal trainers.

Although exact figures were not available, Murray reports a significant increase in the last several years in the number of people seeking personal training certification. It costs $399 to be certified as a personal trainer through AFAA. The examination lasts for three days (Friday through Sunday).

GETTING RESULTS

One person who has experienced the personal trainer boom firsthand is Gene Castellino, a personal trainer who runs Results, a fitness center in Sherman Oaks, California.

For Castellino, becoming a personal trainer was a natural career choice since he had been exercising and eating right ever since his boyhood in Pennsylvania. After graduating from college with a degree in finance, he tried working in corporate America, but missed one-on-one contact with people. In 1993 Castellino moved to the West Coast and worked as a personal trainer for several years.

In April 1997 Castellino opened Results, with the idea of creating a customer-friendly facility that wouldn't be intimidating. Among Castellino's innovations was to limit the number of people working out at any one time, so they would be able to spend more one-on-one time with him or the other personal trainers on staff. He emphasizes education, so people understand the "why" behind certain exercises, rather than blindly sweating it out. He also eschews the long-term contracts typical in the fitness industry, so people won't feel trapped in a never-ending fitness commitment.

Castellino offers three different types of programs for his clients. A package of 6 sessions costs $50 per session; 12 sessions cost $45 per session; and the 24-session package costs $40 per session. A session consists of an hour with a trainer. Following that, the client is free to utilize the cardiovascular equipment. Results hosts approximately 200 sessions per week.

"We emphasize the service side of personal training," says Castellino. "I want to focus on a quality session, rather than running them through a few exercises."

What this means, he adds, is that his clients know that every time they come to Results, they'll receive individual instruction. They won't have to worry about the gym being crowded or not being able to get onto a certain piece of equipment. This knowledge that everything will be the same as it was before instills comfort level in his clients and makes people actually look forward to working out.

ENTERING THE PERSONAL
TRAINING FIELD

If you've got a body like a Greek god or goddess and you want to enter the fast-growing world of personal training, you have several options.

The first is to work with clients in their homes, using their own equipment. The advantage is that start-up costs are low; all you need is the standard home office equipment (computer, printer, fax machine, and cellular phone) to set up your business. Factor in some marketing/advertising expenses, and total start-up costs shouldn't exceed $5,000.

A second method is to work with clients in their homes but take the equipment with you. The drawback is that, unless you drive a vehicle the size of a tractor-trailer, the amount of equipment you can transport is limited. If you opt to go this route, add the cost of a vehicle, its maintenance, and exercise equipment to the $5,000 start-up cost just listed.

Another option is to open your own gym/facility. Naturally, start-up costs are extremely high if you go this route. Equipment costs alone will range between $75,000 and $100,000 for new, high-quality equipment. You can try to save some money by buying low-quality or even used equipment, but remember that these machines will be in almost constant use; low-quality or used equipment may break down frequently. Castellino bought top-quality equipment and has never experienced a breakdown.

As for additional costs, they include the facility (renovations and rental), hiring staff, and office equipment (computer, printer, fax, and so on). In total, depending on location costs, this venture could easily cost between $300,000 and $400,000.

However, personal training is also a well-paying field. Some trainers charge $50 to $100 an hour for their services. If you do not operate your own facility, and have a roster of as few as half a dozen clients, you could make back your initial start-up cost of $5,000 within a year.

If you run your own gym, then obviously it will take longer to recoup your initial investment. However, since this is a business in which you can make $100,000 annually, the breakeven point can come in three or four years.

GROWING THE BUSINESS

If you decide to open your own facility, choosing the right location is key. Placing your gym in a highly visible spot in an affluent area, as Castellino did, will certainly help your business become a success.

This is a business that piggybacks on people's tendency to use such personal-oriented services as gardeners, chefs, and assistants. Selecting a demographic area in which people tend to use these types of services might well mean success for yours. As far as location, Results is on a heavily traveled street in Sherman Oaks, and hundreds of people pass it every day on their way to a freeway. This prime location, and word of mouth, is responsible for Castellino's business growth. He has done virtually no advertising or marketing.

"We have two types of clientele," he says. "Those who come here for years, and those who just want to take it [the training] as a two- or three-month course to get started, because they can't afford to pay long-term rates."

THE FUTURE EXPANSION
OF PERSONAL TRAINING,
NOT WAISTLINES

Since it's likely that more and more evidence will pile up touting the benefits of nutrition and exercise, the personal trainer industry seems to have a bright future.

"I think that the field is going to go through the roof, more than it has done already," says Kurt Murray. "Especially with all the baby boomers [getting older], people are going to need to continue to exercise. There's always going to be a market for it. It's a great thing."

SOURCE

Industry Association

Aerobics and Fitness Association of America, 15250 Ventura Boulevard, Suite 200, Sherman Oaks, CA 91403, (818) 905-0040

Household
Services

Alarm Systems Installer

Job Description: *An alarm systems company installs devices for burglar detection, medical alert, and other home security tools.*

- *Start-up cost as low as $2,000*
- *Potential first-year earnings: $25,000*
- *Breakeven time from initial investment: three weeks to two years*
- *Future growth potential: high*
- *No staffing required*

An elderly Jenkintown, Pennsylvania, woman slowly lowered herself into her bathtub one evening, hoping the warm water would ease the pain of her arthritis. When she attempted to leave, she found herself helpless, unable to rise. Her screams for help went unheeded, and it was the next afternoon before someone rescued her. Terrified of being alone, she asked her son-in-law what might prevent such an occurrence. Three years later, Lifecall was born.

Lifecall Systems Inc., Camden, New Jersey, is a security monitoring franchise that specializes in medical alerts. Had the woman stranded in the bathtub subscribed to Lifecall, she would have pushed a button embedded in a pendant worn around her neck, which would have triggered a series of events: An electronic signal would have activated a unit attached to her telephone, which would have dialed a toll-free number in Ohio. If the victim was within 50 feet of the telephone, she could tell the monitoring center what was wrong. If she was unable to talk, the center's computer bank—armed with her name, medical history, directions to her house, and phone numbers of the nearest ambulance service, police, and her doctor—would automatically call for help.

Medical alert may be the fastest-growing segment of the alarm industry. Fewer than 25 percent of households contain any sort of fire or burglar alarm, according to the National Burglar & Fire Alarm Association (NBFAA). That, according to a spokesperson, means "the potential for the alarms industry is tremendous compared with other products and services. The market is virtually untapped."

EVERYONE NEEDS SECURITY

Fear of crime permeates modern America. According to the 1997 FBI Uniform Crime Report, every 19 seconds a violent crime (murder, forcible rape, robbery, aggravated assault) is committed in the United States. A property crime (burglary, larceny-theft, motor vehicle theft) is committed every 3 seconds. To put it another way, in 1997 there were 2.43 million burglaries and 489,000 robberies in the United States.

If crime isn't enough to scare you out of your home, consider accidents. The National Safety Council estimates 3 million Americans are disabled in home accidents yearly.

While alarms may not prevent crime or accidents, alerting the proper authorities swiftly can mean the difference between a minor incident and a tragedy. Several years ago *Security Dealer* magazine reported 14,000 alarm dealers currently operating. In 1997, according to the NBFAA, Americans spent $14.8 billion on professionally installed electronic security products and services. That exceeded the previous year by more than $1 billion. Those figures do nothing to suggest the possibilities, says Skip Gundlach, whose Better Bottom Lines consultancy helps entrepreneurs get into the alarm business. "There's more business than anybody's taken care of," he insists. "Nobody doesn't need security."

Critics growl that the industry is growing slowly. The industry has barely kept pace with new home starts, when the potential market is virtually all of America. They cite two reasons for this disappointing stat:

- Alarms of the past were expensive and unreliable.
- Even today, the public remains unaware that monitoring services exist.

Problem No. 1 may be a relic of the past. "Maturity is coming about in the industry," says the NBFAA spokesperson. "Manufacturers are making systems that don't cause false alarms, are aesthetically pleasing, and the costs are coming down. There should be considerable growth with a better product at a lower cost."

WAITING FOR THE PHONE

While alarm companies are making converts, signing on customers remains a concern. Skip Gundlach insists all you need do is market your services properly. "The industry is made up of individuals waiting for the phone to ring," he states emphatically. "It has done its dead-level best to starve itself." In Gundlach's book, Yellow Pages and newspapers don't pay. He advocates literally knocking on doors, especially commercial doors, to spread the gospel directly to the consumer.

Tod McQuaid, who operates TEMAC Inc., agrees, but adds that you should approach those doors with caution. Don't frighten merchants with a hard sell when you should be reassuring them that you've come to help. T McQuaid had worked for a large alarm company for 12 years before relocating to Lewisburg, West Virginia, to start his own practice. "When I first came to the area, I dropped my business card with commercial establishments," he recalls. "I told them to call for an appointment." By letting customers come to him, McQuaid made friends instead of enemies and has since installed not only fire, burglar, and medical alarms but also emergency lighting, fire extinguishers, and driveway- and fence-protection devices in banks, hospitals, and residences throughout the mountains of West Virginia.

KNOW YOUR CUSTOMERS

Study the psyche of your customers. Tod McQuaid says that while cold calls targeted residentially may work elsewhere, they are taboo in the small Appalachian communities he serves. He recalls a competitor who tried door-to-door sales. "The sheriff caught him before he hit the third door."

Don't approach the sale of an alarm system the same way as you might sell a vacuum cleaner. "Security is both tangible and intangible," points out Skip Gundlach. Like Tod McQuaid, Ken

Miller contends that people who employ fear tactics see more doors than contracts. His DKW Enterprises, Secane, Pennsylvania, operates a Lifecall medical alert franchise. "These people contacted you. They know they need the product. They've been beaten to death by salesmen for aluminum sidings and insurance. What they need from you is a sincere presentation of what your system can do to help them."

Some installers have success with stuffing mailboxes or buying mailing lists and sending flyers to a targeted audience, such as people over 65 or families likely to have valuables to protect. Miller advertises on local radio and in pennysavers, which, he says, stay in the home longer than daily newspapers. "But it's a mistake to spend $5,000 for a radio ad until you are ready to service the business," he warns, noting that a radio campaign may generate 75 to 100 leads. Although it takes just 15 minutes to install a Lifecall system, Miller allocates three to four hours per sales call. That chunk of time accounts for driving, the pitch, and paperwork, which includes taking a complete medical history. Miller's customers don't mind the intrusion. "The little old ladies make you lunch," he says.

A PERPETUAL-MOTION MACHINE

Alarm business profits can be good—and long-term profits can be excellent. You can sum up the beauty of the security monitoring business in two words: recurring revenues. Once you sell a subscriber, you generate cash flow each month like a utility. Revenues build from a small base like an upside-down pyramid. Explains Skip Gundlach: "A one-person show would have a hard time installing $10,000 worth of systems a month. Those three to six systems would generate monitoring fees of $30 to $150 a month. But that's cumulative. Next month, you install another five systems—and get an additional $100 in recurring revenues."

After six months in business, "I now have $650 a month in residuals," in addition to installation fees of some $2,000 a week, calculates Ken Miller. In his case, the monthly income includes not only monitoring but some leasing fees for the Lifecare systems he installs. His goal is to reach monthly residuals of $2,000 within a year. "Life will be a lot more comfortable," he said. "When I want to take a vacation, I know the money still comes in."

You break even on the sale of the $1,000 to $1,500 systems, making your profits on the recurring revenues. After the installation, responsibility becomes, for the most part, passive. In other words, monitoring centers wait for the equipment to trip an alarm before going into action. Action, you'll note, is no more costly than calling the local fire, police, or medical authorities.

Small and midsize operators turn the responsibility of responding to the alarm over to a monitoring station. For under $10 per month per subscriber, a central monitoring service located thousands of miles away receives any alarms and notifies the local fire and police departments of emergencies; you keep the rest of the $20 to $30 monthly monitoring fee as profit. After you sign on several thousand accounts, you might consider spending the $75,000 or so to staff and equip a monitoring station with computers and phones.

Since consumers rarely change services once the system is installed, entrepreneurs who can build a base of subscribers see profits that mount steadily with each new customer. In general, companies that decide to sell can command anywhere from 15 to 50 times their monthly recurring revenues. Even at those prices, Skip Gundlach tells newcomers who have the capital to buy existing businesses with accounts if they wish to build business quickly.

Installers either sell systems outright or rent the hardware for monthly fees on top of the monitoring charge. The leasing arrangement brings in longer-term profits, unless the customer pulls the plug on your services. It's easy enough to discontinue the monitoring functions, but regaining possession of leased hardware sometimes can be sticky. Although the law grants court orders to retrieve your equipment, most installers don't bother since the cost to enforce a contract often exceeds the value of the hardware. And operators say the problem is no greater for security firms than for other services doing business in private homes, such as servicing built-in vacuum cleaners or swimming pools.

ALL OVER THE LOT

An entrepreneur can still break into the alarm business for under $5,000. With a phone for making appointments and a car to cart the equipment to the installation site, all you really lack are tools to install the systems, sales brochures, and incorporation papers. Most distributors will sell you one or two systems as your orders come in, so you don't have to spend heavily for inventory.

The potential of the business varies, depending on how many alarms you install, the price of the service, and the amount of marketing hustle you employ. The NBFAA estimates that nearly half of all installing firms realized revenues of less than $250,000.

A technician or salesperson heads the typical one- or two-person operation, although a growing number of regionals are amassing war chests to gobble up moms-and-pops, and several national chains are getting into the act. On one end of the spectrum, cable-TV installers and electricians moonlight by installing systems part time. Playing the same game with a quantum leap in advertising dollars, venture capitalists and even some major Japanese electronics behemoths reportedly are scrutinizing ways to pour millions into the security business.

The installation expertise necessary varies with the type of system. Ken Miller, who managed nightclubs before opening DKW, says installing a Lifecall unit is no more complicated than plugging an answering machine into a phone jack. But Tod McQuaid, who climbed an eight-year ladder of installing systems for other companies before starting TEMAC, warns that some microprocessor-based systems require a high degree of expertise. Some full-service companies install everything from sprinklers to closed-circuit TVs, each system needing custom design. Although some states have licensing requirements, McQuaid advocates stricter standards to eliminate the "occasional people" whom he blames for systems that trip too easily or not at all. Both the National Burglar & Fire Alarm Association and local burglar and fire alarm associations provide licensing information and courses.

As an installer, you're responsible for servicing what you sell, but little can go wrong with the simple alarms that most subscribers require. Should a Lifecall system malfunction, for example, Ken Miller unplugs the old unit and replaces it with a new one, supplied free of charge from the franchisor. Because the servicing is so minimal, Miller has installed systems as far away from his Pennsylvania base as Florida and Oregon.

LATCHKEY KIDS

Miller predicts a vast market well beyond the seniors who are the core of his business. Parents with babies prone to illness as well as households with latchkey children represent an untapped potential. In fact, Miller personally experienced the terror of a working parent when his daughter suffered a nasty cut while both he and his wife were working. "I immediately put a system in my house and told her to push the button if she ever had a problem again."

Owners of one-person operations have mixed feelings about nationals. While they may cut into the potential pie, "their TV campaigns and mass marketing may awaken awareness," predicts an industry expert. "The industry is going to expand geometrically once the heavy bucks come in," says Skip Gundlach. Adds Ken Miller: "Particularly in the medical area, I don't have enough competition. Common knowledge isn't to the point yet where people know we exist."

SOURCES

Industry Associations

National Burglar & Fire Alarm Association, 7101 Wisconsin Avenue, Suite 901, Bethesda, MD 20814-4805, (301) 907-3202

Security Industry Association, 635 Slaters Lane, Suite 110, Alexandria, VA 22314-1301, (703) 683-2075

Carpet Cleaner

Job Description: *A carpet cleaner shampoos and cleans carpets for homes and businesses.*

- *Start-up cost as low as $1,000 (if leasing cleaning equipment)*
- *Potential first-year earnings: $35,000*
- *Breakeven time from initial investment: extremely rapid (one month to one year)*
- *Ideal home-based business*
- *No staffing required*

When Bobbie Carter calls to estimate the fee for Carter's Carpet & Upholstery Cleaning Service, she has no guarantee she'll get the job. But she puts her equipment in her minivan just in case. Nine times out of ten, the customer can't resist Carter's enthusiasm: She's sure her cleaning method beats anybody else's in the small town of Franklinton, Louisiana. She clinches the sale by pulling out before-and-after photographs illustrating the miracles she performs. The pitch ends with Carter suggesting she start with just one room. If all goes well, she ends by cleaning carpets throughout the house.

Carpet cleaners say the domino effect doesn't stop with doing multiple rooms in the same house. Joe Wasson, proprietor of Hoosier Carpet Care in Rushville, Indiana, figures "one job well done equals three other jobs because word-of-mouth advertising works so well in this business." Bobbie Carter furnishes an example: "One day I was doing an estimate that led to cleaning the woman's carpeting. The mother-in-law was visiting and had me come to her house after I finished. From there, I did such a great job they asked me to do the carpeting at the jewelry store the daughter owns."

Carter solicits goodwill by leaving a thank-you note with every job and calling back the next day to make sure the customer remains pleased with the job. "I always mention my work is guaranteed and if you have a problem I'll come back."

Recommendations come only if you do a superb job, of course. So make sure you buy equipment capable of results. Joe Wasson stresses the importance of walking through a home with the customer before attempting any cleaning. "Let them know which spots won't come out, and they won't be disappointed," he suggests.

Even though word of mouth is the strongest business builder in this or any other industry, carpet cleaners say you drum up business any way you can, and different methods of securing clients work best for different entrepreneurs. One Colorado cleaner did his first carpet at the bank that loaned him the money to buy his equipment.

Carpet cleaners are split on the value of advertising, although most do some advertising. Bobbie Carter says her best inquiries come from simple three-line ads in the newspaper's classified section. "The ad costs just $26 a week, so one job pays for the ad and that job usually leads to others," she calculates. Carter's vivacity makes her a natural salesperson, and she uses her personal contacts to develop customer leads.

In contrast, Joe Wasson's more subdued personality means he relies more on advertising to pull in customers. Recently Wasson allotted fully 35 percent of his gross—which amounted to $40,000—to advertise anywhere and everywhere. "I use radio, newspaper, leave coupons door to door. I donate my services to raise money for charity."

Wasson also pens a newsletter that he sends to customers every three to four months. "I tell what type of vacuum works best and how to take out certain stains by yourself. Getting my name to the customer periodically reinforces repeat business," he explains. He estimates that "60 percent of customers whose carpets I cleaned a year ago have already called me back to do them again."

Households are just one type of home for carpets. The more ambitious carpet cleaning services send letters and make cold calls on businesses. Commercial accounts offer several advantages. Carpets in an office complex are often much bigger jobs than a single house. Also, restaurants or retail establishments need their carpets cleaned often, and you may land a contract that promises repeat business in exchange for a slight discount. Finally, says Bobbie Carter, "The people who work in a business often hire you once they see what a great job you did on the business's carpet."

How You Charge

Just as carpet cleaners differ in how they approach advertising, they also support two schools of thought on pricing. You can price either by the room or by the square foot. Joe Wasson says he switched from square-foot pricing to room rates to simplify matters. "I was charging about 12 cents a square foot. But I found I often had to make two trips: one to estimate a job and a second trip to do the job itself," he explains. "It was just too time-consuming." So he switched to a flat rate of $17 a room, which he says works out to around 9 cents a square foot. "I can offer the customer a better price and still make more money because I don't waste time," he says. Also, room rates make advertising more effective because many people have no idea how many square feet their rooms contain.

Bobbie Carter disagrees vehemently with Joe's room-rate reasoning, however. She says most people hire her on the spot so she doesn't waste many trips by estimates. Besides, "Is it a 9-by-12-foot room, or 12-by-24?" she asks. "People get mad if you quote them one price then try to charge more if their rooms are too big." Instead, she charges 15 cents a square foot when she doesn't move furniture and 22 cents when she does. "I only weigh 77 pounds," says Carter, who has to hire somebody to move the furniture if customers want rugs cleaned under the bed or behind the chest.

One attraction carpet cleaning offers is the relatively low entry cost. Since you work out of your home, you basically need equipment and a way to transport it. Usually the family car suffices in the beginning, so your budget will cover heavy-duty equipment, which can run several thousand dollars. "I arranged for a loan divided into 48 monthly payments of $107 each for

$4,100 worth of equipment," says Carter. "But business was good enough in the first eight weeks that I made 16 payments and still put some money in the bank."

In addition to equipment, you also need industrial-grade supplies. Of course, you can buy supplies as you go, paying for them from cash flow. Carter used an income tax refund to stock up on $600 worth of cleaning fluids in order to get a bulk discount from the Von Schrader Co., of Racine, Wisconsin, which manufactures her equipment and supplies.

Von Schrader, which provides carpet cleaners who use its equipment with such backup materials as advertising and a toll-free number to answer any questions about carpet cleaning, says entrepreneurs average $30 an hour. Many carpet cleaners begin part time, moonlighting on weekends or evenings until they build enough reputation to quit a day job. Therefore, if you clean carpets part time—say 10 hours a week—you could expect to add $15,600 to your income, minus the cost of equipment and advertising. Full-timers who clean carpets 40 hours a week can gross $62,400. Of course, that kind of hustle leaves little time for such necessities as marketing and travel to and from each job.

PIGGY-BACK

No law says you have to stop with carpet cleaning. Upholstery cleaning is one natural piggy-back service that offers better profit margins even than carpets. "I see carpet cleaning as a way to get in the door," says Joe Wasson, who also cleans upholstery, cars, and full houses.

Another way to increase income is to add employees. Wasson recently invested $3,000 in a second set of equipment and hired an employee who has a car. "I make 10 to 20 percent on the jobs someone else does, and still pay them a good salary," he says.

Adds Bobbie Carter: "I expect to have six to eight trucks on the road eventually."

Closet Organizer

Job Description: *A closet organizer straightens, cleans, and reorganizes messy, cluttered closets.*

- *Start-up cost as low as $20,000*
- *Potential first-year earnings: $100,000*
- *Breakeven time from initial investment: three months to two years*
- *Ideal home-based business*
- *No staffing required*

Entrepreneur magazine estimates that 344 million closets lurk in America's homes. Chances are, 343,999,000 of them are towers of doom, with tennis racquets poised to fall on forgotten prom dresses, or circa-1940 suits rubbing shoulders with paisley bell-bottoms from 1968. Not to mention what's going on in the additional millions of attics, garages, and kitchen pantries—all those storage places where we stuff our long-lost treasures.

MAKING A KILLING

Marty Ginsberg wondered aloud to a friend why somebody didn't make a killing designing a better closet, a closet that could hold a person's possessions in organized splendor rather than keep them in chaos. "I had never heard of California Closet Co. until the friend sent me a newspaper ad he ran across," says Ginsberg, who was a trucking company vice president. "Two weeks later I was on a plane to check out the franchise. Two weeks after that, I quit my job."

Marty and his wife, Ruth, who had raised three kids and managed an office for a group of psychologists, bought a California Closet Co. franchise. They hired a single employee and opened a 2,000-square-foot combination warehouse, showroom, and workshop in Randolph, New Jersey. After three years, they had hired 14 salespeople and woodworkers. Considering the dire need for closet organizers and the growing public awareness of the field, "With work, you should be able to do $1 million in the business," says Marty.

INDEPENDENTS VS. FRANCHISES

The Ginsbergs laid out cash for a franchise and a business address, but independent woodwork designers can start from their homes. You need a van capable of lugging around material, and you might need to lease warehouse and workshop space if you don't have a good-size home garage. Draw up a budget for inventory (most of which you can buy as you go along), tools, and advertising. Barbara Clevenger started Closet Tamers in Fort Wayne, Indiana, by spending $300 to paint a logo on her van. Instead of taking her clients by to see samples in a show-room, she visits their homes with a photo album containing be-fore-and-after shots of her closets.

One advantage of buying a franchise involves the training the parent company provides. Marty Ginsberg had designed a couple of tables and cabinets from his workshop in his base-ment before opening his California Closet franchise, but "it was strictly a hobby," he says, "nothing on a commercial scale." By following the training guidelines provided by California Closets, Ginsberg says he was able to earn while he learned.

California Closet can install a standard eight-foot closet for around $500; extras such as wire baskets or drawers increase the figure. Marty or a salesperson designs each closet separately, depending on the homeowner's needs and budget. Although some independents subcontract the construction, keeping the total job ensures quality and also keeps the profits in-house.

Closet organizers advertise heavily in the home section of newspapers and pennysavers. Less traditional advertising works, too. Take a booth at a home show, for example, or pre-pare slide shows for social and civic clubs.

UNLIMITED VISTAS

Most organizers don't stop with closets, although closets usu-ally provide the bulk of the business. California Closet Co. of-fers a line of accessories that range from hangers, to safes, to ski racks. "I can't buy as cheaply as Bradlees, so I make sure to carry a more sophisticated shoe box," says Marty Ginsberg. "It's something you wouldn't find except at the better stores."

Once you're comfortable with closets, you can expand into other storage areas—one West Coast organizer sells an oak veneer garage storage system for $12,000 or more. Let customers know you will install shelving, drawers, and other storage nooks wherever they need them.

Marty Ginsberg even offers a do-it-yourself kit. "We design the closet and fabricate the pieces," he explains. "Then we give customers written and pictorial instructions to do it themselves."

Ginsberg says he gets his share of high-end customers who can afford to spend $12,000 to redo all 17 closets in the old homestead. But he also gets their less affluent neighbors. "Everybody has the same problem with storage, and the smaller the closets, the more help you need," he says. "When you're out of space, you're out of luck."

Not if you're Marty Ginsberg. Business is so good that he and Ruth tripled the size of the facility within two years of start-up. And recently they moved to Fairfield, New Jersey, and doubled their California Closet square footage again.

Drycleaner

Job Description: *A drycleaner uses non–water-based methods to launder clothes that are not suited for conventional cleaning methods.*

- *Start-up cost as low as $75,000*
- *Potential first-year earnings: $45,000*
- *Breakeven time from initial investment: several years*

The drycleaning business mirrors the mood of the country. In the late 1960s and early 1970s, as America donned miniskirts and cut-off jeans, and as demonstrators took on political issues, drycleaning shriveled. People were not concerned with their appearance. Also, technology brought us polyester, the miracle synthetic that never sees the inside of a drycleaning plant.

Now, however, influenced by the "Dress for Success" ethic, Americans again long for creases in their trousers and blouses of real silk to offset their three-piece suits.

What's to keep the pendulum from swinging away from drycleaners? Simple demographics. Explains Marvel Zuercher, who runs The Habit Cleaners in Berne, Indiana: "Working mothers don't have time to iron even cotton clothes that you can wash." But isn't drycleaning expensive, compared with throwing the sweaters on the gentle cycle? What happens when the country isn't feeling quite so flush? Several franchises hedge by specializing in discount cleaning. For example, Clean'n'Press Franchise Inc., of Phoenix, Arizona, cleans any garment for 99 cents. But even traditional cleaners don't worry much about economic slumps. "No business is depression proof, but this comes close," says Ken Faig, director of education for the International Fabricare Institute (IFI). "In bad times, people don't buy clothes and have to keep the old ones in good shape."

DO IT YOUR WAY

That bigger picture of drycleaning may have been in the back of Marvel Zuercher's mind when she bought The Habit, but really she wanted a job. "I had been a librarian and teacher when I quit to have a baby," she recalls. "When my son went to kindergarten, I wanted to go back, but jobs weren't available. This business came up for sale, so I grabbed it."

Zuercher, with her sunny disposition and combative attitude toward such indignities as cooking grease on wool slacks, has a personality right on target for a drycleaning entrepreneur. "I'd always had some mechanical ability and an interest in selling, which fits in real well with what I do. I just about majored in home economics in college."

Running a drycleaner, she says, is almost an extension of the home: "I can keep my son near me. Brian has a corner of the office where he studies. Summers are slower, so I spend more time at home." True, drycleaners keep long hours, but the three trusted employees Zuercher inherited when she bought The Habit pinch-hit when she wants an afternoon off, and she shuts down entirely between Christmas and New Year's and during a slow week in August.

If you don't know anything about drycleaning, don't despair. Franchises welcome newcomers with open arms. For independents, the IFI hosts a three-week intensive course, and regional trade groups sponsor seminars. For example, the Neighborhood Cleaners Association, headquartered in New York City, spreads its 80-hour curriculum over 10 weeks.

AMBIANCE

There's no rule that drycleaning establishments have to be stark cubbyholes in rundown shopping centers. When The Habit's lease expired, Marvel Zuercher bought an 84-year-old carriage house. Her designer not only turned it into a modern drycleaning plant, he also added such touches as flower boxes and French doors that open onto a drive-under balcony. The brown-and-white barnlike structure reflects the Swiss character of the little Indiana town (population, 3,500). An *American Drycleaner* article praising the 1,800-square-foot structure, which won "Top Ten" honors in the magazine's Plant Design contest, noted its practical advantages: "Promoted subliminally are good looks, cleanliness, and the fact that people feel better when they know they look their best."

Modern equipment, which recycles the fumes and vapors, allows entrepreneurs to locate small drycleaners in previously unlikely settings, such as shopping centers. The *American Drycleaner* magazine, which estimates a typical plant at 2,000 square feet, tracks a trend to units less than half that size that require just one or two operators. Of course, you still need easy access to a parking lot because customers won't cotton to carrying their dirty laundry through a busy mall.

Such an environment costs extra, but you could lease and equip a modest location for $96,000 to $135,000. If you decide to launder shirts as well, budget another $20,000 to $25,000 for additional equipment. For operators who wish to have the expertise of a franchise outfit behind them, a few thousand dollars will give them an affiliation with a group such as Miami-based Dryclean-U.S.A., or One Hour Martinizing, which is headquartered in Cincinnati. To buy an existing business, figure on spending about one year's projected gross revenues.

The IFI says an average plant grosses $191,666 a year. Without taking a salary, figure a pretax profit of 30 percent, or $57,500—if you're average. Cash flow is good, since customers pay (in cash) when the work is done. You may have to bill if you line up large-volume jobs, such as cleaning uniform rentals, but your revenues will increase, as well. Also, decide whether your particular community will support facilities to launder shirts or dryclean furs. If you're unsure in the beginning, you can always subcontract that add-on business with another professional.

HOW TO PULL THEM IN

Drycleaners don't budget much for advertising, unless they intend to lure customers from a competitor. But savvy operators increase business through education. Marvel Zuercher gives tours through her plant to civic and high school groups. "They see how we can clean better than they could at home," she explains. You could also give visiting lectures on topics such as "How to Care for Your Clothes."

Zuercher says the most important marketing tool is to let customers know you care about their clothes. She often jots notes on The Habit stationery explaining how customers might treat similar stains in the future. Or she just tells them when they come to pick up their clothes. "We educate customers so they'll be happier with their investment in clothes," explains the former English teacher. "For example, don't rub a silk tie when you get something on it—just blot it to absorb the moisture. Then take it to your cleaner." She also tells customers when they can wash garments just as well at home. "If they trust me to give them the right information, I may lose a particular sale, but I gain a customer."

SOURCES

Industry Associations

International Fabricare Institute, 12251 Tech Road, Silver Spring, MD 20904, (301) 622-1900

Neighborhood Cleaners Association, 252 West 29th Street, 2nd Floor, New York, NY, 10021, (212) 967-3002

Home Decorating Retailer

Job Description: *A home decorating retailer sells paint, wallpaper, curtains, flooring, and other materials used to decorate a home.*
- *Start-up cost as low as $100,000*
- *Potential first-year earnings: $250,000*
- *Breakeven time from initial investment: several years*

When Bill Elliot decided to begin laying the groundwork for his new life, he quit his job as a cable TV installer and went to work for the Benjamin Moore paint company. His friend and soon-to-be-partner Steve Huggins, a schoolteacher, had worked summers in a paint store. After a year, they had completed enough on-the-job education to open Upstate Color Center. Since the paint line they wanted to carry was already assigned in their hometown, they moved 185 miles to an untapped territory in Easley, South Carolina.

Upstate Color is one of almost a thousand home decorating centers that open each year. According to the National

Decorating Products Association (NDPA), the industry rings up annual sales of $12.75 billion. Is now a good time to be in the business? "We've barely scratched the surface," says Bill Elliot.

CUSTOMERS COMING
AND GOING

Decorating centers draw customers from two sources: homeowners and the building trade. During strong building cycles, you can sell contractors items such as paint and linoleum, and offer homeowners curtains or blinds for their new windows. When high interest rates slow home building, many individuals remodel their old abodes. "Existing housing—most of it over 20 years old—is prime for new exterior and interior design," says a recent issue of *Decorating Retailer*. "And the new residents of these houses . . . are profiled as vitally interested in fashionable home decorating."

The industry association says it takes about $100,000 to open a 2,500-square-foot home decorating store that expects to do at least $350,000 in annual sales by the end of its second year. Smaller stores, of course, cost less, as do shops specializing in one or two product lines, such as paint and wallcoverings. But here's what the NDPA says the average store (which counts 38 percent of its business in paint, 24 percent in wallcoverings, 12 percent in sundries such as drop cloths and paint brushes, 9 percent in floor coverings, 12 percent in window treatments, and 5 percent in "other," such as picture framing, bath boutique items, and art supplies) should set aside:

- $15,000 for fixtures (you might shop for used shelving in good shape)

- $45,000 for inventory (some dealers offer "buy now, pay later" plans)
- $90,000 to $120,000 for operating expenses during the first two years
- $30,000 to $60,000 for accounts receivable if you anticipate dealing with contractors or others who don't pay as they go

Like most other retailing enterprises, a home decorating store takes several years to hit full stride. But the NDPA finds the typical dealer has 1.8 stores and $932,000 in yearly sales. You need the volume, because pretax profits average $21,830.

THE SUPPLIER CONNECTION

While you carry hundreds of different items, you can get them from just a handful of suppliers. Bill Elliot uses just five for the 1,600-square-foot Upstate Color Center: one paint company, two brush manufacturers, and two sundry distributors.

Choose suppliers with care, because manufacturers can be particularly helpful when starting in the home decorating business. Some paint suppliers offer free dealer training courses and help with site selection. A few even help track down financing. However, experience can come only by working in a decorating center. *Decorating Retailer* advises, "If you have a difficult time finding an opening for yourself as a temporary and eager but ignorant deco center employee, contact major paint or wallcovering manufacturers and perhaps they can find a spot for you among the stores they supply."

Some suppliers also advise on store layouts. If you shoot for a homeowner customer base, you may want a pretty shop with model windows showing off the latest in woven verticals and a plethora of in-store displays. If your business comes from builders who buy in bulk, you might opt for a filled-to-the-rafters image. "Some people have a small display area and keep the majority of their paints in a back storeroom," says Bill Elliot, who estimates a 50-50 split between customers and contractors at Upstate Color. "We feel if a customer sees hundreds of gallons of paint, it reaffirms we're in the business."

NOT MUCH WALK-IN TRADE

In areas where rents are high, many successful operators settle for an accessible, but not necessarily prime, location. "We're a block off the main artery," says Elliot. "If you have good products and good service, customers will find you."

Because home decorating products are not an impulse buy— and because profit margins are generally on the skinny side— many entrepreneurs restrict their conventional advertising to a Yellow Pages ad and sporadic eighth-of-a-page ads in the neighborhood pennysaver. If you advertise, be sure to inquire about co-op ad allowances from manufacturers. With their help, advertising may not be as expensive as you think.

Inexpensive marketing works well in the home decorating area. If you have a van, paint it with a bright logo for all the world to see. When the van isn't delivering valances and floor tiles, park where it's visible from a main drag. Contact area builders regularly to remind them you offer discounts for bulk buying. Bill Elliot also calls on local industry periodically. "They paint every year or two and we give discounts for large volume," he says.

SOURCE

Industry Association

National Decorating Products Association, 1050 North Lindbergh Boulevard, St. Louis, MO 63132, (314) 991-3470

Kitchen and Bath Designer

Job Description: *A kitchen and bathroom designer custom-plans and installs kitchens and bathrooms in homes.*
- *Start-up cost as low as $100,000*
- *Potential first-year earnings: $250,000*
- *Breakeven time from initial investment: two to five years*

You rarely see a bathroom without a Jacuzzi any more," says Ann Patterson, who launched City Design in West Des Moines, Iowa, along with her husband, Rick Martinez. "Sometimes you see one Jacuzzi for the parents and another for the kids. I did one $40,000 bath that we turned into a sunroom with skylights and curved glass walls. It had a sunken Jacuzzi, of course. And a fireplace."

OUT OF THE WATER CLOSET

A fireplace in the *bathroom*? And not in Beverly Hills, but in *Iowa*? Needless to say, Americans have brought their bathrooms out of the water closet. And as for kitchens, well, we're putting in labor-saving devices such as microwave ovens meant to get us out of the kitchen. Then we turn our kitchens into entertainment and creativity centers by stocking them with televisions and range-tops that grill. If you want to do your Julia Child number, you can prepare anything from shish kebab to sashimi with professional-quality equipment. But 30-foot-long kitchens aren't just for cooking.

"Something's happened to the way we view kitchens and bathrooms," agrees Russell Platek, a certified kitchen designer and director of education for the National Kitchen & Bath Association (NKBA). As business booms for kitchen and bath designers, more people are setting up shop. "Last year alone our association membership grew by 15 percent," he says.

You can enter the kitchen and bath business as a retailer, designer, installer, or all three. After Ronald Robinson had managed someone else's store for 15 years, he and his wife, Ida, set up Top Notch Kitchen & Bath Boutique in Mount Vernon, Illinois, primarily as a showcase of kitchen and bath equipment. "We do some installing, but an installation takes Ronnie three days to complete," says Ida. "That cuts into the time Ronnie has to sell on the floor." Product sales command a higher profit margin than design or installation because sales is less labor intensive. You can realize as much as 30 percent of revenues as profit. As a result, Top Notch typically designs a kitchen or bath, measures and orders the equipment, and lets someone else worry about installation.

Using another approach, City Design relies as much on design and installation as product. You might have to drop profit margins by as much as 5 percent to pay for the time it takes to install a kitchen or bath, but your overall fees can be higher because you charge for construction as well as products. Another source of income comes through designer fees: homeowners, architects, or contractors ask you to draw the plan but not to build it. On sales of $5 million, a large shop with several designers in a metropolitan area could see profits of $1.25 million.

OFF (BUT NOT TOO FAR OFF) THE BEATEN TRACK

In either case, you must get the customer through your door. Instead of a slot in a high-rent mall, look for visibility with the kinds of customers you need to attract. City Design is one street away from the antiques district, an area with stores and restaurants where "people in the income bracket we serve go to play and shop," says Ann Patterson. These potential customers have seen City Design but don't drop in to browse because it's not on the main drag. "I cannot afford walk-in traffic," says Ann. "I figure to pay for my overhead, I need to average sales of $40 an hour. If I spend half of every day chatting with people who are not interested in buying, I can't pay that overhead."

Even though your average customer buys only once or twice from your shop, their purchase is a big one. Ann Patterson's kitchens average $15,000, and her typical baths cost $5,000. In a major urban area, the averages can be even higher. To make sure the people who put in a custom bath buy from you, it pays to advertise. Francis Jones, executive director of the NKBA, believes in marketing that encourages people to dream up their ideal rooms in the first place. "Our competitors do not come from our industry," he says. "They come from the auto, vacation, and investment industries," other businesses geared to high-income dreamers who eventually carry out their fantasies.

The NKBA's Russ Platek suggests that a mature design firm spend 3 to 5 percent of its gross on advertising and a brand-new firm allot up to 15 percent to get the name out. In addition to advertising in such places as symphony and theater brochures, City Design rides its manufacturer's cooperative plan to advertise on television. Ann Patterson also keeps close ties with architects who refer clients to her since few architects tackle her two specialties.

A WHIFF OF POSSIBILITIES

Because each design is customized to fit a particular home's configuration and a particular homeowner's taste, "we see a product that's not even conceptualized until we do the work," says Patterson. Therefore, your showroom permits a customer to sense the possibilities of a truly interesting kitchen or bath. The NKBA says a minimum-size showroom would need 1,200 square feet, although Top Notch utilizes 6,800 square feet to accommodate its five lines. With just two manufacturers, City Design operates with under 2,000 square feet. Neither store warehouses items. Instead, both avoid high inventory costs by waiting for a customer down payment before placing an order.

A couple of tips on the showroom designs: If you plan to design and install, look for higher-end merchandise and ask for exclusive rights in your area from the manufacturer. "When you have to pay for design time out of the cabinet margins, there's no room for bidding wars," says Ann Patterson. Also, before putting in a sample room, ask the vendor how long till obsolescence: You can only hope for two years before models change. Stocking new appliances every year is common as manufacturers constantly update, but you can sell the floor samples. Cabinets are a different story since they must be custom fitted to exact measurements.

PROFESSIONALS

Salespeople need to be experienced estimators. Most customers have no earthly idea what converting their dreary linoleum scullery into a cheerful dream kitchen will cost. There's no need to give firm figures at this stage, but you must be able to estimate based on the size and age of a customer's kitchen, the appliances needed, and the cabinetry he or she likes. Even in new houses, Top Notch will estimate off a blueprint, "but we won't order until we can measure a job," says Ida Robinson. "Contractors have a way of moving a wall a couple of inches, and that's enough to destroy the measurements."

Before going the extra steps of measuring and designing a kitchen, Ann Patterson asks for a $250 to $500 retainer, although she applies that fee to the final cost if customers buy cabinets from her. "I figure for every hour I spend with the client, it takes two to three hours of pricing, paperwork, and drawing," she explains.

To arrive at a close appraisal, the installer accompanies Patterson to estimate his time as well as the time for such subcontractors as electricians and plumbers. After the installer determines labor and equipment charges, the customer receives a standard NKBA contract that outlines down to each electrical outlet what City Design will do.

City Design asks for 25 percent of its fee when the contract is signed, 50 percent more when construction begins, 15 percent when the kitchen is in working order, and sets aside the last 10 percent for contingencies. "Maybe a special-order tile didn't come in, or one cabinet came in damaged," Patterson explains. "By asking for our fee in stages, the client can't hold more than 10 percent if something goes wrong."

No licenses are required to either install or design kitchens and baths. But you'll need some training. Auburn University in Auburn, Alabama, offers a bachelor's degree in the kitchen and bath field, which includes a minor in business administration. If you're not interested in a four-year program and already have a carpentry, engineering, or art background, check out the NKBA's home study and regional traveling courses for both designers and installers. The association even offers a certification in kitchen design.

SOURCE

Industry Association

National Kitchen & Bath Association, 687 Willow Grove Street, Hackettstown, NJ 07840, (908) 852-0033

Landscaper

Job Description: *A landscaper installs and maintains plants, beautifies the grounds of both commercial and residential establishments, and performs other outside maintenance.*

- *Start-up cost beginning at $15,000*
- *Potential first-year earnings: $30,000*
- *Breakeven time from initial investment: rapid (less than one year)*
- *Potential home-based business*
- *No staffing required*

Landscapers thank Lady Bird Johnson for awakening interest in exterior decorating. In the 1960s, the First Lady's "Beautify America" program prompted citizens to plant trees and trim hedges as never before. The 1970s followed with a more serious concern for our environment; government programs encouraged landscaping to combat pollution and prevent erosion. The latest boom, however, comes from upwardly mobile, two-income families who allot 10 percent of the purchase price of their new homes to sow bluegrass and plant dogwoods. As their country cousins struggle to hold on to their farms, landscapers say they've never had it so good.

And there's still room to grow. "We're way behind the Europeans," says William Doerler, who operates Doerler Landscapes Inc., in Lawrence Township, New Jersey, next door to wealthy Princeton. "The Europeans have planted annuals for hundreds of years. Now the U.S. has discovered petunias and marigolds. Jazzy landscapes are the hottest thing."

Some landscapers employ landscape architects to design layouts; some also sell rhododendrons or birches on a retail basis. But most characterize themselves as service businesses—entrepreneurs who maintain and install plants. "We visit your new house, find your needs, likes, and dislikes, and create a look," explains Doerler. "We're similar to an interior decorator for the outside of your house."

SHOESTRINGS

While you don't need a degree in ornamental horticulture to run a landscaping business, it doesn't hurt; after all, you will be called upon to install irrigation systems and grade slopes. If you don't want to go for the whole four-year program, you can audit some classes at land grant colleges and agricultural schools or work for an established landscaper.

You can locate your business on a couple of acres 20 minutes out of town where the rent is cheapest: Landscapers just don't get off-the-street business. Also, since you are not a retailer, you don't need a visible presence. Many landscapers even begin from their garages, often performing maintenance (mowing, pruning, and the like) rather than planting. Take the case of James Douglas Davis, who operates White Oak Landscape Co.,

Inc., from the Atlanta suburb of Kennesaw, Georgia. "I began on a shoestring," says Davis, who has a degree in ornamental horticulture from the University of Georgia. "My initial capital was maybe $3,000 for a mower, blower, and a used van. I did strictly maintenance in the beginning—cutting grass, pruning, mostly residentials and some condos and banks. You need to build a client base so you can get referrals to do installation."

Within a year and a half, Davis began acquiring equipment, including a one-ton dump truck; he also began stocking plants as his installation business began to grow. "The county zoning commission got after me for working out of my house, so I rented a small lot. I needed more space, so I bought two and a half acres." White Oak has grown to one of the top 50 landscapers in the country, with $2.5 million in sales and between 40 and 80 employees. (During the fall and spring planting seasons Davis doubles his staff.)

Since installations provide large doses of capital, many landscapers strive to develop this side of their businesses. White Oak has charged up to $100,000 for landscaping some ritzy residences and between $50,000 and $200,000 for commercial installations; of that the company nets profits in the 10 percent range. William Doerler adds that, in addition to setting off new homes to best advantage, his company "designs lots of swimming pools and hot tubs into the environment."

But installations swing up and down, following construction cycles. Also, they are one-time deals, unless you convert installations into maintenance contracts. With those drawbacks in mind, most landscapers retain at least some upkeep jobs. "Once you get a maintenance contract, unless you screw up, that's revenue from here on in," points out Doug Davis. Large corporate accounts, of course, are the most lucrative. Some landscapers in the frost belt provide snow-removal services to carry them through the slow winter months.

KEEP THE BUSINESS GROWING

In addition to cold calls to condominium groups and corporations, you can generate business through contacts made at civic organizations. Follow leads from architects, builders, and real estate agents. Label your trucks prominently, and post a sign at each installation project to generate customer awareness of your business.

Your biggest residential customers are those homeowners who can afford your high prices: people who don't cut the grass themselves or hire the teenager down the street. "Our carriage trade is the crowd in their 50s and 60s who don't want to do it themselves, but want a showcase home," says Doerler. He calls them "the Mercedes group."

SOURCES

Industry Associations

American Nursery & Landscape Association, 1250 I Street, N.W., Suite 500, Washington, DC 20005-3922, (202) 789-5980

American Society of Landscape Architects, 4401 Connecticut Avenue, N.W., 5th Floor, Washington, DC 20008-2302, (202) 898-2444

Laundry-Plus
Provider

Job Description: *A laundry provider offers coin-operated wash-
ers and dryers for people to clean their clothes.*
- *Start-up cost as low as $50,000*
- *Potential first-year earnings: $30,000*
- *Breakeven time from initial investment: one year or longer*

After four and a half years as an industrial sales representative on straight commission, Jim Bogen had had it. "I
was putting on 60,000 miles a year, and I was tired. I had
started a family and I wanted something less stressful—I didn't
care what it was."

A friend suggested laundries. "I wanted not so much the income but the lifestyle. I saw basically a self-serve business that
wasn't real management intensive." So Jim Bogen opened a
Duds 'N Suds franchise in Bozeman, Montana, where he now
works just 20 hours a week. His work often consists of mingling
with customers waiting for their rinse cycle to finish. "The atmosphere of my store is that of a living room with a lounge area

and lots of plants and posters on the wall. It's conducive to talking with people. If you take the time to visit, you find everybody has their own stories to tell."

Bogen's venture brought him the lifestyle he craved—and apparently decent income as well. He doesn't like specific talk about profits, but, just 18 months after start-up, Bogen was using his free time to launch a second business next door—a self-serve car wash. "Traditionally car washes and laundries are good business partners. They serve the same demographics and can trade off customers."

START WITH AN OPEN MIND

Indeed, some entrepreneurs combine the two facilities under one banner. The Coin Laundry Association says the number of laundries remains fairly constant—around 35,000. These generate several billion dollars in annual gross revenue every year. But the industry is in the middle of revolutionary change as imaginative entrepreneurs supplant the laundries of the past with new ones. Yesterday's dingy, depressing laundry outlets are fast disappearing. Springing up in their stead are comfortable facilities like Jim Bogen's that combine other services or profit centers under one roof.

"The newer facilities are better designed, prettier. They offer more amenities," says Ben Russell, editor of *American Coin-Op*. Jim Bogen's Duds 'N Suds has a pool table, television, and snack bar that serves soft drinks and packaged Frito-Lay products. Russell says you can add just about anything you want to a laundry service. But the addition typically either lets customers get rid of a second chore while they're doing their wash or makes a boring task fun by adding a social element. He lists the following typical laundry partners: convenience store grocery sales; electronic games; suntan parlors; drycleaning; beer, coffee, sandwiches, or other refreshments. The list goes on and on.

WHAT'S YOUR POINT?

Before deciding what amenities to offer along with wash and dry, consider your customers and whether you want another income producer or just a way to increase laundry traffic. Jim Bogen says even though he devotes just one-third of his shop's 3,300 square feet to his 68 washers and dryers, 90 percent of his revenues still comes from his laundry facilities. But he believes those revenues are higher than the old wall-to-wall machine shops could generate. The attractiveness of Duds 'N Suds invites customers in and brings them back. "We're a freestanding brick-and-cedar building with a split-shake roof. I really think we're the nicest-looking building in town," says Bogen.

Some additional services can be real moneymakers, however. Some singles-bar-*cum*-laundries make better margins on $2.50 Daiquiris than 50-cent dryers. The capital to open and staff a bar pays off only if you serve lots of singles, of course. If you open near a trailer park populated with young families, you might be more successful cordoning off a children's play area. If you cater to working-couple condominium owners, perhaps they'd appreciate the convenience of drycleaning or wash-and-fold services.

DO IT FOR A SONG

All additions are not equally expensive. To entice senior citizens in on slow afternoons, Richard Torp, communications director for the Coin Laundry Association, suggests hiring speakers who aim their talks at retirees. "Help them see it as a social outlet, a chance to get out of the house," he counsels. "You might have free cake and coffee on certain afternoons, or a little entertainment. Create a reason why people should gather."

Jim Bogen spends about 5 percent of his revenues to advertise through direct mail, newspaper, college papers, and door hangers. But, recognizing that people won't drive miles out of their way to do their laundry, he emphasizes the importance of the right location. "Look for university communities and multiple-family housing in lower-income areas," where people are unlikely to have their own washers and dryers. "The most common users of laundries are young singles and people living in crowded conditions, like city dwellers," adds Ben Russell.

LOTS OF HELP FOR A SELF-SERVE BUSINESS

To help him over the start-up hurdles, Bogen opted for the franchise route, becoming the 25th franchisee of the Ames, Iowa–based Duds 'N Suds. He says the parent company helped him bypass some start-up glitches, and its group-buying plan eased start-up costs a bit. Machine distributors represent a deep well of start-up help for the independents who dominate the coin-operated laundry industry. "They install the machines and will help develop a location and lay out a store," says Russell. "Some even build stores from scratch." In addition, distributors service the machine either on a contractual basis or when the need arises.

Start-up costs in large part depend on the amenities you offer. Washing machines can run from $500 for a small top loader to $4,000 for a 30-pound front loader; dryers average $1,200 to $1,500. Some manufacturers also lease their machines. Mainstreet locations (and rents) usually are unnecessary. But you may have to add plumbing to accommodate the machines and comply with local codes. "In some communities, the sewer system tap fee can run $1,000 per machine," warns Richard Torp. "If you have 30 machines, that runs into money."

Most operators learn the basics of repair and call in expensive specialists only for the big jobs. Ben Russell, who operates The Village Laundry in Elmwood Park, Illinois, says repair costs are minimal: "My laundry averages about $3 per machine per month in service charges."

Because laundries remain basically self-serve, labor costs remain low. Jim Bogen keeps two staffers on board for 30 hours a week. A solo attendant handles the balance of the week. "We start at minimum wage, so labor doesn't cost any more than utilities," he says. In fact, some facilities operate staffless for days on end. Some manufacturers promise machines that will accept credit cards instead of coins in the near future, which could reduce the need for employees even further. More likely, because they won't have to worry about handling cash, employees will be free to tend to other chores, such as operating a drop-off service.

Richard Torp figures about 15 percent of all laundries currently offer something more than just machines. But now that the public has experienced the benefits of laundries with pluses, he has no doubt the percentage will increase. Adds Jim Bogen: "Traditionally, customers felt nobody took the effort or time to make the environment more attractive than a bus depot." Now that they've tasted laundry luxury, why in the world would they ever go back to yesterday's unrelieved drudgery?

SOURCE

Industry Association

Coin Laundry Association, 1315 Butterfield Road, Suite 212, Downers Grove, IL 60515, (630) 963-5547

Maid Service

Job Description: *A maid service cleans private residences.*

- *Start-up cost as low as $500*
- *Potential first-year earnings: $15,000*
- *Breakeven time from initial investment: extremely rapid (one week to several months)*
- *Ideal home-based business*
- *No staffing required (initially)*

With over 45 million working women in this country, is there any wonder that maid services are booming?

If you don't mind housework, there's lots to be said for running a cleaning service. "Getting started was so simple," admits Ruby Burgis, who left a personnel management position at Aetna Insurance to launch Personal Home Care in the Atlanta suburb of Norcross, Georgia. Her entry vehicle was an ad in the Gwinett County newspaper's classified section, which landed her "a tremendous response. There's such a need for domestic help," says Burgis.

And the potential? Solo practitioners can't shoot too high, probably no more than $20,000 to $30,000 a year. But add a few employees and let their brooms do the sweeping. If you spend your time managing others and rounding up jobs, you can keep 40 to 50 percent of the take yourself—as profits. The only overhead you need worry about is advertising to collect both employees and clients, relatively simple bookkeeping, a few supplies, and insurance.

There are three aspects to running a maid service. In reverse order of importance, consider:

NEXT TO GODLINESS

Cleaning

"Just because you know how to clean house doesn't mean you know a thing about the housecleaning business," warns a Chicago entrepreneur. "You have to know so much about managing—managing people, managing your time." The importance of delivering a clean house to clients can't be overemphasized, but polishing a house to a shine is the easy part. If you're diligent and pay attention to detail, you can accomplish almost any housekeeping chore.

The key to the cleaning business is organization. To clean efficiently, set and stick to a cleaning routine. Ruby Burgis devised a training program for her maids that begins with a session in her office. There each maid receives a manual Burgis wrote that walks them through the basics of dusting, vacuuming, glass polishing, and bathroom and kitchen scrubbing. Then she accompanies them on their first job to teach by example. Admitting "I hate housecleaning," Burgis cleans right along with employees on their first house or two to show them her own methods. She provides a checklist for clients who want such extras as laundry or window washing, and tacks on extra charges.

Most operators swear by the team system. Two to four maids visit the same houses every week, so they become familiar with the customers' needs. The team divides the chores, rotating tasks among the members from house to house to reduce monotony. Ruby Burgis disagrees with the buddy system, however. "I want people to have their own personal housekeeper who would be in the house for several hours." A good maid can develop a following.

You can either furnish equipment and supplies or ask to use the customer's. Stocking your own cleaning arsenal ensures you have the best ammunition to clean with, and, except for a vacuum, which can cost several hundred dollars, supplies are inexpensive. However, an urban service that relies on public transportation might request that customers provide the equipment so maids won't have to drag mops on buses.

GENERATING LEADS

Finding Clientele

You don't need 60-second spots on prime-time television; inexpensive advertising works just fine in the maid business. You can target specific audiences with flyers stuffed in mailboxes or mailed via zip code. Leave your number on the supermarket bulletin board. One-inch ads in the classified sections of neigh-borhood or pennysaver newspapers often provide the best leads. If you provide company cars, mark them with your tele-phone number and logo.

Maids, while no longer only for the rich, aren't for the lower-income brackets either. Target advertising to professional neighborhoods whose households earn $40,000 or more. Families need more help than do singles.

Follow up those leads promptly and at the customer's conve-nience. You may need to visit people on evenings or weekends to accommodate working people. Some entrepreneurs guess the price for the first visit in order to avoid the nuisance of an estimate trip, but "How can you quote standard fees when a three-bedroom, two-bath house can be 1,800 square feet or 4,000?" asks Ruby Burgis. Also, touring the house with the cus-tomer allows you to sell extras like carpet cleaning.

To price a job, have in mind an hourly fee per employee and guess how long a cleaning will take. Households with children or pets or collections of knickknacks require more time than homes of professional couples who like sleek, modern furniture and who travel constantly on business. Also, you can offer lower prices for weekly cleanings than monthly marathons, since the house had a thorough scrubbing just the week before.

Carry liability insurance to pay for any breakage. The larger maid services also are bonded to cover theft. Although she spends about $150 a month to blanket six employees with both kinds of insurance, Burgis says customers rarely ask whether she's covered. "You need the liability, but smaller services can usually just give references in lieu of getting bonded," she says.

While the bulk of your revenues will come from steady resi-dential clients, you can also discover other sources of dirt to clean. For instance, unless you are very busy, don't turn down one-time cleanings for people who are preparing for the holi-days; you can charge more for one-shot deals, and they some-times blossom into regular arrangements once clients see how their houses sparkle. Be creative in your advertising. One ser-vice suggests gift certificates as presents for new mothers. Burgis does some offices for entrepreneurs whose houses she cleans; but she warns that heavy janitorial work requires con-tracts and a complicated bidding procedure. (See "Janitorial Service," page 47.) Also, network with people who have lots of houses to clean, such as real estate agents who might recom-mend you to clean houses before or after a sale. Or check with apartment contractors who need postconstruction cleaning.

THE MAIDS

Employees—Getting Them and Keeping Them

Don't underestimate the frustrations here. Getting good, reli-able people is tough, and you must constantly refill your em-ployee ranks since turnover is notoriously high in this industry. Ruby Burgis uses the same newspaper to advertise for employ-ees and attract customers. In addition, she asks workers to rec-ommend friends who might want jobs. She also lets the state employment service know when she needs maids.

If you think hiring employees is tough, getting them to stay committed for a long time is tougher. "When a maid doesn't show up, I take the job," Burgis says with a groan. "In a pinch, I've used friends, boyfriends—whoever can help me out." Turnover is a fact of the cleaning entrepreneur's life. But some tricks of the trade make life a little easier.

First, make employees realize their importance. Some franchises issue uniforms to create a professional team spirit.

Second, don't be greedy. Remember, the housekeepers do the hard work, so pay them well. You can outpay most jobs that hire unskilled labor by offering a respectable $10 an hour and still keep an equal amount to cover overhead and profits. Since your maids likely subcontract as independent operators, you don't pay for benefits such as health insurance. Hint: Properly trained employees complete jobs more efficiently, which allows them to squeeze more houses into their cleaning schedule. Since you pay by the job, they make more money and therefore stay on board longer.

Third, offer flexibility. The maids with families particularly like part-time work. If you need more employees to work Friday afternoons, pay them a bonus.

THE MATCHMAKER APPROACH

Ruby Burgis, who started Personal Home Care as a typical maid service, changed her focus to deal with the constant employee turnover issue. Now, instead of taking responsibility herself for maids who clean clients' homes, she matches maids and households. It works this way: After an individual answers her ad, Burgis trains the maid in specific houses that contract with her for services. After a two- or three-week training stint, during which time the maid gets a salary, the maid buys the rights to clean that house as well as others that Burgis lines up. If a homeowner decides within 14 days that the housekeeper is not up to par, Burgis finds a replacement. "A contract is based on the amount of monthly income it will bring," she explains. "If it's a weekly house that pays $50 for each cleaning, I charge $200 for that contract. If the maid does five houses a week, the fee would be $1,000."

As a result of the new approach, Burgis still has to attract maids to train and customers to clean for, but she doesn't worry about a maid quitting after six weeks.

Meanwhile, Burgis points out a side benefit of her business. Since she hates housework, she knows exactly whom to call when she wants her *own* house cleaned.

Self-Storage Operator

Job Description: *A self-storage operator offers various-size facilities where customers store possessions they can't accommodate at home.*

- *Start-up cost as low as $50,000*
- *Potential first-year earnings: $40,000*
- *Breakeven time from initial investment: several years*

Michael Knuppe, who operates 11 AAAAA Rent-A-Space centers from San Leandro, California, holds up an industry survey that reveals just one out of ten Americans even knows what a self-storage facility is. "Think of the untapped potential!" he exclaims. The potential he refers to extends beyond the kind of customers with whom the industry was pioneered: individuals who leased space to store out-of-season water skis in self-storage facilities. Knuppe believes other markets are thirsting to be tapped—whether they know it or not. "Retailers can store excess inventory with us. Doctors and lawyers can keep files. I haven't yet figured out what group can't use us!"

The 18,000 or so self-storage facilities across the country are, simply put, big closets that rent by the month. The 88 percent majority of Americans who don't include the phrase "self-storage facility" in their lexicon might recognize the misnomer "miniwarehouse." But unlike a warehouse tenant, self-storage customers don't share the key with other renters, and the landlord assumes no responsibility for the property stored inside. Also, self-storage facilities take myriad sizes and shapes. Storage is not a type of building but a use of real estate.

The ministorage business began in the late 1960s in the fast-growing South and Southwest, where storage space was at a premium. The climate in those regions didn't require enclosed garages, and new houses springing up often lacked basements. Recognizing the need for storage space, some enterprising individuals divided old sheds into surrogate garages for overcrowded homeowners, and the industry took off. Mike Knuppe, a developer who entered the business when he decided running self-storage centers beat building apartment houses and condominiums, suspects the more lucrative areas will be in "northeastern and southeastern suburbs with populations of 100,000. Then the opportunities could swing back to the West."

REAL ESTATE

Mike Knuppe isn't the only real estate investor who bolted to the self-storage industry. Contractors relate to the tenant-landlord relationship inherent in renting storage facilities and positively gloat over the relative advantages of renting space to boxes and furniture rather than to people. "You don't have to do call-backs on leaky toilets," Knuppe explains. "Also, we used to build properties and try to sell before the interest rates ate us up. Self-storage facilities produce income from the first tenant."

Contractors also understand why the cost of building storage centers often surpasses seven figures. "The average-size facility among our association members runs about 47,000 square feet," says Gail Pohl, executive director for the Self-Service Storage Association. In contrast to the few mom-and-pop holdovers who launched the industry with five- to ten-unit garage spaces, today's entrepreneurs need at least 30,000 square feet of property to build on. Unless you reach the 300 customers to fill all that air, you won't be able to afford a site in a well-trafficked section of town. Those couple of requirements mean the real estate alone could run you $1 million in a pricey suburb.

Then there's the facility itself. "We used to build sheds with doors for $5 a square foot," says Knuppe. Now such elaborate extras as double-paneled bronze doors, indoor-outdoor carpeting, and computerized alarm systems push building costs to $30 to $50 a square foot. Some multistory facilities in cities require elevators and climate control.

Okay, but is it worth it? A lot of heavy investors think so, including some franchises and conglomerates that, rather than assume debt, raise money to build units through stock market public offerings. "The typical return without debt service runs 20 to 25 percent of revenues," says Knuppe, whose operations cover a total of 1.25 million square feet spread out over the San Francisco Bay area. Using his figures, a typical 30,000-square-foot warehouse brings in revenues of about $200,000 a year. Once you pay off your construction loan, you keep at least $40,000, assuming you hire a manager to oversee the property. If you operate the facility yourself, keep another $15,000 to

$20,000 as salary. The Self-Service Storage Association says facilities larger than 35,000 square feet usually justify a manager living on the premises. So if you operate a larger center, you get an apartment in the bargain, worth maybe $6,000 a year.

TAKE IT EASY

Frankly, a single self-storage facility is pretty easy to oversee, say the experts. In fact, many small-town centers combine storage with other services, such as truck leasing. Basic duties include three functions:

- Maintaining the outside of buildings (most facilities are concrete, steel, or other easy-to-care-for material)
- Collecting monthly rents
- Signing on new customers

The industry is still grappling with the question of whom to hire to manage the facilities. Originally, most on-site managers were retired couples who saw in the opportunity a way to supplement their incomes that would put relatively few demands on them. When the period between start-up and full occupancy lengthened (figure on a couple of years to fill all your cubicles), "the management companies hired individuals with sales expertise." So recalls Mike Knuppe, who cuts an 83-person payroll for his 11 facilities. However, the higher salaries that the sales breed demanded—which often included a percentage of the gross—were not justified by the speedier occupancy. Owners who do not manage the facilities themselves now are experimenting with a third approach. "I'm hiring retired couples from the military or with police backgrounds who are not quite as old," says Knuppe. He offers them the same percentage cut he gave salespeople but keeps base salaries lower.

The sales effort should include consumer marketing and a more concerted effort to attract business users, remembering that a whole sea of potential users don't even know you're out there. "Definitely plan on 5 percent of your gross for advertising," Knuppe counsels. In addition to Yellow Pages and direct marketing, companies increasingly add radio and even television in reasonably priced markets.

Once a customer calls, Knuppe says you run an 85 percent chance of closing a sale right on the phone—if you drop everything to hold the caller's hand. "People call a storage center during traumatic times in their lives. There's a death or divorce, or they're getting ready to move, and they need to store items. It sounds corny, but you need to be their knight in shining armor, their salvation in a crisis."

The other sales approach involves calling directly on big potential users, namely businesses. Sell them on the fact that they can free up floor space and stock more top-selling items by stashing slow movers or out-of-season items with you. Once you land a business customer, life indeed becomes easier. "They're longer-term clients than consumers who just use us to store items while they're moving," says Knuppe. On top of that, businesses are more likely to pay on time.

WHAT'S IN THOSE BOXES?

While the delinquency problem may sound scary, industry insiders say only 1 to 2 percent of all customers refuse to pay their bills. And, to make life easier, about three-quarters of all states spell out specific procedures to gain possession of the goods in the event of nonpayment, detailing circumstances in which a self-service center can auction off a tenant's property.

"Unfortunately," admits Mike Knuppe, "I don't know of a ministorage facility that hasn't been caught" accepting illegal items, including drugs and arms. AAAAA virtually eliminated this danger by working closely with the Drug Enforcement Bureau. "They even train their dogs on our facilities." Also, when the manager announces that AAAAA photographs each customer, most unsavory suspects scoot without a word.

As the industry discovers competition, "you need to create a strategic differential." Knuppe's strategy: "To close the gap on the moving experience, I rent trucks and sell padlocks and generally make life easier for those who are moving." Service and flexibility are increasingly important, as well. AAAAA offers 40 sizes of rental units, ranging from $12 to $185 a month, "so price is never the reason not to rent with us," says Knuppe. And some enterprising souls have surpassed merely giving advice; they offer to take over the real headaches. For example, one service delivers modules to a customer's backyard. The customer packs items inside, and the storage company picks up the module to cart it back to the lot. How's that for pickup and delivery?

SOURCE

Industry Association

Self-Service Storage Association, 6506 Loisdale Road, Springfield, VA 22152, (703) 921-9123

Water Conditioning
Dealer

Job Description: *A water conditioning dealer sells products and systems, primarily to households, that remove contaminants from commercial water supplies.*

- *Start-up cost as low as $5,000*
- *Potential first-year earnings: $25,000*
- *Breakeven time from initial investment: one year*
- *High growth potential*

American drinking water has been called a political time bomb. According to the 1997 National Water Quality Survey, one out of five Americans is dissatisfied with the quality of the household water supply. Even more revealing is that one out of three people surveyed believes that the water is not as safe as it should be.

Okay, Americans voice outrage that the H$_2$O flowing so freely from our taps may be poisoning us. But are we doing anything about it? According to the Water Quality Association's latest figures, the answer is a resounding "yes." The 1997

National Water Quality Survey found that 32 percent of those queried currently use a home water treatment device other than bottled water, as compared to 27 percent just two years earlier. But industry observers say we ain't seen nothing yet. RainSoft Water Conditioning Co., which franchises from Elk Grove Village, Illinois, estimates that less than 10 percent of the market for home water treatment devices has been sated. That, say dealers, gives them a huge market as the country becomes more and more aware of the problem. More than nine out of ten households remain to respond to their promises of pure water. "Not every home is a potential sale," says Harold Posey, who operates Posey Fresh Water from Houston. "But nearly every home is."

IT'S A LARGE NEIGHBORHOOD

To show how much faith he has in the growth of his industry, Harold Posey invites competitors to move in next door, saying there's more than enough business to go around. Posey has installed at least 7,000 water treatment units in Houston since he began and insists his own market remains less than 10 percent tapped. With reported sales of $3.5 million, he says he does better than 15 percent pretax profits.

Harold Posey knew he was on to a good thing when he first discovered the water conditioning industry as a vice president at ITT Financial in Denver a decade ago. He was a banker back then, and, "when customers applied for financing, I would get a finance statement on their business. I reviewed finances for water conditioning companies each year and started noticing how fast these dealers were accumulating wealth. I began to compare them with other industries. The more I looked, the more intrigued I became."

Unable to withstand the lure any longer, Posey bought a RainSoft franchise in Houston, where he had once lived. "I remembered how bad the water was—and how dynamic the city." Those two elements convinced him to invest $50,000 to set up shop, which primarily involved marketing.

Even today, Posey budgets 12 percent of gross for advertising and lead development, on top of what he spends on the sales staff's salaries. He builds sales through two approaches: telemarketing to generate leads, followed by direct door-to-door sales to nail down those leads. He turns a battery of six full-time and six part-time telephone operators loose to cold-call potential customers, such as upper-income households or businesses such as restaurants or drycleaners that need especially good water. Only after an operator gets a nibble does the 18-person sales force go into action. "That approach keeps the salespeople in front of qualified buyers," says Posey. "I don't send them to a house on stilts with chickens in the front yard because they won't buy the systems." An average Posey Fresh Water sale hovers around $2,500, which includes a system to soften the water, a drinking-water unit under the kitchen sink, and installation.

Unlike most products, you must customize each water treatment package to a particular client's needs. That means you have to test each tap, since additives differ by water district and household. But thanks to training available from vendors and the Water Quality Association, you don't have to be a chemical engineer to test the water or a mechanical genius to install the units.

You target two basic customers with water treatment

equipment: residential and commercial. Most sales so far involve units to soften water and make it taste better. More expensive units can remove contaminants in drinking water, as well. "Most water supplied by municipalities in this country is potable—meaning safe," says Harold Posey. "But it's not palatable—meaning it tastes *baaad*."

Whether you approach a residential or a commercial customer, and whether that customer is interested in water treatment or water conditioning, you have three basic ways to make money:

- Sales
- Leases
- Service

SALES

To maximize your cash flow, try to sell products outright. Particularly in the early days, a rush of cash from a $750 reverse-osmosis unit feels real good going into the pocket. If you work it right, you don't even have to pay for the inventory until a customer places an order. If you sport a healthy credit rating, many dealers waive their fees as long as you stock equipment in a bonded warehouse. Of course, once it leaves the warehouse on its way to a customer, you'll have to cover the cost of the item.

Large industrial companies and businesses generally prefer to buy equipment rather than rent it. Buyers, they reason, claim depreciation as an expense and spend less in the long haul. In addition to contacting hotels and hospitals directly, you can call on contractors and engineers putting up new sites.

Businesses are particularly good customers for a couple of reasons. Sometimes fees top $100,000 on a single, large installa-
tion. One system to purify water for a hospital's kidney dialysis
machine costs about $30,000, and a hospital usually buys more
than one unit. Also, a business lead often means repeat business.
A contractor who likes your water in a fast food operation
might ask you to outfit a white-tablecloth restaurant as well.

LEASES

"Renting is like prostitution: You sell it and still own it," Harold
Posey says with a grin. It looks like this: You front the $400 to
$500 equipment costs and charge customers $20 a month to use
your unit. Within two years you've collected your entire investment. And, since those $20 payments come in indefinitely,
everything else is gravy. "Leasing is going to be my retirement,"
says Posey, who hopes to increase his lease business from 10
percent of sales to 30 percent in the next year or two.

Homeowners in particular like leasing since the $20 monthly
fees don't sting the way a $700 purchase does. Now that opera-
tors are selling more water treatment systems to middle-income
Americans instead of just the wealthy, observers predict that
leasing represents the wave of the future.

SERVICE

One more way to build residual income involves service contracts. One out of every five Posey Fresh Water customers
spends $10.50 a month on a preventive maintenance contract.
Once a month, Posey's service department delivers salt, which

is used to clean the unit's filters, right to the customer's door. Posey Fresh Water also dispatches technicians to fix anything that might go wrong.

Posey warns start-ups not to promise service until they have the volume to support technicians. He also warns that maintenance headaches throb until entrepreneurs learn proper installation. Once you pass through the learning curve, though, service calls likely will diminish. "I have a lot fewer problems today than I did in the beginning, even though I have 7,000 accounts out there now," says Posey.

Water softening units have, until recently, been the staple of the industry. Now dealers sense an increasing willingness to invest in drinking water systems as well. That's good news for treatment companies, which can make bigger sales by offering both options.

SOURCE

Industry Association

Water Quality Association, 4151 Naperville Road, Lisle, IL 60532, (630) 505-0160

Personal
Services

Auto Detailer

Job Description: *An auto detailer completely and meticulously cleans the interior and exterior of a car, including such typically ignored parts as the engine.*

- *Start-up cost as low as $5,000*
- *Potential first-year earnings: $30,000*
- *Breakeven time from initial investment: rapid (six months to one year)*
- *Excellent home-based business*
- *No staffing required*

During slack times when Peg Mosey sold Fords in Fort Wayne, Indiana, she wandered into the cleanup area to watch the staff polishing and vacuuming cars before putting them in the showroom. "I used to spend two to three hours a week cleaning my own car and I thought, if you use professional products, this is not hard work. It's just time-consuming."

One summer Peg borrowed $5,000, using a certificate of deposit as collateral. She paid $400 for supplies, and bought a buffer and a wet-dry vac. Then she plopped down rent money for the building that was to house her new auto detailing business. With what was left over, Peg bought signs for her own spotlessly clean five-year-old Grand Prix that displayed her phone number and address. Voilà! Car Tender was in business.

THE OLD JALOPIES NEVER LOOKED SO GOOD

According to the Automotive Vehicle Manufacturing Association (AVMA), the typical passenger car on the road today is 7.5 years old, up from 5.5 years in 1970. That's the oldest average since the Korean War. People hang on to their cars because new ones are so expensive these days. According to the National Vehicle Leasing Association, leasing now accounts for more than 30 percent of the average 15 million plus vehicles sold in the United States each year. And, whether new or old, the cars are being better taken care of. According to the International Carwash Association, today there are 22,000 car washes in operation, each serving an average of 71,000 cars per year.

But it costs hundreds of thousands of dollars to build a conveyor or brush carwash plant, and it can take years to recover your investment. Entrepreneurs like Peg Mosey have found an inexpensive way to enter the auto appearance field and are cleaning up. Instead of counting on high volume to bring in the bucks, they charge handsomely for doing an extraordinary cleaning job, one car at a time, by hand. Called detailing, the work they do would make a dress sergeant proud. "I shampoo seats, do the dash with Q-Tips, the chrome with steel wool," Mosey rattles off. "I completely dress the engine, treat all the rubber." Her 29-step process takes up to five hours per car and runs $125.

It's tricky, but you can also ride into the business by way of the executive parking lot. Some detailers outfit vans with the equipment they need and round up BMW and Caddy owners as they leave their cars on the way to board meetings. To set up a mobile shop, you need access to running water and permission from the municipality as well as the company whose lot you camp out in.

If you don't want to go it alone, you have the option of franchising. Boca Raton, Florida–based Tidy Car figures a new franchisee needs $75,000 to $85,000 to open its average 1,500- to 2,000-square-foot shops. That capital covers the $20,000 Tidy Car licensing fee and $15,000 for a store-opening media blitz as well as equipment, inventory, leasehold improvements, and payments on a courtesy van to shuffle customers in and out. Since Tidy Car gives you four weeks of training, you don't need to know the first detail about detailing before signing on. The parent company also teaches you related skills, such as how to install sunroofs.

FROM VOLKSWAGENS TO JAGS

Independent detailers cater to several groups: luxury car owners and corporations, car dealers, or limousine operators to whom image is everything. Peg Mosey has rubbed sparkles onto everything from a '67 Corvette show car where she spent days removing every last speck of dust from the engine (the owner won top points in the cleanliness category), to a 23-foot travel trailer. "That was like cleaning someone's apartment. It took six hours."

Mosey recommends passenger cars go through the complete treatment twice a year and offers discounts to regular customers, such as the Mercedes owner who has her wash his car once a month. But "car dealers are my cushion," because they provide steadier work than the individual owners of Porsches and BMWs. Mosey spends a little less time detailing a dealer's used car but charges just $65. "They can usually get a couple of hundred dollars more at auction for repossessions if the cars are really clean," says Mosey.

In addition to the luxury and car-dealer market, Tidy Car considers all of the 201 million vehicles on the road its potential customers. To entice such volume, it charges a little less than most independents and advertises a lot more heavily. Its franchise material also notes this: "There are many nonretail areas where significant revenues can be generated, such as insurance companies (i.e., flood-damaged interiors), commercial fleet accounts, institutional and government accounts, body shops, car rental companies, and new-car dealers who may purchase Tidy Car services at wholesale prices for resale to new-car buyers as part of their option package."

Gary Goranson, then a regional sales manager for Magnavox of Canada, began Tidy Car 15 years ago. He originally sold his car-polishing and detailing services from a van parked on the street. Tidy Car's more than 400 locations still offer those services, along with such extras as window tinting, rustproofing, and sunroof installations. Goranson's theory: Once you get customers in the door, why stop with just cleaning their cars?

TRAFFIC

Even if you start from your own garage, you might consider leasing a visible location as soon as feasible. How will the drive-in traffic find you if you're tucked away in suburbia? Tidy Car is partial to retail auto malls, but also approves freestanding sites close to major retail shopping areas in an "upscale environment." Other major inducements include a speed limit of 45 mph or less (so drivers have time to see the prominent sign as they pass) and a daily traffic count of 20,000 vehicles.

Although it buys the old saw about location, location, location being the three most crucial aspects of success, Tidy Car says "the next three factors, in order of importance, are advertising, advertising, and advertising." Marketing is even more important if you can't afford a prime Main Street address. Peg Mosey uses flyers, newspapers, magazines, and TV, and gave away a detailing job as a promotion in a radio station tie-in. Tidy Car insists new franchisees set aside $15,000 for a splashy opening ad campaign and follow that up by budgeting 5 to 10 percent of revenues for advertising on a regular basis. Don't be afraid to call car dealers and other potential corporate clients and offer them package rates. The worst they can say is "No thanks."

In her first year in business, Peg Mosey hired an employee to buff the cars and still netted $15,000. She is bullish on the future, noting "the consumer market hasn't been tapped." While the government won't let Tidy Car talk about profitability since each franchisee differs, a spokesperson allows this: "Most of the [older] dealers are remodeling and building new Tidy Car buildings—and buying new cars and boats for their families."

SOURCE

Industry Association

International Carwash Association, 401 North Michigan Place,
Chicago, IL 60611, (312) 321-5199

Automotive Tune-up Provider

Job Description: *An automotive tune-up provider services and maintains cars so they operate efficiently and correctly.*

- *Start-up cost as low as $100,000*
- *Potential first-year earnings: $235,000*
- *Breakeven time from initial investment: rapid (six months to one year)*

One year, following a stint as head nurse at the University of Iowa hospital, Susan Gerber moved with her family to Spokane, Washington. With two small children, she decided she wanted the flexibility of being her own boss. "I explored restaurants (the classic business people want to start) and a children's clothing store (I'd bought enough children's clothing, so I felt I should know something about the field)." But nothing seemed right until she stumbled on the automobile tune-up business. Her husband, Hank, a neurosurgeon, races sports cars as a hobby. "The whole family goes to the races," Susan explains. "So the tune-up business attracted me."

Susan Gerber readily admits her initial reservations: "I knew how to change tires and not much else about cars." But a trip to Precision Tune's Beaumont, Texas, headquarters reassured her that she could manage the business. "They showed us the men who were signing on as franchisees who didn't have an auto background either." To this day, Susan Gerber—who now operates four of her own Precision Tune sites and oversees two others in the capacity of subfranchisor—has never tuned a car. But she's plenty busy managing the books and staff, placing advertising, and handling customer relations. Meanwhile, "our best center did over $400,000 in revenues last year and we did way over $1 million total. Our returns were *very* healthy on that."

OPEC FALL-OUT

Tune-up centers and other automotive aftermarket businesses gained momentum following OPEC's oil embargo in the 1970s. Many operators responded to what Stan Stephenson, publisher of *Chilton's Motor Age Magazine*, calls "the gas-and-go syndrome." Self-service pumps replaced service stations that checked under the hood and operated mechanic bays. "Periodic car maintenance plummeted precipitously," says Stephenson.

That's not to say that drivers don't need their cars repaired. In fact, new computerized auto technology makes do-it-yourself repairs less likely. And busy working couples would rather drive to a quick tune-up center than leave their cars overnight at the repair shop. In addition, people keep their increasingly expensive cars longer—an average of 7.5 years, according to the Automotive Vehicle Manufacturing Association. And today's smaller, four-cylinder cars achieve 11 to 15 percent better gas mileage following a tune-up, according to Precision Tune literature.

In place of full-service repair shops, America has embraced auto specialists: transmission businesses, lube shops, brake stations, tune-up centers, and more. The International Franchise Association's *Franchise Opportunities Guide* lists over half a dozen auto service franchises currently operating.

By concentrating on one specialty, you cut start-up costs dramatically because you don't need sophisticated equipment to diagnose and treat every car ailment under the hood. "Realistically, you'd need $1.5 million to equip and operate a full-service repair center today," says Stan Stephenson. But you can launch a tune-up service for under $120,000. You also don't need a Ph.D. in auto repair if you concentrate on one area. That's a good thing, because "training is getting longer and longer because the technology increasingly is more complex," says Stephenson. Even technicians who specialize need elaborate training to understand today's complex cars. Precision Tune requires mechanics to complete a four-week certification course, followed periodically by in-person or videotaped refresher classes.

FRANCHISE ROUTE

Most newcomers to the automotive aftermarket join franchises or build multiple centers to establish a presence in a market. "It's the pizzazz that separates the franchises from individual operators," says Edward L. Kaufman, an industry consultant. "It's tougher to do business without big company resources for advertising, promotion, signage, training, and a warranty on merchandise." Still, he cites opportunities for individuals with "a serious, professional attitude about fixing a car" and doesn't discourage independents who know their stuff.

But for individuals like Susan Gerber who lack an automotive background, observers recommend hooking up with a franchise. "If you follow their plans, you cannot help but make money," says Stan Stephenson. Industry pretax profits often hit 16 to 22 percent on revenues of $200,000 to $500,000.

Precision Tune recommends franchisees put aside $101,000 to $120,000 in addition to real estate costs to start a tune-up center. That capital covers the franchise fee and equipment for a three- or four-bay facility. Depending on the location, expect to spend another $1,500 to $5,000 monthly to rent an 18,000-square-foot site—or $84,000 to $108,000 to construct your own. Whether your specialty is tune-ups, mufflers, or transmissions, you'll want a visible location with heavy traffic, since much of your business comes from drivers who notice your shop as they chug to work each morning.

In addition, plan on heavy promotion. Precision Tune franchisees commit 9 percent of gross sales to advertising. In markets where air time is inexpensive, or where multiple franchisees band together to share costs, television is the most popular medium, followed by radio, newspaper, and direct-mail coupons.

"There are two kinds of ads," explains Susan Gerber. "We emphasize price through coupons in direct mail or in print." The parent company estimates that the Precision Tune tune-up, averaging $32 to $49 depending on the area of the country, costs "as much as 50 to 100 percent less than competition."

Gerber says another important draw along with price is expertise. "We're qualified to take care of the technical problems of today's cars. We talk about the extensive training of our technicians." Precision Tune ads also point out that their franchisees tune a car in about 40 minutes—far faster than re-pair shops that ask customers to leave their transportation for hours or days.

ALL THINGS TO ALL PEOPLE

Susan Gerber says the very meaning of the term "tune-up" is changing. "People tend to think of replacing the spark plugs and cap and rotor," she says. "But carburetors have given way to fuel injection; new cars don't even have points and condensers. We've made the equipment and training changes necessary to address the different car we tune today." The proliferation of computers in today's cars also makes it much more difficult for do-it-your-selfers to perform maintenance. Consequently, the need for qual-ified, trained, professional tune-up services has grown.

Precision Tune responded to the modern car by expanding its services. In addition to the tune-ups and oil changes the company always offered, its mechanics now replace distributors and perform fuel-injection repairs. Other auto franchises have broadened their menus, as well. For example, some lube shops also repair car air conditioning.

The approach expands the revenue base as it attracts cus-tomers for multiple jobs. "Just as with McDonald's, which now has salads and a fish sandwich, a one-product-line marketing ef-fort is not feasible for automotive shops in the long run," says Stan Stephenson. The balancing act of the future will involve offering just enough services; too many will require the very ex-pertise and start-up costs that pushed general-repair stations out of the business.

SOURCE

Industry Association

Independent Automotive Service Association, P.O. Box 929, 1901 Airport Freeway, Bedford, TX 76095-0929, (817) 283-6205, (800) 272-7467

Beauty Salon Provider

Job Description: *A beauty salon provider performs various services to enhance personal appearance, including haircuts, makeovers, pedicures, and manicures.*

- *Start-up cost as low as $2,500*
- *Potential first-year earnings: $20,000*
- *Breakeven time from initial investment: several months to several years*
- *No staffing required (initially)*

I remember a woman who had horrible eyebrows." Erika Zimmerman, proprietor of Erika's Hair-Um, Inc., in the Chicago suburb of Darien, shudders. "The arch made her look so stern, so I asked if she found it easy to make friends. She was distant with me, too, but she admitted she'd always had a hard time with people.

"Well, I told her there was nothing wrong with her face," continues Zimmerman, lacing positive reinforcement along with recommendations that she reshape the woman's eyebrows. "I said her face was classic, but her eyebrows gave her a domineering look. You know, that woman was so grateful! She said, 'I've had to go through my whole life without someone pointing out what a simple change in appearance could mean!' "

ONE-STOP BEAUTY SHOPPING

Observers suspect beauty shops of the future will fall into two camps: franchises that offer low-cost haircuts and deal in volume; and full-service salons like Erika Zimmerman's that provide, along with cuts and perms and coloring, such specialties as eyebrow arching, skin care, manicures, body massages, and even fitness facilities. According to Business Information Services, the average salon pulls about 31 percent of its gross from haircuts, 17 percent from perms, and 30 percent from hair coloring. That leaves 22 percent from other areas, including nail care, retail sales, and skin care. (In addition, many of the country's 150,000 hair-care salons that do not offer additional services themselves rent space to concessionaires.)

But the dependence on hair care alone appears to be changing. For example, *Modern Salon* says 54 percent of those salons that offered manicures increased their nail-care business during a one-year period. Of course, you can still start with just hair care and grow. But you should have a good idea of which path you want to pursue, since growth will depend on one of two approaches: Either you must pull in lots of customers for hair care, or you can sell more services to fewer customers. Your pricing, your advertising, your equipment purchases, even whether you choose to start as an independent or a franchise may all depend on which star you shoot for.

More evidence that "full service" is replacing strictly haircutting comes from the 1999 Job Demand Survey conducted by the National Accrediting Commission of Cosmetology Arts and Sciences (NACCAS). The survey found that 70 percent of salon owners classified their salon as a full-service shop, while just 13 percent considered it as a haircutting salon.

The study also found that "the salon industry continued to be a job-seekers market." According to the survey data, in January 1999 there were 1,286,000 professionals employed in 296,563 beauty salons, barber shops, skin care salons, and nail salons in the United States. This is in line with information supplied by the U.S. Bureau of Labor Statistics, which predicted that "employment of barbers and cosmetologists is expected to grow about as fast as average for all occupations through the year 2006. Increasing population, incomes, and demand for cosmetology services will stimulate job growth."

Erika Zimmerman gambled on the supermarket over the fast-food approach when she spent $100,000 to create Erika's Hair-Um in a former residential site. In addition to equipment purchases for six hair stations and a skin-care and steam-and-massage room, the cash went for visual effects. Zimmerman gutted the house, knocking out the attic to create a cathedral ceiling and skylights. She also landscaped the outside with pine and apple trees. The entrepreneur felt that establishing a special ambiance would alert customers that she was more than the traditional beauty parlor. "When I opened, there was no such thing as a total-concept salon under one roof," Zimmerman says. "Still, many beauticians haven't visualized the upgrading of the industry." Has the gamble worked? Evidently.

Zimmerman estimates half of her $157,000 gross comes from skin and nail care.

WHERE THE CASH COMES FROM

Your first expense goes not for your own beauty boutique but for your training. Although all states require cosmetologists to be licensed, the qualifications necessary to obtain a license vary. Generally, a person must have graduated from a state-licensed barber or cosmetology school, pass a physical examination, and be at least 16 years old. Public and private schools offer classes in barbering and cosmetology. Full-time programs usually last 6 to 12 months. An apprenticeship program can last from 1 to 2 years.

Most freshman beauticians sign on with an existing shop both to gain experience and to build clientele who will follow when they open their own boutique. While you're working in someone else's establishment, polish skills and learn other elements of your trade, such as skin care and makeup.

A well-run shop can cover rent, utilities, and miscellaneous costs (such as advertising and bookkeeping) through retail sales. Many salons neglect the natural add-on business of selling shampoo, makeup, and even accessories such as jewelry and scarves. Margins are high, the items take up little space, and carefully selected products appeal to customers who are already predisposed to look stylish. The sales pitch can be subtle. You can easily afford to give 10 to 20 percent of the retail price as commissions to stylists who recommend the superior products you stock.

After you cover overhead, your only other expense is the

talent you employ. Most salons pay commissions, splitting the price of each haircut, makeup, or manicure 50-50 with the employee. (In addition, good beauticians often pull a third of their salary in tips.) Some beauty shops even charge stylists for supplies. Another approach is to contract with stylists who rent space from you and charge their own rates.

Depending on your salary arrangements with employees—and whether you count your own paycheck as an expense—expect to keep between one-third and one-half of the fees you collect as profits.

SELLING BEAUTY

Beauty salons typically advertise in newspapers and the Yellow Pages or hand out flyers announcing specials. But letting the services sell themselves is your most effective marketing tool. You can do this in three ways:

- Make each element of your boutique visible. "A customer having her hair permed will see another who's having a body massage and realize how relaxing that looks," observes Erika Zimmerman. "It's contagious. She asks for a massage, too." Ask stylists to recommend manicures while they're coloring a client's hair; throw in a bonus to the employee who generates the most nail business of the month.
- Build steady clientele. For example, instead of selling a facial here and there, package treatments. Zimmerman offers a five-treatment skin-care special for $155 and points out to customers that, if paid for separately, it's a $260 value.

Also, you can call on groups such as nursing homes and

offer to do their hair at a discount during slow morning hours. And don't neglect your contacts. Zimmerman sells gift certificates to a plastic surgeon and a cosmetic dentist. "When they're finished with patients, they send them to us for a complimentary treatment," she explains.

- Involve your customers as salespeople. Some promotions are apparent to the customer. You can give away a free manicure with every three friends the customer brings in. Your other marketing partnership with a customer is less conspicuous— but more effective than any advertising you'll ever buy. Namely, get your customers to recommend your establishment. Hair-Um's skin-care business boomed when Zimmerman packaged treatments not only because of the perceived value, but also because results are much more obvious with weekly skin care than with sporadic treatments. Customers sign on for repeat packages and act as walking billboards. Their friends remark on the glow, and clients recommend Zimmerman.

Knowing the value of word of mouth, Zimmerman and her five stylists take pains to teach clients how to care for their new hairdos or show them how to perform at-home skin-care techniques. The longer customers look good, the longer their friends will ask for recommendations.

SOURCES

Industry Associations

Hair International, 1318 Starbrook Drive, Charlotte, NC 28210, (704) 552-6233

National Accrediting Commission of Cosmetology Arts and

Sciences, 901 North Stuart Street, Suite 900, Arlington, VA 22203-1816, (703) 527-7600

National Beauty Culturists' League, 25 Logan Circle, N.W., Washington, DC 20005, (202) 332-2695

National Cosmetology Association, 3510 Olive Street, St. Louis, MO 63103, (314) 534-7980

Dating Service Provider

Job Description: *A dating service provider matches up single people who are seeking partners.*

- *Start-up cost as low as $5,000*
- *Potential first-year earnings: $50,000*
- *Breakeven time from initial investment: rapid (six months to one year)*
- *Excellent opportunity for people with physical disabilities*
- *No staffing required*

Single men and women represent nearly 40 percent of the U.S. population. Because of the rising divorce rate and the increasing age of the average bride and groom (we postpone nuptial bliss until our mid-20s), the Census Bureau reports that one out of every two households is headed by a single person.

There are two kinds of singles in the world: men and women who already cuddle with a steady, and people looking for Mr.

or Ms. Right. Today's business community is falling all over it-self to bring the sexes together. In addition to computer and video dating services, restaurants, adult schools, and for-profit hobby associations have all gotten into matchmaking. (A restaurant might promote a gourmet night where participants change tables at every course, for example. A class on "Meeting Your Perfect Match" provides dating tips for the outside world, but students have been known to exchange phone numbers be-fore the bell rings.) However, businesses designed specifically for matchmaking also achieve fame and fortune. Many fine-tune their appeal to a particular group. Cities big enough to boast specialty dating companies match blacks, classical music lovers, even the overweight. "People are tired of singles bars," says Susan Hendrickson, who operates the more general-inter-est Georgetown Connection dating service in Washington. "They don't want to pick out men and women the same way they go to a supermarket to pick out apples and oranges."

Hendrickson's partner, and the founder of Georgetown Connection, is her mother, Joan Hendrickson. Like many en-trepreneurs who start dating services, Joan learned from experi-ence just how dreadful the singles scene can be. After spending 23 years of marriage raising three daughters, Joan found herself divorced. "She had never worked before and had no skills," re-calls Susan. "The only job she could find was an interviewer at a video dating service."

Serendipity! Joan's natural warmth and curiosity made her a good interviewer. Her tapes brought out clients' personalities, and she genuinely liked what she was doing. When the business folded a year later, she scraped together enough savings to buy out the previous owners.

NO PH.D. REQUIRED

Joan was no video technician. She didn't have to be. The technical aspects of filming a dating interview are simple, compared with, say, taping a drama or even a training film that calls for following swift-moving action and creative dissolves and fade-outs. Most video dating companies don't splice or edit the interviews. Likewise, you don't have to be a computer programmer to start a computer dating service. But it doesn't hurt to take a course or two at a community college to polish your skills.

A good video interview ignores the vital statistics that Jack is five feet eleven inches tall or Jill is a chiropractor. Your clients read that sort of information in a short bio you furnish with each tape. Instead, the tape should capture personality. Most dating services say a three-minute interview allows a viewer plenty of time to decide whether a meeting would be worthwhile. "We chat for about 15 minutes, but the camera's only on for three minutes," says Susan Hendrickson. "I begin by talking about the weather or myself—I say 'My seven-month-old didn't let me sleep last night.' It relaxes the client. Most people don't know when they're being taped. An interview works best when it is spontaneous."

Susan always asks, "What is your most special quality?" You could also ask about hobbies or faults. What kind of vacation sounds perfect? Who is the ideal date?

KEEP OUT THE BAD APPLES

A dating service's several-hundred-dollar registration fee generally deters kooks. But many services ask new clients to fill out extensive application forms and show a couple of forms of identification so they can verify claims made by suspicious characters. Some services suggest dating partners meet in a public place the first time. What you're really selling at a dating service is your reputation for putting the right people together, so you try to minimize the chances for bad experiences.

The registration fee also marks you as attracting fairly affluent clients. People who can afford you know their prospective dates also have financial wherewithal. Professionals in the dating service field say it's imperative to have a prestigious location for your potential clients, and to furnish the space as tastefully as your budget allows.

Joan Hendrickson decorated Georgetown Connection with colonial furniture from her Reston, Virginia, home. "People are nervous walking into a dating service," remarks Susan. "The stock phrase is 'I've never done this kind of thing before.' Our office relaxes them. The studio looks like a den, with an Ethan Allen couch and a shag rug—except it's got some lights and a video camera in the corner."

You can create ambiance with other touches, as well. Many services provide coffee or wine, and Georgetown Connection tries to know members by name. "If you know their eccentricities and what they like and don't like, it's easier to steer members to dates they get along with," says Susan. One of her clients, Mary, is a busy attorney who doesn't have a lot of free time to view tapes. "If John picks Mary's tape, I call and describe him. She trusts me enough to say 'Sure,' and I give out their phone numbers at that point. If I have any questions, I recommend she come in and view his tape."

A New York City service, Video Chemistry Inc., goes a step further for its harried clients. Each month it mails out a magazine that profiles members. Clients choose tapes from that list, which Video Chemistry mails so they can watch on the VCR at home. For busy new members, the company will tape an interview at their home or office.

DO YOU HAVE ENOUGH ELIGIBLES?

The pivotal question to ask regarding site selection: Do enough singles live in your area? If you charge $500 a year to join your service, figure you need 100 members to gross $50,000. From that you must pay for equipment, advertising, rent, utilities, and salaries (including your own). You may need three or four or ten times that many members or a higher membership fee to meet your expectations. The Census Bureau can tell you how many singles live in your area and local newspapers may also have figures. Check to see what dating alternatives exist. Is there enough business to split between two dating services? How can you be different?

To attract your first applicants, you may have to provide incentives, such as special introductory offers or a get-acquainted wine-and-cheese party. Budget plenty for advertising, as marketing will continue to be important throughout the life of your business. Just as a retailer keeps shelves stocked with merchandise, you must keep a plump portfolio of eligible singles. *How to Capitalize on the Video Revolution* notes that "if you are successful at what you do, you have to expect some of your members will no longer need your services. Therefore, you must constantly be replenishing your supply."

In addition to city magazines and newspapers, some markets offer cost-effective radio and cable-television spots. You also can buy direct-mail lists that segregate the marrieds from the officially unattached. If you specialize in a particular type of date—senior citizens, for example—you may advertise in publications geared specifically to your audience.

Joan Hendrickson courts free publicity. She's been on a national talk show and the front page of the *Wall Street Journal*. Local credits include the Washington *PM Magazine* TV show and the *Washington Post*: "We've lost track of how many times we've been in the *Post*," says Susan. Each appearance adds 10 or 15 members. "Dating services have no credibility," she explains. "This type of publicity erases the stigma."

Will there always be enough singles to support dating services? Of course some areas become saturated with too many services. In such locales, you may set yourself apart by catering to specific populations. But, as a rule, modern society provides a ready supply of singles. Susan Hendrickson points to the member who married a video date shortly after Georgetown Connection opened and recently rejoined after that marriage ended in divorce.

Financial Planner

Job Description: *A financial planner plots the economic future for his or her clients by helping them make sound, informed financial decisions on such matters as investments and retirement planning.*

- *Start-up cost as low as $5,000*
- *Potential first-year earnings: $40,000*
- *Breakeven time from initial investment: rapid (less than a year)*
- *Ideal home-based business*
- *Excellent opportunity for people with physical disabilities*
- *No staffing required*

Case study: Between two professional incomes, David and Samantha earn about $200,000 a year. They have a lovely colonial on 1.5 acres—and a high 30-year mortgage that won't go away. They have a 70-foot yacht, a 17-year-old with her eye on Princeton, and a 15-year-old who wants to take flying lessons. An ex-spouse collects monthly checks, and aging parents may need financial help in the future. And because David's a pediatrician and Samantha's a sole proprietor who refurbishes artwork, neither can count on retirement benefits to gild their golden years. Even the wealthy need financial planning.

Not everyone who sells investment products is a financial planner. Unlike a broker who recommends only stocks, a planner chooses from all sorts of investments: bonds, real estate, venture-capital opportunities, whatever. And instead of just advising on investments, a financial planner takes a client's entire financial life into consideration, including income from all sources and all financial commitments and goals.

BOUTIQUES

Applying a loose definition of financial planners as individuals who sell specific products such as stocks, as many as 250,000 financial planners exist. Regardless of the industry size today, observers believe financial planners may outnumber stockbrokers as we enter the 21st century. "Expect a tremendous influx into the profession," predicts Glenda Kemple, a CFP (certified financial planner) as well as a CPA (certified public accountant).

Why the increase in planners? Classic supply and demand. As the tax bite continues to sting, and as investment vehicles become ever more complicated, even the middle class is seeking out financial consultants. "I expect employers soon will offer affordable financial planning from banks as a cafeteria benefit along with health insurance," says Glenda Kemple, who operates out of Carter Financial Management in Dallas. It's becoming easier to get in the game as insurance companies, banks, and brokerage firms all test the financial planning waters, creating salaried positions in an industry that, until now, has been a boutique field. Universities now bestow MBAs and even bachelor's degrees in financial planning as well as courses to prepare would-be CFPs for the necessary certification test.

DO THE TWO-STEP

Financial planning has two stages: devising the financial plan over a period of a few weeks and keeping the plan on track over a period of years through ongoing monitoring. Assume you're Samantha and David's financial adviser. To write their plan, first you compile all their assets and liabilities, and match them to the family's goals. If the couple has neglected wills or insurance, you help get those in place. If you just happen to be an attorney, you can even draw up the will, although more likely you would just recommend a lawyer. More planners, however, earn licenses to sell insurance. After David and Samantha's financial house is in order, you outline a budget that allots money for investments as well as every other obligation, such as mortgage and tuition payments. "Financial planners typically work with people who have money to save and invest," explains Kemple. "If a client is in financial trouble, we refer them to a credit counselor."

Up to this point, you'd have dealt with the science of numbers. Now comes the "art" of planning. You take that analytical data and match it to Samantha and David's goals and their tolerance for risk. Now you make specific investment recommendations. "I try to blend my suggestions with existing investments and make sure the entire portfolio is diversified between such areas as stocks, bonds, real estate, and so on," says Kemple. Samantha and David's plan calls for both near-term liquidity to pay for their children's educations and investments that won't mature for 20 years to shelter retirement income. Since both are adventurous and can afford to gamble, you suggest they stash 10 percent of their investments in more volatile commodities or even to back that new technology David ran across in his medical research.

For the written plan, you charge a flat fee that ranges from a minimum of $300 or so for a simple plan, to the $30,000 stratosphere for really complicated plans that involve millions of dollars of income coming from various sources that must be divided among dozens of investments and obligations. "Clients feel organized and content when the plan's complete," says Kemple. "The challenge is to keep them on course." Kemple visits with each of her 50 clients three times a year and talks with them monthly. On top of that one-time fee, some financial planners charge annual retainers. Some charge by the hour—anywhere from $50 to $200. Other planners take a percentage of income. Some take commissions on the sale of stocks, bonds, insurance, or other products recommended to implement the plan.

Those fees add up swiftly. "Successful, established planners earn in the six-figure range," says Kemple, who doubled or tripled her CPA salary after becoming a CFP. If you hire associates, your firm's revenues can move into seven figures.

PLANNING TO BE A PLANNER

Most planners have at least a bachelor's degree in some financially related field, such as accounting or economics. But dentists, attorneys, psychologists, and teachers also have become financial planners. Currently, no state or federal laws define financial planner qualifications, although you need licenses to sell specific products, such as stocks, insurance, or real estate.

You may need to register with the Securities and Exchange Commission to become a Registered Investment Adviser.

If you decide you want the credibility (and probably the higher fee) of a certified financial planner, expect to devote a year or two to intensive study. Glenda Kemple completed the 80-hour course work as a correspondence course from the College for Financial Planning while still on her accounting job. Other planners earn certification while practicing, similar to the way in which many accountants achieve CPA designations while working. You have to pass exams in six areas to become a CFP: tax management, investments, insurance, employee benefits, retirement, and estate planning. And it's not over yet: To keep that CFP status, you have to complete 45 hours of continuing education every year.

SETTING UP SHOP

Unlike consultants who work out of clients' offices, financial planners invite the customers in for a visit. Asking a client to have a seat in your living room may be relaxing, but where their future is concerned, clients expect professionalism—so you really do need an office. In addition to secretarial help, busy planners hire "paraplanners" to do some of the grunt work, and you'll need a computer to juggle all the figures. Of course, besides a computer you'll also need software and a modem (since you're going to be constantly surfing the Internet to keep up with the latest financial news) as well as a fax machine and cell phone. After setting aside a little money for marketing, a solo practitioner might spend $20,000 to hang a shingle. You can cut overhead in half, however, by teaming up with other financial planners, much as lawyers or doctors form group practices and share rent, some personnel, and library facilities.

If you know how to plan finances, you're only halfway home: Who're you going to plan for? To attract clients and gain credibility, you might give seminars or write a newspaper column on particular aspects of personal finance. Or send out newsletters to clients and potential clients. Offer an hour of free consultation—provided new clients bring in recent tax returns, balance sheets, and a list of financial goals. This will eliminate "tire-kickers."

Glenda Kemple exchanges referrals with people she calls "strong centers of influence"—bankers, attorneys, accountants, and other professionals monied people rub shoulders with. In addition, she cold-calls on prospects, asking to plan their finances. Kemple is particularly fond of lawyers, who make up about 25 percent of her practice, saying she understands the type of investments that appeal to them. "A lot of planners specialize in just doctors or small business owners," she adds. Others take on a particular age bracket, or just people above (or below) a certain income level.

Whatever the specialty, Glenda Kemple says financial planners meet the most interesting people. People with money, people with influence. But people who, despite their successes, need help with their finances.

SOURCE

Industry Association

The Financial Planning Association (began operation in January 2000), 5775 Glenridge Drive NE, Suite B300, Atlanta, GA 30328-5364, (404) 845-0011

Image Consultant

Job Description: *An image consultant enhances a client's image by improving personal appearance, diction, clothing, and so on.*

- *Start-up cost as low as $1,500*
- *Potential first-year earnings: $20,000*
- *Breakeven time from initial investment: extremely rapid (several months)*
- *Ideal home-based business*
- *Excellent opportunity for people with physical disabilities*
- *No staffing required*

You've seen the makeover in all the magazines. You've read about the importance of looking "right" in *Dress for Success* and *Color Me Beautiful*. It appears that we Americans (1) don't like the way we look and (2) are willing to spend money to turn ourselves into vice-presidential material.

Brenda York, who heads the Academy of Fashion & Image in the Washington suburb of McLean, Virginia, estimates the total field, including speech/public appearance and dress/color consultants, employs 5,000 individuals. And she says we ain't seen nothing yet. With so few practitioners and so many people desperately in need of an improved image—especially professionals looking for an edge on the job—she predicts the size of the field will continue to grow. "People are just now hearing about personal image consulting. When you start from ground zero, you grow quickly."

FROM FAD TO BUSINESS TOOL

The industry began as a service to wealthy women "who sat around their country clubs talking about their consultant," says Brenda York, who founded York & Associates. Today's clients more likely are bound for business success than the putting green and have no time to shop. And now we're talking both male and female clients. "So many women entered the workforce and looked great that men felt they had to dress better as well," says Marilyn Ciccolini, who founded Wardrobe Images Inc., in Tenafly, New Jersey, to specialize in male makeovers.

As a personal image consultant, you help clients look the part of an executive in their chosen industries. (Wall Streeters don a more sober uniform than do Madison Avenue ad executives.) The tasks of image consultants vary, depending on their expertise. For example, they might:

- Analyze clients' coloring and advise on makeup, hairstyle, and coloring
- Shuffle through a client's existing wardrobe, discarding pieces and coordinating what survives
- Shop for new clothing
- Comment on ineffective body language and mannerisms
- Coach clients on speech techniques

For these services, image consultants charge a flat $300 to $600 fee, or $35 to $85 an hour. Some corporations even place personal image consultants on retainer to make over entire legions of salespeople, vice presidents, and other reflectors of the corporate image.

CAPITAL AND CONFIDENCE

But you don't have to do all those things at once—or ever. Some personal image consultants concentrate on one specialty, say shopping, while others branch out in even more directions, such as producing fashion shows. And speech consulting is a major specialty unto itself. Unless you have a lot of capital and self-assurance, Brenda York recommends start-up consultants moonlight part time while holding another job. "Work nights and weekends—that's when clients want you anyway," she says. "If your apartment is inadequate, meet them in a hotel or restaurant or in their home." She also advises tackling one specialty at a time. "First learn color, then makeup, then wardrobe, then men."

Marilyn Ciccolini had the money—about $20,000, which is at the highest end of a personal image start-up scale—and the confidence to plunge in with real commitment. Her background seemed tailor-made for an image consultant. She has degrees in buying and merchandising from the Fashion Institute of Technology in New York and is a psychiatric nurse to boot. Credentials included stints as a manager for the Stern's department store chain and as an account executive for Liz Claiborne. Before setting up shop, Ciccolini spent a year researching the industry. She read numerous books on personal image consulting and talked with competitors listed in the *Directory of Personal Image Consultants*. She also took Brenda York's two-week, $2,500 "How to Start Your Own Fashion & Image Consulting Business" course.

To avoid competition in the New York City area, and to follow her own inclinations, Ciccolini decided to consult exclusively for men. "I love men's clothing. It's better made than women's. Also," she adds, "men are more receptive than women who have been raised with fashion and have definite ideas about what they like."

From the beginning, Ciccolini tailored means to ends. "I'm selling a package," she reasoned, and it was essential to "package myself well." She custom-designed stationery and business cards and printed brochures and back-up information to distribute in seminars. She incorporated in New York and New Jersey and outfitted an office attached to her home. She also hired a press agent to get publicity and invitations to do seminars.

GETTING CLIENTS

"When I first started, I ran an ad," Marilyn Ciccolini recalls. "I attracted more people who wanted to work for me than I did clients." When you're selling your services as a consultant of any sort, clients want assurances that you are truly expert in your field. They ask for recommendations rather than check out the Yellow Pages. "Advertising just doesn't work," says Brenda York.

Instead, network. Discount services for colleagues and acquaintances in order to build a referral base. People will ask who your clients are, and you should get permission to use clients' names. Says York, "Everybody is a potential client, because everybody is interested in looking better."

Get your name out to a wider audience by speaking to social and civic groups. Those speeches are freebies, but you leave business cards and brochures with members of the audience who may contact you later. You can charge for speaking to business groups. York checks the *Washington Post* business calendar, which lists upcoming trade-association meetings each Monday. In addition, "I call people who are planning meetings to tell them I'm available to speak on 'Polishing Your Professional Image.'"

Marilyn Ciccolini sells to both corporate sponsors and individuals by calling cold, explaining her services, and asking for an appointment. "The bestselling tool I have is explaining you can look great year round and only spend four hours doing it." Those four hours include an initial two-hour interview in which Ciccolini and the client talk about budget, measurements, and the proper image to project. Ciccolini likes to meet in the client's office so she can see how his peers dress. She spends another hour at the client's home going through his wardrobe. Ciccolini discards what doesn't work, and catalogs what does so the client knows which shirt and tie match which suits. The final hour is spent at the store where Ciccolini awaits with a tailor and a number of suits from which to choose. Although the client has put in just four hours buying maybe $1,000 worth of clothes, Marilyn has spent up to ten hours, for which she charges $60 an hour.

Because of her proximity to New York, Marilyn has no shortage of potential clients. Personal image consulting works best with a ready pool of executives close by. In rural areas you might offer variations on the theme. For example, Linda Hunt consults from her Greenburg, Vermont, dress shop, Linda's. In-shop advice is free, but she charges a fee for visiting clients' homes to check out their existing wardrobes.

ADD-ON SERVICES

You won't get rich in image consulting because you're limited to hourly fees that average $50 (more in urban areas). But many personal image consultants push their income well into six figures by developing business boosters, such as conducting seminars. "Figure you do wardrobes twice a year—for spring/summer and fall/winter," reminds Brenda York. "Color analysis is a one-shot situation. You have to figure out what to do the rest of the year." York & Associates sells makeup in custom blends for clients in a makeover at 100 to 150 percent markups. Scarves, books, even clothing present other possibilities.

Some beauty salons and retailers pay consultants 10 to 15 percent commissions for sending along clients. But York warns against buying everything from one store. "Then clients don't need you. Next time they just go to the store's shopper."

Also, don't let commissions sway you into recommending items the client doesn't need. If your goal involves bringing clients back every season, get the most value for the budget they've set. "If a recent college grad can spend only $350, I say let's get a nice suit," says Marilyn Ciccolini. If you dress your client well—and if the client has the talent and drive to go along with the new image you've created—next season you'll have a bigger budget to work with when the client returns with a raise and a new title.

Mediator

Job Description: *A mediator negotiates disputes (divorces, child custody, and so on) so that they do not have to be brought into court.*

- *Start-up cost as low as $5,000*
- *Potential first-year earnings: $40,000*
- *Breakeven time from initial investment: rapid (six months to one year)*
- *Ideal home-based business*
- *Excellent opportunity for people with physical disabilities*
- *No staffing required*

Susan and Jim handled the first four years of their divorce with relative harmony. They share joint custody of Kimberly, who alternates weeks with Mom in town and Dad in the suburbs. But Kim enters first grade in September. Susan argues that the magnet school in town provides an exciting, challenging curriculum, while Jim wants Kim to attend the suburban school, with its fresh, open-air setting. Kimberly will live with whichever side wins, since she can't shuttle between schools.

"It's fascinating that neither thought of the third school district that lay between them," says John Haynes, who practices family and business mediation and also teaches courses in the subject at The Haynes Mediation Training Institute. Both of Kimberly's parents agreed to move into the central district—Susan on the north side closest to the city and Jim on the west edge, within walking distance of his previous home. While both adults compromised, each kept what they really wanted: joint custody of Kimberly.

GROWING DISPUTES, GROWING SOLUTIONS

A recent article in the *Dallas Morning News* cited 20 divorces per 1,000 married women. With the breakup of each marriage comes conflict: not only the personal animosity, but also the practical decisions of what happens to the children, the house, alimony, and joint property. About half the states in the country, as well as local jurisdictions in other states, require couples to seek mediation before they file for separation or divorce.

Business disputes are no less cumbersome. Thanks to clogged courts, the average civil suit takes 42 months—nearly four years—before litigants get their day in court. "And you can't get to court with less than $5,000 or $10,000 paid by each side in legal fees," says John Haynes. Mediation is not yet mandatory in business or interpersonal conflicts; but as the debt crisis threatens more farmers, Minnesota and Iowa both require mediation in disputes between bankers and farmers.

Several other states recommend the process even though they don't require it.

Mediation began in America as a tool in labor-management disputes. The practice is much more widespread in some European countries, such as Norway, where it is perceived as an alternative way to settle many forms of disagreement. While everyone agrees that no U.S. mediators practiced full time until the late 1970s, nobody knows how many hang shingles today. John Haynes, author of *Divorce Mediation* (Springer, New York, 1999, $29.95), estimates that 10,000 divorce mediators practice but says those figures are meaningless because the field is growing so rapidly. He says he expects to see an increase as more states require mediation and more people see it as an alternative.

Indeed, mediation does seem to be growing as experts suggest. The American Arbitration Association (AAA) said that it handled more than 95,000 cases in 1998. And arbitration isn't just confined to personal matters, either. According to the AAA, nearly 400 companies and 4 million employees worldwide turn to them to resolve workplace conflicts.

DEFUSING

Mediation offers a route to solving conflicts outside the legal arena. The step defuses volatile situations before angry litigants waste time—and money—in court. No judge decides who's right and who's wrong; instead, the enemies themselves devise solutions to problems. Unlike a lawyer who pledges allegiance to one side or the other, the mediator acts as a referee, helping to resolve the conflict in the interest of both sides.

Businesspeople who would rather not air their trade secrets appreciate mediation because it occurs behind closed doors rather than in the open courtroom.

Those states that require mediation offer two alternatives: court-appointed mediators who practice out of courthouses or private practitioners. As of this writing, no state licenses mediators. However, the Academy of Family Mediators accredits only lawyers and members of such helping professions as social work and psychiatry as divorce mediators, and many courts use academy standards to define whose mediation is acceptable. In addition to lawyers, many ex-businesspeople practice business mediation.

How It Works

Mediators charge $20 to $100 an hour, per side. The average divorce mediation runs 12 hours over the course of six weeks. A business issue might be solved in two hours if the issues are clear-cut and unemotional. A complicated environmental case involving the public as well as private and government groups could take years. Typically, the first one-hour session orients both sides to the process. In divorce situations, the mediator gives both husband and wife forms to fill out, asking what each expects future incomes and expenses to be. From there, the parties return for two-hour sessions until both sides agree to the issues at stake: parenting responsibilities and how to divide the marital assets, for example. At that point, the mediator writes a document in plain English that the couple takes to an attorney, who turns it into a legal separation or divorce agreement—a step that makes the decision binding. "Lawyers we use in New

York charge $350 to do the filing," says John Haynes. "That compares with retainers of $2,500 both the husband and wife would pay if a lawyer did the whole procedure."

YOU CAN WHOLESALE

John Haynes estimates a mediator in a metropolitan setting seeing clients 20 hours a week, 48 weeks a year grosses $75,000, which accounts for cancellations due to bad weather or illnesses. You can do better if you include bigger corporations as clients because they don't balk at stiffer hourly fees. "Figure a New York rent and telephone costs $20,000 a year; $55,000 isn't bad for 20 hours' work a week." Haynes advises sharing offices with other mediators, lawyers, or therapists to cut overhead. "You also can move from wholesaling to retailing." By that he means hiring other mediators to work on an hourly basis. As manager of the practice, you keep $60 out of the $100 fee. Haynes Mediation operates two full-time offices as well as two that it rents one day a week. Revenues amount to $250,000 a year.

Breaking into the business part time is also an option. Professionals, such as social workers, attorneys, or consultants, can continue practicing until they build a clientele. Individuals can sign on with groups, such as the American Arbitration Association or the Center for Information Technology and Dispute Resolution, which offer business mediation. Approach existing mediation practitioners and courts that might want to use your services. Ask other professionals for referrals. "Don't go to family lawyers since this would take away their divorce business," advises Haynes. "Instead, talk with tax or corporate lawyers. They'll be overjoyed to give you the business and keep their clients for wills and other things." Also, make the rounds of PTAs, local mental health agencies, and civic and business clubs. Haynes Mediation also advertises in local law journals.

John Haynes, who once worked as a labor-management negotiator, says his greatest satisfaction comes from helping families through all sorts of rough situations. He recalls the case of the daughters who couldn't agree on what to do with their ailing mother. "Two daughters wanted Mother to stay home, but the third argued she really needed the attention of a nursing home. We finally agreed Mother should go to the nursing home, but we developed a calendar of visitation. One daughter visited Mother each week to ensure she kept contact with her family. Again, we found the third alternative between the two extremes."

SOURCES

Industry Associations

Academy of Family Mediators, 5 Militia Drive, Lexington, MA 02421, (781) 674-2663

American Arbitration Association, 335 Madison Avenue, 10th Floor, New York, NY 10017-4605, (212) 716-5800, (800) 778-7879

Personal Assistant

Job Description: *A personal assistant performs routine errands for clients, such as grocery shopping, picking up drycleaning, and so on.*

- *Start-up cost as low as $3,000*
- *Potential first-year earnings: $40,000 to $50,000*
- *Breakeven time from initial investment: extremely rapid (as little as one month)*
- *Excellent home-based business*
- *No staffing required*

In the past only celebrities had personal assistants—people to perform all those mundane chores that they didn't have time to do or considered beneath them, such as waiting in line at the supermarket, buying birthday gifts, and driving Fido or Fluffy to the vet.

Today, however, the concept of the personal assistant/errand service has been transplanted from the glamour and excitement of Hollywood to Main Street, U.S.A. According to the *Dallas*

Morning News, personal assistants are "reaching more people than ever before." People from all walks of life are seeking someone to perform those exact same tasks that the stars shun. The result is a growing increase in the number of personal assistants hired by people all across the country—and an opportunity for entrepreneurs who don't mind performing those everyday duties to establish a business with excellent growth potential.

THE DRIVING FORCE

Just like the personal chef and personal coach professions, the personal assistant industry has boomed because of one universal truth: Time is important, and how people manage it has become even *more* important. To working people everywhere, the question is how best to use their free time: run all over town doing errands, or relax with family and friends? It isn't difficult to figure out which choice people are making and, consequently, why the personal assistant industry is growing so rapidly.

"I do whatever people don't have time to do themselves," says Laura Elizabeth Cribbs, a personal assistant based in Adelphi, Maryland. She performs a wide range of tasks for her clients, including going grocery shopping, taking pets to the veterinarian, and selecting gifts for spouses, relatives, and bosses. She's even planned vacations for some clients.

To become a personal assistant, you must be both resourceful and reliable. If your client asks you to go grocery shopping, for instance, you must be able to find appropriate substitutes for any unavailable items on the list. By the same token, if you're asked to "pick up something nice" as a birthday gift for a client's wife, you must be able to shop for something that suits her, not you. If you don't know the client's spouse or partner well enough, you must ask the right questions to uncover tastes, habits, hobbies—all without seeming too nosy. The line between personal assistant and busybody can be dangerously thin, and you must walk it with the skill of the Flying Wallendas—or risk a professional fall.

KEEPING THE BOTTOM LINE HEALTHY

Start-up costs are low for establishing a personal assistant/errand service business. (The two descriptions are often used interchangeably.) It's an ideal home-based business, thus avoiding the need and associated costs for an outside office. Even a computer, which is de rigueur for most home-based businesses, is not absolutely necessary in this field (although the increasing use of e-mail means that you really should have one, because your clients probably do and expect to be able to reach you that way). However, both a cellular phone and a pager are necessary, so that you can easily stay in touch with your clients (and vice versa), especially when you're on the road.

Make no mistake, on the road you will be. Laura Elizabeth Cribbs spends much of her average seven-hour workday in her car. Before you start a personal assistant business, you might want to trade in that old refugee from a junkyard you've been driving for something with a little more comfort and size. Cribbs uses a Jeep Cherokee; the extra space comes in handy when she chauffeurs family pets to the vet.

Another possible start-up expense is becoming bonded and insured. Bonding and insurance protects you in the event of theft, accident, or other mishap. Many personal assistants are bonded and insured, while others, such as Cribbs, are not, in order to reduce costs. The cost is anywhere from a few hundred into the thousands, depending on the type of insurance selected.

Although placing advertisements in local newspapers is one way to publicize your business, Cribbs primarily built hers up by word of mouth, again with an eye toward cost containment. (For that same reason, she doesn't accept credit cards for payment.) She finds that the lower her overhead costs, the more likely people are to use her.

"If you start spending money on advertising and other things, you have to raise your prices," she says. "Then people won't use you as much."

If you can keep your start-up costs minimal, it is possible to see a return on your initial investment within one month (as Cribbs did).

DO THE CLIENT SEARCH

The most important component in building a personal assistant business is finding your target audience. Obviously, this is the type of industry that busy executives and other working people want to utilize. To introduce herself and her services, Cribbs bought bulk supplies of candy, which she wrapped in cellophane to make small, individual gift packages. She left these "goodie bags," along with her business cards and brochures, in numerous businesses and office complexes in her area. After people discovered the baskets and read her brochure, some became clients.

To increase her business's visibility, she donated her services for a charitable auction and received numerous inquiries from potential clients. Time-stressed new brides and new mothers are other groups that often require her services.

For those contemplating starting their own personal assistant business, Cribbs offers some advice: "If people want to put their energy into it, [they should] take a day, dress nice, and go to [a lot of] businesses and drop off their brochure," she says. "You can build up so much business that way."

Like many other personal service–oriented businesses, how successful you will be, and how much you can charge, depends on the region where you live. Cribbs, who lives in the Washington, D.C., area, charges $15 an hour (one-hour minimum) for her services and acknowledges that she could charge as much as $25 per hour if her business was based in Los Angeles. In large cosmopolitan areas, it's possible to make $40,000 to $50,000 annually as a personal assistant.

Although she has been in business in Maryland only since early 1997, Cribbs already has built her client list to 45. Fifteen utilize her services on a regular basis (usually weekly), while the rest call on her more sporadically.

A personal assistant's workload follows the ebb and flow of the calendar. Cribbs's busiest time is around the holidays and during the summer, when people are more active and have less time for common chores.

CREATIVITY AND FLEXIBILITY ARE KEY

You need two key qualities to establish a successful personal assistant business: the first is an affinity for people, since you interact with them constantly. The second quality is creativity. Sometimes clients won't be clear about what they want you to do, and you have to figure it out yourself. Creativity also comes in handy when you perform a service such as gift-wrapping. Here clients expect something special—not something that they could have done themselves or had done at the local mall. The more you impress your clients with your resourcefulness and inventiveness, the more likely they might become steady customers.

To achieve success, you also must be flexible. On some days Cribbs is busy from the moment she walks out the door until late into the evening; on other days her workload is more relaxed. In general, however, a personal assistant has to be ready to respond to a client's needs at a moment's notice. If you can, and if you use some flair to spice up those boring chores, you, too, could be a success as a personal assistant.

"Most people can't afford to have a personal assistant, like you always hear of movie stars doing," says Cribbs. "The service that I offer them is someone who can be just that, but on an hourly basis."

Personal Chef

Job Description: *A personal chef prepares meals one or two times per month at clients' homes, providing enough food for two to three weeks.*

- *Minimal start-up costs (as low as $4,000)*
- *Potential monthly income: $3,000 to $4,000 after 60 days*
- *Potential yearly income: $40,000 to $50,000*
- *Breakeven time from initial investment: extremely rapid (as little as two months)*
- *Excellent home-based business*
- *Flexible schedule*

L ove to cook? Tired of your day job?

If the answer to both questions is "yes," then you may be a prime candidate to join the burgeoning home-meal industry by becoming a personal chef—a profession that *U.S. News & World Report* called "a hot-track" career, and *Entrepreneur Magazine* labeled "one of the hottest trends in today's marketplace."

Eat, Drink, Man, Woman — Immediately!

According to the United States Personal Chef Association (USPCA), in 1992 there were approximately 15 personal chef services in the United States. Two years later, the number rose to 450. By mid-1999, there were 3,000 personal chef services in the United States, and applications to join the USPCA were pouring in at a rate of 100 per month.

Why have personal chefs suddenly become so popular? Time—or rather, the shortage of it—is one factor. Back in the days when Father knew best and even the best-dressed housewife wore an apron, Dad went off every day to earn the daily bread, while Mom stayed home to cook it.

Today, of course, things are very different. Usually both parents are working, leaving no one home to rattle pots and pans until the end of the day. According to the USPCA, almost 80 percent of Americans decide what's for dinner after 4:00 P.M.

Another reason that personal chefs have become all the rage is that we, as a society, have gotten used to immediacy in our lives: We want everything *right now*. However, this philosophy, when applied to eating, usually results in something barely appetizing or marginally healthful, such as fast food. Eventually, both our bodies and minds rebel, and we seek more nutritious alternatives—but we still want them *right now*.

"[We say] 'Where can I get a healthy meal that is still convenient and fast, yet affordable?'" says David McKay, executive director of the Albuquerque-based USPCA.

Did someone say "personal chef"?

For as little as $7 or $8 a meal per person, a personal chef will come to a client's home, prepare several dinners, and leave them in the refrigerator or freezer. When the hungry clients come home, all they have to do is choose a dinner, heat it up, and dig in. Best of all, it's nutritious and delicious food, not some artery-clogging fare picked up at the drive-through.

Is it any wonder that the personal chef industry is flourishing?

Gratuity Not Included

As the saying goes, if you can't stand the heat, get out of the kitchen—as well as the personal chef business. A typical USPCA personal chef has 10 to 20 clients and cooks for each client one or two days per month. During each visit, the chef makes two to four servings of several different entrees and side dishes (enough to last two to four weeks).

However, to succeed as a personal chef, you have to be able to juggle numbers as easily as you do multiple entrees, so that excess costs don't devour your bottom line. Unlike other personal service professions, the amount a personal chef can charge is dictated not by location so much as by the types of meals prepared. The trick is to charge enough to make a profit while making your services cost-effective for your clients.

For instance, McKay's wife, Sue, who is a personal chef, charges a family of five (husband and wife, plus three children) $340 per visit. For this amount, the family receives 10 dinners. At that rate, each dinner costs around $6.80 apiece. Contrast it with the expense of the same family dining out, where the cost, with beverages and tip, could easily reach between $12 and $15 per person.

SO YOU WANT TO BE A CHEF

"Becoming a personal chef is a very attractive home-based business," says David McKay. "It's one of the few businesses in the food service industry that you can legally operate from your home [since all of the cooking is done at the client's residence]."

McKay estimates initial costs between $3,000 to $4,000 to begin a home-based personal chef business. Since a chef normally earns between $3,000 to $4,000 per month, a figure that McKay says most USPCA chefs reach in their second month of operation, start-up costs often can be recouped within approximately 60 days. A personal chef can expect to make between $40,000 and $50,000 per year.

One reason that initial costs are low for this business is that all paperwork can be done at home, in a small office or even at the kitchen table. In addition, no special equipment is required. (Most chefs use their clients' utensils.) All a chef needs to begin is some basic cooking equipment, a telephone, a computer, and—of course—recipes.

The USPCA offers training in how to become a personal chef. Training costs run as little as $500 for a two-day course to $1,700 for more intense and lengthy sessions. The association provides member support, either via the Internet or through one of its 40 local chapters across the country. The USPCA also offers a certification process.

According to McKay, the average personal chef is a service-oriented individual between 35 and 55 years old. Sixty percent are female, 40 percent are male, and only half have formal culinary training. The overwhelming majority of personal chefs are single owners/operators of their business. For many, becoming a personal chef was a career change. Often someone who loves cooking got tired of playing the corporate game and sought something different, or a chef who cooked in a major restaurant or hotel grew tired of working long hours and holidays but wanted to remain in food preparation.

COOKING UP A STORM

For Vickie Kurlick of Rivervale, New Jersey, becoming a personal chef was certainly a career change. Disillusioned by the long hours and stress of her corporate job, Kurlick resigned and opened her business, The Traveling Gourmet, in January 1996. Besides her love of cooking, one of the things that attracted her to the personal chef field was the low start-up cost.

"Starting your own business is always a risk-taking venture," she says. "My start-up costs were minimal. From start to finish, my start-up costs were under $4,000." She recouped it in just four months.

An additional expense can be the cost of getting both a bond against theft and liability insurance, since personal chefs are usually alone in their clients' homes. This protects you in the event something gets stolen or damaged at the home.

Although she initially advertised in newspapers, Kurlick quickly discovered that being a personal chef was a business that thrived primarily on word of mouth. She also realized that people were reluctant to hire her until she became a familiar face. In order to meet people, she did cooking demonstrations so that people would recognize her and become aware of her business. Slowly her client list grew; today she has 14 customers and wants to hire an assistant so that she can take on more of the many prospective clients who are clamoring for her services.

A personal chef obviously requires a keen sense of organization, so work time is spent cooking, not running around searching for ingredients. Kurlick doesn't cook on Mondays. Instead she dedicates the day to organizing her menus for the upcoming week and doing bulk shopping for nonperishable items. On a cooking day she stops at the grocery store for perishables before arriving at the client's house no later than 10:00 A.M. Depending on the variety of meals she makes, Kurlick spends approximately four hours in the client's kitchen.

On each visit, she cooks five entrees and five side dishes, and divides each into two, for a total of ten entrees and ten side dishes. After cooking she wraps the food, labels it, and puts it in the freezer. She leaves detailed reheating instructions, along with suggestions for side dishes. She visits half of her clients every two weeks and the other half monthly.

For families she cooks more "standard" food (chicken, spaghetti and meatballs, meat loaf, soups, and so on); childless couples tend to prefer more gourmet fare. She does not repeat an entree unless the client requests it.

Kurlick charges $290 per visit unless there is a specific dietary restriction, which bumps the cost up to $325. She also offers a sliding scale for children: those under 5 are free, ages 6 to 10 are $25 per visit, and those 10 and older cost $50. For those whose palates crave unusual foods, she charges her normal rate, plus the cost of the specialty item. Her expenses are minimal, primarily consisting of recyclable, microwave-usable containers she uses for food storage.

"I want my clients to feel as if they're eating in a restaurant, but with the comfort of home," Kurlick says.

If that type of philosophy agrees with you, then maybe you can cook up a great business for yourself as a personal chef.

S O U R C E

Industry Association

The United States Personal Chef Association: (800) 995-2138

Personal Fiduciary

Job Description: *A personal fiduciary provides financial expertise utilizing a more personal, people-oriented style than traditional financial experts.*

- *Start-up cost as low as $1,500*
- *Potential first-year earnings: $20,000*
- *Breakeven time from initial investment: extremely rapid (several months)*
- *Ideal home-based business*
- *Excellent opportunity for people with physical disabilities*
- *No staffing required*

For someone who deals with figures all day long, Sal LaGreca has a million stories. Consider the one about Elaine Freedman. Sal had been executor for her husband's estate and was managing the widow's assets when he got a phone call from the police that 70-year-old Elaine had been in a car accident. No, she wasn't hurt, but her car was blocking two lanes of traffic. And she was scared. "She refused to get out of the car until I arrived," says LaGreca, who got in his car and sped 20 miles to the scene of the accident.

"My business card says I do fiduciary accounting and taxation," continues the Edison, New Jersey–based entrepreneur. "That means I do for individuals and law firms what bank trust departments do: manage assets, act as power of attorney, prepare income tax returns, do accounting for settlements of estates, offer investment advice." But where bankers strive to keep a strictly business relationship, personal fiduciaries often get involved in their client's well-being. Since he has access to checkbooks belonging to people not always able to look out for themselves, LaGreca gets personal: "I make sure my client at the nursing home has enough sweaters or another client's house gets cleaned regularly. In another situation, I arrange to have a woman taken to church every Sunday."

WHERE THE MONEY COMES FROM

Not to get mercenary, but fiduciaries do get paid for their missionary work because they charge an hourly fee. It's crucial to keep accurate time sheets where you record everything. Sal LaGreca, for example, gets $50 an hour whether he's preparing a client's income tax report or depositing someone's jewelry in the bank.

But income is not restricted by how many hours you can squeeze in between dawn and midnight. As a fiduciary you also are paid when you act as executor of estates. In New Jersey, executor fees amount to 5 percent of an estate's first $200,000 (or $10,000), and 3.5 percent on the excess. For a $400,000 estate, an executor might spend 50 hours preparing an accounting that answers such questions as: What assets did the deceased have?

How did the executor distribute the assets? Did the executor pay all taxes? Were any investments made for the estate? What problems arose and how were they handled? The executor receives $15,000 for the work that went into that typical 40-page accounting.

If you want to tackle personal bookkeeping or tax preparation, take specialized courses. Investment advisers can register for courses leading toward financial planning certification. (See "Financial Planner," page 430.) But a fiduciary incorporates snippets of all those fields into one job. Experience in estate administration or taxes—such as you might garner with banking or legal training—probably provides the best fiduciary background.

Once you have the know-how, setting up shop is as easy—or as tough—as getting clients. Sal LaGreca was working as a trust officer for a large New Jersey bank when he began thinking about going on his own. "I'd always paid for vacations or the kids' tuitions by doing tax work for individuals on the side," says LaGreca. But then he and his wife, Joan, decided they'd like to buy a house. So LaGreca mentioned to a couple of attorneys he knew through the bank that he was willing to handle their clients' taxes. "Joan and I worked all day long at the bank and spent nights doing the outside work," says LaGreca, who worked on tax preparation while Joan, who was also a bank officer, typed his correspondence. The bottom line: "We had the down payment for our house in three to four months."

It took just one other piece of evidence to convince LaGreca to leave a $36,000-a-year-job and such perks as a company car and a big entertainment allowance, which he spent to bring in bank customers. "Banks expect you to bring in so many wills or investment accounts," he explains. "Right after I'd worked myself to death during tax season, I brought in business from another bank. They were paying $25,000 just for us—which really meant me—to do the tax work." Recognizing that he might as easily pitch that $25,000 account for himself rather than for the bank, LaGreca decided he was through hustling for an employer.

CLIENT TYPES

Fiduciaries service three types of clients, each responding to a different sales pitch:

- Banks (usually smaller institutions), which don't have the in-house personnel to fully meet their depositors' needs
- Attorneys who come in contact with tax and estate work but would rather concentrate on the legal rather than the accounting headaches
- Individuals who have a tax or estate problem, usually referred by one of the first two sources or another individual. Once they sign on as tax clients, you can ask if they need someone to act as power of attorney or executor of their estate.

With ammunition in hand, Sal LaGreca approached his employer as his first account. "I saw that a CPA firm had charged $8,000 to do the accounting on one particular estate we'd farmed out. I looked at the records and figured I could have done it for $2,000." The discrepancy, he explains, involves overhead. If you start from a desk in your basement, as LaGreca did, and employ a part-time typist who works out of her or his home, you can keep nearly all of your $50 per hour fee. In contrast, a large accounting firm with marble walls and on-line computers and a backup librarian might count $25 of a $75 fee as profit.

Somewhat to LaGreca's surprise, the bank agreed to send accounts his way. Instead of a competitor, they saw an unofficial, outside partner who could help them service accounts that no one on staff was equipped to handle.

LaGreca sent out formal business announcements and made the same pitch to other banks and attorneys. To gain visibility with potential clients, he became a trustee for the state's Estate Planning Council, made of lawyers, accountants, and bankers; he also spent $1,000 to host a hospitality suite at the annual meeting of the New Jersey Bankers Association Trust Division. "It's hard to say how much work I got from that party, because business tends to dribble in as banks need you," says LaGreca. "But because they had been to my hospitality suite, the bankers remembered me when I called on them to solicit business."

LaGreca's goal was to make $30,000 during the last six months of his first year. "We surpassed that," says the entrepreneur. "Then we said let's make $50,000. We broke $72,000." Figuring on the same income for his third year, LaGreca broke $72,000 in the first six months.

Now that LaGreca is contemplating hiring a part-time fiduciary to help with the overflow, he hesitates to put a figure on future goals. "Never in my wildest dreams did I think the business would take off like this," he says.

Pet Sitter

Job Description: *Pet sitters spend days and evenings caring for pets—playing, walking, and feeding—in their owners' homes while they are away.*

- *Start-up cost as low as $5,000*
- *Potential first-year earnings: $40,000*
- *Breakeven time from initial investment: rapid (several months)*
- *Excellent home-based business*
- *No staffing required (initially)*

It's a fact of life: Neither people nor their pets like strange places. Unfamiliar sights, sounds, and smells get our pets and us anxious and make us feel nervous and tense. People and their pets are much more relaxed at home, surrounded by comforting sights and sounds. Yet for a pet owner who is going to be away from home for an extended period of time, there never used to be an alternative to boarding the pet in a kennel or similar place so it could be cared for properly.

Now there is an alternative—a pet sitter. For a fee, the sitter comes to your home while you're away and lavishes the same loving attention and care on your pet as you do when you're there. (And you know you do. There's no sense denying it. We all treat our pets as surrogate children.) The advantage for you is that you don't have to feel guilty about boarding your pet. The advantage for Fluffy and Spot is that they get to sleep in their favorite place, play with their favorite toys, and eat their favorite food even when you're away. Think of all the slobbery affection you'll get when you return! (Except from your cat, which will pretend that it didn't miss you when you get back even though it did. That's just the way cats operate.)

Before you dismiss pet sitting as an industry that's going to the dogs, consider this: In the United States, pet sitting is estimated to be a $20 to $35 million industry. From 1993 through 1998, the number of pet-sitting businesses increased an incredible 753 percent!

DON'T LOOK AT ME LIKE THAT

Why are Americans spending a lot of money on pet sitters? As Aretha Franklin might say, it's all about r-e-s-p-e-c-t.

"Society today has a new respect for animals," says Patti Moran, founder and president of Pet Sitters International (PSI). "We've begun to give our pets human traits, and just like you would for a real child, you want only the best for your pet. They're seen by many as surrogate children and as true family members."

Another factor boosting the industry has been the growing fear of crime by homeowners. By bringing in mail, opening blinds, and turning on lights, pet sitters give vacant homes a lived-in look.

Although kids have been taking care of their neighbors' pets since the vacation was invented, it has only been since the late 1980s that pet sitting has become a full-time professional business. Within the past five years, it has blossomed into a full-fledged industry. According to a 1998 survey, 76 percent of the 33 million American households with pets used some type of pet care when traveling. Of these, 30 percent use a pet sitter, while 22 percent use a kennel or veterinarian. This means that pet sitters are visiting approximately 7.5 million U.S. homes annually.

CRITTER CRAZY

By her own reckoning, Patti Moran was one of the first to establish her own professional pet-sitting business. She began Crazy 'bout Critters in 1983 in Winston-Salem, North Carolina. Without guidelines to follow, Moran figured out what she needed completely on her own. Her start-up costs—which couldn't have been more than $100—were limited to supplies (a pooper scooper, paper towels, pet treats, and garbage bags) and some brochures explaining her business and the services she offers.

Although Moran's business was new, she used an old tool—networking—to find clients. She visited vets, groomers, pet stores, and travel agencies in her area, introducing herself and her business and leaving behind her brochure.

Within four years, she had become so successful that she wrote a book, *Pet Sitting for Profit—A Complete Manual for Professional Success*, that launched the careers of numerous other pet sitters across the country. It also made Moran the "mother" of the pet-sitting industry. Today PSI has over 2,400 members, and Moran, besides heading PSI, also runs her own company that produces pet-sitting products, such as diaries that enable pet sitters to record details of each visit.

IS THERE A FLUFFY OR A FIDO IN YOUR FUTURE?

Obviously, if you're not an animal lover, becoming a pet sitter would be a bad career move. Besides a fondness for animals you also must be responsible, dependable, have a wealth of common sense, and—perhaps most important—maintain a good sense of humor.

"Not only will pets do the darndest things, but clients will ask the darndest things." Patti Moran laughs. "It keeps the job interesting. You never know what you may run into [as a pet sitter]."

That last statement should be taken seriously. Although a majority of pet-sitting jobs involve "standard" pets such as dogs and cats, you never know when you'll be asked to sit for a parrot, a tank of fish, or some other creature.

"The more unusual [the pet], the more the need for a pet sitter," says Moran. "At least, you can take a dog or cat to a kennel."

You can establish a pet sitter business anywhere. While a metropolitan area obviously is home to a lot of people and pets, folks who live out in the country also need someone to take care of their horses, goats, or pigs.

To launch your own pet-sitting service, figure on start-up costs between $3,000 and $5,000. This includes the cost of obtaining a bond against theft (approximately $60 to $100 annually) and liability insurance (approximately $350 annually). Many pet sitters obtain these because they have keys to their clients' homes, and so this covers them in case of theft or other problem at the home. The bulk of your initial expense will be on office equipment (computer, printer, fax machine, cellular phone), plus printing costs for contracts and other forms. (Signing a contract with your clients protects you in the case of a pet's injury, sickness, or death, and also spells out your duties in writing.) PSI offers accreditation programs that cost between $85 and $299, depending on level, experience, and degree of difficulty.

According to PSI, most pet sitters charge an average of $12 per visit. Each additional dog costs $3, while each additional cat costs $2. Some sitters charge hourly rates that vary from $8 to $24, depending on the number of pets and additional services required.

Another PSI statistic states that customers have pet sitters care for their pets an average of 15 times per year, and each customer averages 115 professional pet sitter visits per year. PSI estimates that a pet-sitting business with a staff of four can generate annual profits between $40,000 to $60,000 within three to five years. If your business follows this formula, you can recoup your start-up costs in as little as three months.

A WATCHER OF WHISKERS

Carole Lini of Ewing Township, New Jersey, began her pet-sitting business as a part-time venture in 1989. A veterinarian technician by trade, Lini saw how unhappy many pets were when they were boarded and realized that there was a need for a pet sitter. Within two years, she had enough clients to become a full-time pet sitter. Today her business, Whisker Watchers Inc. (which is affiliated with Happy Tails of Mercer County, New Jersey) utilizes two private contractors, four part-time employees, and three full-timers to help manage its growing roster of two- and four-legged clients.

"When I started this business I had no idea it was going to take off the way it did," she says.

That success, however, comes with a price. Lini warns that anyone who begins this business has to be prepared to work long hours and be on call 24 hours per day. She gets calls for pet care at any hour of the day, ranging from people who are stuck at work and going to be home late to someone unexpectedly going into the hospital. Another casualty of her busy schedule is her automobile; in 1998 Lini put 90,000 miles on her car.

Lini grew her business by putting up flyers in supermarkets and leaving them at travel agents and real estate agencies. She also placed ads in local papers; the more often her ads appeared, the better response she got from them.

"You really have to be diligent [in the beginning] and promote yourself," she said about starting a pet-sitting business.

Lini meets with her clients—both human and animal—beforehand, in order to put both at ease. While her normal rates are similar to the average quoted by PSI, she structures her price according to the duties she is called on to perform. On average, she charges $15 per visit and spends approximately 30 minutes in the home. Her "nonhuman" clients run the gamut from dogs and cats to fish, birds, horses, and even some pot-bellied pigs. She tries to travel no more than 15 or 20 miles to get to a client's home.

"You have to be dedicated, reliable, honest, and present yourself well [to succeed in this business]," says Lini. If you can do that, pet sitting is one of the few businesses in which the rewards can be both financial and spiritual.

"There's nothing more rewarding than going into a home and seeing the pet—their love is unconditional," she says.

A BRIGHT FUTURE

While no industry or business is truly "recession-proof," pet sitting may come close. Many people put their pet's welfare ahead of their own, and so even if the economic climate falters, it seems likely that people will find a way to continue spending money on their pets. Combined with the fact that pet sitting as an industry has barely scratched the surface of its potential client base, it's understandable why this industry is considered to have enormous potential.

"I think the future looks very bright for this profession," says Patti Moran.

That sound you heard was a thousand tails wagging gratefully.

SOURCE

Industry Association

Pet Sitters International, 418 East King Street, King, NC 27021-9163, (336) 983-9222

Skin-Care
Aesthetician

Job Description: *A skin-care aesthetician offers facials, mud packs, and other treatments to help promote healthy skin.*
- *Start-up cost as low as $6,000*
- *Potential first-year earnings: $42,000*
- *Breakeven time from initial investment: six months to one year*
- *No staffing required*

A major crop of baby boomers is rapidly approaching the dreaded age of 50. In addition to worrying about the paunch, they're now seriously scrutinizing their wrinkles. "I predict skin care will become bigger than the hair business," asserts Ron Renee, chairman of the International Association of Aestheticians.

With approximately 25,000 licensed skin aestheticians (skin-care specialists) operating, compared with many times that number of cosmetologists (hairdressers), Ron sees great opportunity ahead. "We're a changing society," he says. "By the turn of the century, 30.6 million Americans will be over 50 years of age. The majority of those will be women—the most frequent skin-care salon visitors." Many of those women work and not only want to look their best on the job, but have the income to afford facials, which average $30 apiece. In addition, many aestheticians act as makeup artists, sell custom-blended skin-care and beauty products, treat acne, and offer leg and bikini waxing and body wraps.

According to a study of the skin-care market from June 1998, the "aesthetics industry is experiencing extraordinary growth. Aging baby boomers are creating new markets for middle-age and elderly clients."

PICKING UP THE KNOW-HOW

With just a few exceptions, each state requires licensing for aestheticians. But requirements vary drastically and, according to skin-care specialists, don't cover all you need to know. Many states expect an aesthetician to be a cosmetologist. (See "Beauty Salon Provider," page 417.) Training for cosmetology can last anywhere from 300 hours during an eight-week crash course to 1,500 hours over nine months, but most programs devote only a class or two to skin care. Professional aestheticians are more comfortable with states that require degrees specifically in skin care; some states require both cosmetology and aesthetics degrees. In the past few years, a few schools have opened specifically for aesthetics.

Hairdressers, the first to the skin-care starting line, already possessed the degree (if not the expertise) to break into the business. Some doctors, particularly dermatologists, soon added facials to their practices, sometimes hiring aestheticians to provide the actual skin care. Nurses caught on and got their own aesthetics licenses.

I'LL SCRATCH YOUR BACK

You need relatively little capital to hang a skin-care shingle because you can ride the coattails of other professionals, such as hairdressers. Although such giants as Christine Valmy and Georgette Klinger operate very successful stand-alone salons, the Aesthetician International Association recommends that entrepreneurs lease space in a beauty shop or other establishment that offers traffic and complementary services. Judy Davidson, who operates D'Lair Facials and Cosmetics in Hair Panache, Flossmoor, Illinois, praises the symbiosis of the services. "The clients' hair is trashed when I get through with them. They just walk over to the sink for their shampoo." She swaps referrals with hairdressers and manicurists. Some aestheticians build relationships with dermatologists or family doctors who send clients their way. "And a recommendation is everything in this business," emphasizes Davidson. "Would you trust your face to a newspaper ad?"

Unless you are going with a multiple employee operation, you need no more than an eight-by-ten-foot space to house your treatment table or bed as well as your equipment—steamers, magnifying mirrors, lighting, cabinetry, and a sink. If you're renting space from another establishment, you can keep start-up costs under $10,000. Just set partitions around your area for privacy. Davidson, who has been both a hairdresser and a public relations entrepreneur, picked up a lot of used equipment, particularly such small items as apothecary jars, gowns, and towels, when she started D'Lair in 1984. But be careful where you cut corners. "You need a good, comfortable bed," recommends Ron Renee. "Use music and light therapy. The secret is to put the client to sleep while you're giving the facial. If someone spends 90 minutes in discomfort, they won't want that experience again." As with any personal service, your business is built on repeat customers.

CONCESSIONS

Although most beauty shops balk at the complications of actually running a skin-care operation, often they are happy to lease aestheticians space at reasonable rates since skin-care offers clients another reason to frequent a particular shop. "I stock five manufacturers in makeup and three in skin care and custom blend everything," says Judy Davidson. "Beauty shops don't want to keep track of the inventory, ordering, bookkeeping. Also, beauty salons pay their employees commissions, and I don't think I could make a living on commissions alone. I need the markups on products I sell to survive. Maybe 70 percent of my revenues come from selling products."

Davidson makes those product sales to clients who come in for regular facials, acne treatments, or makeup consultations. She suggests that aestheticians in locations such as her suburban Chicago site could expect $40,000 in revenues the first year, keeping $15,000 as pretax profit. As you build a steady customer base, revenues should increase and profits should jump even faster, since such costs as rent remain fixed. At some point, you may want to add another treatment room or two.

Only Your Aesthetician Knows For Sure

Unlike a hairdresser, who can assume an avant-garde look and bouncy attitude, an aesthetician should project a professional manner. Much of what skin-care specialists do involves consulting: Use this moisturizer to treat your skin, try that face pack to fight acne, or try this blush to enhance your coloring. Clients are paying for your expertise. For example, to custom blend a foundation, Judy Davidson mixes matte and oils in proportions suited to the client's skin type. Then she adds tints and color developers to match the skin color. "The foundation may only run me $3, but the client pays $22.50 for my expertise."

While some aestheticians emphasize makeup, Davidson takes the European attitude that "if you have just $100 to spend, take care of your skin first." As products and techniques continually improve, the rewards for both her clients and herself escalate. "People come in saying 'My face is so raw it hurts,' then return a week after I've given a facial and they've followed my home-care suggestions. It's so satisfying when they say 'I can't believe it's improved so much!' "

Source

Industry Association

Aesthetics' International Association, 3939 East Highway 80, Suite 408, Mesquite, TX 75150-3355, (972) 932-7026

Vocational School Operator

Job Description: *A vocational school operator teaches job skills and prepares students for a host of occupations.*

- *Start-up cost as low as $60,000*
- *Potential first-year earnings: $60,000*
- *Breakeven time from initial investment: six months to several years*

Donald Beardsworth likes to say the secretarial students he attracts at the International Business College in El Paso, Texas, and its six Southwestern branches "qualify for everything but the IRS." About 80 percent pay for 100 percent of their tuition through government loans and grants; many students are on welfare and some lack high school diplomas. A few have college degrees but can't find a job. "My philosophy is to give them six to nine months of training, period. If they don't have a high school diploma, we give them a GED [general education diploma] prep course and take them to the testing center so they get their equivalent. We get them off the welfare rolls and onto the tax rolls."

EDUCATING THE PUBLIC PRIVATELY

Like Don Beardsworth, most presidents of vocational and trade schools are pragmatic sorts. But you don't have to scratch too deep under that tough exterior to find caring educators who provide the computer-repair or truck-driving education a public school doesn't. Proprietary schools supply about one-half of the postsecondary vocational education in this country, according to the Association of Independent Colleges and Schools, an accrediting body. As high schools move further to basics (reading, writing, and arithmetic), their curriculums have even less room for typing, bookkeeping, auto repair, or electronics.

The market for vocational school graduates remains strong. According to the Career College Association's *Private Career College Fact Book 1998–99*, the 725 member institutions that belong to the group educate more than a quarter of a million students annually for employment in more than 150 occupations.

Workers' desire for a fast education is tantamount to a hunger: the recognition being, to put food on the table, the breadwinner needs to acquire new skills. Displaced assembly-line workers learn to repair robots. Former steelworkers learn to retrieve information from databases.

TO START OR BUY

Despite the need for private-sector education, starting a school isn't easy when you factor in paying rent, recruiting teachers and students, buying equipment, and winning accreditation. (The exception may be small cosmetology schools that take just a handful of students at a time. Start-up costs are minimal, and the school receives income from cutting customers' hair as well as from tuition. The drawback? Cosmetology schools operate in a highly competitive field.)

For the most part, "It's easier to start by purchasing a school," says Joseph Thompson, president of Antonelli Institute of Photography and Art, a Plymouth Meeting, Pennsylvania, school that offers two-year associate degrees in photography, art, and interior design. He explains that the accrediting groups will not consider a school until two to three years after start-up. And even then a school must prove it is financially stable to get a stamp of approval. Why is accreditation so critical? "Students cannot get government funding unless the school is accredited," Thompson explains, noting about 40 percent of his students receive grants or loans. "And if you attract affluent students whose parents pay the tuition, they look for accreditation to make sure you're giving a good education and getting jobs for the students."

Thompson, a former photo-lab operator, says to check the *Wall Street Journal* ads and business brokers to see what schools are on the block. Costs vary, depending on whether the school has a campus and how much equipment it owns. A school that teaches medical technicians, for example, pays more for teaching tools than a school for models. But, as a rule-of-thumb, expect to spend $1,000 per student to buy an accredited institution. In addition to students, your purchase price also buys such assets as instruments or equipment, a library, instructors, curriculum, and sometimes real estate, so you'll want to check on the conditions of each.

Don Beardsworth spent just $75,000 for the then 75-year-old International Business College nearly 20 years ago. "When I took over, it had 154 students," says Beardsworth, a former banker who worked in admissions departments for two midwestern vocational schools. "Now we've got 1,900 students and seven locations. I wouldn't take $3 million for the school today." Recently the school made 8 percent pretax profits, or about $480,000, on $6 million in tuition revenues.

THIS IS THE WAY WE GO TO SCHOOL

Because you offer fast education, those students you inherit when you purchase a school won't be with you for long. Don Beardsworth starts new classes every three weeks and must replace his entire student body every six to nine months. Therefore, advertising and recruiting are crucial. "The main school has 600 students and 5 admission specialists," he explains. "They go to high schools to give demonstrations and explain financial aid. They invite students to come for aptitude tests." (About 5 to 7 percent don't pass.)

Schools with high class turnover usually budget 10 percent or more of revenues for advertising: newspapers, radio, direct mail, even TV. Afternoon television soap operas could be renamed "trade school traumas" considering all the vocational-school advertising breaks.

Above all, recruiters sell students a new life after school—a new job and a new career. "You'll be out of business real fast if you don't place your graduates," warns Beardsworth. International Business School has at least one job developer on each campus who constantly calls on employers to line up interviews. Placement is why people pay $10,000 for a two-year education at Antonelli instead of about $4,000 at a community college, adds Joe Thompson. "We tell students we teach more, faster. We use the latest techniques. Our graduates go out and start their own photography studios or get good jobs."

To keep that competitive edge, a school needs two things: good instructors and up-to-date equipment. Trade schools generally offer instructors and administrators at least competitive salaries and benefits. Since trade schools are more involved with recruiting and placement than their public sector cousins, you may need one administrator for every instructor on board.

KEEPING CURRENT

Look at your market frequently to see what changes are taking place, and change your curriculum accordingly. For example, many southern California schools give business courses in Asian languages. All executive or medical secretaries who graduate from International Business College can operate word processors and input data. An adequate response to the business environment requires having the latest teaching equipment. You don't have to buy it, however, since many manufacturers offer lease packages. Don Beardsworth says he spends about $150,000 to outfit each new 50-student branch school. As long as you keep the same curriculum and student-teacher ratio, branches automatically receive accreditation if the parent school has passed muster.

What about the future of trade and technical schools? Proprietary schools receive much of their tuition indirectly through government funds to students, and no one knows from year to year what Washington has in mind for students. But increasingly, older Americans are switching careers after their first choice fails them in some way. More and more, they look to private education to help them make that switch.

SOURCE

Industry Association

Career College Association, 10 G Street, N.E., Suite 750, Washington, DC 20002-4215, (202) 336-6700

Wedding Consultant

Job Description: *A wedding consultant helps a bride and groom plan either all or any part of their wedding.*
- *Start-up cost as low as $5,000*
- *Potential first-year earnings: $40,000*
- *Breakeven time from initial investment: rapid (one year)*
- *Future growth potential: high*
- *Excellent home-based business*
- *No staffing required*

It's a sad but accurate commentary on modern life that everybody's busy nowadays. Between work, business trips, shopping, meeting friends, managing schedules, and the 1,001 other details that people deal with every day, life often seems to fly by in a blur.

With all that going on, who's got time to plan a wedding and deal with florists, caterers, dressmakers, musicians, printers, limousine drivers, photographers, and everyone else involved with making wedding magic? The answer is: the wedding consultant.

For nothing more than a moderate fee, a wedding consultant will make all those problems go away for the prospective bride and groom. While the future Mr. and Mrs. count down toward the Big Day, a wedding consultant tackles the seemingly insurmountable mountain of detail that needs to be resolved before that day arrives. While the wedding consultant is down in the trenches, dealing with fussy florists and jaded caterers, the happy couple float blissfully above the fray.

Is it any wonder that more and more brides- and grooms-to-be are clamoring for the services of qualified wedding consultants . . . and that the wedding consultant field is booming as a result?

"People e-mail me through our website [all the time, saying]: 'I want to become a wedding consultant. How do I do that?' " says Rosanne Falduti, executive director of the National Association of Wedding Professionals, Inc. The association receives several calls a month inquiring about becoming a wedding consultant or planner.

Although it may seem as if the wedding consultant profession is relatively new, actually it has been around for some time. Its roots are in the field of event planning; once you've planned a major trade show and figured out the logistics of where and how to get a gigantic arch made out of 10,000 balloons, it's not too great a stretch to organize a beautiful wedding.

However, the field has become more prominent in recent years, due to several factors. One of these is the increasingly frantic pace of life. Many people can't even cook for themselves at the end of the day, let alone tackle a strategic nightmare like planning a wedding.

"Life has gotten so hectic," Falduti says. "People just want someone to come in and take over."

But even more critical to the burgeoning popularity of wedding consultants is the removal of mothers from the equation. Years ago, when the majority of women stayed at home, planning their daughter's wedding was the ultimate event in the life of many mothers.

Today, however, the typical mother-of-the-bride is more apt to be working or pursuing her own dreams and ambitions. With a mother's schedule often just as chaotic as her daughter's, it's easy to see why the client rosters of wedding planners are growing.

FLEXIBILITY IS KEY

A wedding planner must be versatile. He or she must be prepared to do whatever the client wants, from planning the entire wedding to just organizing a small part, such as the flowers or the photography. Wedding consultant Sue Totterdale offers several options to prospective clients.

"I have three packages," says Totterdale. The first is similar to a consultation, in which, for $45 per hour, she sits down with the client and points the way toward getting the proper vendors.

The second and most popular package is more inclusive. For $600, Totterdale recommends vendors, makes certain that everything is running on schedule, and ensures that the ceremony rehearsal, the rehearsal dinner, the reception, and other events all go smoothly.

The third package is the most inclusive and the most expensive. Totterdale handles every detail of the wedding, leaving the bride and groom little to do but show up on time and exchange their "I dos." She prices this service similar to a gratuity, charging 18 percent of the total cost of the affair. With the cost of an average wedding between $20,000 and $25,000, the fee generated by this third package can be substantial—particularly if the happy couple adds a tip, as often happens.

LOCATION, LOCATION, LOCATION

However, a word of caution before you run out and get your "wedding consultant" business cards printed: Not every part of the country is fertile territory for this type of business.

"Using a wedding planner is a demographic thing," Rosanne Falduti pointed out. "If the area can afford it, then they'll use it more than the areas that can't afford it."

Where you're located also affects the prices that you can charge. Totterdale says that if she lived in a more populous area, such as Miami, she could raise her rates to be comparable to what others in the area charge.

"You have to keep it [your rates] competitive," she says. "I found out that if you charge by the hour, or charge a percentage [of the total wedding], nobody will hire you. They want to have a fixed cost."

COOL UNDER PRESSURE

What qualities make a good wedding consultant? One of the most important qualifications is having a good, solid background in the hospitality industry, so that you can handle the logistical arrangements that a wedding requires. There are so many aspects to planning a wedding that a novice can't hope to know them all—and that's exactly what clients will be counting on you to provide.

Hospitality industry experience also gives you familiarity with vendors, and knowing which are reliable and which aren't is critical to the success of both your job performance and the wedding itself. Vendors are just as eager to please wedding consultants as they are the bride and groom, because they know that reputation is everything in the wedding business.

"They [the vendors] know that if they don't show up on time, if they're not ready on time, then I'll never use them again," Totterdale says.

A wedding consultant also has to be fast on her feet and be able to adapt to any situation without panicking or disturbing the ceremony that's going on around her. In a pinch, Totterdale has fashioned a bride's throw-away bouquet from individual flowers and a piece of ribbon when the florist forgot to provide one and also cooked nonstop for several days when a bride's mother forgot to get a caterer.

It goes without saying that a wedding consultant has to be a detail-oriented, organized person. You also have to be an even-tempered, "people person," someone who can get along with the diverse personalities of brides, grooms, mothers, mothers-in-law, vendors, clergy, and a hundred other people.

NETWORKING IS KEY

Networking skills are essential to succeeding as a wedding consultant. Business associates give you referrals and vice versa. Having a strong network within your local wedding industry can make or break your business. Just ask Sue Totterdale.

Before starting her own event planning/wedding consultant business, Totterdale and Co., in 1995, Totterdale was the executive catering director for a major hotel in her area. When the hotel expanded its activities into weddings, Totterdale gained both the experience and the contacts that helped her business thrive when she went out on her own.

By her own account, Totterdale has done over 800 weddings. Currently she handles about two dozen weddings per year, although she admits that if she pushed, her reputation is such that she certainly could take on more clients.

"This is a wonderful home-based business," Totterdale says. Although some consultants who combine weddings with other services, such as event planning, have an office, many others, like Totterdale, operate out of their home.

What makes the wedding consultant business even better is that it requires little in the way of special equipment, so start-up costs are low. A good computer is necessary, one with a color monitor, color printer, and powerful-enough modem to hasten Internet access and downloads (for all those color pictures of flower arrangements and cakes that the bride saw in some magazine). To facilitate customer communication, an e-mail account, cellular phone, and fax machine are also necessary.

Subscriptions to the major bridal magazines are also important to a wedding consultant, since brides-to-be read these publications and reference items they see in them. Additional start-up monies should be allocated for brochures, business cards, and other marketing expenses. Registering for and attending bridal trade shows is another necessary expense, because it gets your name out and your face known, and keeps you in touch with trends and new vendors.

So if you've got a hankering to get folks hitched, the wedding consultant business may be right up your "aisle-way."

Real Estate

Home Inspector

Job Description: *A home inspector examines residences to determine their condition and discover any problems before the structure is sold.*

- *Start-up cost as low as $25,000*
- *Potential first-year earnings: $50,000*
- *Breakeven time from initial investment: one year or longer*
- *Ideal home-based business*
- *No staffing required*

Consumer movements dug the foundations of the home inspection industry as home buyers rebelled against the *caveat emptor* creed. The framework went up as housing prices soared. "People don't give real estate away. Buyers can't afford to come up with another $2,000 or $10,000 if they find their roof leaks," says Ronald Passaro. When he started Res-I-Tec Inc., a Redding, Connecticut–based home inspection service 20 years ago, "only myself and one other guy were doing inspections in Connecticut. Now there must be 40 or 60 companies."

Lending institutions contributed the bricks and mortar to the home inspection industry as they began requiring house inspections before they would grant mortgages. Simultaneously, states began enacting laws requiring sellers to disclose what was wrong with their properties, so sellers began calling on inspectors, too. "Inspector reports became a negotiating tool on the price of housing," says Kenneth Austin, president of HouseMaster of America, a Bound Brook, New Jersey, franchisor of home inspections services. If an inspection indicated that the heat pump was gasping its last, the seller might be persuaded to knock off a few thousand.

BOOM TIMES—FOR A FEW

According to one source, there are approximately 168,000 licensed real estate agents in the United States. Compare that to the 3,900 real estate inspectors, and you can see that there is a major need for inspectors.

"If you go by the names of new inspectors in the phone books, the industry doubles each year," says Ron Passaro. "But a lot of part-timers drop out when they realize inspectors are liable if they make a mistake." Regardless of the swinging door syndrome, opportunities in the home inspection field are huge. According to *Entrepreneur* magazine, ten years ago home inspectors were involved in around 10 percent of home sales. Today, however, they affect between 40 and 50 percent, and the figure is expected to double over the next five years. While inspections are a standard part of any real estate deal in some parts of the country, other areas are just now catching on.

Just as the potential liability holds down start-ups (be sure to factor insurance into your start-up costs), so does know-how. Several universities have designed courses with the guidance of the American Society of Home Inspectors. But most inspectors have taught themselves. And they need to know everything from how to evaluate a home's structural soundness to how to identify strengths and weaknesses of swimming pools and kitchen appliances. A working knowledge of plumbing and electrical wiring is fundamental. Passaro hires only registered architects, engineers, or people with a building background as inspectors. Even then, Res-I-Tec puts them through a 13-week formal course before letting them tackle solo inspections.

HouseMaster of America has similar requirements before accepting inspectors into its 54-hour course. But you don't have to know a HVAC from a min-vac to spend an average $20,000 for a HouseMaster franchise. "We really prefer a marketing background—someone who can sell the service," says Ken Austin, noting that you can hire and train qualified inspectors to check out plumbing and evaluate septic systems. Because the inspector you hire keeps only about 25 percent of an average $200 inspection, an owner who also sells the service should net at least that much after paying for overhead on a modest office.

HOME-BASED OFFICES

Many inspectors hold start-up costs down by beginning either from home offices or as divisions of established companies connected with home repairs. (However, the American Society for Home Inspectors frowns on inspectors who make repairs, saying an inspector who benefits from a report could face conflicts of interest.) If you opt for an office, you don't have to spend much on decor or location. "This isn't a walk-in business," says Ken Austin. "Home inspections are ordered over the phone so no fancy office is required."

Even in the beginning, unless you and your partner or spouse plan to handle all the tasks, you'd better allot some start-up cash as salary for at least one other person. HouseMaster recommends three bodies: one to sell, one to inspect, and one to manage the paperwork back at the office. (Each inspection requires a professionally typed report.)

Real growth comes as you add employees. You can perform a home inspection only during daylight hours. And since each inspection takes two to three hours—not counting travel time— even a high-energy individual can't inspect more than three houses a day. If you can line up enough jobs, a solo practitioner can bring home $70,000 or so, leaving some time to market services.

To outgrow that home office, you'll need to drum up business, which is where a marketing background comes in handy. A few inspectors advertise directly to the public on cable TV and in newspapers. But that's an expensive, scattershot way to peddle to the small audience who plans to buy a home. Instead, most inspectors build relationships with real estate professionals. Call on Realtors, corporate relocation departments, attorneys, and lenders. "Let them know you're there," says Ron Passaro. Some inspectors graduate to commercial properties as well.

Expect some big changes in home inspections during the 21st century. "Several states are looking at licensing," says Passaro. "If they give anyone a license who sends in $1, that could destroy the industry." He points out the potential room for abuses by incompetent or unscrupulous inspectors. A slipshod inspection is little better than no inspection at all. "But if

licenses require education and set ethical standards, it could enhance the industry," by winnowing out the unfit and enticing
more home buyers to spring for an inspection.

SOURCES

Industry Associations

American Society of Home Inspectors, 932 Lee Street, Suite
   101, Des Plaines, IL 60016-6546, (800) 248-2744
International Society of Home Inspectors, 141 Robert E. Lee
   Boulevard, Suite 262, New Orleans, LA 70124, (888) 921-
   4744

Manufactured Housing Contractor

Job Description: *A manufactured housing contractor builds homes that are constructed at a factory and then placed together at a site, rather than building at the site from the ground up.*

- *Start-up cost as low as $12,000*
- *Potential first-year earnings: $300,000*
- *Breakeven time from initial investment: from several months to two years*
- *No staffing required*

People tell the story of hairdresser Harold and his brother Ronald, a computer programmer, who inherited two acres of undeveloped land. Rather than sell the parcel for a fast buck, they decided to develop it themselves.

Neither brother had a construction background, but Harold had bought a modular home the previous year. He had watched his dealer truck in the two segments and lift each by crane onto the foundation he had hired a subcontractor to build. The dealer's crew had joined the sections together and waterproofed the roof, all before the sun went down. "I saw no reason we couldn't do the same thing—buy factory-built modules and hire experts to add the 10 percent of essentials that don't come from the factory, like the foundations, plumbing, and electrical work," says Harold. The fifth bank the brothers approached agreed, giving them 75 percent financing, collateralized by the valuable land, on the $500,000 construction loan. By the end of their first year in business, the ten townhouses they ordered from a New Hampshire factory had each sold at around $100,000. The brothers figure they pocketed $200,000 above the price they were offered just for the land. "We used the money to buy more land in the next county, where we're doing it all over again," says Harold, now president of H & R Bros. Homes Inc.

The modular concept that is making the brothers' fortunes consists of fully constructed sections of houses, complete down to the wallpaper and light fixtures. According to the National Association of Home Builders, in 1996, 37,000 modular homes were produced. The association added that "forecasters see the modular housing industry continuing to increase its market share." Additional statistical support for the manufactured home industry comes from the U.S. Census Bureau, which reported that in 1998, "manufactured home shipments represented 22.7 percent of all new single-family housing starts and 29.6 percent of all new single-family homes sold."

WHY BUILDERS LIKE MODULARS

Sales of modular housing spurted ahead in the Northeast when interest rates began falling seven years ago. "When the market sprang back, contractors discovered that anybody who could tape drywall had gone to Houston to work," says Shepard

Robinson, publisher of *Manufactured Housing Newsletter*. "With no skilled labor to be found, developers turned to factory work."

Modular housing appeals to both the building community and consumers. "Contractors don't have to buy $10,000 in lumber with no home buyer in the wings. You can wait until you have a customer," explains Robinson. Factories that construct modulars in the quality-controlled atmosphere of a manufacturing plant also eliminate traditional building problems such as on-site vandalism and weather delays. For the most part, factory labor is less expensive than construction crews, so employee costs are lower.

You can build on speculation, like the Harold and Ronald, or you can operate as a dealer. Speculating requires a higher initial capital investment since you must purchase the land and modules and subcontract site-work. Dealers invest less—maybe $50,000 to $150,000 in a model home or two to show customers what they are buying. But if you are lucky enough to line up a buyer on the basis of brochures, you can start in the business with just enough cash to hire a crane crew to put the module in place and a finishing crew to join the modules together.

Here's how dealers work: "We take a $2,000 to $3,000 deposit from a customer and give the whole thing to the factory," explains Bob Brann, president of Shoreline Modular Homes Inc. in Madison, Connecticut. Shoreline pays the factory in full when it ships the home four to eight weeks after the order is placed. The dealer either employs or subcontracts with a crew that lifts the house onto the foundation supplied by Shoreline. Another crew spends a few hours joining the modules. At that point, the customer's mortgage kicks in, and Shoreline receives its cash immediately. "It's almost a cash business," says Brann.

WHY HOMEOWNERS BUY MODULARS

Customers like modular homes because they arrive months faster than a home built to order and because "brick for brick, a modular home costs 25 percent less than traditional construction," says Bob Brann. A typical modular sells in the $50,000 range; transportation costs, site preparation, finishing fees, and land costs might bring the homeowner's ultimate cost to $100,000. By contrast, an average site-built home runs around $140,000.

Modular home sales do not swing as wildly as do traditional home starts. "When interest rates reach 20 percent, sales drop, but not as fast as the rest of the home building industry," says Brann. "People who would buy site-built homes save 25 percent on construction by coming to us, so they can afford a home by going modular. We get a larger share of the market, and they buy bigger houses."

Shoreline sells "every kind of home, up to 3,000, 4,000 square feet," continues Brann. "Contemporary, traditional." Highway laws allow transportation of modules up to 14 feet wide and 60 feet long. Bob figures a two-story colonial might cost $35 a square foot, or a total price of $81,000 (plus foundation and land costs).

CATHEDRAL CEILINGS
AND GREENHOUSES

Today's modulars are indistinguishable from site-built versions. Deluxe Homes of Berwyck, Pennsylvania, Shoreline's supplier, offers a dozen pages of options on its single-family homes, ranging from whirlpool tubs to cathedral ceilings with skylights. "To satisfy a real custom market, we'll add a $3,000 greenhouse available locally," says Bob Brann. "We just tell the factory where to put the opening and we add it on-site."

Brann sells about a third of Shoreline's 200 modular homes each year to developers, who buy for speculation. One customer specializes in whole developments containing 20 to 50 modular homes. The developers deal through Shoreline rather than directly with the factory to avoid the headaches of erecting the modules. However, most manufacturers will either subcontract an erection crew or recommend a local crane operator. "Builder markups are whatever the market will bear," says Brann. "We've sold houses for $100,000 that the developer turns around and sells for $200,000 or $300,000 after they add the lot. Most look for a 10 percent return."

Shoreline, which collected pretax profits of around $500,000 on revenues of $10 million, scatters its houses from Delaware to Rhode Island, although its six model-home sites are all in Connecticut. Bob Brann says the only constraint is the lot size and configuration, and Shoreline has gone to interesting lengths to accommodate location. "Modules are heavy," says Brann, "so we've reinforced some bridges to bring them across. Once we lifted a module over an existing apartment building." He recalls a customer who was quoted $500,000 to build the home he wanted on Block Island, Rhode Island. "He spent about $100,000 on our package, plus another $3,800 to rent a barge for a house that's probably worth a half-million in that market," says Brann.

If you're selling a completely erected modular home, advertise the same way you would for a traditionally built model: in the classifieds and through real estate brokers. It's a little trickier if you're lining up buyers for homes still at the factory. Shoreline spends $4,000 every year (not counting the cost of the home) to put up an entire house at the New Haven Home Show. "It's expensive PR, but we get a lot of sales over the course of the year," says Brann. When the four-day show ends, Shoreline dismantles and reassembles the house elsewhere either as a model or as a completed home with a for-sale sign in its front yard.

Modules offer applications in the commercial market as well as in the residential. Northeastern cities have purchased modulars as low-income housing projects. And Salt Lake City built a gymnasium and surrounded it with a dozen 60-foot-long modules and called it a school. "Modules built the school in half the time," says James Birdsong of the Home Manufacturing Council. "Also, if the population shifts, they can transport the school to a new site."

In addition to single-family homes, Shoreline offers duplexes, townhouses, and apartment flats that can be stacked in all sorts of configurations. "You could join together 400 units, or a dozen here, then add a space, and join another dozen," says Bob Brann, who lives in half of a manufactured duplex and rents out the other half. "People are just starting to see the potential for modulars."

SOURCES

Industry Associations

The Building Systems Council of the National Association of Home Builders, 1201 15th Street, N.W., Washington, DC 20005, (202) 822-0200, (800) 368-5242

Manufactured Housing Institute, 2101 Wilson Boulevard, Suite 610, Arlington, VA 22201-3062, (703) 558-0400

Real Estate Agent

Job Description: *A real estate agent sells homes, commercial establishments, and other types of structures.*
- *Start-up cost as low as $4,000*
- *Potential first-year earnings: $20,000*
- *Breakeven time from initial investment: six months to one year*
- *No staffing required*

When you bought that colonial last year, one of two thoughts undoubtedly crossed your mind. Either "I'm sure glad that's over!" or "That was an exciting experience. . . . It might be interesting to be a real estate agent."

You're not alone in wanting to enter an industry so tied to the American dream of owning one's own home. The National Association of Realtors counts approximately 1 million real estate agents. These agents have their hands more than full, thanks to a robust economy and low interest rates that have fueled the housing market to explosive new levels. In June 1998, according to the federal government, sales of new homes climbed 3.8 percent to a record 935,000-unit annual rate. This was the fastest pace since record keeping began in 1963, said the Commerce Department. While observers expect sales of commercial properties to suffer during the next few years because of tax law changes, real estate agents expect home sales to remain strong. Regardless of what interest rates do, "we still see a strong demand for housing," says Elizabeth Duncan, director of media relations at the National Association of Realtors. "Households are still being formed and they need a place to live."

A TWO-YEAR RUNWAY

Because real estate is a regulated industry, the entry path is well marked. Although exact requirements differ depending on the state where you practice, you must follow three steps to open your own brokerage firm:

- Licensing. Community colleges and universities offer evening or night courses to prepare you in several weeks or months to take your state's test, which leads to a license.
- Apprenticeship. After you get a license, you sign on as a salesperson with an established broker for two years or so, a step most states require. During your training, you learn what the schools don't even attempt to teach you, so choose your mentor carefully. Not only should you look for an agency with abundant listings so you can make a living while you learn the ropes, you also should ask about benefits such as in-house training programs. "Most agents are independent contractors who set their own hours and are their own bosses—under a broker's guidance," explains John Major, a

- Coeur d'Alene, Idaho, broker. Agents get paid on commission, so put aside some money for groceries, rent, and so on to tide you over until your first sale. While commissions differ depending on the sale price of the house and the amount of advertising the client requests, residential commissions average 6 percent.
- Brokerage. Many agents never take this step, but if you want your own office, you'll probably be ready to become a real estate broker after a couple of years of apprenticeship. The state licensing board looks at your performance record—the number of listings you've handled and the sales you've closed—and may set requirements for continuing education. Now you can hang your own shingle and hire other sales agents if you wish. You can opt for a simple, one-person office or a computerized, multiperson franchise. (Currently about 18 percent of all agencies are franchised.)

If you want to offer elaborate enticements to bring in buyers, such as Video listings and limousine tours, factor those costs into the start-up budget. You also may want to set aside money to design a website and advertise your own agency, as well as the houses you sell. Many brokers routinely distribute newsletters or flyers to homes in their territory in hopes of someday picking up the sale when the owners decide to move.

People make fortunes by building large real estate brokerages. But according to the Department of Labor's 1998 *Occupational Outlook Handbook,* the average salary of a full-time real estate agent was $31,500 in 1996. The middle 50 percent of agents earned between $20,500 and $49,700. The top 10 percent earned more than $75,400, and the lowest 10 percent earned less than $12,600.

Technology is also affecting the real estate profession,

particularly in the area of start-up costs. Whereas the cost of opening a one-person agency might have been as little as $1,000 a decade ago, today's beginner is likely to spend about $4,000. Why? Because besides the usual office equipment, experts advocate that first-timers get a digital camera, computer, cell phone, e-mail account, and website, as well.

According to those who generate salaries way above the norm, the best brokers have three things going for them: product knowledge, a willingness to hustle, and an inborn sales ability.

KNOW YOUR BUSINESS

Product knowledge boils down to understanding your market, the particular ranch or split-level you represent, and, perhaps most important, the financing climate.

The albatross hanging around the neck of every real estate agent is interest rates. Even when money is plentiful and consumers can borrow at reasonable rates, today's real estate agent must understand the thousand-and-one financing techniques available. Those who don't risk attracting home buyers who can't find the money to buy a home. But if you're savvy, you may be able to steer buyers into financing packages that will let them buy even in difficult times. For example, you might explain the benefits of seller financing to a couple who could afford to accept monthly installments on the sale of their home.

"Agents don't just talk the financial lingo but actually act as a go-between between the lender and buyer," says Elizabeth Duncan. "The agent has to understand the implications of a mortgage. Would a couple be better off with a 15-year mortgage that they can pay off faster with a lower interest rate? Or would lower payments over 30 years be better?" Bone up on current financing by talking with area bankers and even take courses if necessary. Most large franchisors provide continuing classes in financing techniques.

"A smart real estate agent may not know every financial structure available," admits John Major, "but knows where to look to find financing." He says good agents in his small Idaho town keep in touch with up to ten lending institutions. "I've seen agents fail because they make only one phone call to a banker who won't lend to the customer. Then they just give up without calling more banks. There are lots of reasons why banks won't loan money, so you have to know everything about the bank and about your client." For example, some banks shy away from commercial loans, and the client may want to turn that quaint Victorian into a restaurant. Or possibly the client forgot to tell you he is unemployed, so meeting the monthly mortgage may be iffy.

Lenders will jump at the opportunity to talk with you, either in their offices or in yours. "After all," says Major, "the bank is in the business of lending money." A chat every six months suffices in stable periods, but you'll have to gauge the current financing climate.

HUSTLING

Next comes a willingness to devote time and energy to your practice. Not only must you unload your current listings in the least time possible, but you also must line up a steady stream of new clients. You must be visible: An attractive office on Main Street will draw more buyers and sellers than a dilapidated back-alley storefront. Check with the local government to see the ratio of realty offices to houses before setting your sights on a particular site.

Once you're established, don't wait for clients to sniff you out. Call and write area homeowners to offer free appraisals. Send postcards to everyone within a six-block radius when you get a listing. Even if they're not in the market to sell this month, that family with the Cape Cod may remember you when the time comes.

EMPATHY

Finally, those who succeed in the real estate business display a natural affinity for buyers and sellers. If you have sold cars or insurance or dresses, you have a leg up in the real estate business. Although a home is the biggest purchase most consumers ever make, "sales is sales," insists John Major.

In addition to uncertainties about the flow of credit, a few other outside forces rock the real estate business from time to time, so an even disposition and a supply of Rolaids make life easier. Notably, even in the best of times, the industry is seasonal. "We do a tremendous business in the spring and summer when everything's beautiful," says Major. "But we only sell to skiers in the winter."

The best agents make the most of drawbacks, planning winter vacations or using slack times to take—or give—courses in various real estate activities. For example, some states require a different license to sell industrial or commercial property as a major part of your business.

While anyone in realty decries the notoriously cyclical nature of housing, Major insists the business isn't much worse than others. "Housing fluctuates to the economic pitch of the nation. When everything else is down, so is housing. But there's always a market, even in economic downturns.

"Consider the supply-demand factor," he continues. "There will never be any more land created than what we have now. But everyday, more babies are born. New families are created. They all need housing."

SOURCES

Industry Associations

National Association of Realtors, 430 North Michigan Avenue, Chicago, IL 60611, (312) 329-8200

National Association of Real Estate Brokers, 1629 K Street, N.W., Washington, DC 20006, (202) 785-4477

National Association of Residential Property Managers, 6300 Dutchmans Parkway, Louisville, KY 40205, (800) 782-3452

Real Estate Appraiser

Job Description: *A real estate appraiser determines the value of property and structures for various reasons including mortgages, foreclosures, and tax assessments.*

- *Start-up cost as low as $7,000*
- *Potential first-year earnings: $75,000*
- *Breakeven time from initial investment: rapid (three months to one year)*
- *Ideal home-based business*
- *No staffing required*

W e're really real estate detectives," says Robert H. Heffernan, founder of Professional Appraisal Associates, in explaining what an appraiser does for a living. "We use our knowledge of the market to determine what a particular piece of property is worth."

Heffernan's list of customer types runs the gamut. For example, properties must be assessed for:

- Banks, every time they grant a mortgage or foreclose on a home loan
- Lawyers, when they distribute an estate or represent clients in a marriage or business partnership breakup where the couple must divide real estate
- Individuals, who want an uninterested party to tell them the true value of a home before they buy or sell, or before they contest real estate taxes
- The government, each time it condemns property or re-assesses taxes
- Insurance carriers, before they agree to property-damage settlements

"Some appraisers specialize in one segment, or take just residential or commercial properties," says Heffernan. "But we wanted a large base to cover the market fluctuations that occur in real estate. Residential may slow down while commercial sales are still strong. Or banks that don't grant as many mortgages when interest rates go up may foreclose on more properties." Heffernan's strategy works. In less than a decade, Professional Appraisal Associates has grown to one of the largest services in the Northeast with 25 appraisers and 7 secretaries.

In general, however, the real estate appraisal field is expected to grow about as fast as the average for all occupations through 2006, according to the Department of Labor's 1998 *Occupational Outlook Handbook*. As with real estate agents, full-time appraisers averaged $31,500 in income in 1996.

THE ART AND THE SCIENCE

There's a whole method to the madness of pricing real estate that goes way beyond looking up prices in the classifieds. Some standard industry approaches are as follows:

1. The Cost Approach (or, count all those nickels and dimes). First you count all the individual components of a property, including what was originally paid for the land as well as the sticks and the bricks. You don't have to be an engineer since you don't inspect for construction flaws. (To learn more about inspection, see "Home Inspector," page 493.) But you do need a rudimentary knowledge of construction prices. Next, assume what it would cost to build today. Then you subtract the depreciation since the land was bought and the building was constructed. Voilà—the cost of the property.

2. The Market Data Approach (a/k/a checking out the Joneses). Look for sales within the community that compare with the real estate under scrutiny. Of course, you must add any appreciation or depreciation that has taken place since the comparison property sold. Then you adjust for differences in size, quality of construction, and location within the community. (An ice cream stand on the corner of Main and Second streets would go for more than one in the middle of the block.)

3. The Income Approach (or, how much cash can this cow generate?). This approach assumes the owner might want to rent out. You find what similar houses or storefronts lease for as well as what improvements other landlords make to attract renters. That guideline suggests what your client might make as net income prior to mortgage payments.

Of course, if no income-producing properties exist in the area, appraisers don't bother with this last approach. Otherwise, they are expected to use all three techniques to arrive at a fair market value.

Since every deed is recorded at the courthouse, all you have to do is find a property roughly equivalent to the three-bedroom, two-bath townhouse you're assessing. Then you assume your client's property is worth about the same, right? Wrong. "Identifying sales is easy," says Bob Heffernan. "Determining the reasons why a property sold for what it did is the difficult part." For example, sellers who allow buyers to space out payments on installment plans likely ask for more than sellers who make a lump-sum sale. Or, say negotiations for an industrial plant stretched over two years; the deed may read one year, when the purchase price was actually agreed upon two years earlier.

The only way to dig up such clues is through detective work—typically talking to the buyer and seller or the attorneys and real estate brokers involved in the sale. "People wonder why we get our fees," says Heffernan. "They pay for our judgment and ability to track down meaningful numbers."

LEVERAGE

Once you pin down an assessment, you can use the figures to help you assess other, similar properties—within a reasonable time period. Most lenders require residential property comparisons no older than six months, although commercial figures stay current for as long as a couple of years. But if you have to assess two homes roughly equivalent in size and value, you need do the homework only once. Such an economy-of-scale assessment of many similar properties can cut down on how much time you spend following paper trails.

Bob Heffernan says Professional Appraisal Associates takes between four and eight hours to assess an average residence. If he's doing the assessment for a bank that supplies much of the backup information and provides a fill-in-the-blank—type form, he charges between $150 and $300, depending on the difficulty of the assessment; a homeowner who wants a written narrative likely pays $400 to $450.

Appraisals for commercial real estate can take much longer than those for residences, depending on the size of the property and the number of tenants. "A typical northeastern commercial property would run $2,000 to $5,000," says Heffernan, "but I've seen them up to $40,000."

Although few appraisers charge strictly by the hour, most figure a top-of-the-profession appraiser makes $100 to $125 an hour, while a less experienced junior staffer commands $50 or so.

Generally, the most successful practices fall into two categories: solo appraisers with no overhead, and large (15 to 30 people) firms. It's those in-between firms that have the most difficulty meeting expenses, because they have overhead but no economies of scale. "A 3-person operation needs as much data as a 100-person firm," says Heffernan. "It is inefficient to run."

Let's look first at a one-person start-up. You can easily operate from a spare bedroom equipped with a telephone. You'll need a tape measure to count off feet and a camera to record the general look of a property. The family car can provide transportation. If you type your reports, buy a computer with word processing software; an alternative is to contract with a part-time typist. A Yellow Pages listing catches the eyes of individuals who need appraisals. Also, you may advertise with tasteful announcements in professional bank and legal journals. With such low overhead, approximately 75 percent of your gross—which might reach $70,000 annually—equals profits.

WHEN IT'S TIME TO GROW

Once you add a partner or a second appraiser, you'll probably need office space and a full-time secretary. "We figure half of the fees we charge goes to salaries, both secretaries and appraisers," says Bob Heffernan. "Overhead—cars, insurance, supplies, rent—leaves profits anywhere from nothing to 25 percent." Grow as fast as you can, because the smaller firms may have to struggle at the lower profit ranges until they can add enough associates to achieve those economies. Marketing becomes a crucial part of your strategy, as you need to attract more clients if you are to add appraisers.

Also: You need to hone your detective techniques. For example, instead of wading through court documents to find comparison properties, establish contact with real estate agents who will let you peruse their files. Many outfits join county real estate organizations that often provide regularly updated sale prices and descriptions of properties.

Some appraisers migrate into real estate brokering, although others consider this a conflict of interest. But nothing says you can't put some of your profits into real estate investment and even development of properties. After all, considering the homework you've done, who knows a community's real estate needs better than you?

SOURCES

Industry Associations

American Society of Appraisers, 555 Herndon Parkway, Suite 125, Herndon, VA 20170, (703) 478-2228

Appraisal Institute, 875 North Michigan Avenue, Suite 200, Chicago, IL 60611-1980, (312) 335-4100

The Foundation of Real Estate Appraisers, 4907 Morena Boulevard, Suite 1405, San Diego, CA 92117, (800) 882-4410

Real Estate Auctioneer

Job Description: *A real estate auctioneer sells property at auctions for banks and other agencies such as the federal government.*
- *Start-up investment as low as $500*
- *Potential first-year earnings: $100,000*
- *Breakeven time from initial investment: extremely rapid (immediately to six months)*
- *Ideal home-based business*
- *No staffing required*

L arry Latham's construction business was being suffocated by 20 percent interest rates. He was a couple hundred thousand dollars in debt when he heard a stranger talking about how he made $300,000 in a single day, auctioning off dock property for the City of New Orleans.

The banks were in as much trouble as Larry. They'd foreclosed on home mortgages and were stuck with property they couldn't sell. So Latham, who had kept his broker's license and knew the real estate business as well as anybody, figured he had some potential partners to launch him into the real estate auction business, whether they knew it or not. He approached the very banks that held his six-figure IOUs. "I said, 'I know you've got real estate you'd like to sell. I can sell it for you real fast. All you have to do up front is give me $1,000 per house for advertising.'

"I guess the banks wanted to give me a chance to get out of debt so I could pay them back," Latham muses. Anyway, they turned the advertising money over and authorized him to show the houses. Sure enough, during the next year, Latham auctioned off 28 houses that the banks had been unable to unload. He received a 10 percent commission on each house, which ranged in price from $12,000 to $60,000.

Armed with his new track record, Latham graduated from knocking on the doors of bankers he knew, to doors of unfamiliar financial institutions. Then he let the government know he could get rid of the property it had collected in lieu of taxes. "That first year I sold a half-million dollars worth of houses," says the entrepreneur. A decade later Larry Latham Auctioneers still operates from tiny Moulton, Alabama—as well as from 14 branch offices scattered from Washington, D.C., to Los Angeles. Annual listings amount to a quarter-billion dollars. Of that, Larry Latham Auctioneers lands commissions of between 6 and 10 percent (about $15 million), compared with average commissions of 6 to 7 percent that real estate brokers command. The auction industry gets higher fees because property is sold faster.

LOW OVERHEAD— HIGH POTENTIAL

Unlike art or antique auctioneering, which requires a facility where you can store and display your inventory, real estate auctioneering demands little overhead—unless you grow to Larry Latham's scale. (For a look at auction houses, which sell everything from comic strip illustrations to the Duchess of Windsor's jewelry, see "Auction House Dealer," page 595.) You won't accumulate as much as a two-by-four in inventory. Somebody else fronts the advertising costs, and you can start as a part-time, solo auctioneer operating out of your own home and car.

Is it lucrative? Because you often auction estates (as well as the house itself), which consists of a person's entire worldly possessions, says Dick Dewees, who runs the Missouri Auction School in Kansas City, "you can get a percentage of the average person's life savings in a day or a week. Next week you can sell another estate. You can make as much as an average person saves in a lifetime in a year."

All an auctioneer has to do is bring in the sellers and let them fight each other like bargain hunters at a going-out-of-business sale. "Americans are the most competitive people in the world," says Larry Latham. "All you do is create a market by telling the public you're going to sell to the highest bidder."

Auctioneers admit that some real estate goes for less than the owners would like. But they also insist other properties command premiums. Individuals decide to auction their houses because it's fast—and they gamble it might be more profitable. Auctions are to traditional real estate listings what Seattle Slew is to the old gray mare: fast. "Auctions create an urgency," says Latham. "Sometimes people won't buy a house on the market, hoping the price will go down. But once it's on the auction block, somebody else will buy it if you don't." While a real estate broker may advertise a home every week and still not sell it for months, an auction company advertises it once or twice, holds an auction, and somebody walks off with the deed.

Larry Latham scoffs at the notion of competition. "Business

will grow at 100 percent a year for the next five to ten years," he says. "We honestly cannot keep up with the demand—we turn down three out of five properties. The smaller guys pick up some of them, but they get too busy to handle the overflow."

Real estate auctions, whether for a $10,000 vacant lot or $10 million estate, follow the same basic eight steps. You

1. Round up some real estate
2. Advertise
3. Show the property at the set time
4. Legitimize the property (verify the facts)
5. Arrange financing (optional)
6. Host the big day
7. Close on each sale
8. Get your commission

STEP 1: FINDING THE MERCHANDISE

If you're selling the Taj Mahal, you'll generate enough interest and commission to base the entire auction around that single piece of property. Otherwise, plan to bundle anywhere from a handful to a few hundred smaller sales together. Contact banks and other property holders that have houses, farms, or commercial or industrial property to sell. You can even go to real estate brokers and offer them a listing fee for turning a house over to you. Larry Latham signs four-year contracts with groups such as the Department of Housing and Urban Development (HUD) to auction blocks of houses monthly in different sections of the country.

Almost all real estate auctioneers operate on consignment,

meaning you sell somebody else's property without ever taking title. However, occasionally an auctioneer willing to tie up a few dollars for a few days can gamble. "I've seen guys buy a plant the board of directors was afraid to auction," says Dick Dewees. "They pay $1.2 million and the auction company sells the plant and the equipment in pieces for $1.5 million."

Unless you state that an auction is "absolute," the sale is at the owner's reserve, meaning the owner can refuse the winning bid as too low. "Any decent auctioneer wants everything sold at absolute auction and asks for that," says Dewees, who calls minimums "pure foolishness. Properties bring 10 to 15 percent less if bidders know the owner can refuse their bid." He says serious bidders will not invest the time to really scout out properties—for example, bring in an engineer to inspect a house ahead of time—if they know it might not sell at the price they're willing to pay. Therefore, they bid low, guessing they may have to invest more in after-purchase improvements.

STEP 2: FINDING THE BIDDERS

In order to push prices high, you must create a critical mass of buyers, all anxious to outbid each other. Instead of placing a one-inch ad buried in Sunday's paper, you "blast with a big ad," says Dick Dewees. In that ad, you list your properties, their addresses, the open-house times for prospective buyers, and the time and place of the auction. You also explain extra information, such as whether financing is available (and from whom) and what buyers must do to qualify.

Some auctioneers also advertise on radio and TV, or with direct mail and telemarketing. If Larry Latham thinks a property is ripe for development, he sends brochures to lists of real estate investors. For residential properties, he mails to people already living in the area. "We figure they know friends or family they'd like to locate in the same neighborhood," he explains. For the most part, the sellers pay for the advertising up front.

STEP 3: SHOWING OFF

If the property is unoccupied, the auction company usually shows it at the advertised open house. If the seller still lives in the house, the owner hosts potential bidders. Many auctioneers print brochures describing each home (3 bedroom, 1½ bath, 2-car garage on ½ acre. Special features: skylights and Jacuzzi). Bidders use the open house to assess what they think the property is worth and often visit several listings.

STEP 4: TYING LOOSE ENDS

This step is where that intangible—expertise—comes in. If you sell real estate, you must be familiar with the market in general as well as that particular home. In the period between taking the listing and the auction, you also check out titles to ensure the house is truly free to be sold. Your reputation depends on verifying the facts. If you advertise a factory at 108,742 square feet, it had better be 108,742 square feet and zoned for industrial usage, or you can be sued for misrepresentation.

Larry Latham has enough business to be choosy. He refuses auctions in deeply depressed real estate markets, for example. While the dips may not be as treacherous as in traditional real estate sales, auctions still suffer the cyclical peaks and valleys other real estate experiences. "Also, if you take a property built over a toxic waste site, it reflects on you. I wouldn't touch it, even if the seller is willing to take 50 cents on the dollar. They should be negotiating the problems in a private sale, whereas we would advertise those problems to the public and ruin the market."

STEP 5: FINANCING

Lining up financing is an optional step, but Larry Latham says it pays off. You get commissions faster if banks are eager to participate and buyers don't renege if they drop a down payment at the time of the auction. Latham calls on banks or savings and loans and tells them of the blocks of houses he auctions on a particular day. His ads and brochures specify which institutions will finance and at what rate. Latham's auctions require anyone attending to bring a cashier's check. This tactic assures that the auctions will be full of bidders rather than the merely curious.

STEP 6: THE AUCTION

Depending on how many bidders you expect, you rent a hall, which could be a hotel room, convention site, or the municipal auditorium. Auctions of large estates are held on the property. When Larry Latham expects 1,000 bidders to bid on 100 properties, he might employ 3 or 4 auctioneers and 10 "ringmen," or individuals walking the floor to catch bids. In addition, a dozen people working the desk register bidders, making sure each has a cashier's check.

To auction real estate, you must be a licensed broker. (See "Real Estate Agent," page 505, for how to become a broker.)

Some states also require an auctioneer's license. (See "Auction House Dealer," page 595.) If you don't call the auction yourself, you can hire auctioneers who receive either a flat fee or a percent of each sale.

STEP 7: WRAPPING IT UP

After the auction is over, Larry Latham leaves a skeleton crew of three or four people to work with the buyers' lawyers to close each sale. This step may stretch over six weeks as buyers and lenders get together. Except to sign papers, the seller never has to appear.

STEP 8: MONEY

As soon as the buyer takes title, you get your commission check from the seller. Commissions vary depending on:

- The local real estate market (you usually do a point or two better than brokers in a given area)
- The price of the property (a $10 million ranch sale often carries a lower percentage but higher absolute fee than a $50,000 house)
- Deals you make with the seller (for example, Larry Latham takes a smaller commission to auction 300 houses for a single client than he does for selling 100 houses)

From that commission, you reimburse yourself for the cost of renting the auction hall and personnel salaries. For small auctions that you call yourself on the premises being sold, overhead may be zilch. "If I didn't have the overhead of 40 employees and 14 offices," says Larry, "I'd try to sell seven houses a week. If they average $50,000, I've made $35,000 at the end of that week."

Instead, Larry Latham Auctioneers concentrates on volume. Dick Dewees recalls a Phoenix auction he and his son, also a certified auctioneer, called for 112 of Larry's houses. "A thousand people showed up and the fire marshall wouldn't let anybody else in the municipal auditorium, so another 2,000 people stood outside on the steps. These were the same houses that brokers had listed for two, three years, mind you."

Dewees zeroes in on a particular Phoenix property: "I remember one house we auctioned for $120,000. The developer who originally built it a few years before couldn't believe it, because he was selling brand-new ones with identical floorplans and new microwaves and air conditioners for $117,000. He wanted to know who made the runner-up bid of $119,000 so he could sell a new house to that person."

Dewees says timing is crucial in an auction, because you need as many bidders as possible to create competition. "If you sell residential property, you want a weekend or evening sale so both the husband and wife come. If it's a commercial sale, you auction during the week because businesspeople go to the lake on the weekend. Mondays aren't good, though, because businesspeople want to go through the weekend mail and get the crew started. If you think an investor might buy a property, you sell on Wednesday or Thursday. That's the doctor's day off, and doctors have more disposable income than any other group." Finally, says Dewees, "in the State of Oklahoma, the cardinal rule is you never ever have a Saturday afternoon auction during football season."

What happens if it rains? "That's great," says Dewees. "Farm bidders can't get into the field to plow. The guys who usually go to the lake would just as soon be indoors."

Real estate auctioneers say almost any property that two or more people want to buy makes good auction material. Half of Larry Latham's sales are residential, 20 percent are farms and ranches, and the rest are commercial properties. "We do $10,000 houses and $200,000 houses," says Latham. But the splashiest auctions are the really big multimillion-dollar deals. Take, for example, the Big Sky Movie Ranch in Simi Valley, California.

Backed with a $420,000 advertising budget provided by the Getty estate, which owned the ranch, Larry Latham Auctioneers began marketing the 7,000-acre ranch, primarily to foreign investors, four months before the June auction. The *Los Angeles Times*, *USA Today*, and the *Wall Street Journal* all carried front-page stories on the sale of the Movie Ranch, which hosted filming of such television shows as *Gunsmoke* and *Little House on the Prairie*. In May, 3,000 people paid $5 a head to attend a barbecue there, proceeds going to the YMCA. The publicity created excitement and didn't hurt Larry Latham's reputation as an auctioneer *extraordinaire*, either.

Come the big day, two dozen people bid on the ranch, which was divided into four parcels. When the final gavel sounded, the estate sold for $35 million. Larry Latham Auctioneers collected about 6 percent, or $2.1 million.

SOURCE

See "Auction House Dealer," page 595.

Relocation Consultant

Job Description: *A relocation consultant specializes in helping professional people find new homes when they are transferred to another part of the country by their employer.*

- *Start-up cost as low as $3,000*
- *Potential first-year earnings: $15,000*
- *Breakeven time from initial investment: several months to one year*
- *Ideal home-based business*
- *No staffing required*

Brad and Arlene, who both work for large corporations with branches across the country, always kidded about who would make vice president first. In their case, it was Brad, and both were thrilled with his promotion. There was just one drawback, and it was a stinker: Along with the higher salary and prestige came a transfer to his company's St. Louis office.

The couple visited St. Louis and liked the Midwest. Nevertheless, they aren't so sure they want to leave family, friends, and Arlene's good job for what amounts to a foreign country. Brad's company has been in this situation enough times to know it can lose a good employee faced with such choices. To ease the dilemma, Brad's boss says he'll be getting a call from a relocation consultant. If Arlene wants, a career counselor will also help her find a new position in St. Louis. With such hand-holding, the couple decides to join the thousands of people who move to new cities each year. According to the Employee Relocation Council, companies in the United States relocate an average of 210 current employees and 99 new hires annually. The average costs to relocate the employees are: $40,676 for homeowning new hires, $11,491 for renting new hires, $53,696 for homeowning current employees, and $15,604 for renting current employees.

A GUIDE TO THE BRAVE NEW WORLD

" 'Relocation consulting' is a generic term that encompasses anything having to do with assisting transferred employees," says Anita Brienza, manager of public relations for the Employee Relocation Council. When she says "anything," she includes

- Finding a moving company
- Arranging for a pet's transportation
- Describing the types of neighborhoods in the new town and possibly lining up real estate to choose from
- Suggesting schools, churches, hospitals, daycare centers, and nursing homes—any support organization that a family might need
- Brokering and even buying the house in the old neighborhood

- Stress counseling
- Spouse job-placement assistance

Of course, you can mix and match among those responsibilities or add your own services. Except for career counseling, which really counts as its own unique specialty (see "Career Counselor," page 41), most relocation consultants concentrate on knowing their territory better than anyone else in the whole world. "I sell my knowledge of an area and of its real estate practices," explains Terri Fisher, of Fisher Hornor Associates, Westfield, New Jersey. Even though you don't actually sell homes, you need a real estate license to offer such counseling. However, you can pick that up in several months. (See "Real Estate Agent," page 505.) "I've hired people without real estate background who had experience with being transferred themselves," Fisher says. "They know from experience exactly what has to be done and have the empathy to help clients through the process."

Typically, relocation counseling works this way: The corporation calls the relocation consultant with the name and phone number of the employee on the transfer track. Then the counselor contacts the employee for an initial telephone counseling session. "We determine how the employee and family feels about the move and discuss the housing and personal requirements," says Fisher.

HOLDING THE BUYER'S HAND

For employees who want to buy, relocation consultants discuss the home-buying process and actually qualify them for a mortgage by asking about their income and debts and assets. Then comes the "art" part, as you ask about lifestyle and what the couple wants in a community. "Clients might want schools with a certain curriculum, or an idyllic rural area," says Fisher.

Any good relocation specialist worth the moniker knows which areas sound appropriate for the income level and lifestyle the clients describe. Some consultants actually broker houses themselves, although Fisher considers that practice a conflict of interest since some agents tend to favor their own properties. Instead, before the client comes to town for the house search, Fisher lines up real estate agents who cover the areas she selects for her client. Then she describes exactly what her client's dream house should include. The real estate agents plan an itinerary of houses to tour. Fisher accompanies the client on the first day's tour to make sure that she properly conveyed the client's preferences. "New Jersey's idea of rural might be different from that of someone from another part of the country," she explains.

Since she's done the homework ahead of time to identify which neighborhoods seem perfect and has screened real estate agents for efficiency, Fisher's typical client buys a house in only four days. "It always blows my mind, but then we've eliminated the wasted time that clients usually spend looking at inappropriate houses and communities," she says.

Most relocation consultants receive their commission from the real estate agent rather than the corporation, a practice that brings everybody knocking on the consultant's door. Corporations like you because they have employees who have found housing quickly and efficiently and can now concentrate on the new job. Real estate agents are happy to pass along anything from 25 percent of the broker's commission to 1 percent of the sale price of the house because you bring them interested, qualified buyers. Buyers like you because you act as an objective party who protects their position and speeds along the house-hunting process.

Taking the Rental Route

If the employee wants to rent, you take a different approach. "We ask if they're interested in an apartment, house, or condo," says Terri Fisher. "We learn what size family they have and what commute time would be acceptable. We determine whether the family has pets and the length of the lease they're looking for. Some families want to rent for a short time until they're ready to buy, for example."

With all the particulars in hand, a day or two before the client comes to town you call landlords to see what units are available and sketch an itinerary. Then you meet the clients at their hotel or the company and give the grand tour. On the way to each rental, point out schools, shopping centers, and community amenities. "By the end of the day, clients know what's available and they're usually ready to sign a lease," says Fisher.

When you relocate renters, as opposed to home buyers, corporations will pick up the tab for your time. You can expect anywhere from $500 to one-month's rent as your fee.

The better you know your area, the less time you spend on research. With more time, you can sign on more clients and boost your potential income. An efficient relocation consultant can expect annual fees in the $30,000 to $50,000 range. But you can leverage that fee in a couple of ways.

LEVERAGE

Most obviously, you can hire staff or subcontractors and increase the number of clients your firm relocates. You also can
do a real volume business by targeting large accounts, such as a
corporation that's moving a whole division to your area. Each
one of those transferred employees needs to find a new home.

Terri Fisher says her firm relocated one such group from
Manhattan to New Jersey over one year. "This move involved
researching the new area for the corporation and gathering current information on schools, housing, daycare, senior citizen
facilities, places of worship, recreational activities, and so on."
Using that information, Fisher presented an orientation program to give the transferees a visual introduction to the new
area and its offerings. "A 'Relocation Center' was set up at the
company's Manhattan site, and each of the 300 employees
whose jobs were affected was eligible for a personal counseling
session with one of our consultants," recalls Fisher. Home buyers were referred to real estate agents while Fisher Hornor
Associates found rentals for those who wanted to rent. For such
a comprehensive service on this scale, a relocation firm could
gross several hundred thousand dollars.

You can also offer other services, such as lining up moving
vans and storage. Terri Fisher goes beyond furniture rental to
lease everything a renter needs to set up house—pots, pans,
linens, and all the odds-and-ends every household needs. "If
the move is permanent, the client is better off to buy," explains
Fisher. "But for the short-term moves, we'll stock an apartment with everything necessary. We even put the dishes away
and make the beds so all the client has to do is come in and
unpack the clothes from the suitcases." In addition to serving

corporations bringing in executives for short-term assignments, Fisher's household-linens rental service gathers leads from real estate agents, furniture rental companies, and even other relocation companies.

Fisher stresses the importance of developing contacts with corporations and real estate agents and says not to be afraid to tackle even the most finicky clients or difficult cases. She remembers one lead she received from another relocation company that only handled mass moves. The assignment had its difficulties. "The family was looking for short-term rental, and landlords don't like to give leases for less than a year. They also had a dog, so on the surface the assignment was not appealing."

But Fisher found the family a furnished house and saw rewards beyond that one-time fee. "In talking with them, I found the husband was going to be president of a healthcare facility and was going to bring in people to work for him. They were only renting because they planned to buy a house in the near future. So I got additional business in the long run."

SOURCE

Industry Association

Employee Relocation Council, 1720 N Street, N.W., Washington, DC 20036, (202) 857-0857

Retailing

Children's Clothing Boutique Retailer

Job Description: *A children's clothing boutique retailer stocks unique, high-end clothes for kids.*

- *Start-up cost as low as $60,000*
- *Potential first-year earnings: $120,000*
- *Breakeven time from initial investment: several years*

Today's upscale children's retail market is a shopkeeper's fantasy come true. As discounters clothe the masses and department stores scrape margins on midprice points, children's boutiques flourish by offering $150 Giorgio Armani blazers in size toddler 2 or $650 Krizia sequined "cocktail" dresses for the under-six set. And 200 percent markups on $900 christening gowns can cloak a lot of mistakes.

Demographers and social scientists say the American baby boom generation is bringing up its own babies with panache. With mother working, modern parents possess the money (and perhaps the guilt) to buy their kids the best, including the best clothes. Two sets of statistics suggest that the population of children is growing and that an increasing number of parents can afford to clothe their darlings with the help of Ralph Lauren and Liz Claiborne:

- The increasing preteen population. The Census Bureau counts 44.7 million children under age 13. Whether the birth rate continues to climb or not, existing kids need a fresh closetful of clothes every year to grow into. In response, the children's clothing market has been growing faster than a five-year-old grows out of his or her jeans. According to Reuters Business Report, in 1998 children's clothing sales earned $30.1 billion, a jump of 3.8 percent over 1997 and an 11.5 percent increase over 1996.
- Affluence. The IRS tells us that 14 million households (16 percent of the U.S. population) have incomes of $50,000 or more. In addition, the government counted 10,800 individuals with annual incomes of $1 million or more.

KIDDIE CACHET

"I cater to—I hate to say it—yuppies," admits Dorothy McNish, who named her Little Rock, Arkansas, boutique after granddaughter Elecia Michelle. "People want top quality for their children—something everyone else doesn't have. These women waited longer to have children. They've been in the workforce and have money to spend. They don't think twice about spending on their children. When they see what they want, they buy it."

Indeed. Dorothy does carry a line of Philippine smocked dresses in the $32 retail ballpark. But bestsellers include $80 to

$350 French and Italian matching sets and "little dresses" for up to $800. Three years after start-up, Elecia Michelle was grossing nearly $20,000 a month and Dorothy was close enough to profitability to taste it.

Doris Cerutti, the grande dame among pricey children's clothing shopkeepers, allows that Cerutti's "used to be practically alone. Now there must be 20 children's shops in a 20-block radius." But for Cerutti, on the upper-crust, Upper East Side of Manhattan, competition has been healthy as business has continued to grow. In her case, a shop on every corner merely legitimizes the trend; parents accept a $120 price tag on a pint-size Burberry raincoat without blinking. Meanwhile, numerous affluent areas still lack a glitzy kids boutique, forcing moms (and grandmoms) to make semiannual pilgrimages to Madison Avenue or Rodeo Drive.

Discounting the hordes of wealthy, middle-age matrons who decide it would be "fun" to open a "sweet little shop," one consultant claims some successful shopkeepers live better than heads of large department store chains. "If you're an astute merchant and religious about working, retailers can live like barons," he insists.

IMAGE: YOU ARE WHAT YOU WEAR

Because you must locate in affluent areas to be near your clientele, rent may be on the high side. Your most expensive element in start-up, however, will be inventory. A very small boutique can go easy on the decor and squeeze in for $60,000 or so. But opening a bigger store with adequate stock in an urban high-rent district may cost $250,000 or more.

If you want to operate an exclusive children's clothing store, you must look the part. The most important aspect of image is simply the merchandise on the floor. "Make a statement with your clothing," insists Doris Cerutti. If you intend to sell top-of-the-line clothing, "don't reach out for the masses," echoes Dorothy McNish, who worked in ladies' and children's stores before opening her own boutique. That's not to say you shouldn't stock basics like overalls and jeans, but make them unique since no boutique can compete with K-Mart on prices. "We're not a museum," says Maggie Chafen, who carries $24 Esprit short sets as well as $300 Joan Calabrese dresses at her Dottie Doolittle boutique. "San Francisco residents are not kings and queens. Real people don't send their children to school in $200 dresses, but they want one for parties."

Like other apparel retailers, children's merchants spend a lot of time scouting out new merchandise. Chafen, who opened Dottie Doolittle fresh out of business school, estimates she spends $150,000 annually to stock her 2,000-square-foot store by shopping Europe twice a year as well as New York. Dorothy McNish not only filled her store but also decorated it on a $62,000 shoestring. Acknowledging it's vital to keep a full stock, she and her husband, Bill, "do" New York markets four times a year, and Dallas, home of another major merchandise mart, once. They hit the local boutiques as well as the apparel shows to see what competitors sell.

Doris Cerutti advises new shops to "get attached" to a buying office. For a stiff fee, these professional clothing buyers, most located in New York, will help determine the number of items you need in each size, the amount of inventory—all manner of things.

Vendors also court the boutiques, making client rounds once

a season. McNish credits designers with providing helpful hints and putting her on the track of other sources of merchandise. It won't hurt to ask for exclusive rights to a line within your trading zone. You might even get them.

IMAGE: WE'VE GOT THE LOOK

The other component of image is the shop's decor. Rugs and mirrors create enough of a look for some retailers, but exclusive boutiques need a one-of-a-kind look that would impress an interior designer. Dorothy McNish has thought out the 1,200 square feet of Elecia Michelle, complete with "pale gray carpeting and pale, pale, pale pink walls," in minute detail. Take just the window display, for example: "We're in an old bank building with windows from the roof to the ground. A banister identifies the display area and keeps children out of the window. We lay merchandise on an easel and a white bench. Stuffed animals sway on a little swing when the air conditioner blows. I always keep ferns or fresh flowers or decorated baskets in the windows."

However, remember that children (and their parents) are your customers and strive for a comfortable, safe setting. "I hire people who like kids," says Maggie Chafen. "I don't want a tense atmosphere." You surely want toys for the kids to play with and to strive for subtle childproofing: Hang rather than fold merchandise for easier maintenance; dangle those charming mobiles high from the ceiling where kids can see but not touch them.

WE DO IT ALL FOR YOU

Upscale clothing stores for all sizes exude an almost snobbish pride in their service. Create a personal relationship with customers through such touches as alterations, gift wrapping, delivery, and maybe even special ordering. "In department stores, you find your clothes and bring it to one of 14 cash registers," says Doris Cerutti. "We're the opposite. We have one register and 14 salespeople. Our customers feel it's important to have someone help outfit their child in 13 minutes so they can get back to their apartment or country house." Steady Cerutti customers buy from their own salesperson, who is familiar with their children's sizes and tastes.

Even smaller shops like Elecia Michelle, which Dorothy McNish runs with just two saleswomen, see one-on-one attention as crucial. "When we get a shipment, we call a customer to say we have such-and-such. 'Would you like to come in?' Then we put that merchandise aside. People spend $600 to $1,000 a trip. I couldn't survive without the call list."

Doris Cerutti goes one step further: Her sales staff delivers samples for customers who like to shop at home.

The question remains: Will today's affluent moms and dads abandon upscale children's boutiques and designer clothes from Betsey Johnson in favor of JCPenney and Oshkosh? The editor of *Kids Fashion* doubts children's clothing will ever be the same: "Women learned to dress when manufacturers first began mass production of clothes. Men caught on in the '50s when they got beyond black suits and white shirts. The only thing left was kids—and Europe has been way ahead of us for years.

"Whether the boom will continue, no one knows," he says. "But the trend is here to stay."

SOURCES

Fashion Markets

Bayside Merchandise Mart, 150–160 Mount Vernon Street, Dorchester, MA 02125, (617) 825-4040

Dallas Apparel Mart, 2300 Stemmons Freeway, Dallas, TX 75207, (214) 637-2171

International Kids Fashion Show, 485 7th Avenue, Suite 1400, New York, NY 10018, (212) 594-0880

Florist

Job Description: *A florist sells flowers and houseplants, creates floral arrangements, and offers a variety of other products and services relating to flowers and plants.*

- *Start-up cost as low as $15,000*
- *Potential first-year earnings: $1,000 to $5,000 per month*
- *Breakeven time from initial investment: several years*

When a florist thinks of heaven, Holland comes to mind. "You imagine bicyclists carrying a loaf of bread and a bunch of flowers," says Marcia Schaaf, proprietor of Schaaf Floral in Minneapolis.

In fantasizing what could be, consider that the average European spends $50 on flowers every year, compared to just $20 spent in the United States. But there is hope: The Society of American Florists (SAF) reports that posies are much more popular than they used to be. The total retail sales of floral items has surged to $15 billion.

Season by season—or rather petal by petal—Americans are

developing a love of flowers. Tradition continues to dictate floral displays at holidays and such festive and somber events as weddings, proms, and funerals. But the real sales increase comes from Americans' increasing fondness for occasional arrangements gracing dining room tables for no particular reason at all. Citing the ad campaign launched by the Society of American Florists, Drew Gruenburg, SAF director of communications, says Americans today are more likely to "Give Flowers to Someone Special: Yourself."

ARTISTS BEWARE

While the future of the flower business does sound rosy, florists average yearly revenues of around $209,182. Of course, some florists can tap larger markets. C. S. Cosentino's single, supermarket-size shop, Cosentino's Florists, in Auburn, New York, brings in more than $500,000 annually. Ken Royer's Flowers Inc., with 11 units throughout Pennsylvania Dutch country, generates $6 million in annual revenue. "The margins are there," says Royer. "All you have to do is get enough volume."

C. S. Cosentino, who also consults, warns would-be florists that "if you're an artiste—if you love flowers—stay away. If you're a businessperson who enjoys flowers, you have a chance." You must first and foremost recognize that you're in a business to make money, not flower arrangements. Strive for volume through advertising and location and trim costs through business savvy.

Unlike other retail establishments, flower shops create on the premises. "Flower shops are not Eliza Doolittle selling flowers from a stand," explains an FTD spokesperson. "You have to take the raw product, flowers, and manufacture a product—a bouquet or other arrangement—on the spot." Thanks to the florist's skill, a couple of nosegays and a few sprigs of baby's breath become a special anniversary gift.

Because of such variables as labor talent and product perishability, it's hard to control markup. Ken Royer's solution to the problem is an assembly-line approach that has earned him the moniker "the McDonald's of the Flower Industry." During holiday periods, Royer employs 40 people to create designs in a central location. He posts a "menu" of arrangements at each store and then advertises specific items such as a Daisy & Mini (carnation) Basket. This way he cuts labor costs, saves money by buying in volume, and passes the savings on to his customers by selling many flowers with price tags well below the usual $18 to $20 minimums set by competitors. For example, Royer's chain sold 1,400 Candlelight Centerpieces for $12.50 each during one Christmas season. While a single store can't match his volume, it can adopt a modified version of Royer's assembly line. Offer fewer arrangements, but promote those so you sell baskets and baskets of each item.

SHAKING OUT THE COBWEBS

Until recently, the traditional florist aimed at reducing overhead rather than building business. Take advertising. While the 3.5 percent of sales that Ken Royer devotes to direct mail, newspapers, and cable TV isn't overly generous by other retail standards, it's about 2.5 percent more than most florists set aside. And florists generally ignored the rule of thumb that location holds the key to success. In fact, since customers traditionally ordered most items over the phone for delivery to a hospital, the practice was to pick the least expensive site available.

Bucking the old traditions, modern florists are trading up to the high-profile, high-rent districts, which is pushing the cost of entry higher. You still can outfit a small, neighborhood shop for $50,000, but really elaborate urban sites can run to $300,000. In addition to scouting out the clientele in your prospective location, consider the other businesses in the area that will attract customers. For example, C. S. Cosentino reports that a successful Florida florist placed most of his 30 shops within a quarter mile of a McDonald's. "They already did the site selection for him," he explains. That florist basks in walk-in traffic.

The industry also is polishing its interiors. "The florist has a beautiful product to sell, and we're finally putting it where the public can see it," says Drew Gruenburg. Ken Royer hopes to rent franchisees a $225,000 prototype shop he developed under the name Flower Link. Compared to the dark cubbyholes associated with flower shops of the past, this store is astounding: a brick building with an atrium entrance, exposed wood ceiling, mezzanine, and drive-through window, all of which is splashed throughout with the colors of hundreds of flowers, of course.

The flower industry offers more start-up help than most small-business fields. Consultants, colleges, and trade schools offer both design and business courses, and numerous publications publicize the latest industry developments. FTD and Telefloral, the two largest wire services, offer management as well as creative advice through hundreds of seminars. (Wire services aid shops in fulfilling the 15 percent of business that comes from out-of-towners. The customer simply contacts a local florist, who calls the head office of the wire service he or she subscribes to. The wire service relays the order to a member in the distant town, and a clearinghouse settles accounts between the parties once a month.)

THE BASICS OF JUGGLING

Entrepreneurs point to five different areas in which you need to develop skills to successfully run a flower shop.

1. Selection and care of your product. "Trial and error is expensive when you deal with perishables," warns C. S. Cosentino. "You must know how to handle flowers—how to cut them underwater, which preservatives to store them in, a myriad of things." If you're big enough, you can order flowers directly from importers, local greenhouses, and growers in the California and Colorado "flowerbaskets." However, most small- and medium-size firms secure their lilacs and birds-of-paradise through wholesalers.

2. Flower arrangement. Although both art and science combine to create a centerpiece, ironically, design skills may be the easiest to learn. Scores of community colleges and even some four-year colleges offer courses.

3. Customer relations. While all retailers deal with customers, florists encounter people at such emotional times as weddings and funerals. You must react sympathetically to a bereaved relative one moment and hold the demanding hands of a parent of the bride the next.

4. Delivery. In the beginning, you can sign on with a delivery pool or hire a part-timer with a station wagon. However, costs mount as volume grows. Marcia Schaaf, who owns five

delivery vehicles, also subscribes to a pool whose driver drops orders outside her normal zone for a fee.

5. Collections. Some florists honor just the major credit cards, but those with house cards say the paperwork and cost of collection is worth the trouble to build a loyal clientele. "We mailed out 15,000 of our own cards when we opened our last store," says Ken Royer. "It's an invitation to buy in the store."

Schaaf says 70 percent of her credit purchases are on her own card. Because in-house cardholders represent a sort of inner circle of ready-made buyers, many florists direct advertising pieces to them. A computer that spews out address labels allows Schaaf to send out periodic circulars to her 4,000 or so cardholders.

THE COMPETITION

New variations of the flower shop are appearing all around: supermarkets, stands at the entrances to subways, and mall-based kiosks. Besides the 27,341 retail florist shops in the United States, the Society of American Florists estimates that there are 23,000 supermarkets with floral departments and 10,857 retail nurseries and lawn and garden supply stores that also sell the beautiful buds. Instead of cutting into the floral pie, however, these retailers create consumer awareness of flowers for everyday and might even signal a need for a good florist shop in an area.

Despite the notion in the industry that competition is healthy, C. S. Cosentino recommends that new florists specialize. He points to a florist who advertises to the 8,000 to 10,000 offices in Syracuse, New York. A bevy of weekly customers builds volume quickly. Marcia Schaaf likewise developed a "good corporate base" in Minneapolis and traces her best leads to her community involvement. Since she is on the board of the city's chamber of commerce, all the businesses know her.

Another lucrative specialty is parties. Approaching caterers to discuss your strengths doesn't hurt, although Schaaf says a little reputation goes a long way in the party game. "Consider each wedding you decorate a showcase for your talents; do something unique that caterers will remember the next time they recommend a flower shop."

Like other retailers, florists work long hours and weekends. Nevertheless, says C. S. Cosentino, "because what we do is a craft, the hours don't seem as long."

SOURCES

Industry Association

Society of American Florists, 1601 Duke Street, Alexandria, VA 22314, (703) 836-8700

Wire Services

American Floral Services, 3737 Northwest 34th Street, Oklahoma City, OK 73157, (405) 440-6000

Florafax International, 8075 20th Street, Vero Beach, FL 32966-1320, (561) 563-0263

FTD, 3113 Woodcreek Drive, Downers Grove, IL 60515-5420, (800) 736-3333

Garden Center Provider

Job Description: *A garden center provider sells outdoor gardening and landscaping supplies as well as decorative items for the yard including shrubbery, trees, and flowers.*

- *Start-up cost as low as $36,000*
- *Potential earnings: $240,000*
- *Breakeven time from initial investment: one to three years*

In Atlanta, several massive garden center chains stock thousands of azaleas and tulip bulbs in their multiacre lots, and they buy mulch by the dumptruck. But those people who want to buy exotic perennials like candytuft or other, even more unusual flowers make the trip to tiny Funkhouser's Garden & Gift, a 1,500-square-foot, closet-size store with just 2,000 square feet of outdoor selling space. Explains proprietor Bill Funkhouser: "The mass markets carry the bestsellers. They run full-page ads. We're not going to compete with them. So we carry the unusual." That approach earned Funkhouser's sales of $250,000 in its second year of business.

Do-It-Yourself Flower Power

Americans are dressing up their yards with a vengeance. According to a survey in *American Demographics* magazine, Americans spent $26.6 billion on their gardens in 1997, a 17 percent increase from 1992. Gardening supplies and services represented the fifth biggest outlay of household cash, right behind computers. Those aged 60 and over were the most likely to get their hands dirty outside. Households that spent the most time outdoors were those headed by college graduates, who forked (or plowed) over an average of $503 per year on gardening and supplies. The "flower power" generation has a couple of choices: Either hire a landscape contractor to plant the holly, or do it yourself. Both segments of the garden world are thriving. (See "Landscaper," page 374.)

As Bill Funkhouser's situation illustrates, garden centers come in all sizes, with any number of specialties. You could open with $36,000 or $180,000, depending on your size, whether you locate in a high-rent shopping center or a suburban back road, and the inventory you carry. "A lot of centers are almost equipment shops: power equipment, lawn mowers," explains J. D. Causey, who runs Causey's Garden Center in Wilmington, North Carolina. "We're 70 percent greengoods. We call ourselves a retail nursery center."

Many wholesale nurseries or equipment distributors will help sketch out a floorplan, depending on your specialty and the amount of cash you have to spend. Keep the needs of your local clientele and climate in mind. For example, Causey's Garden Center stocks large planters for decks and patios to cater to the outdoor-living orientation of its coastal region. A

Tucson garden center carries Sonora cactuses that would not last a week in Milwaukee. Furthermore, mall sites lend themselves to portable merchandise, such as hanging baskets, while you need easy car access to sell 50-pound bags of topsoil.

While the garden center business has never had more room for growth, it pays to differ from department stores and supermarkets that have started carrying Ficus trees and tomato seedlings. Since you probably can't match discount prices, customers come to you for just a handful of reasons:

- Your wide selection
- Your expert advice on what to buy or how to plant
- Unique merchandise they can't get elsewhere

SELLING KNOW-HOW

Bill Funkhouser has built his business on two of those criteria: His shop is known for its expertise, and he specializes in the unusual. Funkhouser, who has a degree in horticulture, teaches employee classes twice a week so the three-person staff understands what they sell. In addition, he is highly visible in the community, speaking to garden clubs and teaching free Saturday lectures in his office on such topics as "Perennial Gardening in Atlanta" and "Herbs for Shady Areas." As Funkhouser puts it, "We sell information as much as product."

Funkhouser's sends customers to competitors for what he calls "the woodies" (trees and shrubs) and saves his precious space for items the gardeners can't get elsewhere, primarily perennials, wildflowers, and herbs as well as some statuary and hanging baskets. "The books on perennials were written for the

Northeast, so we do a lot of educating that contradicts the 'experts.' Most perennials do great here if you put them in the shade, but we especially look for heat-tolerant plants."

Garden center entrepreneurs usually find the consulting tasks more rewarding than bothersome. J. D. Causey says it adds a social element to business. "We deal with a lot of retirement couples who've just moved to the area and want to brighten their yard. We help them be creative and sort out problems like which plants like shade and sandy soil. We ask them about the architecture of their house so we can complement it with the plants we suggest. For example, formal shrubbery like boxwood is appropriate with Federal architecture, while Hollywood juniper would be best with ranches."

Location first attracts homeowners to your store; in addition, most garden centers set aside about 5 percent of revenues for advertising, primarily in newspapers with a smattering of direct mail and radio. Causey's even takes some television spots. "We're in a three TV-station area where rates are practical," says Causey. "You wouldn't do TV advertising in Philadelphia or Miami."

Bill Funkhouser sends newsletters to 5,000 customers, mainly those who write checks over $20 and anybody requesting they be put on the list. The mailings sell a few pansies, but mainly they keep customers interested in gardening. "At Christmas, we say, 'Here are some plants that make nice gifts,' but the newsletter's main value is information, such as what diseases Black-eyed Susans suffer from, when they bloom, and the amount of water they need."

MONEY GROWS ON TREES

Although they are perishable, greengoods usually provide the best margins, as much as 80 percent. Less profitable books, chemicals, and tools may have margins about half as high.

Both hard goods and plants have to be rounded up. J. D. Causey buys from some 40 different sources, most of which he discovers at trade shows. "We get greengoods from 500, sometimes 1,000 miles away," he says. "Nurseries call to say they're making deliveries in our area and ask what we need." The amount of stock varies with the season. Causey's may carry $30,000 worth of inventory in the winter and double that in the spring and fall. Causey tries to turn the inventory about eight times a year.

The best way to sell a showy garden product is to let it sell itself. Funkhouser's installed two tiny, 2-by-15-foot gardens to showcase its plants. The approach works so well that Funkhouser is looking for a larger location so he can add more display gardens. "Take platycodon," he says. "It has beautiful blue flowers that bloom in profusion. In photographs, the blues come out pinkish purple. But there's no way we can get enough of them when people see how beautiful they really are."

SOURCE

Industry Association

American Nursery & Landscape Association, 1250 I Street, N.W., Suite 500, Washington, DC 20005, (202) 789-5980 ext. 3012

Large-size Apparel
Retailer

Job Description: *A large-size apparel retailer sells clothing and fashion accessories for individuals whose weight is above average for their particular build.*

- *Start-up cost as low as $50,000*
- *Potential earnings: $200,000*
- *Breakeven time from initial investment: six months to three years*

As America gets older, it gets heavier. According to new guidelines recently issued by the National Heart, Lung and Blood Institute, 55 percent of adult Americans, or 97 million adults, are overweight. Despite the bulging numbers of weight-reduction centers (see "Diet Clinic Provider," page 304), trend watchers indicate we now accept a few extra pounds as an inevitable fact of life. Making the most of it, though, we'd like to toss out those polyester pant suits and look fashionable.

And since we're willing to pay for it, capitalism is responding: Shops for both tall and heavy men and boutiques for full-figure women are proliferating. Designers who long ignored this market are creating chic dresses and slimming suits for it. Vendors are carrying not just larger versions of clothing initially cut for average sizes but whole lines geared specifically to the needs of heavier individuals.

ROOM FOR GROWTH

"Eventually, stores for larger-size women will have as much competition as everything else," says David C. Keller, former CEO of Wieboldt Stores Inc., the $200-million department store chain headquartered in Chicago. However, "Department stores will continue to appeal to regular sizes and discounters will be all over the lot. It will take years before the larger-size category becomes over-stored."

Keller and two partners opened the first Fashionfull in Buffalo Grove, Illinois, citing a couple of enticements beyond scads of customers and a dearth of competition: Specialty stores achieve higher margins and have bigger tickets than do stores for a more general market. "Our customer can't go everywhere and find the merchandise that fits her, so she is not as concerned with price," says Keller, who was counting on 5 to 10 percent pretax profits—about double what department stores expect—on first-year sales of $250,000. Because the customers are willing to pay top dollar, "We don't have to run as many sales." One consultant to start-up retailers adds, "If you're a size 42 and find a store with beautiful dresses you can wear, you'll buy three at a shot. You'll travel miles out of your way to get there. Large-size stores achieve better margins on much higher average ticket. What's to lose?"

TURN, TURN, TURN

With higher tickets and fatter profits, breakeven comes faster. Also, since you can operate with a smaller store, you can create faster turns. That means you don't have to tie up as much cash in inventory. Fashionfull, at just 1,500 square feet, looks for six turns a year, compared with less than four at a department store. "We get new merchandise in weekly," says David Keller. Such volatility creates a retailing excitement that brings regular customers back often. "The store has a different look every week."

Because the store is small and because you turn inventory so fast, you can get into the business with a slender pocketbook. And since customers arrive for the merchandise rather than the ambiance, don't plow too much cash into expensive fixtures. Keller and partners opened Fashionfull on just $50,000. For this store—and the other five they plan for the Chicago area in the next two years—the trio chose a strip center rather than an enclosed mall. "Rent at enclosed malls in the Chicago area runs $30 to $35 a square foot, compared with $18 to $22 at a strip center," says Keller. "Strips don't provide as much traffic, but walk-in isn't where we get our business anyway. Advertising and word of mouth gets us our customers."

Fashionfull advertises freely in newspapers that cover the northwestern Chicago suburbs and is experimenting with a 20,000-piece direct-mail campaign. The names aren't sorted by size, Keller says, "but we expect those households who wear smaller sizes will have mothers or friends in our size range."

FLEXIBILITY IS YOUR
STRONG SUIT

If you concentrate on selling just one category—apparel for women size 16 and up—you get good at buying the right merchandise quickly. But David Keller says to have an open mind and a readiness to respond to customer suggestions. "We didn't realize we had so many working women in our area and weren't carrying suits at all," he says. "In the first few weeks we had quite a few calls, so now we carry suits." If you're located far from the major apparel marts—New York/Chicago/Dallas/California—you might not be able to react as quickly to customer demand for certain types of merchandise. But, at least in the early days, you might budget for a buying service in New York, or keep cash in reserve for fill-in buys to complement your opening stock.

Of course, try to know as much about your customers as possible before opening your doors. Shopping-center operators conduct demographic studies; ask your landlord what income, age, and population brackets live in your neighborhood. If you know customers have high incomes, for example, you might buy pricier merchandise.

YOU'RE SPECIAL

Many of the same rules apply to running an apparel shop for larger sizes that apply to operating any sort of specialty shop. For example, go heavy on service. Because you appeal to a relatively select group of people, chances are you won't have hundreds of customers in the shop at one time. Encourage your sales clerks to offer assistance and advice on accessories. Make an effort to know regular customers by name, and even call big spenders when you get in a shipment with merchandise just right for them. Your advantage over larger stores, besides the clothing itself, is the extra attention you lavish on customers.

However, clothing stores for this demographic differ from other stores in a few key ways. "We hire saleswomen who are on the heavier side," says David Keller, saying they have greater understanding of the fashion needs of a customer who might resent a 98-pound clerk. His partner, Caroline Frowe, a former Wieboldt divisional merchandise manager, wears a mere size three. "I kid her to stay out of the store," says Keller.

You also have to tread gingerly about how you refer to customers who may be sensitive about their size. "Don't talk 'big' or 'fat,' although you imply it," advises Keller. "Be careful in naming your store. We advertise 'Size 16 and up' rather than 'large sizes.'"

Pet Store Owner

Job Description: *A pet store owner sells cats, dogs, tropical fish, and so on. In addition, the store provides food and other pet care items.*
- *Start-up cost as low as $85,000*
- *Potential earnings: $210,000*
- *Breakeven time from initial investment: six months to three years*

Jerry Pass says if you want to gauge a shopping center's customer draw, visit the pet store. "If the pet store isn't busy, you know the mall is dead." That's not to say pet stores outsell dress boutiques or bookstores or ice cream stands—although typical pet store pretax profits of 20 percent beats most retailing returns by a long shot. But other than W. C. Fields, whom can you think of who could pass that doggie in the window without stopping to "ooh" and "ah"? Getting those customers into your store is easy: Just locate in a heavily trafficked area.

Apparently lots of those pet store window shoppers also leave with a kitten or cockatoo. Nearly 60 percent of families in the United States have pets. The American Veterinary Medical Association counts 112 million cats, dogs, fish, and other creatures that Americans take into their homes. Our fondness for our furry, finny, and "feathery" friends have sent pet industry sales skyrocketing to $20 billion.

SALES ALIVE

Pet stores offer warm and cuddly rewards you just don't get in other businesses. But loving animals doesn't qualify an entrepreneur to open a pet shop. "Many people get in as hobbyists— and 95 percent of those will fail," warns Jerry Pass, who says you need as much business sophistication to run a pet shop as for other forms of retailing. In fact, pet shops are far trickier in one significant aspect: You sell a living thing. That means somebody must visit the store to care for the animals seven days a week—even on Christmas and Thanksgiving when everybody else shutters their stores up tight. Also, you lose a certain amount of your stock to illness. "The public doesn't understand if a pet gets sick two days after they bought it," says Pass. If you buy one hamster carrying a deadly virus, you could lose your entire rodent stock. "You have to be a retailer, a merchandiser, and a vet, all rolled in one."

Pass Pets, which operates from a St. Louis, Missouri, base, largely solved the illness problem by putting a veterinarian on retainer at each of its 31 stores in six states. The vets make store calls twice a week, train the staff on which vitamins to dole out, and take any contagious critters to their clinics. Pass Pets also quarantines all new puppies for seven days before moving them in with other stock. Since addressing the illness question a couple of years ago, Pass says his pets have a 90 percent better health record.

TAKE AWAY THE BEASTS

Another way around the disease problem: Don't sell pets. "If you took the animals away, the pet business would be a piece of cake to operate," says Pass. He laughs, but some retailers run pet supply stores that do a brisk business without a beast in sight. Take, for example, Lick Your Chops, a Westport, Connecticut, chain that calls itself "a complete department store for animal people." The decidedly upscale chain sells little sweaters and sequined collars and obedience-school graduation cards, but Lick Your Chops specializes in nutritious animal food (no additives or scraps) at about triple the price of supermarket brands.

The concept of a health food store for animals was born when Susan Goldstein's golden retriever, Leigh, quit responding to cortisone injections for his painful hip dysplasia and arthritis. Susan and her veterinarian husband, Robert, discussed putting Leigh to sleep or subjecting the seven-year-old dog to major surgery. Susan, who was studying nutrition and working for the Foundation for Alternative Cancer Therapies in New York, suggested a last-ditch campaign: She put Leigh on a diet of brown rice, fresh vegetables, meat, vitamins and minerals, and distilled water. Within six months, Leigh's symptoms disappeared and Susan began toying with the idea of Lick Your Chops. When Leigh was still going strong at 17, the chain consisted of three company-owned and two franchise stores, a retail outlet in New York City's Bloomingdale's department store, a mail-order division, and a manufacturing subsidiary.

99

66

Pet supply stores have one major drawback. They work only in the most populated areas with an affluent population. You can cut inventory and floor space and get rid of all those animal headaches—assuming you can do enough volume on supplies alone. Of course, animals are what attract most entrepreneurs to the business in the first place. So, if you want to keep the pets—but minimize your stock—open just a fish store, or buy a franchise that specializes in nothing but puppies instead of a full-service pet shop. While a specialty pet store still copes with living products, you deal with just one fish distributor or only a handful of puppy breeders instead of a variety of sources.

YOUR GRUBSTAKE

A 2,000-square-foot store stocks about $30,000 worth of inventory (meaning pets and supplies). You buy that merchandise from various services: puppy and kitten breeders, bird importers, fish farmers, and a couple of dry-goods and accessory distributors. Mix and match inventory for a while after start-up to see whether local pet buyers are more partial to parakeets or Pekingeses. In addition, Jerry Pass says to put aside $200,000 if you want to open first class in a heavily trafficked mall. Part of this stake goes to adapt a location to handle your merchandise. For example, Pass Pets installs high-speed ventilation fans to eliminate odors. "What mall wants you as a tenant if you smell?" asks Pass.

You can cut your opening budget nearly in half by opting for a decent strip center rather than a mall. But expect lower revenues. The highest-volume mall shops can sell $1 million worth of goldfish and their ilk a year, compared with about $200,000 for the average freestanding or strip-center boutique.

In some cities, those high-volume mall sites just aren't available. And even where they are, you need all the sales you can get to pay for the overhead. Increasingly, pet stores employ advertising to increase awareness. Many pet food and accessory manufacturers offer cooperative advertising plans, so Hartz-Mountain might share your promotion expenses.

Two demographic trends hold bright promises for pet stores in the near future. The two most populous groups of pet owners tend to be youngsters and senior citizens. It just so happens that those two segments are growing faster than the rest of the population. "Polly want a parrot?"

SOURCE

Industry Association

Pet Industry Joint Advisory Council, 1220 19th Street, N.W., Suite 400, Washington, DC 20036, (202) 452-1525

Pool Supplies Dealer

Job Description: *A pool supplies dealer sells everything needed for a pool: chemicals to keep water clean, toys, filters, automatic cleaners, and other equipment.*

- *Start-up cost: high*
- *Future growth potential: extremely high*
- *Breakeven time from initial investment: several years*
- *Stable business in a growth industry*
- *Some staffing required*

It's official. Americans are in love with their swimming pools.

Of course, what's not to love about something so wonderful as a swimming pool—the water shimmering like glass, the incredibly refreshing feeling one gets from diving into the cool, crystal clear water, and the utter relaxation of just floating away a hot day.

But just imagine how your perception of a swimming pool would change if instead of the water sparkling like a diamond in the sunlight, it looked like swamp water from the Everglades.

Who keeps pool water from looking like that? Pool supply dealers, of course, with their numerous water-purifying, algae-fighting chemicals. As the number of pools in the United States continues to increase, so does the need for pool supplies. It's a business that is riding the crest of an ever-growing wave.

WATER, WATER EVERYWHERE

Pools are in—the ground, that is.

According to the National Spa and Pool Institute (NSPI), there are 7 million pools in the United States. In-ground pools lead the way with 3.8 million, followed by aboveground with 3.2 million.

Sales of in-ground pools have been steadily rising in the United States. In 1996 yearly sales of in-ground pools in this country totaled 149,936. Two years later the figure jumped to 172,184. NSPI spokesperson Suzanne Stearns credited a one-two punch of a strong economy and advanced technology with the increase in pool installations. Since the average income of an in-ground pool owner is $67,000, it makes sense that a bur-geoning economy would help spur pool sales. But what does technology have to do with swimming?

"Today, automated pools are the norm," Stearns explains. "Pool maintenance is less time-consuming." This means the once-dreaded chore of vacuuming the pool has been largely taken over by machines, thereby removing one significant ob-stacle to purchase.

A wildcard factor in skyrocketing pool sales has been the heat. Whether it's due to global warming, El Niño, or just a freak of nature, several summers in the 1990s were extremely hot and dry, and people naturally turned to pools for relief. In

Texas, for instance, the blazing summer of 1998 sent pool sales soaring; some dealers reported increases of 40 to 50 percent from the previous year.

Both in-ground and aboveground pools need a chemical kick to keep the water clean and suitable for swimming. According to the NSPI, the top-ten in-ground pool markets in the United States are: Los Angeles; New York; San Francisco/Oakland/San Jose; Tampa/St. Petersburg; Phoenix; Miami/Ft. Lauderdale; Dallas/Ft. Worth; Orlando/Daytona/Melbourne; Philadelphia; and Boston. The top ten for aboveground pool ownership is: New York; Pennsylvania; California; New Jersey; Illinois; Michigan; Florida; Massachusetts; Ohio; and Texas.

EVERYONE INTO THE POOL . . . SUPPLY STORE

North Shore Pool Supply in Wakefield, Massachusetts, for example, has been in existence for over 25 years. In 1987, Chris Callanan purchased it, figuring that he could use his retail background to grow the business.

He was right. Today, North Shore Pool Supply is doing four times the dollar volume it was when Callanan bought it. He has expanded both the sales staff and store capacity. According to Callanan, the last four to five years have been banner ones in the pool supply industry. His business has doubled during this time.

START-UP COSTS

As you might suspect, start-up costs for a pool supply business are extremely high. In merchandise alone, expect to pay from

$75,000 to $100,000 initially. Then there's the store rental, fixtures, computer system, and other necessities. With all this to consider, start-up costs can be as high as $300,000. On top of that, Chris Callanan advises a new pool supply business owner not to expect to draw a salary for the first year, while the business gets established. Thus, you also should have a year's savings tucked away for living expenses. As a result, breakeven time can take five years or longer.

Other initial expenses include advertising and the cost of a computer specialist to install your system and software. Since the computer will be used to log inventory control, sales, database management, and numerous other chores, it's best to let a professional handle the installation.

To cut costs, consider starting small, and letting the growth of the business dictate how much merchandise to order and stock, rather than the other way around. Since money will be limited the first year or so, try to have family and friends lend a hand to save staffing costs.

BUILDING A BUSINESS

Although the location of your business will not affect your basic service—selling pool supplies—it will affect other aspects. For instance, pool supply companies in warm-weather states, where pools are open year-round, have service contracts with customers to maintain their pools. However, in states where the pool season is much shorter, such as Massachusetts, such contracts are rare.

"The rates you need to charge for weekly service [in cold-weather states] don't keep someone employed all year round," says Chris Callanan. "Then you're faced with the decision of sending out unskilled people [for maintenance]. I don't think that does a lot for your reputation."

However, what Mother Nature takes away, she also gives back. In states where weather conditions compel people to open and close their pools, this task can generate revenue at the beginning and end of the pool season. In Massachusetts, Callanan begins opening pools in early April and starts closing them in September. Pool closings continue through November to early December.

Another way to keep business humming during the off-season is to diversify your merchandise. Callanan, for instance, began selling spas and accessories several years ago. Today they account for approximately 40 percent of his business.

Keeping your merchandise unique also will help your store prosper. Callanan stocks products and items that his customers cannot find at a mass merchandiser, such as unique toys and flotation devices beyond the water guns and rubber rafts typically available. He uses this philosophy during the holiday season, as well, when he turns his store into a Christmas gift shop featuring hand-blown glass ornaments and other items not available at most retailers.

"I have the same approach with the pool business," says Callanan. "I don't sell the same old thing."

KEEPING IN THE SWIM

With pools popping up in backyards across the country, it's almost inevitable that you'll encounter competition. Advertising is one way to keep your name in front of customers, although the cost can be high, particularly if you're in a metropolitan area. (Billboards in the Boston area, for instance, cost $10,000 per month.) North Shore Pool Supply has found that sending periodic mailings to their customers has helped bolster business.

"We work very hard at maintaining a [direct mail] database," says Chris Callanan. "Anyone who comes in to purchase anything is entered into it."

A WET AND WILD FUTURE

The pool supply business seems more recession-proof than most. As Callanan points out, if the economy slumps, there might not be as many new pools constructed, but people will still want—and need—to maintain their existing pool. Thus the future for the pool supply industry seems as crystal clear as the water that they—and possibly you—work so hard to maintain.

SOURCE

Industry Association

The National Spa and Pool Institute, 2111 Eisenhower Avenue, Alexandria, VA 22314, (703) 838-0083

Professional Women's Clothing Retailer

Job Description: *A professional women's clothing retailer sells female attire for the workplace and other formal occasions.*

- *Start-up cost as low as $200,000*
- *Potential earnings: $200,000*
- *Breakeven time from initial investment: two to five years*

The story of Just Grand, a clothing store for professional women located on Grand Street in St. Paul, started out, well, just grand. Then its partners hit a too-fast expansion period that put them on speaking terms with Chapter 11. But the moral to the story—hang on and learn by one's mistakes—makes for a happy ending. "We can't expand now because we have so much debt to service from our previous attempt," says partner Marilyn McNutt. "But once we pay that off, we will grow. We know now where to avoid mistakes, and we also know from the success of the remaining store that the concept is valid. We'll do lots better next time around."

McNutt and her three partners can hardly be blamed for

pursuing their concept so enthusiastically. Looking at the changing role of women, it seemed they couldn't lose. The U.S. Census Bureau reports 36 million American women work full time outside the home. Increasing numbers of these women abandoned the "pink ghetto" of low-paid clerical jobs to enter the executive ranks. And the one piece of advice every business woman's magazine shouts to this day is: Use your newfound income to dress the part.

Just Grand opened intending to dress the executive woman with panache. "The professional woman doesn't want navy blue suits with white shirts and red ties," says McNutt, who taught sales marketing before joining Just Grand. "She wants to look good without being too traditional. She wants something classy that she can wear for three or four years without tiring of it."

HOME SWEET HOME

After four years, based on the reception working women gave to the pilot store, the partners decided to grow. Within nine months, they opened seven stores. The next year, only the original remained. "You always hear about the importance of location," says Marilyn McNutt. "But unless you experience a bad site, you can't believe how important location really is."

The concept of an executive clothing store for females has one drawback: Department store buyers also want to dress the professional woman. Recognizing that competition, you've got to locate smack dab in the middle of lots of professional women; know your merchandise and present it in a way that makes boutique shopping convenient, and offer superior service.

Just Grand's most serious expansion mistake involved

locations. The entrepreneurs spent a lot of money getting what they thought were good locations in expensive shopping malls. But they found that not just *any* foot traffic will do. Shopping malls in the suburbs may be great for a cruise-wear shop, and might stock some executive wear if the demographics are mixed, but malls that draw primarily from middle-class neighborhoods may not attract enough women who need $75 silk blouses. You may be better off in the financial district of at least a midsize town, but check your customer base carefully. McNutt recommends camping out in a location before committing to a professional woman's boutique. Study the type of shopper and ask the landlord to produce demographic information, including the type of households and income levels in the area.

Malls are okay if your customer can get in and out easily and enough executives frequent the area. It may be a stereotype, but the traditional female executive isn't a shopper. She wants to get in, buy her wardrobe, and get out. So don't settle for a middle-of-the-mall spot that means she has to park six blocks away. This convenience is one of your prime draws over department stores.

Paying for the location that will make a professional women's clothing store work admittedly will make a dent in your purse. Your merchandise doesn't come cheaply, either. Plan on a start-up ante of at least $200,000. And like other clothing stores, margins are tight. The only way to get rich in retail clothing is to build a reputation or open several stores. While they are still paying off their debt service, Marilyn McNutt and her partners squeeze salaries in the $20,000 range and haven't declared a profit. But if your debt load is less, partners might figure on a $30,000 to $40,000 salary and profits of $6,000 to $25,000, depending on the size of your store. A solo owner might bump up the salary, although another salesperson will have to come aboard.

YOUR MERCHANDISE

Just as your customer hasn't the patience to discover a shop hidden in a less-than-prime location, she doesn't want to wade through racks of clothes to find a hidden treasure. Your clothing should portray an image. Display clothing already accessorized with a suede belt and pearls. Don't be mysterious. Know exactly what appeals to your customer and don't stock lots of superfluous items in an attempt to be all things to all people. After all, that's what department stores are for.

Just Grand has fine-tuned its merchandise mix since those early days. Separates (blouses, skirts, and jackets) make up 60 percent of the shop's sales, dresses account for 15 percent of the business, and the rest goes to accessories. "Our customer doesn't really buy suits," says McNutt. "She wants the flexibility to mix and match, and she'd rather buy a skirt and jacket that go with other pieces of her wardrobe." Also, "our customer is older [typically in the 26 to 46 age bracket] than shoppers in a junior's department. She is not necessarily the same size on the top as the bottom, so separates make more sense," adds McNutt. Instead of sizes 6 and 8, Just Grand inventories more 8 to 12.

Any specialty store makes a mistake when it tries to compete with department stores, which can better absorb price markdowns. So the 1,800-square-foot Just Grand attempts to carry different items from its competitors. "If a vendor tells me I'll love a particular dress because Dayton-Hudson just bought a slew of them, I say 'Thanks, but no thanks,' " says McNutt. Just

Grand also doesn't stock 15 of the same blue worsted in different sizes. "We are a neighborhood store," she points out, meaning vice presidents don't fancy meeting their outfit in the elevator on the way to work.

MAKE YOUR STATEMENT

A specialty boutique spells its trump card: s-e-r-v-i-c-e. "Lots of people have a nice selection, but we're known for helping the customer decide what's right for her," says Marilyn McNutt. The ratio of sales help to customers is higher than a department store's because of the personal attention each customer requires. "You need a lot of sales help to mix and match the separates we stock. We don't let customers get out of the store without suggesting they might want a particular scarf for that new outfit." Not only do such suggestions build profitable add-on sales, they also prove to customers that someone pays attention to their needs.

In addition, Just Grand offers free wardrobe counseling by appointment. (See "Image Consultant," page 436, for suggestions on how to master this specialty.) Partner Kadie DeMay outfits about 30 customers every season. When you realize each may spend $1,000 to $1,500 per wardrobe—each season—you'll understand why this is a profitable service worth the bother. DeMay keeps a file on what each client bought last season and encourages them all to bring items from home for her to accessorize.

You also should consider offering alterations. This doesn't have to be a hassle. Just Grand pins hems and other minor alterations in-house and sends the garments for quickie alterations to a tailor. "We offer the service for free," says McNutt. "After all, men's stores don't charge for tailoring, so why should we?"

McNutt says Just Grand won't make the mistake of haphazard expansion again. But she does see a chain of women's professional clothing stores in her future. Her reasoning: "We have a wonderful product. The concept works."

Pushcart Retailer

Job Description: *A pushcart retailer operates old-fashioned pushcarts, usually specializing in a particular item or related group of items that can't typically be found in stores.*

- *Start-up cost as low as $6,000*
- *Potential revenues: $100,000*
- *Breakeven time from initial investment: several weeks to several months*
- *Excellent opportunity for people with physical disabilities*
- *No staffing required*

When the leasing manager approached Karen Richards about selling her decorative rubber stamps from a pushcart at Faneuil Hall Marketplace in Boston, she flatly refused. "I was selling the stamps along with batik ties at craft shows," she recalls. "I had no idea how to display or produce in volume. I didn't know the first thing about business matters like insurance and taxes. And I didn't *want* to know."

TRY IT FOR JUST TWO WEEKS

But Richards relented when the leasing manager gave her a two-week lease at $220 a week plus 10 percent of sales. Inkadinkado Inc. was born with 300 stamps on a pushcart. "Opening a retail operation is like going on the stage," Richards says. "You're all set for public humiliation. You're sure you're going to get booed—that nobody will buy."

Instead, Richards sold . . . and sold . . . and sold. "I began trying to talk people *out* of buying." She laughs. "I promised I'd ship them stamps free of charge. Anything to keep from running out of inventory. I had this two-week commitment and I was terrified I'd run out of stock."

The mall opened at 9:00 A.M. and didn't close until 9:00 P.M. "So all night I made stamps from a factory that let me use their tools, and all day I talked people out of buying," recalls Richards. Nowadays, she's more than happy to sell her stamps. Inkadinkado still operates the Faneuil Hall pushcart, but that's in addition to a manufacturing business, a wholesale operation, a mail-order catalog, and an importing subsidiary with 30 total employees and a gross of over $1 million a year.

THE PUSHCART RENAISSANCE

Pushcarts aren't what they used to be when rag peddlers and knife sharpeners roamed dingy city streets as mobile entrepreneurs. Observers generally credit Faneuil Hall Marketplace with reintroducing the pushcart theme—and sprucing it up to add color and excitement to shopping malls across the country. Today pushcarts and kiosks purvey a range of fun products:

They sell flowers and ceramic jewelry; teddy bears and Christmas tree ornaments; handmade leather belts and anything in the color purple.

If you're thinking of setting up a retail shop, consider some advantages of selling from a pushcart:

- Minimum investment. Rates have gone up from the days when Faneuil Hall first opened, but the average mall now leases a pushcart for about $1,000 a week plus 10 percent of weekly sales over $1,500. You need no fixtures and maintenance is minimal. You do need inventory. Inkadinkado recommends pushcarts selling its stamps start with a $5,000 wholesale batch of stamps, which will retail from $10,000 to $12,000, depending on how much markup you tack on. That stock could last anywhere from two weeks to a month, depending on how fast pushcarters sell.

- Cash flow. You shoot for volume sales, since most pushcart items sell in the $10 range. (As Karen Richards puts it, "Who's going to buy a diamond bracelet from a pushcart?") But this Arrangement means you get wads of cash in every day. If your start-up budget is tight, use this month's cash to finance next month's inventory. In addition to your best-sellers, you may want to stock a few larger, relatively expensive items as well. Not only will a $200 picnic basket, prominently displayed as your centerpiece, add a few substantial sales, it will also attract attention to your less costly wicker items. Most established pushcarters take credit cards to encourage high-ticket sales.

- The best location in the house. Malls usually place pushcarts and kiosks in first-floor sites that only a store with a well-known brand name as well as big bucks to cover first- and last-month rent deposits could afford.

- A short-term commitment. If you're a schoolteacher who wants to spend summers retailing those wonderful silk flowers you design, check out a pushcart.
- Intimate customer contact. "We now consider our pushcart a laboratory cart," says Richards. "When we have 20 new unicorn designs, we see which ones sell before we ship them to our wholesale customers. Faneuil Hall says 1 million people a month go through the mall. The customers give you great feedback—'This stamp is too small, or can you make this one in orange?'" Indeed, a pushcart is a great place to test an entire concept before investing in a store. Sports Etc., a shop stocked with Boston sports team paraphernalia, began as a Faneuil Hall pushcart.
- Likewise, you can test a mall from a pushcart. Let's assume you want to open an earmuff store but wonder whether a particular mall is right for you. Why not see what kind of sales you can eke out from the pushcart before signing a two-year lease?

AUDITIONS

Increasing numbers of malls lease pushcarts. Still, as competition among peddlers grows, you have to work to get a good cart in a good mall. Malls have no obligation to lease you space and expect two contributions from pushcarts: They should add an unusual or unique flavor to the shopping environment and generate profits for the mall. Some pointers on winning the pushcart lease:

- Unless you're wedded to the idea of selling pottery or leather, pick a more unusual product where competition is nil.

- If you're turned down for December (and can afford a slow month), apply for January. Once you prove you can sell under poor conditions, the mall will invite you back for the good times. Or, if your first-choice mall turns you down, apply to another. After a couple of months, take your profit record to your first choice again.

- Malls like track records and may ask what similar operations gross, so do as much homework as possible. Some pushcart vendors franchise, such as the Purple Panache, which sells all sorts of purple clothing and knickknacks. Inkadinkado offers "unfranchises." Explains Karen Richards: "We put dealers through a free three-day training program on how to merchandise. They get a monthly newsletter and discount below the wholesale price for buying with us." Inkadinkado, which takes no fee for the service, asks that prospective dealers line up a location and buy $5,000 in starting inventory before attending its training.

- Check out the retail shops in the mall and don't compete. If a shopping center already has an art gallery, you won't get past the lease manager with a stand selling similar artwork. Many malls reject food kiosks for the same reason. Instead, display a complementary product. For example, assume a mall has no toy store but a nearby retirement population. Your pushcart may offer a perfect solution for grandparents wanting to buy Christmas gifts.

- Present your case professionally. Before visiting with the mall's leasing manager, "sketch what the kiosk will look like and add some color," suggests Richards.

EASY STREET

You can make a nice living selling from a pushcart. But unless you have an incredibly hot product and locate in a very high-traffic area, a pushcart won't make you rich. Because mall hours are long, you probably will hire an assistant, whose salary cuts into your gross. Also, malls like to create excitement by changing pushcart vendors constantly; so you probably can't get a lease for more than six months a year—and probably not six consecutive months. You can, of course, work full time by setting up your wares at a different (noncompeting) mall during off-seasons.

If a pushcart isn't the means to a more than comfortable financial end, you can build up experience and capital operating your pushcart and start a store. Or, like Karen Richards, you can branch out by pushing your cart items to other retailers. If selling to other retailers isn't successful, what's to rule out an empire of pushcarts—a franchise, perhaps, selling all manner of items from pushcarts all over the world?

Rental Center
Supplier

Job Description: *A rental center supplier enables customers to rent, rather than buy, a wide variety of objects for use around the house and outdoors, for both work and recreational purposes.*

- *Start-up cost as low as $90,000*
- *Potential earnings: $150,000*
- *Breakeven time from initial investment: three to seven years*

At the close of World War II, thousands of soldiers received their discharge papers in California. Plans to vacation for a couple of weeks under the palm trees soon led them to settle down amid opportunity and sun. The California housing boom that followed catalyzed a new industry: rentals. Equipment-rental stores sprang up to supply new contractors with equipment to build houses for the transplants. Soon the new centers discovered that homeowners would rent Rototillers to dig their gardens and wheelbarrows to cart away the rocks, so they expanded their inventory to reach a wider audience.

From Construction Equipment to Champagne Glasses

Currently, the American Rental Association (ARA) estimates that over 7,000 rental companies scattered across the country carry everything from heavy construction equipment to champagne glasses. While the phenomenon has taken time to spread east, recent rental growth has been inspiring. Today consumers can rent everything from baby carriages to sump pumps and construction cranes.

The rental boom stems from many sources, ranging from the mobility of American society to growth in the number of small homes and apartments with no room to store infrequently used items. And with the cost of fix-it help today, Americans are more likely to tackle whatever's broken themselves than to hire a professional. More and more, rental companies supply the tools.

Depending on your store's size and whether you choose an expensive urban setting or a less costly suburban locale, expect to spend $90,000 to $350,000 to set up shop. Most of that capital pays for inventory—the items you rent out. General-rental centers typically carry $300,000 to $500,000 worth of stock, using a rule of thumb that says that they should see $1 in rental fees for each dollar spent on inventory. In other words, if you spend $300 for a storage shed, expect it to bring in $300 in rental fees over a year's time. If you keep the shed for five years, renters pay for it five times over.

Paying for the Goodies

Depending on your arrangement with the manufacturer, you don't have to shell out the full price of a $30,000 backhoe up-front. If you're willing to pay their interest rates, many manufacturers of large equipment happily accept monthly payments. "We finance equipment just like you would a car," explains Jeanne McElroy, who runs Resource Rental Center Inc. of Council Bluffs, Iowa, with her husband, Jim. After the 35 to 40 percent down payment, you cover equipment costs with installments from rental income.

While you might not be able to round up enough cash to finance all the goods you eventually want to carry, you can start small and grow gradually, adding (and replacing) inventory as your cash flow allows. Lanny Anderson founded Anderson Rent All in Ithaca, New York, 20 years ago with just $7,500. (He cautions that, if starting today, he would multiply start-up costs by ten due to inflation.) That capital bought a skeleton inventory of rental items, which he added to as revenues grew. Recently Anderson realized up to $32,000 profits on revenues of $400,000 after subtracting his own salary.

The McElroys expect their community's growth to push their revenues of $400,000 (with net income of $64,000) to the half-million-dollar mark. "A lot of out-of-state contractors are bidding on a new shopping complex being built within a mile of us," explains Jeanne McElroy. "They don't bring their heavy equipment with them." Instead, they rent everything from earth movers to concrete pourers for hundreds of dollars a day.

INVENTORY FROM SOUP TO NUTS

Teaching skills serve rental entrepreneurs in good stead. You need product knowledge and the talent to explain to your customers the workings of up to 1,000 pieces of equipment—from air compressors to typewriters. Be sure to ask the manufacturer's sales representative for full demonstrations when you take possession, and be patient when explaining items to renters. "If customers don't get expert instruction, they're either going to have difficulty with the equipment and be dissatisfied or injure themselves," says Richard E. Detmer, author of A *Practical Guide to Working in an Equipment Rental Business* (available from the American Rental Association for $15.00). "Either way, they won't be back."

For inspiration on which items to stock, rental entrepreneurs shop equipment and hardware trade shows and talk to manufacturers' representatives. The best hints come from customers. When a half-dozen people request a wheelchair, for example, it may be time to investigate medical equipment. While someone in Jeanne McElroy's position might stock a lot of construction items for a construction boom, a center in a university town might rent out lots of typewriters around the end of the term.

Inventory mix does not always fall into place automatically, even for those who know the business, so be prepared for some trial and error. You might want to stock a limited number of products and wait to see which categories prove themselves. McElroy, along with her sister, ran her parents' rental store in Omaha for several years. Even with that background, McElroy had a few surprises when she and her husband took some cash and about $65,000 worth of equipment from the Omaha store and qualified for a $100,000 Small Business Administration–backed loan to open their own shop. Instead of the homeowners she rented to in Omaha, she found a Cedar Bluffs customer base of light contractors—"groups of five guys who built apartments on speculation." Instead of $2 hedge trimmers and $10 snow blowers, she found herself renting giant backhoes for $160 a day, plus the trailers to haul them on for another $10.

To learn the needs of your community, read between the lines in local newspapers and check with the local chamber of commerce. Look for statistics on age, income levels, homeowners vs. apartment renters, and large building projects. McElroy cautions that high-income homeowners tend to hire out their jobs. General rental stores tend to do better in middle-income areas with more do-it-yourselfers.

In contrast, if a lot of college kids live in the area, go heavy on party items. (For a separate look at stores that specialize solely in party items, see "Party Rental Supplier," page 677.) Lanny Anderson's party business represents his fastest-growing source of revenues. Providing 25 percent of his total income, it already equals his construction business. The other half of his business comes from homeowners. In addition to supplying local fraternities and sororities, Anderson's party tents and punch bowls attend a lot of weddings. "A lot of people now have weddings at home or in the park," he says. "They do it themselves rather than go to the country club."

SOMEONE HAS TO BE MECHANICAL

You can break down the rental business into front-of-the-store functions, such as dealing with customers and manufacturers, and backroom responsibilities, which usually means maintenance. "Someone has to be mechanical, because equipment constantly needs repair," says Dick Detmer. A long fuse helps, too. "People will take a $700 chain saw meant for cutting firewood and try to cut tree roots out of the ground." Detmer groans. "Do you know what that does to equipment?"

Customer use and abuse reduces a tool's life span. You have

to assume a continuous reinvestment. Some stores levy a refundable 5 to 10 percent deposit to cover damages or loss, which helps cover the costs. Jeanne McElroy simply assumes she must replace $20,000 pieces of construction machinery every three years or so and homeowner tools, such as lawn mowers and chain saws, annually. Knowing that, she prices rentals high enough to get her money's worth. Some competitors keep the equipment for five years, replacing just the motor when it blows. "But," says McElroy, "we think the image of new equipment is worth the price. The industry has a reputation for being way too junky." Her tactic of establishing a quality image encourages repeat visits to Resource Rental Center.

Rather than absorbing the losses associated with the rapid turnover of equipment, McElroy profits by selling used tools to customers who liked what they rented. "Some people say you'll lose your rental customers if they buy the equipment, but we sell them a service agreement to keep them coming back. You have to be flexible."

Rental stores thrive on repeat business; customers who catch on to the advantages of renting are loyal. Dick Detmer estimates the same consumers come back for either different equipment or the same item an average 15 to 20 times a year; contractors, who comprise one out of every four of Lanny Anderson's clients, come in every day. Especially when you consider this type of repeat potential, it pays to keep customers satisfied. Working on community relationships pays, too. Detmer says he invited grade-school kids to the store he ran in upstate New York for field trips. They told their parents about the experience, and his business increased. He also recommends product demonstrations to local service clubs.

THE POTENTIAL

Industry spokespeople feel the rental business needs to get its message across more clearly. "People are conditioned to think about buying," says Dick Detmer. "They just don't consider renting." Most rental-store owners are happy to recite the benefits of renting: Why buy a snow blower you drag out of the basement once each February? When visiting Grandma, wouldn't it be simpler to rent a car seat for the baby rather than lug yours on the airplane? In addition to a national marketing effort led by the ARA, many local entrepreneurs are increasing their advertising. Lanny Anderson puts aside 5 percent of his budget to advertise in the newspaper, Yellow Pages, and on the local radio stations, and to set up and staff displays in malls. The entrepreneurs say that, with a little effort on their part, America is bound to discover renting.

SOURCE

Industry Association

American Rental Association, 1900 19th Street, Moline, IL 61265, (800) 334-2177

Sales and Marketing

Auction House Dealer

Job Description: *An auction house dealer sells items to the highest bidder.*

- *Start-up cost as low as $500*
- *Potential earnings: $15,000*
- *Breakeven time from initial investment: immediate to six months*
- *No staffing required*

In her third year as a business major at Washburn University, Susan Stucke faced up to her own particular reality: "My father ran his own business and I'd been raised to be real independent. I couldn't see myself working for somebody else the rest of my life. So I decided I'd have to start my own business."

But everything required money—which Stucke just didn't have. "When my father suggested auctions, I was skeptical," she recalls. True, she had enjoyed attending auctions all her life, and she could open an auction house for the price of the first month's rent. A two-week course at the Missouri Auction School in Kansas City (which now runs $425) convinced her.

The enthusiasm of the instructors, all successful auctioneers in their own right, lit the bonfire. "The day I came home from school, I rented a building," says Stucke, who is now entitled to the honorary title of "Colonel," a holdover from colonels who auctioned off their mules at the end of the Civil War. Stucke quit college, "which I didn't need anyway," and worked full time in a retail store. But she spent nights and weekends scouting for merchandise and rounding up audiences. That first year Stucke Auctions in Topeka, Kansas, auctioned off about $250,000 worth of everything from "trash to treasures." Stucke soon devoted full time to the auction house. After ten years, business topped the $1 million mark, not counting what she made at on-site auctions or freelancing as an auctioneer for other auction concerns. On-line auctions are also a growing marketplace. According to *Time* magazine, on-line auctions accounted for $4.5 billion in sales in 1999, and are expected to account for $15.5 billion in sales by 2001.

JUST A SALES TOOL

Experts trace auctions (the word comes from the Latin *auctio*, meaning gradual increase) through Greek literature, as far back as 450 B.C. Some categories—art, tobacco, horses—have sold at auction for years, causing many auctioneers downright amusement at the way auctions are turning the country upside down. Today just about anything two or more people want to buy can be sold at auction. "Auctioneering is merely a method of selling," clarifies Dick Dewees, who runs the Missouri Auction School in Kansas City, and takes weekend auctioneering jobs. And a growing number of auctioneers who raffle off everything from $20,000 Persian carpets to $2 baseball cards agree. (For a look at real estate auctions, probably the hottest segment of the industry, see "Real Estate Auctioneer," page 519.) In her regularly scheduled auctions twice a week, Susan Stucke says with pride she'll auction anything from cardboard boxes of garage-sale leftovers, to tractors, to estates. She also schedules specialty auctions: coins every Wednesday and once-a-month events devoted to antiques and restaurant equipment.

To set up an auction house, experts suggest five steps:

1. Learn what Dick Dewees refers to as "the auction method of selling" (including talking fast)
2. Establish an auction house
3. Gather merchandise
4. Attract bidders
5. Hold the auction

STEP 1: TALKING FAST

Several auction schools train auctioneers, and, if you want, you can receive certification from the Auction Marketing Institute. Dick Dewees's Missouri Auction school needs just two weeks to turn out auctioneers. "We take people who already know the product to be auctioned, so we don't teach you about your field of expertise," explains Dewees. "We teach you the auction method of promoting." That basically means advertising—and how to talk fast.

Explains Dewees: "I can say 'one-and-a-half'—that's four words. Or I can say 'one-naff' twice as fast. Crank that into a chant and raise and lower the voice with the help of a PA system, and you sound like you talk a lot faster than you really do." By the third night at school, Dewees's students call a real auction. "They might not be good yet," he says, "but they get through it." After a few more sessions, the technique becomes second nature, he insists.

To be sure, you can't be a wallflower and call auctions. While being a bit of a showman helps, true loudmouths lose credibility. Auctioneers want to project a sense of fun and urgency and their own confidence in the product. Auctioneers, like public-speaking instructors, say the basis of confidence is knowing your stuff. If you're auctioning pens, you'd better understand the difference between a Bic and a Cross. "You'd be amazed at how many just plain people get a microphone in hand and take charge," says Dick Dewees.

STEP 2: SETTING UP HOUSE

Unless you auction fine art or expensive antiques, you don't need a classy storefront. Instead, look for lots of traffic and easy access. "The better your location, the less you spend on advertising," points out Susan Stucke.

Your house needs a theaterlike arena as well as storage and display space for the merchandise. You also need office space and public rest room facilities. Stucke recommends the optional restaurant or food stand. "People can't bid when they're sitting down at McDonald's," she says. "Also, hot dogs and Cokes provide a little extra income." A small start-up can squeak by with 1,500 square feet (plus parking and loading facilities), while large auction houses easily gobble up five times that space.

Check out competition and population draw from nearby communities to see how many auctions your particular region will support. Much depends on how often local residents frequent auctions. Topeka (population 120,000) supports numerous houses because consumers regularly buy and sell through auctions. Susan Stucke estimates three out of every four members of her typical audience are regular customers. Such loyalty lets her do two sales a week.

STEP 3: GETTING THE GOODS

"It's amazing where you can find merchandise," says Stucke. Basically, general houses auction items from individuals (such as someone who wants to sell an old car), dealers and collectors, and repeaters (such as bankers and attorneys who must dispose of estates or arrange distress sales). When Stucke first began, she called newspaper want-ad numbers, suggesting that advertisers who failed to sell their television or washing machine through the ad bring it by Stucke's. She made the same pitch to people holding garage sales.

But those stray air conditioners and sofas require a lot of legwork. And often you can get stuck with junk. (Stucke solves the junk problem by taking 30 to 50 percent commissions on items that auction for under a certain price.) Your time might be better spent in establishing long-term, high-volume relationships. For example, banks and lawyers might hesitate to assign large estates to a new auction house, but they may send one or two pieces your way. Later on, they can become prime sources of merchandise, and even whole estates. Stucke also contacts miniwarehouses and moving companies that repossess property that owners don't claim. Other sources include retailers who take bicycle or lawn mower trade-ins and even car dealerships.

If you're successful, sellers will start knocking on your door, so the merchandise canvas gets easier. "As soon as I get booked up for the Wednesday auction, I tell sellers to come back again in time for the Saturday auction," says Stucke. "When I come in on Thursday morning, I have eight or ten pickups full of stuff in the lot so they'll be first in line for Saturday." The seller is responsible for getting the merchandise to your door, and the buyer pays to cart it away.

Some auctioneers actually buy large lots of merchandise from close-out sources or overseas contacts. Then they refurbish the individual pieces and auction each item separately. While you tie up capital for the month or so it takes between buying and selling the goods, 100 or 200 percent returns aren't uncommon.

More typically, however, auctioneers accept goods on consignment. While fees to the seller average 15 percent, commissions range anywhere from 5 percent on really large estates to 50 percent on low-end items. Art auctioneers traditionally take 10 percent commissions from both the buyer and seller. In some cases, sellers ask for estimates of what their Remington (painting or typewriter) will bring. If you're qualified, you can eyeball the merchandise yourself; otherwise call for an expert appraisal and pass along the cost of the seller.

STEP 4: BRINGING IN BIDDERS

"Getting an audience is the least of your problems," insists Susan Stucke. "Everybody has auction fever now. I just have to let people know I'm having an auction—I don't even tell them what I'm selling. They'll come out of curiosity."

In areas of the Midwest where auctions are a way of life, radio stations and newspapers regularly devote an advertising section to auctions. If you're hawking expensive items that might draw national attention, consider advertising in specialty publications. Many houses use direct mail, either to the general public or to a list of regular bidders.

If you're selling items that attract a middle-income audience, just let the folks know the theme of the auction. For example, you might sell general household goods, or antiques in the $100 to $1,000 range. But to attract heavy bidders to a collector's sale, you'll need to detail your inventory piece by piece. For example, Leslie Hindman Auctioneers in Chicago sends glossy, illustrated catalogs to regular bidders of art or estates. Each item is described and carries an estimate of what the appraiser expects it to bring. Prices usually fall somewhere between wholesale and retail.

Whether you're dealing with Louis XIV antiques or circa-1960 refrigerators, buyers like to inspect the merchandise. You have to invite all those prospective buyers to your premises beforehand so they can examine the goods. Dick Dewees emphasizes the importance of merchandising: "If you pile pieces of jewelry in a heap they won't bring as much as if you lay the better ones on black velvet."

STEP 5: THE EVENT

Until this point, a very busy entrepreneur could handle all these tasks—from renting the auction hall to bringing in buyers and sellers—alone. Now you need support: typically two or three "ring" people to display merchandise and take bids while you auction; a cashier to take the money; and a clerk to record transactions and settle accounts with the sellers. For really big auctions, or specialty events requiring expertise, you need a second—or third—auctioneer. The good news is you don't need a bloated payroll. Just subcontract with all these people as freelancers.

Most auctions sell 60 to 100 items an hour, and most last no more than five hours. The audience (not to mention the auctioneer) simply tires if you go any longer. If you land a really big estate, stretch the auction over several days.

Different auctioneers use different techniques to keep the audience's attention. Susan Stucke alternates one large, expensive item with a lesser item at her general auctions. In large estate auctions, Leslie Hindman's catalogs note the order items go on the block, so buyers interested in a particular sapphire don't have to sit through the Chippendale antique segment of the auction.

WHERE DO YOU GO FROM HERE

You can make a good living from an auction house, but most auctioneers don't stop with the business their auction houses generate, no matter how robust it grows. Unless you specialize in a particular category—autographs or fine wines, for example—shoot for the big, single-estate sales. You can hold those at your facility or on location. "Outside sales have so much more potential because you don't have overhead," explains Susan Stucke. On top of the regular commission fee, many auctioneers charge advertising fees to bring the bidders to the site.

With the proliferation of auctions, many medium-size houses have more business than they can handle. When you're not auctioning your own account, chances are you can sign on with somebody else. For example, Stucke receives expenses plus $300 to $1,000 a day to call business liquidation auctions for an Atlanta firm. She has so much fun calling auctions she even does some for free. "I call charity benefits like the Muscular Dystrophy Foundation," she says. "I donate my time, but I get to travel, all expenses paid, to the really fabulous resorts of the world."

SOURCE

Industry Association

National Auctioneers Association, 8880 Ballentine, Overland Park, KS 66214-1985, (913) 541-8084

Consumer Show Organizer

Job Description: *A consumer show organizer gathers retailers who specialize in one particular field or type of product. The organizer also provides activities for attendees.*

- *Start-up cost as low as $12,000*
- *Potential earnings: $50,000*
- *Breakeven time from initial investment: one to four years*

"Mindy Odegard and I had planned our pregnancies together and had daughters six weeks apart," says Deborah Rothman, president of Baby and Family Fair of Santa Monica, California. "I had been practicing law and she was in retailing, and neither of us wanted to return to our professions. So we started Baby Fair to fulfill the fantasy of finding all the baby products and information together in the same place where you could also change diapers and play with the babies."

Rothman is reminiscing about the launching of Baby Fair, which has now expanded to include products and seminars aimed at toddlers and preschoolers as well as infants. That first show attracted over 100 exhibitors and 1,500 consumers to the Santa Monica Civic Center. Rothman continues: "That first show attracted a total media blitz because of the wall-to-wall bellies," since many browsers were more than a little bit pregnant. Other consumers came with their tiny families in tow. "That was also the weekend where the term 'stroller gridlock' was invented."

THRILLS, CHILLS, AND EXCITEMENT

Baby and Family Fair doesn't sound much like a hardware show, or a plumber's convention, or any other exhibition staged by a trade organization, does it? Trade shows (see "Trade Show Organizer," page 638) increasingly are serious undertakings, meant to educate members of an industry and provide a forum from which to do business. Consumer shows, on the other hand, combine education and sales with a lot of fun. For example, Baby and Family Fair has story time and play areas for the kids along with booths displaying Aprica strollers. Whether you run a boat show or a flower fair, you're as much a part of the entertainment world as the theater up the block. To make it fun, you might decide to offer extras, such as food or raffles. In fact, exhibitors may agree to donate prizes.

Of course, there are a host of similarities between consumer shows and trade shows. For example, both shows nail down exhibitors in much the same way: through direct mail and telemarketing to lists bought through trade publications and associations. But a consumer show can survive with fewer exhibitors since your audience likely is local and therefore the hall you rent may be smaller than the mammoth (and expensive) caverns trade shows need. Depending on the type of show you run, you also can call on local businesses; for example, food shows can ask local restaurants to participate along with national distributors. In addition to contacting national toy companies, Deborah Rothman asked her daughter's gym to exhibit.

Following the practice of trade conventions, consumer-show exhibitors buy booth space before the show, which allows you to pay for auditorium space, advertise to the public, and cover setup costs with exhibitors' money rather than your own. "A convention center gives you empty space, and you do what you like with it," explains Mike Hallal, vice president of Mitch Hall Associates in Westwood, Massachusetts, which throws open its computer shows to the public. Setting up a show could mean elaborate decorations, carpeting, and flowers, or it could mean just stark booths. You provide these amenities yourself or hire organizations that specialize in show setup.

THE GATE

Unlike a trade show, consumer expos get to charge admission. Mitch Hall's shows attract 30,000 people at a shot, all willing to pay $15 to shop the booths—or a very hefty $40 to attend seminars. These fees, mind you, come on top of $2,000 booth fees for maybe 600 booths. And they come twice a year since Mitch Hall stages the expo both in Boston and San Francisco.

Of course, Mitch Hall can command such fees because the shows deliver—they deliver consumers for the products and products for consumers. You probably can't get such prices from either exhibitors or the public on your first convention. But as the show's reputation grows among both segments, your prices rise. If a Jacuzzi manufacturer generates solid sales and leads from your home show, it will be easy to sign the firm up next year—or for extra stops on your five-city tour.

To deliver those customers, you have to advertise. Unlike a trade event, consumer shows spend huge sums to advertise in local papers, on the radio and television, and to hobbyists in specialty publications. Baby and Family Fair spends $50,000 to $75,000 to advertise in every city it visits. And don't neglect free publicity. Most city magazines and newspapers carry a calendar of events. Also, invite reporters to cover the show, which will help build your reputation for next year.

TAKE IT ON THE ROAD

Once you get the formula down, you can duplicate the show elsewhere. If your idea works in one place, likely it will fly in another, as well (unless competition gets there before you do). Some of the groundwork is already done since exhibitors might agree to buy booths in different cities. After all, a whole new group of customers will view their wares in each city. During their third year in business, for example, Baby Fair toured seven cities. If your show is at all specialized, however, make sure you put down stakes in the right places. Mitch Hall chose the high-tech Boston and San Francisco markets for its computer show.

Craft Wholesaler

Job Description: *A craft wholesaler makes and sells unique items at the wholesale level.*

- *Start-up cost as low as $500*
- *Potential earnings: $100,000*
- *Breakeven time from initial investment: very rapid (one month to six months)*
- *No staffing required*

Faced with a recession that was depressing his kitchen remodeling business, Bill Campbell decided to register for an interior design course to pass the time and complement his business skills. One day he came on a class on how to make pottery. "I found myself handing over $10 to enroll. That class changed my life because it showed me something I really wanted to do badly."

Campbell spent the next five years studying pottery at the university level. Then he plowed into an "irrelevant" job for four years in order to save enough money to practice his art full time. "My new wife and I moved to Cambridge Springs, Pennsylvania, with $3,000 and a mortgage on our house and a mortgage on the building where I was going to make pottery and Jane was going to make jewelry. Somehow we got through that first year. I did some retail craft shows and one wholesale show. They weren't terribly exciting, but I got some orders and I learned how to display my work and how to present myself with a business card and catalog."

The next year Campbell returned to the wholesale show where retailers from across the country shop for crafts to sell in their stores. By 3:00 P.M. he had $10,000 in orders for the functional, beautiful pottery he makes. "I was so excited that when I went to call my wife, first I forgot the phone number, then I couldn't remember her name."

Today, Bill Campbell's Factory Studios sells by wholesale somewhere between $500,000 and $1 million worth of pottery (he won't be more specific) to 400 retail outlets up and down the East Coast. Like most craftspeople who have hit the big time, Campbell skirts questions about how many potters work for him. "When you have more than one employee, artisans start accusing us of being a factory."

THE WHOLESALE CONNECTION

Bill Campbell is one of thousands of craftspeople who might have struggled below the poverty line a decade ago. Today department stores, catalogers, and galleries snatch up ceramic jewelry and hand-blown goblets to sell to "Americans fed up with the garbage that's been dumped on us," says Wendy Rosen, whose Wendy Rosen Agency Inc. stages the two largest whole-sale-only trade shows for craftspeople in the country. (See "Trade Show Organizer," page 638.)

Until Rosen and a few other individuals dreamed up whole-sale craft shows, artisans sold one brass bracelet or hand-carved buckle at a time from booths at crafts fairs. Alternatively, they knocked on retail doors, hoping to interest the local men's shop in 20 or 30 belts. But retailers who order quantities in the thousands changed all that. "When I first began my shows, exhibitors [artisans] averaged $30,000 to $50,000 in production a year," recalls Rosen. "Now $1 million isn't uncommon and $150,000 is average. Many clients have doubled and tripled volume."

Michael Scott, editor of the *Crafts Report*, which reports on business aspects of the artisan colony, estimates "at least 100,000 people make all or part of a living through crafts." Pointing to universities that teach jewelry and pottery making (a few have even added business courses in the art department), he notes, "The attitude toward making money in crafts has changed. Once starving was considered a part of the artistic experience. Now it's acceptable to make a very comfortable living as a craftsperson."

LIFESTYLE

While artisans work hard, they get to organize their business on their own terms. As an artist, you work when and where you please. "I'm a powder skier," says Jan Mayer, who located Kriska Painting on Silk in Salt Lake City for easy access to the Alta ski slopes. "I don't care if it's my busiest season; when the powder comes, I take a day."

Jan Mayer and partner Christine Boiral (Kriska herself) make delicate hand-painted scarves whose vibrant colors and abstract designs remind him of the geography of Bryce Canyon. Mayer acknowledges that he probably could make more than the $20,000 to $40,000 he keeps out of Kriska's $500,000 annual revenues—if he wanted to compromise his lifestyle. "Most of my employees make as much as I do," he says, noting that Kriska's profit-sharing plan gives employees a pride in their work and a sense of responsibility that allows him to travel up to six months a year on business and pleasure. In fact, he often combines the two; he recalls a seminar week in Ixtapa, Mexico, where artisans spent days windsurfing and evenings organizing a crafts equivalent to the Good Housekeeping seal of approval.

CRASHING THE GATE

The best place to meet retailers who will turn your hobby into your profession is at a wholesale show or the crafts section of a gifts show for wholesale buyers. Some craftspeople win acceptance the first year they apply to the shows, but you may have to build a reputation first. Show juries judge the worthiness of your work, and, depending how crowded your particular craft is, weed out competition. If you can't crash one of the premier shows your first year in business, don't despair. You still can make contacts and build a reputation through smaller shows. You can even take your windchimes or wall hangings directly to stores.

Booth fees run from $100 to $600, depending on the show. Bill Campbell and his wife, Jane, set aside another $1,000 for large multiday shows to cover transportation, food, and lodging. In addition to a sampling of your wares, bring brochures and catalogs. Set aside several hundred dollars to design and print the material. Spell out prices and terms in black and white, and picture your quilts or jewelry in glossy four-color.

CAN YOU MAKE 100 JUST LIKE THAT ONE?

The most exquisite craftsmanship in North America won't entice retailers who doubt that you can deliver on time, in quantity, and with consistent quality. Buyers want assurance that you can reproduce the quality they see at the show. While your craft represents your creative side, the printed brochure gives them a sense of your professionalism.

Craftspeople steer "true artists" away from the wholesale route, warning that you must ask employees to replicate a single pattern many times. Artistry often takes a backseat to delegation, leading many high-volume craftspeople to characterize themselves as designers rather than artisans. Bill Campbell insists he lacks "an ethereal sense" about his pottery, which retails from $12 to $50. Instead of crafting museum pieces, "I try to create a feeling of celebration when people use my pottery," he explains. "I want you to smile when you reach for an incredible salad bowl. And you won't have to guess at the function of my pottery. It's onomatopoetic—a fish platter looks like it's meant to serve fish."

Sergio Lub, an Argentinian native who makes brass and copper bracelets in Walnut Creek, California, recalls the moment of insight that changed his show behavior. "I realized that to make money at the shows was not my main objective. My real goal was to meet retailers, get to know who they are so they would commit themselves to represent me." Instead of waiting anxiously in his booth for orders as exhibitors do at retail fairs, Lub began walking the aisles to meet retail buyers. "If I open just one new account, the reorders cover the show costs and much more."

Most big-time craftspeople attend 8 to 12 shows a year, including some traditional fairs for the public. Although wholesale orders account for 90 percent of the Factory Store's revenues, "fairs are where the market is tested," Bill Campbell says. "Listen to the public. They're a mean jury—'This handle's too big.' 'Have you got this in blue?'" Remember that, unlike the purist, you're designing for bulk sales, so you must respond to the public whim.

After you take the public's pulse, listen to the other craftspeople. More than in most other fields, artisans share secrets that work for them. "Shows are an opportunity to pick the brains of people next to me," says Jan Mayer. "Network. The most successful people in the country are at these shows."

Mayer and his artisan contacts often trade lists of wholesale accounts so they can approach likely retailers after the shows are over. The most successful craftspeople are marketers. They send brochures and call on gallery owners or museum shop buyers on their own turf. Mayer's three-person marketing division also holds the hands of about 600 old friends—retailers who already carry Kriska scarves. "Retailers need help; they're very busy people," acknowledges Mayer, who has a toll-free phone number to encourage orders.

ON APPROVAL

Sergio Lub, whose $15 to $40 bracelets sell in approximately 600 museum shops and galleries, developed a way to entice new accounts aboard. Basically, he trusts them with credit by offering his bracelets "on approval." Traditional artisans, possibly because they lived on the poverty level, expected up-front payment for their wares. But many retailers shied away from contracting with craftspeople, fearing their reputation for unreliability.

Lub's no-lose solution gives retailers a display case with $1,000 worth of bracelets for a month or two on a trial basis. If they don't sell, ship them back. If customers like the bracelets, a retailer knows within 30 or 60 days and pays at that point. Now the only way Sergio Lub Inc. does business is on approval. Returns equal about 5 percent of sales, but the policy has significantly multiplied the accounts willing to try his wares. "It's better to sell 100 pieces and lose 2 or 3 than to sell just 10 and lose none," Lub says.

On-approval policies have limits, however. Lub draws the line at difficult-to-ship work, such as big pots and fragile glass items that must be packaged very carefully.

GROWTH ORIENTED

Even as the crafts world evolves from its cottage-industry roots to the big time, most artisans never consider marketing. But both Sergio Lub and his good friend Jan Mayer offer retailers co-op ad campaigns; they pay half the cost of any ad that features their products. "I have a $20,000 ad budget, which many consider unrealistic. If I wanted to cut back on advertising, I could double my salary. But," says Mayer, "I'm growth oriented."

Apparently, promotion helps. Stores that advertise Lub's bracelets see an average 30 percent increase in business. Ad costs eat about 10 percent of the extra income, which, Lub points out, "gives us a return of almost ten to one." He also notes that craftspeople make good copy for newspapers interested in alternative lifestyles. Since an interesting story sells more items than an expensive ad, approach the press with how you weave baskets.

WE'RE DIFFERENT

Even as they move into the mainstream, craftspeople still differ from most businesspeople. While all manufacturers worry about quality control, for example, artisans take it to the extreme. Sergio Lub includes a lifetime guarantee with every brass or copper bracelet, even the $8 children's line. If it breaks, return it for repair or replacement. And while competition surely exists among artisans, it is more subtle than in other industries. Craftspeople talk about the familylike atmosphere of their field. Artisans also value such traits as integrity. "Over the years, I've probably taken $50,000 worth of checks at the Columbia University Show, which is right next door to Harlem," says Jan Mayer. "I never got a bad check."

One continuing debate involves the very prosperity crafts now enjoy. To grow large, artisans must hire employees to duplicate their work. Some diehard craftspeople argue against what they consider assembly-line tactics. Even businesspeople

like Bill Campbell admit that "part of our strength is the uniqueness of our crafts."

The question remains: How many times can a crafts maker
duplicate an item before it loses its uniqueness? Some million-
dollar shops are convinced they still have room to grow before
compromising their artistry.

SOURCE

Industry Association

American Craft Council, 72 Spring Street, New York, NY
10012-4019, (212) 274-0630

Direct Sales Operator

Job Description: *A direct sales operator sells products to consumers without benefit of a retail store, by door to door, over the telephone, or other methods.*

- *Start-up cost as low as $1,000*
- *Potential earnings: $20,000*
- *Breakeven time from initial investment: a few months to one year*
- *Ideal home-based business*
- *No staffing required*

The pioneer ancestor of the Avon Lady was the Yankee peddler who brought goods from the East to the little houses scattered across the prairies. Modern-day descendants of these traveling merchants have created a $23.17 billion industry, according to the Direct Selling Association. Nearly 70 percent of these sales are made at the home, by a workforce that is overwhelmingly composed (99.8 percent) of independent contractors.

Garage Classics

Despite the move from covered wagon to station wagon, a great many things have *not* changed in the direct selling industry. Importantly, it remains a low-cost business to enter. "You don't need $2,000 a month to lease a retail store or capital for half a million pieces of direct mail," says Robert H. King, chairman of Consumer Marketing Services Inc. of Hollywood, Florida. Since the sales staff receives commissions instead of salaries, you don't need to worry about payroll and withholding taxes and fringe benefits. After the initial inventory purchase, additional product can be purchased using income from sales. "No other retail approach allows you to bootstrap the way direct sales does," observes King.

Indeed, King, who left the chairmanship of the direct-mail encyclopedia firm World Book Inc. to start his own direct sales consulting firm, jokes that "my partner and I were discussing plans to start our own ladies undergarment direct sales business, when he said, 'We'd better buy a garage,' When I asked why, he said 'Because all the successful direct selling companies started in a garage.'" In Consumer Marketing's first year as a direct sales operation, King did not object to losing $37,000 on sales of $250,000 because of the potential to earn $250,000 on $1.5 million in revenues the very next year.

King can afford to wait 18 months for profitability and is investing in a computer system and warehouse with his eyes on explosive growth. But "direct sales has always been a distribution channel where you can exchange perspiration for start-up capital," he says, pointing to all those success stories that start with a tiny nest egg.

For example, Rita Berro Kasdon started Concept Now

Cosmetics in Santa Fe Springs, California, by cashing in a $6,000 life insurance policy. Kasdon put aside $1,000 to support herself and her two children until cash started flowing, and spent the rest on cosmetics inventory. "I couldn't afford to have the lab [that formulated the cosmetics] apply the labels," she recalls, "so I stuck them on at the warehouse myself." Today Concept Now supports 6,000 sales reps in the United States, Canada, Mexico, and Southeast Asia. With global sales expected to top $10 million, Kasdon plans on taking the company public.

One element that makes direct mail profitable is that money isn't tied up in inventory or bad debts. From the beginning, Concept Now required its salespeople to include a money order or cashier's check when placing an order, and used that capital to buy from suppliers. "There are no accounts receivable in this business," Kasdon explains. "I've never borrowed because it isn't necessary."

WHAT SELLS?

Before plunging into the direct selling world, consider what you're selling. Experts suggest choosing between two categories of products:

- Big-ticket items that have a unique feature which a trained salesperson explains directly to the consumer. For example, Bose Corporation sells stereo equipment door to door, which allows its sales crew to show how such a compact system can deliver superior sound. Some companies precede door-to-door sales with phone solicitations. Many big-ticket companies expect customers to pay in installments. So if you choose to hawk computers, you may need more start-up cash to buy inventory than a company that requires immediate payment.

■ Small-ticket items with high markups, such as costume jewelry, cosmetics, and health food products. What you lose in the price of the merchandise you make up in volume since customers buy these types of goodies repeatedly. Since a salesperson with minimal training can explain the less complicated benefits of these products, this segment of the industry relies on part-time representatives who typically sell to friends and coworkers as well as door to door. Parties, where several consumers are invited to see a product at the home of a host or hostess, are another popular approach.

A CAST OF THOUSANDS

Success rests with encouraging a sales staff to knock on doors. "Incentives are important in any business, but extraordinarily important in direct sales," says Bob King. To keep a steady flow of salespeople pounding their beats, expect to sponsor contests, travel, and recognition programs.

When starting Concept Now, Rita Berro Kasdon decided that, to attract a sales force in the face of savage competition from other direct sales cosmetics firms, she would offer a "far more generous" compensation plan than competitors. "Therefore, I was willing to take very little out of the company in the beginning. I only drew $700 a month for the first year, while one of CNC's top salespeople earned over $50,000 during her first year." Concept Now kept interest high with such promotional bonuses as gold Cadillacs, diamond and gold rings, diamond watches, and trips to Hawaii. Kasdon's strategy of practically giving away the store in an effort to develop a strong, loyal sales force worked! Concept Now recorded a $25,000 profit during its first year in business.

Look at it this way: Instead of spending a bundle to lease a store and advertise directly to the consumer, you give that money directly to the sales reps. You can recruit your first salespeople through newspaper advertising. Consumer Marketing even offered some minimum-income guarantees to encourage sales reps to sign on in its first year. But your best source of sales help soon becomes other salespeople.

No matter how motivated each individual representative is, you need increasing numbers of sales people to grow. Successful direct sales firms encourage representatives to view new sales reps as a source of opportunity rather than competition. In using incentives to recruit, beware of illegal pyramid schemes. Your sales crew must legitimately buy products, either for their own use or to sell to customers, before you can reward individuals who brought them into the ranks. This prohibition against doling out dollars dates to the 1970s, when the industry earned a sleazy reputation from companies that paid "salespeople" who didn't sell to enlist other "distributors" who didn't distribute. Instead, each new recruit bought a required initial storehouse of inventory, then, rather than sell products, rounded up new recruits. Their commissions came not from the sale of products rotting in the basement, but from inventory fees paid by the next batch of recruits. Like a chain letter, pyramids are illegal.

It is perfectly legal, however, to pay a recruiter a percentage of the recruitee's sales, and direct sales compensation packages can get pretty elaborate. Explains Kasdon: "If you're a friend of mine and talk me into distributing, Concept Now pays you 5 percent on everything I sell." Once retail volume exceeds $800 a month for 12 consecutive months, the salesperson takes home an extra 4 percent of her friend's sales. But income opportunities don't stop there. If a recruit sponsors additional salespeople, the initial sponsor gets a percentage of all the sales made by people her recruit enlists as well. And so on. Concept Now's literature assumes that a salesperson working just six hours a week can host eight parties a month. If customers buy an average $150 worth of cosmetics at each party, the rep earns $600 a month. An executive director who sponsors 20 salespeople earns $4,856 for the same 24 hours she puts in, since her income is leveraged by the work of other reps, also working an average of 24 hours a month.

PROFIT CHUNKS

Sales commissions and related recruiting and incentive fees eat up the greatest chunk of your margins, followed by product costs and administration costs. As you grow, you can add computers to track inventory, billing, and commissions, or you can farm out those chores to firms that specialize in direct sales time-sharing. Likewise, some entrepreneurs hire warehouses to distribute their goods, although others would rather sip snake venom than entrust distribution to outsiders. "If the parent company doesn't deliver those goods to the sales representative quickly and in good order, they'll hear about it," Bob King says. "A lot of companies set 24- or 48-hour deadlines for the turnaround time after the receipt of the order."

In the end, most direct sales companies look for pretax profits in the 20 percent range, which beats the spangles off of a retail store's 3 to 5 percent profits. Since the commissions must be high enough to attract a sales staff, "you need a product that doesn't cost much relative to what you can sell it for," advises Rita Berro Kasdon. Bob King says a product that costs more than 40 percent of your sales just doesn't qualify as a direct sales item.

Women typically represent both the direct sales customer and the salesperson. As women increasingly enter the workplace, observers see some changes ahead for the industry. For one thing, instead of visiting homes, more representatives are selling in offices and factories. The Direct Selling Association estimates one out of every five Avon Product sales takes place in the workplace. In response to the changing marketplace, Tupperware developed a 20-minute rush-hour office party.

In addition, direct sellers are adopting other approaches to supplement door-to-door sales. Some organizations mail catalogs to customers and potential customers. A few are adding retail locations but retaining the personal attention consumers can't get anymore in most stores.

But those are auxiliary approaches, meant only to increase the effectiveness of the lone sales representative. "Those additions can come later," says King. "The field is still open to an entrepreneur with a product the marketplace genuinely needs."

SOURCE

Industry Association

Direct Selling Association, 1666 K Street, N.W., Suite 1010, Washington, DC 20006-2808, (202) 293-5760

Rubber Stamp Designer

Job Description: *A rubber stamp designer creates stamps, craft projects, and scrapbooks that have intricate, whimsical, decorative, or humorous designs on them and are used for self-expression and just plain enjoyment.*

- *Start-up cost: approximately $10,000*
- *Potential first-year earnings: $30,000*
- *Future growth potential: high*
- *No staffing required*
- *Artistic business that allows for freedom of expression*

Do you wish you were in a more creative business? Are you frequently struck by flights of whimsy? Do you add a little flair to the letters when you sign your name? Are you perpetually doodling little cartoons of smiling suns, friendly flowers, and adorable angels? Do you enjoy arts and crafts?

If the answer to any or all of these questions is "yes," then you might be ready to make your mark in the rubber stamp business, which the *Dallas Morning News* called "one of the fastest-growing crafts in the United States and Europe."

STAMP ME FIVE

If all you know about rubber stamps is that your kids used to stamp them all over everything (paper, the walls, clothing, and your outgoing mail), it's time to wake up and smell the ink. Today the rubber stamp industry—yes, *industry*—is hotter than a volcano.

Nowadays it's not kids but adults who express themselves with rubber stamps. Devotees use them to create their own greeting cards, gift wrap, bookmarks, stationery, and a variety of other paper-based items. Serious stampers use them for everything from handmade door knockers and pillows to ceramic tiles, blinds, wall borders, and scrapbooks (sometimes called memory albums). The uses of rubber stamps are limited only by your imagination.

Rubber stamping is so hot there are trade shows, conventions, publications, and Internet sites all dedicated to the art of rubber stamping. There hobbyists can sell and swap stamps, trade ideas on usage, and tell people how much enjoyment they get from stamping.

CHOOSING A METHOD

There are two basic methods for starting a rubber stamp business. The first is to limit your business strictly to designing (that is, drawing) the stamps and use outside vendors for the actual production. The second is to do both the design and production yourself.

The advantage of the first method is simplicity. You can't find an easier and quicker way to start a business than one that requires just pencil, paper, and imagination. However, the disadvantage is the expense of using outside vendors. The benefit of the second method is that you can control many aspects of design and production, thus eliminating unexpected (and costly) vendor delays and mistakes. The bad news is that this method means high start-up costs and requires a significant amount of workspace.

Susan Brown, owner of Wood Cellar Graphics in Coleridge, Nebraska, operates a rubber stamping business for which she performs most of the work herself. She began her business in 1986, as a part-time venture. A printer at her workplace asked if she was interested in making business-related rubber stamps at her home. Always a creative person, she soon realized that she might also be able to make her own artistic rubber stamps to sell.

She began slowly, attending craft shows and placing small classified ads in country lifestyle magazines to sell stamps, meet customers, and build her business. After a few years, demand for her stamps had become so great that she went into business full time.

Although at one point she had a store and several employees, Brown scaled her operation back to a home-based business. During a typical week she receives orders for between 500 and 600 stamps. This figure is almost double the number she received just three years ago—an indication of how rapidly the rubber stamp industry is growing.

MAKING STAMPS

Making rubber stamps is a complicated process that requires multiple steps and specialized equipment. For example, Brown starts by designing the stamp. She then sends the artwork out to an engraver, who makes a special plate that contains the design in a raised image. (Engraving is a highly specialized skill and the only part of the entire production process that Brown does not perform herself.)

Once the engraved plate is returned, a special molding material is put onto it. Then the plate is inserted into a machine called a Vulcanizer. It has a hydraulic jack and two heating element plates, one on top and the other on the bottom. The Vulcanizer pushes the engraved image into the molding material. The mold is then covered with rubber. The Vulcanizer plates heat to approximately 350 degrees, and the hydraulic jack presses them together to vulcanize the rubber and attach it to the mold.

After the stamps are made, they are mounted on wood. For this Brown buys white maple at a cost of $2.50 per board foot. (She usually buys 500 board feet of wood at a time.) Her partner Ken Krei uses an electric saw to cut the wood to the proper size.

Vulcanizers come in different sizes. A new, large machine like Brown has, which can make between 20 and 30 stamps at a time, costs approximately $1,800. The specialized rubber used to make the stamps costs $150 for a 50-pound roll. However, thousands of stamps can be made from one 50-pound roll. This keeps the cost of making individual stamps low.

Stamps are priced according to size. The stamps at Wood Cellar Graphics range from $4 for a 1¼″ × 1¼″ stamp to $12 for a 5″ × 6″ stamp. Stamp design spans a plethora of interesting and unusual images, from simple yet elegant pictures of birds and animals, to beautifully detailed flowers, to extraordinarily intricate illustrations of desert sunsets and a Christmas tree.

STUDYING THE STAMP MARKET

One critical factor in operating a rubber stamp business is to study the stamp market with an eagle eye. Tastes change quickly; a design that is hot today may be just a fading memory next month. The trick is to learn which designs have staying power, such as angels, and which have the longevity of pet rocks. Susan Brown constantly analyzes the market, a task that has been made easier by the Internet.

Along with studying the market comes planning. While it's nice to catch the popularity wave, there's no reason why you can't generate one yourself. Try to determine what stampers like, and, if possible, develop some signature designs that combine perennial themes with individual expression. Brown attributes the continuing popularity of her stamps to their whimsical, country flavor.

Above all, be patient. Making quality rubber stamps takes practice.

"The first [stamps] I did were just awful." Brown laughs. "They were pretty horrible. I wonder why anyone bought any!"

STAMPING OUT HIGH COSTS

Starting your own rubber stamp business can be costly, particularly if you venture out on your own. The special equipment and materials needed to begin probably will cost in the neighborhood of $5,000. Set aside additional money for a computer, advertising, and producing a catalog, and total start-up costs could be $10,000 or more.

There are ways, however, to reduce that amount. One is to sell stamps at craft shows and similar venues instead of spending heavily on advertising; the cost of vendor registration usually is far less than taking out ads. However, if you feel that you must advertise, consider taking out small ads in magazines devoted specifically to the rubber stamp industry rather than in higher-profile magazines, where ad rates tend to also be high. The downside, however, is that since every ad in specialized rubber stamp publications touts a company selling rubber stamps, it's easy for your message to get lost. To publicize her business, Susan Brown turned to that most modern of marketing tools, the Internet. She built her own web page with a program she purchased and is pleased with the customer response.

Another way to cut costs is to buy a used Vulcanizer, which can cost as little as a few hundred dollars. With the variety of Vulcanizers available, even buying a smaller one will help keep costs low. However, the trade-off is that a smaller machine can make far fewer stamps than a larger model.

Although start-up costs for a turnkey rubber stamp business like Brown's can be high, you can potentially earn around $30,000 per year. At that rate, the breakeven time on an initial investment of $10,000 could come within a few months. However, due to competition and a crowded marketplace, your business is likely to grow gradually. Thus it will take longer to recoup your initial costs.

STAMPING: FAD OR FUTURE-ORIENTED?

With an industry such as rubber stamping, which is based on want rather than need, there is always the danger that the boom could go bust overnight, similar to the dramatic contraction suffered by the baseball collectibles industry in the mid-1990s. Susan Brown, however, doesn't see that happening.

"I think that the attraction of rubber stamps is that people can create something with them, like a work of ark," she says. "Even if you can't draw a straight line, you can create something with rubber stamps. Because of that, I think that the industry is going to continue to grow. People keep coming up with new things to do with them, and a lot of people are just getting involved in it."

So if all this sounds good to you, then maybe you can stamp your way to success—in the rubber stamp business.

Telemarketer

Job Description: *A telemarketer sells items exclusively over the telephone by calling people at home.*

- *Start-up cost as low as $6,000*
- *Potential first-year earnings: $40,000*
- *Breakeven time from initial investment: six months to two years*
- *Ideal home-based business*
- *Excellent opportunity for people with physical disabilities*
- *No staffing required*

The whole world talks about productivity, but business hasn't done much to make selling more productive," observes Lee Van Vechten, publisher of the *Van Vechten Report*, a newsletter for managers of corporate telemarketing groups. As you might guess, Van Vechten offers a solution to the high cost of selling: telemarketing. If you make sales calls—or at least weed out prospects—over the phone rather than via an interstate highway, costs tumble. "McGraw-Hill said that field selling cost about $260 per presentation," says Van

Vechten. "The average cost of a business-to-business telemarketing presentation is about $18."

WHO DOES IT?

Telemarketers sell stationery to businesses or carpet cleaning to consumers. Operators make an appointment for a salesperson to call in person or ask, for example, what you like or dislike about *Newsweek* magazine. Operators standing by at an 800 telephone number offer fix-it advice on your washing machine or take orders for the genuine cultured pearls advertised on Channel 3. Lee Van Vechten's definition, however, covers just about everything: "Telemarketing is intensive use of the telephone in the business environment."

Telemarketing companies range from in-house, multifloor departments at large corporations (JCPenney employs around 4,000 telemarketing operators answering toll-free numbers) to individuals who make calls part time from the kitchen telephone. With the industry still young, "nobody's developed statistics on its size, partially because we're a moving target, we're growing so fast," says Sandy Pernick, who runs The Direct Response Corporation. However, telemarketing has yet to reach capacity. The industry is still inventing methods of operation. *U.S. News & World Report* predicts that by 2001, 8 million people will make their livelihood through telemarketing. Van Vechten estimates that just over 2 million telemarketing operators are making calls. "Expect geometric growth," he says.

Impressive growth is exactly what has occurred. According to the American Teleservices Association, telephone marketing for business-to-business sales is expected to grow 10.5 percent annually, while for consumer sales the growth rate is anticipated to be 8 percent. In 1997 telephone marketing accounted for $238.6 billion in business-to-business sales and $185.9 billion in consumer sales. Nearly 100 million people in the United State (one out of three) buy goods and services over the telephone each year.

NO MORE $250 START-UPS

Sandy Pernick invested $250 to launch The Direct Response from her Des Plaines, Illinois, home. She spent $100 for incorporation, printed some letterhead, and put three people on residential phones. Today the company employs 105 and achieves revenues over $1 million.

Although occasional successes still start from home, the cottage industry is fast turning professional. The good news is the cost of telephone equipment, WATS lines, and long-distance charges are all skidding downward. A well-run company can easily keep 20 percent of revenues as profits. The bad news is corporate customers have been stung once too often by telemarketers who have disappeared overnight without a trace, leaving customers who call the 800 number to follow up on their order with the message: "This service has been disconnected." Pernick, who was a supervisor for another telemarketer before starting The Direct Response, recommends telemarketing only to entrepreneurs with a direct-marketing background. "Businesses look for a professional image, for stability," she says. For you, that means showing clients the permanence that comes with fancy equipment and employees rather than a card table in a basement.

Your First Telemarketing Client: Yourself

Of course, you still can start small by convincing local businesses to use your services. Locate customers the same way you will operate for them: through telemarketing. After you call prospective clients, many will request a brochure, so be sure to have professional-looking literature ready to mail.

Sandy Pernick asks clients for yearlong contracts. "Educate clients to the fact that stopping and starting a program is counterproductive," she says. "If a program works, keep it on full time. Consider it part of your marketing plan." Such long-term contracts do wonders for her scheduling. If in January she knows she will have a minimum level of business in July, she can take on new projects so she doesn't have to lay off staff.

Except for the image issue, you can start a service that only makes outbound calls with just a phone or two. Or you can get fancy by buying an automatic dialer that calls each number in sequence and plays back a recorded message. Traditional equipment that also accepts incoming calls is less expensive—but you need more of it since you also need employees. Telemarketing is both an equipment-heavy and people-intensive industry. "The industry has a personnel turnover rate of 150 to 200 percent," Pernick warns. "Historically that's because we've been part-time employers and attracted transient workers like students." Her solution is to hire only full-time, permanent employees.

Others argue that turnover is so high because telemarketing leads to burnout. It's hard making 100 phone calls a day. Norm Pensky, who runs Adds Telemarketing from South Pasadena,

California, counters this problem by switching people to new assignments often and making sure people take coffee breaks.

BEFORE THE PHONE RINGS

Sandy Pernick insists the actual phone call is the least important aspect of a telemarketing campaign. "You have to plan what to say, decide who to say it to, establish what time to call, and afterwards you have to analyze what people said. That requires more than just subjective opinions. You need number-crunching and you'd better be able to produce an automated report."

Most clients have a good handle on what they want from a telemarketer, but it's up to you to execute their plans. Pernick charges a flat fee for a script (often written in conjunction with the client) and training of her personnel (the client gets involved to impart any technical expertise). Then she charges by the "communicator hour." The industry norm ranges anywhere from $35 to $75 per operator per hour, based on how involved the conversations, the area of the country, and the size of the contract.

Some clients provide lists of contacts, while in other cases the telemarketer finds the most appropriate list. A good way to find customers for your clients is to rent names from publications or associations. If you're calling current customers, completion rate of the questionnaire should be fairly high. But when you make cold calls, only 2 percent may be positives. But, adds Lee Van Vechten, "Most of those rejection calls last less than 1.5 minutes, so those 98 calls who don't buy go quickly."

Van Vechten offers some advice to keep from getting the

phone slammed in your ear. "If the customer knows your company, identify yourself. But the consuming public doesn't like telemarketers from organizations they don't know. So, instead of saying 'I'm with Hal's Meat Packing,' ease your way in. Say 'Good evening, this is Lee Van Vechten. I'm curious, do you think freezers save you money on groceries?'"

Don't be afraid to change your script, but do so early on. Pernick does test runs with two to four callers, then makes any alterations. You won't get meaningful statistics if your approach is haphazard throughout the calling period.

THE LOOMING SHADOW

While everyone agrees that telemarketing has explosive growth in its future, observers also say government regulations will shape the industry. Bills pending state by state may limit the types of consumers that telemarketers can ring up. Other bills may restrict the hours you can call. Sandy Pernick notes that most legislation is aimed toward outbound consumer telemarketing; that is one reason she restricts her business to inbound consumer calls or business-to-business telemarketing.

But others say government won't be able to stop the momentum. Telemarketing supporters say telephone selling works. In the future, more and more consumers will become comfortable with the concept, and more businesses will adopt telemarketing because it is inexpensive. With that in mind, experts expect telemarketers will work with legislators to create a good climate. Telemarketing may undergo subtle changes, they say, but the concept is here to stay.

SOURCE

Industry Association

American Teleservices Association, Inc., 4605 Lankershim Boulevard, Suite 824, North Hollywood, CA 91602-1891, (818) 766-5324, (800) 441-3335

Trade Show Organizer

Job Description: *A trade show organizer gathers a group of manufacturers within the same industry in one venue so that they can hold demonstrations of new products, network, and pursue other sales and marketing strategies.*

- *Start-up cost as low as $10,000*
- *Potential earnings:$20,000*
- *Breakeven time from initial investment: two to five years*

David Cheifetz did not want this chapter written. Companies like his Conference Management Corp. of Norwalk, Connecticut, which stages trade shows for industries as diverse as genetic research and fashion accessories, have been "one of the best-kept secrets around," he says. Like other service businesses, trade shows benefit from high cash flow and no inventory. But trade shows possess another advantage: Unlike most manufacturing, retailing, *or* service businesses, trade shows operate with no accounts receivables; all the money comes before you deliver a product. Whether David Cheifetz likes it or not, competition is catching on. Trade shows are proving enormously popular with businesses, which point to the fact that it takes just half the cost to close a sale that began at a trade show ($550) as compared to a typical sales call ($997). According to the Center for Exhibition Industry Research, over 90 percent of businesses say that exhibitions are "extremely useful" sources of purchasing information. Over 80 percent of exhibiting companies use trade shows to achieve their sales objectives. With statistics like these, it's plain that trade shows aren't a secret anymore.

CASBAH

Trade shows are little more than elaborations on ancient Middle Eastern bazaar themes: manufacturers displaying wares for browsing buyers. Modern operators refined the trade shows into a 20th-century selling tool aimed at corporate buyers who stock up en masse.

Trade associations and other nonprofit groups once dominated trade show management. Such an environment, says David Cheifetz, provided "remarkable business opportunities for astute businesspeople, since the kinds of people attracted to nonprofit fields are not terribly aggressive promoters." Professional managers, including individual entrepreneurs, publishing groups, and ad agencies, now operate about 60 percent of the country's expos with more than 10,000 square feet of exhibit space—and nobody even knows how many "tabletop" shows are set up in hotel hallways and suites for small events. These professionals either manage a trade group's operation for a fee or own shows outright.

UP-FRONT DOLLARS

You can stage a small tabletop show in a hotel for around $10,000. If you can guarantee a hotel enough rooms, sometimes you can negotiate free exhibit space. On a more ambitious tear, a multi-industry extravaganza staged in a major convention center could cost you around $30,000, assuming you handle all the details yourself. If you hire specialists to decorate a show, for example, add anywhere from $500 to $2,000 to your out-of-pocket expenses. A small show might charge $50 for an exhibit table, while the biggies can go for ten times that. Both kinds of shows return profits with margins of 20 to 50 percent.

You can start with little up-front capital because your customers—exhibitors—foot most of the bills. Explains Wendy Rosen, whose Baltimore-based Wendy Rosen Agency Inc. throws two annual wholesale-only trade shows for artisans (see "Craft Wholesaler," page 608), "Most businesses don't see the cash until 120 days after they provide service when the wolf's at the door. But a trade show doesn't need up-front cash because exhibitors pay for their space ahead of time." Rosen staged The Buyers Market of American Crafts on a $500 overdraft from her checking account. Some 85 exhibitors took booths in a suite she rented at the New York Hilton Hotel; 500 merchants showed up, eager to buy crafts to sell in their department and specialty stores. Five years later, 900 pottery makers, jewelry crafters, and woodworkers paid for booth space at her shows, as 10,000 attendees went through the gates. Rosen's two shows together bill about $1 million annually.

You don't need venture capital or even large bank loans to get into the business, but you do require time. Since popular convention centers like McCormick Place in Chicago and the Jacob Javitts Center in New York book space at least 13 months before an event (and up to 10 years for very large expositions during popular times of the year), you should start planning your show 18 months to 2 years ahead of its due date.

STEPS

You follow five steps to launch a trade show, regardless of whether you invite 200 people or the entire state of Rhode Island:

1. Before making any commitments, test the concept. A telephone and letter canvas asks prospective exhibitors if they would buy booths and attendees if they would travel to such a show. While testing a first-time concept, many operators hold onto their jobs just in case the idea doesn't fly.

2. Assuming that a high percentage of contacts say they'd jump at the chance to be in your show, line up blocks of hotel rooms and convention-center space. Since a significant cut of their action is the tourist dollars conventioneers spend, popular convention centers managed by municipalities often shy away from brand-new shows. You might have to hold your show in a second-tier city until you establish a reputation. Wendy Rosen says one sure way to get space involves planning a show for an unpopular time. "Every convention center in the country wants business between December 24 and January 1. Tell a convention manager if you cut me a good deal or take care of my insurance, I'll bring you a convention that week."

3. Print a brochure explaining the "who, what, when, where,

and why" of your event. You can buy mailing lists from trade organizations and publications to supply the names of potential exhibitors. Follow up with sales calls to nail down booth commitments.

Direct mail, telemarketing, and printing costs during these first two steps range anywhere from $2,000 to $15,000, which is money you need ahead of time. From here on out, however, exhibitors foot the show bills. David Cheifetz points out that exhibitors are far cheaper to round up than attendees because they represent a smaller universe.

4. As exhibitor fees trickle in, turn your attention to the people who will visit the booths. Create a program. A typical agenda involves lining up speakers, devising seminars, and arranging special dinners and spousal events. Along with a list of exhibitors, use this program as the calling card to draw the gate.

5. Begin a marketing attack with trade journal and regional newspaper ads and mailings to prospective attendees. Pointing out that a small ad in the *Wall Street Journal* can run $7,500, Cheifetz admonishes, "Use your money wisely."

Unlike consumer shows, most trade shows do not charge gate fees. (Compare "Consumer Show Organizer," page 604.) Revenues come from what's left over from booth fees and, sometimes, from selling services (such as seminars) to attendees. Additionally, successful shows sometimes sell lists of attendee names.

MORE ART THAN SCIENCE

Once you've lined up acceptances from exhibitors and attendees, organize every aspect of the show in minute detail, from when you'll need cleanup crews to the menu at the awards banquet. Running a trade show "is more art than science," insists Russell E. Flagg, whose New York City–based Flagg Management Inc. runs events ranging from French fashion to ultralight aviation. Flagg, who started his own company after working for two large exposition companies, says contingency plans are crucial. Know in advance what to do if the power fails; if the union assembling the booths strikes; if an unexpected snowstorm grounds transportation.

Exhibition managers emphasize that one disorganized or meagerly attended show kills a concept forever. Who will return next year if this show was a disaster? What organization will hire you to manage their one big event if another expo you ran fizzled? The moral of the story: Don't skimp or cut too many corners.

Organization is key to everything. Like a boy scout, a trade show manager has to be prepared.

Hint: If you opt to learn the ropes as an employee of an existing firm, realize that most shows happen just once a year. It pays to join a major organization that puts on dozens of annual expos. The largest operator, Cahner's Exposition Group of Stamford, Connecticut, staged 230 shows worldwide in one year alone.

PARCELING OUT THE CHORES

Most large operators choose to mount the entire show, overseeing chores that range from direct mail tests of the concept to providing tablecloths at the convention hall. However, you can buy every type of expertise for a fee. For example, for anywhere from 85 cents to $2 per person, you can hire an organization to sign in registrants, equip them with printed badges, and provide a computerized list of attendees for next year. "A wonderful cadre of professionals will write brochures, oversee the mailing, put on conferences," says Russell Flagg. "They won't work on dreams, though. Instead of costing you $20,000, it might cost you $150,000 to run a show."

Unless you're shooting for a one-shot deal, expect to lose money on that first event (or two). Although a show's budget may eat up only half the revenues garnered from booth sales, you need the profits to start immediate preparation for next year. "Sink every cent into promoting the show," advises Wendy Rosen. "Exploit the momentum you built for next time."

After the industry accepts a show as an expected annual event, promotion becomes much easier—and profits skyrocket. "You don't have to reinvent the wheel each year," says David Cheifetz. "A good show is like a Mercedes. The salesman doesn't have to tell you it's a fine car. But he still has to sell his product."

BUCKING THE ODDS

Trade show managers fall into two groups: professionals who sight opportunities to throw parties, no matter what the field, and insiders in particular industries who organize a group of friends into a trade show. Wendy Rosen, for one, is proof that outsiders can achieve success. Equipped with a publishing and advertising background, she was designing business cards and order forms for artists when she dreamed up a forum where craftspeople could present their silkscreens and brass bracelets to the retail world. Rosen's almost overnight success came through instinct and application of her talents, a sure-fire idea, and perhaps some luck. Most important, her show brought exhibitors tangible results. "When I first began my show six years ago, exhibitors averaged $30,000 to $50,000 in production a year. Now $1 million isn't uncommon and $150,000 is average," she says. Because of ready access to a wholesale market, "Many clients doubled and tripled volume."

Probably any industry large enough to support a large expo already has one, but don't let that stop you. If David Cheifetz sees room for a better-managed show or a second event in a different area of the country, he rises tactfully to the challenge: "We call the association and tell them we'll stay as far away chronologically and geographically as possible. We ask for their endorsement, but we go ahead if we don't get their cooperation."

Rosen suggests getting in on the ground floor with shows in growth industries. And if you can't do it all, do what you can. "Call up the small associations and offer to handle the marketing, direct mail, or advertising for their meetings," she says. "If an industry is building, you can build along with them."

By segmenting large markets into specific niches, Russell Flagg stages shows for such hard-to-reach audiences as New York lawyers hungry for computer software. "Both sides know the show is not for the general public but targeted to their needs, so they come," explains Flagg, whose dozen shows produced revenues of $1.2 million one year.

As travel grows increasingly expensive, observers forecast fewer massive blockbuster shows. Instead, expect greater numbers of smaller shows scattered across the country. Trade Show Bureau executive director Bill Mee points out that expos have already changed from out-of-town stag-club parties to serious business events. "It's expensive to go to shows, expensive to participate. Now you go for the purpose of doing business."

SOURCES

Industry Associations

Center for Exhibition Industry Research, 2301 South Lake Shore Drive, Suite E1002, Chicago, IL 60616, (312) 808-2347

International Association for Exposition Management, P.O. Box 802425, Dallas, TX 75380, (214) 458-8002

The Trade Show Exhibitors Association, 5501 Backlick Road, Suite 105, Springfield, VA 22151, (703) 941-3725

Travel and Entertainment

Bed and Breakfast Innkeeper

Job Description: *A bed and breakfast innkeeper provides a place of lodging, often in an older, Victorian-style home, in which breakfast is served to guests.*

- *Start-up cost as low as $250,000*
- *Potential earnings: $60,000*
- *Breakeven time from initial investment: two to four years*
- *Ideal home-based business*

Bed-and-breakfast scene No. 1: You and your spouse sip sherry with a fascinating parcel of guests around a cozy fireplace. The conversation leaps from nuclear disarmament to the very best boutiques in Paris. As the guests say good night, anticipating mouthwatering brioches the next morning before a day of cross-country skiing, one woman pauses. "Your inn is absolutely charming," she says. "Can you book the same room for my husband and me next fall? We'll be back for the foliage."

Bed-and-breakfast scene No. 2: Balancing a tray of orange juice in one hand and a coffeepot in the other, you smile bravely at the unshaven guest who is complaining loudly that there's no hot water for showers. Your partner abandons the stove to greet a new guest, despite the fact that check-in time isn't for another six hours. The newcomer turns out to be an unannounced travel writer, who wonders why smoke is coming from the kitchen.

Proprietors of bed and breakfast inns agree that the above scenarios are not only plausible but might well happen at the same inn during the same week. More than most other small businesses, innkeeping represents a total lifestyle commitment. It's almost like a marriage—the vows of "for richer or poorer, in sickness and in health," come true every day for innkeepers of about 15,000 B&Bs in North America.

BUYING A LIFESTYLE

Many B&B converts are corporate fast-trackers who equate the deed to an inn with a ticket away from urban hassles. Many husband-and-wife teams see innkeeping as a way to spend more time with their families. Pat Hardy bought the Glenborough Inn in Santa Barbara, California, after running a 24-hour crisis hotline. "I was trying to figure out how I could be a working parent and still be present for a teenager," she recalls. In addition to working in-house, Hardy has a full-time housekeeper who doubles as a baby-sitter when the need arises.

Innkeepers say they can mold their lives to suit their business needs—within limitations. You might take in a matinee on a lazy weekday, or host your daughter's scout troop. Hardy sometimes sneaks weekday ski trips; Joan Wells, who operates the 12-room Queen Victoria in the New Jersey seaside resort of Cape May, devotes afternoons to community projects.

The trick is to arrange your free time to the flow of the business. For example, Joan and her husband, Dane, are not beach people. So, during their busy summer period, they don't long to hit the beach just minutes from their door. Says Joan: "If you're a skier, open an inn in Cape May. Then go to Vermont during your slack season."

Note: The expense of that Vermont getaway could well be on the business if you stay in a B&B. Accountants say visits to competitors fall under the category of research. Also, you can claim meals in neighborhood restaurants as business expenses. After all, you've got to be able to tell guests about area attractions.

WHAT MEASUREMENTS?

Because innkeeping is a way of life as well as a business, throw out all the regular sales and profit measurements when considering a B&B. Factor in the purchase of a home as well as a company when you figure start-up costs. A plus, however, is that you're allowed business deductions for such everyday costs as heating and air conditioning. Kate McDill and Deborah Sweet structured the Chambered Nautilus Bed & Breakfast Inn in Seattle as a partnership, which allows them to deduct 90 percent of their overhead. "If we were a corporation, we could write off 100 percent," says McDill, but then the partners would each pay taxes as well as the corporation. The Chambered Nautilus, whose six guest rooms and four porches overlook snowy Cascade Mountain peaks, grosses around $100,000 a year with net expenses of $85,000.

"We have a few personal expenses—some clothing, a few groceries, some medical bills," explains Joan Wells. "But the company pays for everything else, including the upkeep on our car, a pension, and most of our food. You just get taxed on what's left over anyway."

Wells's Queen Victoria supports a better living than most inns, with an annual take of over $200,000 and expenses of $150,000. Even though most B&Bs operate on skinny profit margins, they don't give rooms away. The Queen Victoria's rate sheet resembles a train schedule, with rates varying with the season and the size of the room. A carriage house on the property that includes a Jacuzzi, wet bar, and separate parlor rents for $220 a night during peak season.

Many innkeepers devise secondary incomes to supplement their room rates. Pat Hardy and her partner JoAnn Bell operate a consultancy for new innkeepers called Inn Transition. Carl Glassman sells the work of local artists from the Wedgwood Inn, which he operates in New Hope, Pennsylvania. Kate McDill uses her kitchen for catering and opens the sitting room during the day for corporate retreats.

WHERE DOES IT ALL GO?

Income evaporates in a B&B faster than water in a hot skillet. "Things you think will cost hundreds of dollars cost thousands," says Joan Wells, who spends $3,000 every three years or so to replace worn towels and sheets. "There are two things you don't mess around with," she instructs. "Lumpy beds and no hot water." Wells constantly upgrades expensive antique furnishings, such as iron and brass beds that she covers with colorful quilts. "People are particularly hard on chairs," says Wells, a one-time executive director of the nonprofit Victorian Society, referring to her "graveyard of Victorian chairs stored in the basement."

And neither budget nor time allows more outside help. "My partner and I joke about calling maintenance when the toilet breaks," says Kate McDill, a restaurant chef before opening the Chambered Nautilus. "It helps to have a rudimentary knowledge of electricity and hammers and nails. Otherwise you spend a lot of money you can't afford."

EAST VS. WEST

The cost of an inn usually parallels other properties in an area. Kate McDill and Deborah Sweet spent $210,000 for their circa-1915 inn, followed by $50,000 to remodel, plumb, wire, and furnish it. Pat Hardy figures $20,000 to $30,000 per guest room buys an inn in an out-of-the-way East Coast or mountain locale, compared with $30,000 to $60,000 on the pricier West Coast, where suitable property is rarer. Most buyers secure a mortgage on top of a down payment.

In addition to the purchase, Hardy assumes renovation will cost $20,000 to $50,000 per room. A typical inn is a drafty old mansion that was not built to host overnight guests. So makeovers generally add baths, refurbish the kitchen, and decorate. Since spending $165,000 to buy The Queen Victoria ten years ago, Joan and Dane Wells have laid out $200,000 for building improvements as well as $100,000 for furnishings. Hint: Check the tax laws, which often favor renovation of older structures.

Mary E. Davies, proprietor of Ten Inverness Way, says a California inn can get away with four or five guest rooms, because year-round good weather produces 60 to 70 percent occupancy rates. "In New England," she says, "you need a minimum of eight to ten rooms because occupancy is more like 40 percent." You have to be prepared to take care of the demand when it arises; otherwise you won't reach profitability. According to a Laventhal and Horwath study of California inns, city properties that attract business travelers during the week fill their rooms 70 percent of the time, compared to 50 percent occupancy at rural inns where Monday-to-Friday vacancies are common.

Your first requisite as an innkeeper is flexibility. "If you can't deal with crisis and change hats with aplomb, do not get into the business," advises Hardy, who points to tasks that run the gamut from bookkeeping to housekeeping. While being a good cook helps, breakfast is an easy meal to make—which makes B&Bs easier to run than country inns, which serve dinners. Says Hardy: "I know people who bring in croissants and serve fresh fruit and coffee."

The Queen Victoria's six-person staff alleviates some of the pressure on its innkeepers. But one member of the Wells team tries to be on hand at all times. They hire an "innsitter" to run things during occasional family getaways, and they also take separate vacations. "It's hard to get away together because someone needs to mind the store," says Joan. "Also, we work together all the time, so it's not a bad idea to get away alone."

DICKENS

Kate McDill lists creativity as another necessary trait: "You have to create a feeling. Atmosphere is why guests come to a bed and breakfast instead of a Holiday Inn."

Innkeepers' creative juices particularly flow when it comes to attracting guests into their homes. Most B&Bs budget little for advertising beyond guidebook listings, which everyone says is essential. However, Joan Wells sends a steady stream of press releases to travel sections of newspapers and magazines; as a result, each year her scrapbook grows by 15 to 30 articles that mention The Queen Victoria. One annual gala began when a Dickens scholar read *The Christmas Carol* to a few guests beside the inn's Christmas tree. Seven neighboring inns joined in the Dickens Extravaganza. Area restaurants offered Victorian feasts, artisans demonstrated how to make Victorian Christmas tree ornaments, guests trimmed trees, and The Queen Victoria boasted a full house during a week that once was quieter than Scrooge's Christmases. Today the Dickens Extravaganza is part of Cape May's annual Christmas celebration, when the seashore town is as packed with visitors as it is during the summer, and the B&Bs fill up months in advance.

SPLIT PERSONALITY

Many inns maintain a dual identity: turn-of-the-century quaintness in their public rooms and stainless steel kitchens and personal computers behind closed doors. With the help of a computer containing the tidbits she picks up from guests in casual breakfast chitchat, Joan Wells targets particular guest types. For example, she mails announcements of Cape May birdwatching weekends to former guests she knows are birdwatchers. In addition to bookkeeping, the computer also serves as a word processor on which Joan composes a newsletter that guests receive twice a year.

Innkeepers are people who like people, and most say they haven't been disappointed. "It's a very personal business and you get to know some wonderful people," says Kate McDill, who became best friends with a woman who stayed in the

Chambered Nautilus before moving to Seattle. "About once a week someone leaves us a gift."

Innkeepers rarely complain about obnoxious guests. "The kind of person who agrees to share a bathroom is comfortable with other people," guesses McDill, who also speculates that types who commit credit fraud prefer the anonymity of a large hotel. "I've had only two things stolen in two years," she reports. "One woman took a washcloth by mistake and mailed it back."

RESEARCH

Before shelling out your life's savings to buy an inn, stay in as many B&Bs as possible. You may get better results if you visit during the week or off-season when the innkeeper has more time to answer questions. You also can offer a consulting fee. Courses on innkeeping are taught by consultants and some community colleges. The Wedgwood Inn offers an apprenticeship program; a kind of "hands-on" internship that runs from three days to two weeks, the program is a more formal way to follow the advice that innkeepers always offer: "Go to work for an inn before you buy one."

Before setting your heart on a particular property, check the local chamber of commerce or visitor's bureau to determine tourist traffic. Are area occupancy rates high enough to support your mortgage? Make sure local zoning ordinances permit B&Bs. But don't be afraid of other B&B competition. "It works like a shopping mall," says Joan Wells, referring to the score of inns that make up Cape May. "A critical mass builds that attracts customers."

Speaking of a critical mass, Mary Davies estimates 600 to 800 B&Bs clustered in California—compared with just 200 in the early 1980s. Consultant William Oates suspects Vermont hoards well over 200 B&Bs, or double the number a few years ago. The proliferation has helped travelers to view an inn as a legitimate alternative to mass-market hotels rather than a novelty vacation experience.

And bed and breakfasts are not just your Victorian mansion, complete with widows' walks if not ghosts. As those properties become harder to buy, proprietors have converted yachts, a lighthouse, and a Louisiana plantation into B&Bs.

SOURCE

Industry Association

American Bed & Breakfast Association, 1407 Huguenot Road, P.O. Box 1387, Midlothian, VA 23113, (804) 379-2222

Limousine Provider

Job Description: *A limousine provider drives clients to their destinations in a luxury car.*

- *Start-up cost as low as $15,000 (down payment on one car)*
- *Potential earnings: $39,000*
- *Breakeven time from initial investment: six months to one year*
- *No staffing required*

On St. Patrick's Day, one of our corporate accounts rented two stretches," relates Ron Goldman, who runs Presidential Limousine Ltd. in Chicago. "They really did the town from 4:00 P.M. until 4:00 A.M. The bill was well over $1,000—that's $1,000 for riding around in a *car*, mind you. But the client called the next morning saying he had a great time. So many other fields are thankless, even when you do a great job. But we get accolades."

THE GREAT LIMOUSINE
PROLIFERATION

Why the hoopla? To borrow an economics term, the business is supply driven. Maury Sutton, an expert in the limousine business, points out that the six manufacturers churning out stretches in the late 1970s produced just 1,600 limousines a year; now about 50 so-called coachbuilders buy Lincolns and Caddys, saw them in half, and add the three- to eight-foot inserts that make them stretches. These new suppliers have pushed production to 6,000 limos a year.

Not only are there more cars, but they are cheaper, says Sutton, who estimates a 54-inch stretch Lincoln Towncar cost about $45,000 in the "old days." A current model of that same car costs about $40,000—"and it's probably a better vehicle," he says. If you pay in $1,200 monthly installments, you can get into the stretch limo business today for under $15,000. That sum includes a down payment, license, insurance, a car phone, and some advertising. If you start with a three-car fleet, triple those expenses. Since you pay drivers only when they are on the job, salaries aren't a major concern. If you decide to pay for the cars up-front and claim depreciation, start-up costs could run $45,000 per car, depending on the options you collect. Another route is to buy snazzy used limos.

Your permit often will cost less than a taxi permit. For example, a New York medallion cab license costs about $75,000, while a livery license costs a mere $100 or so.

STRETCH STATUS

But no matter how accessible the limousine business is, operators wouldn't make it out of the garage if the public saw limousines as just for the rich and famous. Increasingly, however, all those 13-foot celebrity wagons roaming the streets act as their own advertisements for the public at large. *Limousine & Chauffeur Magazine* says 75 percent of the limousines sold today are bought by livery services rather than individuals. Instead of wiring mom and dad flowers, the kids are chipping in to charter a limousine to take them to an anniversary dinner. More important, corporations are opening up limo accounts. "You can work weekends doing weddings," says Sutton. "If you charge $50 an hour, you can gross $3,000 a month driving part time. But if you decide to make it a business, you've got to get the corporate accounts."

Corporations call more regularly than a consumer who uses limos as vehicles to fantasy land. Ron Goldman, who says 65 percent of his business comes from regular corporate-clients, points to one 300-member law firm that charters a presidential limo two to three times a day. "The lawyers are always going to the airport, or clients are coming in," he explains.

MARKETING LUXURY TO THE MASSES

Advertisements in the Yellow Pages bring in the consumer crowd. "We run the largest ad we can get in the Chicago Yellow Pages," says Ron Goldman. "That ad pays for itself by the second month. The phone rings off the hook with people wanting to take Grandma to her 70th birthday party in a limo." Let caterers and party planners know you're available for their clients, as well.

You can also hook up with other merchants and jointly advertise in newspapers or on the radio. For example, one Los Angeles service arranges "Cuisine by Limousine." Flat-rate packages start at $80 a couple, and include a cocktail in the car, a rose for the lady, and a three-course meal at a restaurant. Although three-quarters of the tab goes to the restaurant, an organized chauffeur can shuttle diners back and forth all evening.

THE BREAD-AND-BUTTER BUSINESS

Tracking down corporate business involves writing and calling executives to bid on jobs. You may have to knock $5 or $10 off the hourly rate to land the big users, whom you bill just once a month. "In effect, it's a sales business," says Ron Goldman. His sales pitches underscore the convenience a limousine brings. For example, he stresses to real estate agents that a limo frees them to sell a property rather than worry about traffic and parking. The practice can be extended in any number of directions. If a salesperson plans to drive customers around in your car, the prestige factor will be at work, so mention your well-stocked wet bar. High-pressure firms in congested cities view limousines as offices that drive down the street. Some fleets outfit the passenger compartment with desks, telephones, and even computers rather than televisions and compact disk players. Entertainer Ed McMahon says limousines, with their roomy compartments and tinted windows, are great for changing into a tuxedo.

THE OUT-OF-TOWN CROWD

Many executives become attached to limousine luxury and book the stretches on out-of-town junkets. Presidential's ten-car fleet stays busy with convention business. "Not just picking them up at the airport," says Ron Goldman, "but driving them and their sales reps and clients around while they're in town." As a member of the convention bureau, his company gets a list of all exhibitors at Chicago's conventions. Presidential shoots out letters to each, inviting them to hire a limo at $50 an hour. One exhibitor at a recent home improvement show hired two limos for the three full days of the event to ferry its sales staff and customers around town. The bill: $3,500. The customer expressed such satisfaction with the squeaky-clean cars and affable drivers that Goldman expects him to come back with the same arrangement annually.

Satisfied customers likely will recommend your company to their friends. You also can join a formal referral network through the National Limousine Association. Developing your own contacts by calling limo services in other cities also has a good return rate. You can collect a finder's fee from customers you refer, or just expect grateful entrepreneurs to reciprocate when their clients visit your town.

At $50 an hour, a busy limousine brings in $100,000 a year, from which an owner/operator can expect to collect $65,000 in pretax profits, not counting tips. A second car will cost you a chauffeur's salary (often not much above minimum wage, since the driver expects to make most of the income from tips).

However, that second and third limo assures extra business. Each time a potential client calls when your car is in the shop or is already booked, you run the risk of losing future business. Some entrepreneurs make their entire living by taking care of another company's overflow business. Generally, the referring company bills the client and keeps 20 percent of the hourly rate.

CHARLOTTESVILLE, VIRGINIA, AND JUNO, ALASKA

The limo business started with New York corporate execs, then leapfrogged to California producers and stars, and is now appearing in other major cities. Even small towns support limo services, particularly if they have an airport and industry or a wealthy population. Maury Sutton says several operators make a nice living in Florida by escorting wealthy matrons to the supermarket once a week. David John, Cadillac's director of Fleet and Leasing, expects annual improvement in the market as tougher drunk-driving laws steer more partygoers toward limos and as parking costs rise in big cities. He also points out that couples continue to spend lavishly on weddings and proms.

The trend is toward longer and more elaborate limousines. Although an understated, 30-inch stretch was once de rigueur, Sutton says 60-inch (that's five feet!) of stretch added to a typical Fleetwood is now the norm. One New York outfit includes among its fleet two white Lincolns, each with three bars, two TVs, two video-cassette recorders, and one laser disk player. The 40-foot-long monsters seat 12 passengers inside and 2 in an outside rumble seat. Even though your chauffeur will never find a parking space, customers who rent the mobile home–size limo expect to spend $1,800 to get to a New Year's Eve bash. The services of a hostess who pours complementary drinks is included.

S O U R C E

Industry Association

National Limousine Association, 901 North Pitt Street, Suite 220, Alexandria, VA 22314-1536, (703) 838-2938

Miniature Golf
Operator

Job Description: *A miniature golf operator runs a course that allows customers to play only the putting portion of golf but with unusual obstacles, unique hole designs, and other impediments thrown in to make the game more challenging.*

- *Start-up cost as low as $75,000*
- *Potential earnings: $50,000*
- *Breakeven time from initial investment: several years*
- *Enables creativity to flower*

Tommy Crouch and his family saw fantastic miniature golf courses when vacationing in Myrtle Beach, South Carolina. The brightly colored, life-size fiberglass animals towered above the palms in places with names like Jungle Lagoon. According to Charles Grove, who designs such courses and supplies 20-foot-tall pirates and giraffes that drink from running streams, Myrtle Beach has 64 mini-golf courses up and down its main strand. Says Grove, "It's not unusual to see 40 people in line to get in, just like at the finer restaurants."

A GATOR GOLF EMPIRE

Tommy Crouch had succeeded at several careers, beginning with accounting. "But I kept thinking about those golf courses," says the Hope, Arkansas, proprietor of Gator Golf Inc. "I knew Silver Dollar City, a tourist town on the Arkansas/Missouri border, didn't have a golf course, so I teamed up with a partner to put one in." When the partners asked for $150,000 to build on leased land, "The bank said, 'First of all, we don't know how you could spend that much on miniature golf, and second, if you did, we don't know how you'd make any money.' "

Crouch and his partner chipped in and literally built the first Gator Golf course themselves. They hired construction employees and followed plans supplied by Charles Grove. Crouch ran the tractor himself. "Well, that first year we made $154,000 in profits," he recalls. "I sold my interest to my partner and did it all over again in another tourist area, Pigeon Forge, Tennessee. Then I decided to go big time, so I sold that one and built a $350,000 mini-golf course in Orlando, Florida. I didn't like Florida, so I sold that one and now I'm buying land to do another in Hot Springs, Arkansas."

Crouch cleared $75,000 for his interest on the first putting course he sold, $50,000 on the second, and $200,000 on the third. This time around, the bank finally decided to back him with $500,000. Is there money to be made in miniature golf? Just ask Tommy Crouch.

The 1990s were a boom decade for miniature golf. After several decades of stagnation, the industry came roaring back with a vengeance as the end of the century approached, growing at an annual rate of about 20 percent during the '90s, according to the Miniature Golf Association of America.

MANAGING FROM A HAMMOCK

As he approaches 50 and wants to slow his lifestyle a bit, Tommy Crouch plans to operate the Hot Springs Gator Golf Course himself—sort of. "I'll continue living in Hope, which is 75 miles away. I can get an assistant manager and be home most of the time."

According to those in the industry, not much can go wrong when you run a miniature golf operation. "A water park needs about 60 employees," says Charles Grove, who analyzes clients' locations and will help secure funding and walk the client through a host of local zoning permits. "Even a big putting course can get by with a half-dozen employees. A husband and wife can do it alone, except for the long hours. So I suggest you hire a couple of presentable teenagers. Insurance is minimal compared to other amusements. The operation is just real simple."

But the best part of the cash-only business is the profits. Grove tells clients, "As a rule of thumb, an ideal location with a good customer draw should gross the cost of the facility during the first year." Depending on how much interest land and construction loans eat up, Grove figures the owner of a $300,000 facility will keep pretax profits of 40 or even 60 percent of revenues—$120,000 to $180,000. Tommy Crouch says he knows people who do better than that. "If you have a $300,000 gross, your operating expenses are only about 20 percent of revenues, so you have $240,000 left over from which you pay out the principal."

HERE'S THE HITCH

Ah, but that principal . . . To support the colorful theme courses Tommy Crouch and Charles Grove operate, expect high entry costs. The monster pelicans and cascading waterfalls require a large tourist population to pay for them. Land costs for the two acres that Grove considers minimal for an 18-hole course and parking usually run in the half-million-dollar range in high-traffic tourist areas. Often you can lease land, but course construction still adds another $200,000 to $350,000.

Even so, Grove says it's not unusual for a young couple with about $42,000 to build one of his facilities by rounding up the rest from outsiders. "They get their in-laws involved and a couple of neighbors, which creates a viable financial base to approach the banks. The couple sets up a corporate structure with the provision to buy their partners out in a few years."

Of course, eventually the couple must pay for the entire cost of the park, plus interest. You can buy into the more traditional mini-golf course with fewer filigrees for under $100,000. The less expensive parks need fewer players to reach breakeven, so you can look for less expensive landlords. Putt-Putt says a 36-hole course needs 30,000 people living within a three-mile radius, or 60,000 within five miles. Including land and a franchise fee of $10,000 (you also pay 3 percent of gross ticket sales to the parent), "you could reasonably expect to open a 36-hole course for approximately $130,000 and a 54-hole course for $195,000."

Smaller courses cost less, although Putt-Putt discourages sale of its 18-hole variety these days, saying return on investment is better with the large variety. In addition, some entrepreneurs have experimented with mini-miniature courses in shopping malls, although the owners also complain of high rents.

Your Own Billboard

Regardless of the type of course you build, you must be accessible and visible. Rhett Sandsburg doesn't bother to advertise Doublegolf in Myrtle Beach, South Carolina, since 99 percent of his business is from tourists. "We're between two stop lights, so traffic slows down in front of the course. People can see us because we have a lot of frontage on the road." Drivers can't miss props like the ten-foot mama elephant and her eight-foot baby, so Doublegolf acts as its own advertising.

Unless you operate in the deep South, miniature golf is a seasonal business, which doesn't bother successful operators one bit. Sandsburg uses Doublegolf's four-month recess for maintenance. "That's when we redo drainage on some holes, put back shrubbery, reshingle any huts, repair animals, or replace carpeting," he says.

Besides, after all that hard work, you could probably use a break. "You're open 15 hours a day, 7 days a week during the season," says Tommy Crouch, who, incidentally, doesn't like to play either golf or miniature golf. "So even though it's easy, you tend to burn out. But on the last day of October, you close and enjoy Thanksgiving and Christmas. In February you take care of any repairs and, by April 1, it's time to open again."

SOURCE

Industry Association

Miniature Golf Association of America, P.O. Box 32353, Jacksonville, FL 32237, (904) 781-4653

Party Planner

Job Description: *A party planner handles all the details for any social affair, including suggesting the theme, hiring caterers, florists, and so on, and obtaining all other necessary elements.*

- *Start-up cost as low as $500*
- *Potential first-year earnings: $20,000*
- *Breakeven time from initial investment: one month to one year*
- *Ideal home-based business*
- *Excellent opportunity for people with physical disabilities.*
- *No staffing required*

Last week we planned a kidnaping," relates party planner Patricia Watson, who runs Magic by PTS Inc. "The 70 Dean Witter executives knew they were going to a party, but they didn't know they'd arrive at a speakeasy (our warehouse) in a fire engine."

When Watson says "Let's plan a party," don't expect Chuckles the Clown and ice cream for a dozen six-year-olds. "We arrange the unusual—that's what makes us Magic." Her

$2-million-a-year Dallas-based firm stages "a couple hundred" parties a year, primarily for corporate and convention clients. The extravaganzas range from a Chinese New Year in June (complete with a dragon parade and rice-eating contest) to Mardi/Gras costume parties. Magic's warehouse full of props holds a full-size merry-go-round and 15-foot-tall toy soldiers. In addition to local entertainment, Watson has booked Dolly Parton and Tanya Tucker. For show business blasts, she contracts with a Joan Collins or Tom Selleck look-alike. Chow runs the gamut from haute cuisine to barbecue. It seems no true party planner is limited by anything other than imagination—either your own or your client's.

THE WHOLE MEGILLAH

Using her own definition of a party planner as someone "capable of dotting every 'i' and crossing every 't,' " Patty Watson estimates that only about 500 true party planners operate across the country. So, if you're in an area that likes to throw parties, there's probably room for another party planner. Magic started as an offshoot of a tour business Watson ran for conventioneers and their spouses. But before that, she was a mother and teacher, professions that "basically prepare you for the impossible," she says.

What does Watson mean by "the impossible"? Well, "Party planners conceptualize the whole thing," she explains. "We create the props, arrange the location, send invitations, handle the RSVPs, line up caterers, flowers, food, entertainment, and absolutely anything else that's necessary."

Party planners either plan the entire bash, or plan and

execute. If you're restricting activities to pure planning, the price of admission to the business involves lining up customers and subcontractors, such as balloon decorators and caterers. Lease props from a rental store, let the caterer provide the serving personnel, and you can also hire freelancers of all sorts: a '50s party might need a cheerleader to lead cheerleading contests, or a part-time actor to host bubble-gum blowing tournaments. Since the client pays the planner who doles out the various fees, be sure to ask for a hefty enough deposit to cover whatever up-front commitments you make for entertainment, decorating, food, and so on.

If you have some expertise and capital, decide whether you want to handle some functions in-house. For example, many planners also cater, plan business meetings for corporate clients, or rent anything from tents to coffeepots. Each additional operation brings in revenues—but also requires expensive equipment and personnel. Most planners accumulate some props, which, if you grow large enough, will need to be stored in a warehouse. Also, you'll need office space.

While you can certainly start from home, some party planners create magical offices with props stashed in every corner. When you reach this stage, invite clients to your premises before planning their parties. The setting will spark all kinds of ideas.

Likewise, as you grow, you'll need vans to transport all those props to party sites. Splash the vans with a logo that you also use on your correspondence, business cards, and the back of such party favors as photographs. While you should fade into the background during the party, you can advertise your presence as you set up.

PARTY PEOPLE

To get started, call folks all over town involved in parties. Those same photographers or florists you book for your parties can provide leads on clients. Let hotels know you can either help out their banquet managers on elaborate projects, or work directly with their customers. Call on convention planners and ask if you can assist them—or any of their exhibitors who might want to throw a private party. If you have an idea of which corporations throw the most elaborate to-dos, send them a brochure or call office managers to suggest they throw a Winter Wonderland theme party this Christmas. You'll not only create ski slopes in their corporate dining room, you'll also pick up the key executives in horse-drawn sleighs.

Try to get commitments months in advance so you can plan in a more leisurely fashion and get better prices for your clients. Patty Watson likes to have eight months' notice for $100,000 parties, although Magic has staged parties for hundreds of people in a couple of weeks. "They just cost more, not only because we have to put more people on the arrangements but because you can't buy in quantity and you pay exorbitant freight costs," she explains. "For instance, if we know we're going to need 100 dozen white roses six months ahead of time, we buy a field and get a better deal."

Set your charges by working backward. Determine how much each element—from catering to props—will cost. Then tack on the cost of your own overhead and profits of 20 to 40 percent, depending on what the market and your client allows.

Before booking a $100,000 party—or even a four-figure wedding reception—clients want references and examples of what you do, so you have to build a reputation. Ask influential contacts to stop by before or during the murder mystery to see the Victorian set you created. Offer to help a charity plan its next luau, and take pictures of the affair. You could split the cost of a professionally produced videotape with a bride and groom if they'll let you use an edited version as a sales tool. The expense of planning a party for free and taking photographs or videos of the event will pay off when you land that big account. If you can put aside a few thousand dollars, kick off your own business with a gala.

THE CLIENT'S ALWAYS RIGHT

To create the right mood and get the touches right, ask clients what they hope to accomplish with the party. If you host a new-product kick-off, perhaps strolling fortune tellers might end each palm-reading with visions of the Caribbean vacation that the corporation will award to the top sales team. If you plan a retirement party, ask about the guest of honor's hobbies and interests, and make theme suggestions around those.

Be sure to outline in detail any outrageous ideas. For example, a gorilla serving during the coffee break might enliven the dullest seminar. But a client who hopes to sell financial services to customers intrigued by what they've just heard on the podium might not appreciate the disruption.

A couple of character traits spell disaster for party planners. If you're a rigid "go-by-the-book" sort, forget party planning. Not only will your imagination be challenged before every party, but you'll have to improvise around unexpected glitches during each event. Also, since you deal with a myriad of details and various subcontractors, disorganization is death. Patty Watson sums it up nicely: "If you've ever planned a 50th wedding anniversary, a dinner party for 100 guests, a graduation, a wedding, and an inaugural ball—and if they've all occurred on the same day—and they've all occurred in the same place—you can do this. You can be a party planner."

Party Rental Supplier

Job Description: *A party rental supplier specializes in renting items exclusively for parties, such as chairs, tables, tablecloths, and so on.*

- *Start-up cost as low as $50,000*
- *Potential earnings: $75,000*
- *Breakeven time from initial investment: 9 to 18 months*

According to Patrick Chose, who runs San Francisco Party rental center and C&M Party Props in nearby Walnut Creek, the "Cabot-Smythe" family does a lot of entertaining. "Mr. Jenkins, the manservant, will call, and in his proper British accent say, 'Mrs. Cabot-Smythe just informed me she is having 80 of her dearest friends over tomorow night.'— Their dining room is just large enough to accommodate 80," Chose adds as an aside. "The first thing he always orders is 80 of our $8 chairs for a rental fee of $640. The Cabot-Smythe mansion is large, but nobody's got room to store 80 chairs."

Patrick Chose, as a matter of fact, has 17,000 square feet of showroom and another 8,000 for warehouse space. And that's enough room to store 5,000 chairs. Not to mention commercial-size tents that conventions rent for $10,000 a day and all the decorations you need to transform your living room into an Oriental theme party. "If you count the linen I stock in 34 colors and all the frilly toothpicks as separate items"—he shakes his head—"I've no idea how many items we stock."

IT'S A GOOD LIVING

Pat Chose does know that running a party rental store is a business for imaginative people who like to have fun and want to make a good living.

Chose's two stores have brought in profits "higher than the 16 percent" industry norm on revenues of about $1.6 million. Chose, who is one of the granddaddies of what the industry calls "pure party rentals" (no tools or other general-rental items offered), opened his Walnut Creek store in 1959 and a second store 25 years later in San Francisco, which his oldest son Jay now manages. Younger son Andy oversees the Walnut Creek shop.

San Francisco Party sits just around the corner from Moscone Center, and that prime location plus a large stock of inventory contributed to top-of-the-line start-up costs of $100,000. Consultant Donald Charbonnet figures you can open the doors to a small store for $40,000. Compared with general rentals (see "Rental Center Supplier," page 586), "party is more profitable, and you can break even quickly," he says. "You can rent a chair you bought for $8.50 for between 50 cents and $1. The rent pays for the chair quickly and there's little that can go wrong with a chair. But a general-rental store stocks an electric jackhammer that might cost $1,000 and is a delicate piece of machinery. Even though you rent it for $50 a day, the return on investment is not as fast." Because party renters usually keep items 24 hours or less, Charbonnet says a store with $50,000 worth of inventory should shoot for $100,000 in annual revenues, or twice what a general-rental center could hope for on the same inventory base. In party, your inventory buck buys a lot more.

SWITCH TO PURE PARTY

Those numbers suggested why numerous general-rental stores either switched entirely to party or added party sections to their lines. While contractors might not rent construction equipment as frequently during recessionary times, renters reasoned people always entertain. Indeed, instead of holding the wedding reception at a hotel, they may move it to the backyard. A rental center can provide everything from dinnerware for 100 to a parquet dance floor. Pat Chose says an average wedding reception rents $2,000 to $2,200 worth of goodies from his store.

HIT THE SPOT

Keith and Pat Klarin, who operate the Party Corner in Shrewsbury, New Jersey, and Party Line (which son Ronald manages) five miles away in Eatontown, say their Jersey shore patrons are great party throwers. Summer and holiday times keep busy a 20-person staff consisting primarily of college students. During slower winter months, 10 people run the business. Before you open a party store, make sure you can count on an affluent clientele. For the most part, you should locate in well-to-do suburbs or business districts. "Party rentals won't support an entire store in some suburban communities," warns New Orleans entrepreneur Don Charbonnet, although they may still represent profitable segments of a general-rental business. Rather than waste valuable retail space on items that don't command large volume, Charbonnet's 13 general-rental centers display samples of party goods and stock rental items in a central warehouse. "We can deliver to the customer's house in an hour." Also, some party centers take highly visible shopping mall cubbyholes just big enough to exhibit one of each rental item that they warehouse in low-rent districts.

Pat Chose says his suburban and urban customers represent two entirely different animals. "The San Francisco store does a tremendous commercial business through the week but not much on weekends. At Walnut Creek, individuals throw the parties on weekends." This difference allows Chose to swap merchandise between the two stores as the need arises.

THE MIX

Pat Chose's two stores also emphasize different inventory. In Walnut Creek, C&M Party Props stocks 12 garment racks, and most of the time keeps 11 on the floor. Most people attending parties in homes stash their minks in closets or in a spare bedroom and don't need garment racks. But in San Francisco, where offices hold parties in commercial settings, "we own 100 garment racks, and most are gone all the time." Also, commercial clients paying with corporate bankrolls spring for higher ticket items. "They want our $8 chairs, not those that rent for $2," says Chose.

Party rentors shop trade shows to come up with inventory, a job that's become easier the last few years. "Manufacturers like silver companies looked down their noses at rental centers until they began to see the potential of selling to us," says Chose. "Now they take booths at the trade shows." He says a recent ARA trade show devoted 140 booths to party exhibitors, compared to zero eight years earlier.

Pure party centers may get 40 percent of revenues from disposable items they sell rather than rent. Keith Klarin calls paper goods "a very lucrative business," pointing out that they don't need maintenance. Pat Chose pays particular attention to the colors paper manufacturers feature, and often buys rental inventory in matching shades. "The manufacturers featured lavender a year before every bride knew she had to have that," he says. "The manufacturers do the research for you."

Coming up with inventory to amuse all your customers is as much art as science. Rather than buy items that you may lend out just a couple of times a year, you may want to tap colleagues. For example, for Mardi Gras nights, you may want to subrent roulette wheels (and occasionally even blackjack dealers) from a theatrical supplier. Shop your competitors and offer to trade novelty equipment back and forth.

Customers will suggest some of your most imaginative items. One client wanted an unusual buffet, so Chose asked a prop house to build a "Winter Wonderland" table, complete with icebergs and various levels where dishes perched. "The client virtually pays the cost on the first rental," says Chose. "Then the friends see it and maybe pay a fee of 20 percent of the original charge the next time around." Given two weeks' notice, Chose will consider customizing anything that's practical for storage.

One of his favorite rental items is coffins—real ones that he rents for $35 a day. "We have eight coffin bars that are mounted on sawhorses and hold ice and bottles. The fraternities love them. For coffin buffets, we suggest they put in things like cold cuts and headcheese."

CONSULTING

Anyone in party rental takes consulting seriously. "The average person planning a reception for 100 has never had more than a couple of people over for dinner," Pat Chose points out. "We suggest things, like do you have enough coffee servers." In addition to winning grateful thanks from customers, such guidance also lands the rental center another $2.50 (for a stainless steel pitcher) to $45 (for a 100-cup silver samovar).

Pat Klarin acts as the Party Corner's resident party consultant. In addition to helping customers pick out the china and linen combinations, she recommends caterers, entertainment, and photographers. She typically visits the client's home to case the layout and offer aesthetic counsel if tents are involved. For a fee, the Party Corner even decorates. "There is a 15 percent surcharge if you want us to do the whole party, which involves lining up the caterer, the band, the flowers, and so on," says Keith. "But if you just want some random recommendations, the advice is on the house."

Rentors consider consulting just one of the services, along with deliveries and tent-raisings, which command fees on top of the rental price. Keith Klarin gives customers a number where they can reach someone from the Party Corner day or night. "Maybe the caterer didn't order dessert plates. They panic. We'll get a call at eight o'clock while the entree is being served and we rush the dessert plates over."

Such accommodation makes good business sense. Each reception for 100 people represents a potential selling ground for future parties any one of those 100 people may mount. This is your chance to show people who never considered renting how nice the experience can be.

As far as advertising goes, list under both "Parties" and "Rentals" in the Yellow Pages. Pat Chose sends "what's-new letters" describing innovative rental items to banquet managers at hotels and clubs. He also scans the newspaper society columns. "If the Symphony Committee is throwing a kick-off party in June, we call to see if we can be of service. If they cater it, we call their caterer."

CATERING TO CATERERS

The real business comes not from the occasional bar mitzvah but from frequent party throwers like the Cabot-Smythes and, especially, from caterers. "Once you get a caterer, they're with you for life," says Don Charbonnet. "They bring lots of repeat business."

Pat Chose set aside a special caterer's conference room when he designed his San Francisco store. The room, available free of charge, is chockablock with samples from the store's floor to encourage impulse sales. "Most caterers work out of their back pockets and never want the client to see their small kitchens," he reasons. Because caterers book the room eight to ten times a week, San Francisco Party profits not only from the caterer's business but also from the extras clients pick up on the way out of the store.

A few party rental centers have grown to legendary proportions. For example, Don Charbonnet speaks in awe of one

40,000-square-foot pure party rental center in Chicago. "Of course they service McCormick Place [one of the largest convention centers in the country]." The company's revenues aren't published, but Charbonnet can guess: "They have union drivers that make $30,000 a year."

SOURCE

Industry Association

American Rental Association, 1900 19th Street, Moline, IL 61265, (800) 334-2177

Tour Operator

Job Description: *A tour operator plans, organizes, and often leads groups of people on unusual and adventurous tours both in the United States and abroad.*

- *Start-up cost as low as $250*
- *Potential earnings: $25,000*
- *Breakeven time from initial investment: several months to one year*
- *Ideal home-based business*
- *No staffing required*

On a brilliant Vermont spring day, John Freidin and a couple of other professors from Middlebury College embarked on a biking weekend. As the sun splashed through the delicate new leaves, making a dappled pattern on the road ahead, Freidin breathed the crisp air and reveled in the exertion of pedaling the Vermont hills. He could practically taste the contrast to his workday life: his sedentary duties as a professor of history and education. His only conscious thoughts concerned the scenery around him, with a slight anticipation of the good meal and pleasant night's sleep at the country inn still hours down the road.

The next moments changed Freidin's life. "In the middle of the first afternoon, I got a flash that people would like to ride like this if they could stay in a cozy inn and get lots of good food." He reasoned that not everyone knew Vermont's country roads as well as he, and would welcome help in plotting routes and booking inns the right distance down those roads. Voilà! Vermont Bicycle Touring was born.

Freidin recently sold his Bristol, Vermont–based company for an undisclosed sum but, he says, "a price I was very happy with." Now he's taking time off to consult, sail, and visit family and friends he neglected while he was nurturing his business to annual revenues of $1.6 million. During those years, he was indeed busy: Vermont Bicycle Touring escorted 5,200 people a year on bike treks throughout Vermont and bordering states. Most clients come from the Northeast megalopolis, but Freidin's fame has spread throughout the fragmented tour operator network. "Freidin did it right," says a somewhat reverential Will Weber, founder of Journeys International Inc., of Ann Arbor, Michigan, an "adventure tour" outfit that arranges Tibetan treks and East African safaris.

TRIAL-AND-ERROR MANAGEMENT

By doing it right, Will Weber means managing a tour operation like a business. John Freidin went so far as to write his own 50-page rule book that he distributed to employees. In it he explains what to do in unusual situations, such as when a cyclist fails to bring a check. (Two possibilities: Either call Western Union with the client's credit card to get cash wired directly to

Vermont Bicycle for a fee charged to the client; or show the customer how to write a perfectly legal check on a blank piece of paper.)

For the most part, the far-flung tour guide industry has few rules and a seat-of-the-pants management style. Unlike the related travel-agency business, tour operators have no industry associations trade publications to guide them. Each new operator invents what works for the particular tours he or she conceives, which can range from two-hour mule rides in southwestern parks to round-the-world sails in schooners. Some plot "mundane" tours like six stops in ten days on a European vacation for schoolteachers. Others take scuba divers to the Great Barrier reef. But all operators devise boilerplate itineraries and orchestrate all the details, from air travel to accommodations. Entrepreneurs either lead expeditions themselves or arrange for guides. Successful tours shoot for 10 percent pretax profits after salary, but the revelation that you can make money doing what outsiders consider a continual vacation can be slow in coming.

ALL THIS AND MONEY, TOO?

Many dabblers lead excursions for the sheer fun of it, or as a way to pay for their own trips. They simply fail to recognize they can make a respectable living from a kayak and therefore don't pursue such business concerns as advertising or employee relations. Many operators are either young with few financial obligations or have other sources of income. Let's see how John Freidin did it.

After the weekend of the fateful "flash," Freidin acted decisively: "I immediately researched my first bike route and ran classified ads in *New York Magazine* and *Saturday Review of*

Literature." From the few inquiries he received, he persuaded three New Yorkers to take a debut trip in early August; approximately 75 cyclists signed up over the rest of the season, which lasts as long as Vermont's stunning fall foliage does. "Fortunately," he says wryly, "I was still drawing a salary and didn't have to make a living." The next year, Vermont Bicycle Touring made a little money, and within three years, "I was making more than I could as a teacher."

THE POWER OF THE PRESS

What happened to John Freidin is a boon to most entrepreneurs but almost a necessity to success in the travel field: Vermont Bicycle Touring got publicity. One cyclist told a friend about his trip—a friend who happened to be the editor of the *New York Times* travel section. Soon blurbs appeared in travel sections of the *Boston Globe* and other publications. Freidin admits the publicity "fell into my lap," but you can prod notices by sending press releases and invitations to travel writers. Advertising helps, too, especially if you pinpoint publications that appeal to your particular clientele. Will Weber, for example, prefers *Natural History Magazine.*

WHO WANTS TO GO?

Unlike travel agents, who compete for the greatest possible volume of *local* clientele, tour operators see the world as their neighborhood. If you offer helicopter ski tours in British Columbia, for example, you may be better off advertising in *Ski Magazine* than in the Vancouver newspaper. Knowing only a tiny percentage of the locals will ever book from them, Journeys International does not even list in the Ann Arbor phone book. "Our clients are from all over the world—Mexico, Hong Kong, Japan," says Will Weber. "It's the old global village thing." While such a far-flung clientele may be hard to round up in the first place, it represents a more stable base. "If the largest local business should close down, we don't worry that it'll affect our market," says Weber.

Most operators court steady repeat business, whether they lead $300 bike trips or $3,000 adventure tours. "On every trip, at least a couple of people have been with us on previous trips," says Weber. "We really try hard with the final dinner to leave a good impression." The best leads on new vacationers are referrals of satisfied clients. Journeys International asks participants which friends might be interested and adds their names to its mailing list.

SEND US $3,000 . . .

Will Weber's complicated operation, with revenues "of more than $1 million," began the year he and his wife started graduate studies after returning from Nepal, where Will had been in the Peace Corps. "There was nothing at the time that was affordable and offered the cross-cultural experience. All the groups stayed in Western hotels. Our idea was to experience the everyday life you can only get if you mix with the culture," explains Will, who later received his Ph.D. in natural resources.

Will and Joan Weber posted announcements on University of Michigan bulletin boards and landed a radio interview. The process took months. "When two grad students suggest people send them a $3,000 check and offer to take care of all the arrangements . . . well, you just don't have much credibility," admits Will. But ten people eventually signed up, which "basically paid our way back to see friends in Nepal." Unless you are prepared to be satisfied with only the free trips and can forsake financial profits, Will recommends "either money for lots of advertising, or patience."

You also need contacts. "I remember trying to get help from the airlines" in booking a group rate, says Will. "Nobody was interested in talking to us until a man from Air India came out in his big car and took us to lunch. He asked why we didn't advertise, and we admitted we had no money. But he liked our enthusiasm and believed we were worth a gamble. So he gave us $50—'Here, take this and run an ad,' just like that." Needless to say, Journeys International booked not only that first trip but many subsequent flights on Air India. When trying to drum up clients or contacts, dress the part and act as professional as your budget permits. Printed brochures, for example, add to your credibility.

WHO WILL LEAD YOUR TOURS?

Once you grow beyond leading all tours yourself, you must find knowledgeable employees who stay around for more than a year. Many operations are seasonal, providing income only during the six-month tourist season or for the half-dozen 16-day safaris a tour group books. If you're the owner, you either stockpile enough profits to see you through the dry months or book counterseasonal tours. But if you're an employee, your options are more limited.

To keep employees aboard, John Freidin created a byzantine bonus system, based on the number of days a tour guide worked

and the number of people taking trips. More seasoned operators earned higher salaries, says Freidin, who now consults for
others interested in starting tour operations. Many Vermont
Bicycle employees hold traditional jobs during the week and
lead tours on weekends for the joint motives of additional income and the opportunity to pursue their cycling hobby.

Freidin found local newspaper ads attracted appropriate
guides, probably because "the type of person who chooses to
live in Vermont likes exercise and the outdoors." In addition,
don't neglect your own customers. They've already demonstrated their love of your business by paying money to participate, and the most knowledgeable or athletic may be good
employee prospects. Freidin says he got a surprising number of
unsolicited inquires "from people who took tours and decide
they'd like to work for us."

Familiarity with your territory—whether it's Kenya or
Colorado—helps in finding employees. The Webers tapped
sherpas they knew in Nepal who arrange local travel and accommodations, in addition to serving as guides. Some operators contract with established guide operations or book part of
a tour through travel agencies. But Will maintains that such
profit-sharing eats at margins and also crowds you out of the
experience you're trying to provide. "How can you recommend
a particular guide whom you don't even know?" he asks.
Journeys International employs only locals. The practice keeps
costs down, even if you pay American wages. And natives bring
a wealth of intimate knowledge no outsider can ever attain. A
U.S. guide leading Americans leaves vacationers with an
American experience, Will argues.

While you should probably understand birdwatching before
you lead a group of birdwatchers to the Galápagos Islands, you
don't have to live in Bangkok to offer tours in Thailand. Just

hire someone who knows the territory. Before Journeys International establishes a new destination, Will visits the country, sometimes taking a tour with an existing company. Such scouting serves two purposes: "You need some personal credibility—the ability to talk to people about your own experiences." Also, visits allow him to shop for the right local employee.

YOU CAN BUY A BOAT OR START WITH ZIP

No average start-up cost exists in tour operations. Will estimates he spends $10,000 to set up a new trip, including $2,000 for promotion and mailings and $2,000 for an on-site visit. His computer helps him write itineraries and sort mailing lists and contacts with airlines and travel agencies through which he writes tickets. Launching windjammer cruises off Maine could be far more expensive; you must buy, rent, or (if you're really handy—and patient) build a seaworthy vessel.

However, many operators start with no capital at all, using deposits from customers to finance early costs and profits from the first trip to buy additional equipment and advertising. Let's assume you are an experienced whitewater expert who leads excursions down the Snake River. Your basic equipment includes a raft, life jackets, and cooking implements. After a couple of springs building a reputation in Idaho, you might put together an expedition to the Rio de la Plata in Argentina. If you are unsure of details, subcontract with an existing operator. You provide the river expertise and, on that first trip at least, let the old hand arrange travel and accommodations. Next time around, pull the entire package together without the partner. Eventually you may establish a local office and employees while you scout out new rivers and new expeditions.

THE AGENCY CONNECTION

Most tour operators are not travel agents, although a growing number of agencies also devise tours. In order to collect airline fees and issue tickets, an agent must meet certain standards of financial responsibility, business experience, and personnel requirements, which may be beyond most tour start-ups. However, you may want to strike up relationships with various travel agents. If you agree to fork over a share of your bookings, agencies will book their customers on your tours. Or you can turn one specific aspect of your tour, such as airfare, over to an agency. Journeys International writes airline tickets through agents, splitting the commissions 50-50. Because it gets a cut of the airfare, the company can hold land costs to about $50 a day.

It's true you will get your share of freebies, although most operators turn down more trips than they take. Will Weber cites as reasons both business demands as the company grows and the desire to spend time at home with wife Joan and five-year-old daughter Robin. However, the whole family came along on a 16-day family excursion one year. The experience was so successful from both business and personal standpoints that Will plans to schedule one or two family outings a year from now on. When the founder of Journeys International speaks of family trips, he's not talking about a week at Disneyland. His Family Trek was to Nepal.

Journeys International's local representatives met the ten-person group in Kathmandu. After two days in a small local hotel, the participants took land vehicles 200 kilometers to the

Himalayas. "Every night we set up camp after an easy walk—three, four, or five hours," recalls Will. They eventually climbed to a comfortable 8,000 feet. The weather was balmy, although snow one night added to the experience. "The villagers had seen Westerners but never Western kids, so they were real curious. Every afternoon we tried to learn Nepali songs and teach them English ones." At dusk, the group moved into tents where they talked about the majestic vistas and hospitality of their new friends, and played games with the children. Nepalese chefs who were part of the expedition prepared five-course dinners. Soon the group went to sleep, anticipating a wake-up call in time to see dawn frame the mountains.

Videographer

Job Description: *A videographer documents various events for posterity, such as weddings, bar and bat mitzvahs, and other special occasions.*

- *Start-up cost as low as $1,500*
- *Potential first-year earnings: $25,000*
- *Breakeven time from initial investment: one month to two years*
- *Ideal home-based business*
- *No staffing required*

A CTION: You pull back from the white lilies to the lilac softness of the bridesmaids. You glance at your sound equipment when Aunt Minerva begins singing "Oh, Promise Me." As you zoom in on the groom's sober handsomeness, you nod to your assistant in the corner to pan the crowd. The camera catches the tears on Granny's cheeks and the giggles from the nephews in the second pew. As the organ sounds the opening chords of the "Wedding March," you direct your video recorder at the rear of the chapel.

ROLL 'EM: You point the camera at Rutherford Beauford Smythe, the richest curmudgeon this town has ever seen. He recites the bit about being of sound mind and body in a straightforward manner, but leans forward with a gleeful gleam in his eyes when he mentions his brother and only living heir. "Just wanted to let you know, Rodney, that I meant it when I called you a good-for-nothing. You may have bamboozled Mother, but not me. You're not getting a cent of my millions, because I'm leaving it all to the Society for Siamese Cat Research."

VIDEO FOR FUN AND PROFIT

Video technology has opened opportunities to a new group of professional videographers. Some assignments require highly skilled artistry, such as taping a high school talent contest where baton twirlers and disco dancers perform under rotating lights. Other situations—taping a legal deposition or an interview for a video dating service, for instance—mostly demand a steady hand or a tripod and some bright lights.

The possibilities in video production are limited only by the imagination. In addition to traditional filming forums, such as recording news and entertainment events, videographers now tape consumer specials, such as a bat mitzvah. In the legal realm, states increasingly allow videotaped depositions and "day-in-the-life-of" tapes that show how an injury affects an accident victim's daily routine. Real estate agents show clients videotapes instead of driving them from house to house. Manufacturers send training videos as part of their product package. Trade associations and universities, job applicants and video dates—everybody sees video as a vehicle to get their point across.

HERE'S THE RUB

Video possibilities may be unlimited, but to turn them into a living wage, you've got to convince buyers they need your service. Videographers may spend as much time educating the public about their services as they do on assignments.

As a videographer operating in the booming video revolution, you've got a choice. Either you can work part time at videotaping, or you can create full-time opportunities by selling as if your livelihood depends on it.

WEEKEND WORK

Especially if you concentrate on the consumer end—taping parties, weddings, or even household possessions for insurance purposes—you can start part time. Most assignments fall on weekends anyway. Professional videographers recommend working with party providers to advertise your services by placing signs or business cards in their shops. For example, bridal shops, florists, printers, and so on are all frequented by couples planning their weddings. If you want to reach people throwing parties or gala affairs, try putting your information at catering halls or gourmet food stores that might cater such events.

You can track down the party givers yourself. Check the society pages of your newspaper for engagement announcements and synagogue records for upcoming bar and bat mitzvahs.

Match their names with addresses from the phone book, and send them a flyer explaining your services.

You don't need much capital to start because companies rent equipment. As for the advantages of renting, "You're always assured of getting the most up-to-date machines," writes Canape. "You never have to worry about repair and maintenance. You don't have to worry about storing your gear or insuring it."

The disadvantage: Renting can be expensive. When you build enough volume to warrant purchasing equipment, select brands that will be compatible with pieces you plan to add later. In addition to the basics (a camera, player, and color monitor), you may start with lights and sound equipment and a van to lug around all the paraphernalia. If you don't want to spring for editing equipment right away, you can rent editing facilities— or even farm the work out to editors—for $25 to $75 an hour, depending on how fancy you want to get. Outfitting a sophisticated production and editing studio and hiring an assistant or two might push start-up costs to $250,000.

JUMPING IN WITH BOTH FEET

If you decide to enter video production full time, chances are you've studied the technique either in college or with a production company. Some manufacturers provide fairly sophisticated training, as well.

While consumer taping can be lucrative, the anniversary or sweet-16 party you tape is a one-time affair. Likewise, legal taping may offer repeat business from a few clients but probably not enough to pay all the bills in the beginning. So don't specialize in your first year. Instead, start with a variety of assignments from as many avenues as possible. If you keep your sales hat on the same rack with your creative hat, you may come up with video opportunities potential clients haven't thought of before.

There are three ways to make money in this business: charge a lot for single assignments, resell the same tape many times, or cultivate repeat customers. Single windfalls come primarily to those who build massive reputations. Clients include cable networks and local television stations that need extra footage. Multiple sales—beyond commercial hits like aerobic tapes— require marketing imagination. For example, Gruenberg Video Group Inc. of New York City sells video yearbooks to high school students. Entrepreneur Paul Gruenberg trains student crews at various schools to tape events during the year. He hires freelance editors to pull visions of proms and pep rallies into a final, $30 product, complete with background music and clips of newsworthy events of the year.

TAPING ATTORNEYS

But most videographers look for repeat business: for example, relationships with attorneys. If you pursue the legal market, first bone up on what's acceptable in your state. Some states don't allow video wills. Others restrict what can be taped during a deposition or the manner in which it can be photographed. For example, most courts prefer a stationary camera to zooms and fade-outs.

To tap the legal market, mail an introductory letter to lawyers whose names you've rented from a local bar association or chosen from the Yellow Pages. You can advertise in local legal journals, although Jerry Fried, president of Ace Audio Visual Co. in Woodside, New York, warns that telemarketing or direct mail can be expensive. "I feel our service is need-based. When the customer needs the service, they look you up in the Yellow Pages." Ace advertises in the Yellow Pages under legal services, videotaping, and audiovisual equipment.

Once you get an attorney's attention, delineate the advantages of video: For example, you can tape patients who are too sick to appear in court. If there's reason to suspect a will may be contested, an attorney might suggest a video version. The judge can decide whether he or she was competent when making the will by seeing and hearing the deceased.

In addition, "Most [legal] videographers say the best way to get started is by associating yourself with a court reporting service" that takes depositions, says Charlene Canape. "Most lawyers still insist that a written record be kept in addition to the video record."

VIDEO BARTERING

In the beginning, you may have to tape a few events for free so you'll have sample videotapes to show. Why not offer your services to professionals whose help you could use? For example, tape the accoutrements and handiwork of a caterer who might recommend your services. Record a party for an advertising company executive who will help you design your brochures.

When taping an event, Canape recommends that you get specific orders from the person who commissioned the tape. "Are there certain activities (a toast, a receiving line, the arrival of an important guest) that you must be sure not to miss? Are there certain people who should be photographed more than others?" Visit the scene ahead of time to see what lighting is needed. If you're shooting a wedding, check with the church to make sure your equipment is permitted.

Since video equipment is easy to use, many people will tape their own events. But "a video involves more than just letting the camera roll," says Jerry Fried, referring to "script writing, setting up scenes, adding titles in the editing, setting up locations." Just as shutterbugs who squeeze off millions of shots turn to professional photographers for formal portraits, it's a sure bet that video hobbyists will call on professional videographers.

"Whodunit" Producer

Job Description: *A "whodunit" producer puts on murder mysteries for clients.*
- *Start-up cost as low as $1,000*
- *Potential earnings: $20,000*
- *Breakeven time from initial investment: several months to one year*

I t's 1927 . . . the Jazz Age. Flappers in short skirts and strings of pearls sip champagne from teacups (Prohibition, remember?) and dance with escorts wearing striped trousers and morning coats. One hundred friends and assorted characters are welcoming world-famous musician Rock Barrett back to his hometown. Rumors circulating about the attempt made on Rock's life don't dim the festive mood—that is, until gunshots leave Rock in a pool of blood. Stretcher-bearers whisk away the dying musician, followed by his hysterical fiancée and his old friend Henri De La Mer, the famous French detective. Murder is afoot.

600 A YEAR

You're in a murder mystery weekend. Created to entice arm-chair sleuths to English seaside resorts during the off-season, murder mystery weekends crossed the Atlantic in the 1970s. In addition to strictly amateur productions, at least half a dozen professional troupes stage whodunits in hotels, trains, cruise ships, resorts, restaurants, and even trade shows. David-Michael Kenney guesses professionals commit 600 such crimes a year. His Philadelphia-based company, DMK Productions Inc., produces the *Jazz Mystery*, in which Henri De La Mer solves the murder described above.

DMK alone produced 66 mysteries in one recent year, con-tributing about a third of the company's $175,000 in revenues. (The company also stages operas, cabaret shows, and other forms of entertainment for corporate clients.) Murder mysteries that involve the audience as unscripted characters are a form of entertainment that Kenney calls "participatory special events." Kenney, who has been a stage manager since age 17, explains: "People watch 125 satellite stations on TV, not to mention videotapes. You can even shop at home through the tube. There's no reason to leave the house. We bring people into your establishment."

PULLING IT ALL TOGETHER

To be sure, not all murder mysteries are as elaborate as DMK's, which writes all its scripts specifically for the occasion. For $7,000, DMK gives a client seven Equity actors who stage five acts between Friday evening and Sunday brunch. The guests—

sometimes as many as 100—receive their own character bios with hints on costumes and personality type. For the first-night soirée, DMK provides a five-person jazz combo; on the second night, a ragtime pianist performs.

While creativity is the absolute key to devising an outstanding whodunit, attention to professionalism adds the polishing touches. For example, the wireless microphones that the actors wear during the prime-rib dinner, cocktail parties, and Sunday brunch alone cost DMK $400 per weekend. Lighting to focus attention on the proper action runs another $100. Now that David-Michael Kenney amortizes the cost of costumes, props, and scripts over all his performances, he keeps 20 percent, or $1,400, as pretax profits from each performance. But, not counting marketing, a start-up company might need $15,000 to pay for all the essentials for that first production, including the renting of facilities for rehearsal and the buying of costumes.

Of course, some mysteries are far less expensive to stage. Amateur actors rounded up from local universities don't command Actor's Equity wages. Some productions follow a basic outline but no real script, so royalties to playwrights are not a consideration. (The plot can't duplicate a famous Agatha Christie novel, however; the guests would already know the murderer.) You can ask the hotel to provide its own music. And single-evening performances need fewer props and costumes than do three-day affairs. But the more elaborate the production, the more a hotel or cruise ship can charge its guests, and therefore the more you charge as a production company.

PUBLICITY STUNTS

The Mystery at the Palace weekends began as a publicity vehicle to create an image for the newest jewel in the Trusthouse Forte chain. "Mystery weekends spread the word of who we are and what we do in an upscale way," explains the director of public relations for Philadelphia's elegant Palace. "Mysteries started as a PR event, and now they are a profit center." The hotel has other expenses on top of the $7,000 fee to DMK, such as salaries for hotel employees, food and beverage costs, and advertising. But at nearly $500 per couple, the Palace brings in $25,000 for each of the seven to nine mystery weekends it stages each year, not counting what guests spend on such extras as cocktails when they meet to compare clues in the lounge.

"But I warn hotels they won't make money until they commit at least three weekends," says David-Michael Kenney. "People don't respond to the first advertising as well as they do after word spreads. Also, collateral costs are high. Printing alone runs $1,500 for items like name tags, notes we slip under doors, and bios for 120 different characters."

SELLING THE SIZZLE

Kenney says you have to sell the benefits once a hotel manager or cruise ship entertainment director realizes the actual cost of the extravaganza. "I recommend they borrow from their advertising and promotion budget to pay for the weekend. The event brings people in to sample the accommodations and meals, which generates long-range business. The Palace has found many of its guests are decision makers for corporations. They're involved in selecting meeting facilities or accommodations for VIP guests. Mysteries showcase the hotel." They also generate publicity. Two networks have filmed segments of the Palace's weekends; Kenney screens those videotapes as a selling tool.

If all goes according to plan on the initial mystery, managers and employees get hooked and usually come back for more. "It's a morale builder," says Kenney. "We use a real waiter who has been paid to kill the detective. He says: 'Henri, I have something for you,' and pulls out a gun." Employees fight over who gets to work weekends and can't wait for rehearsal. Kenney, who assumes the role of Slim, the Maintenance Man, to allow him to cue hotel employees unobtrusively, says getting the manager involved is a key to repeat business. "If the manager has the personality to pull off the role of manager in the script, jump right in and ask him to play the part."

ALL THE WORLD'S A STAGE

David-Michael Kenney expects murder mysteries to survive a long run and points to contracts he has gotten from clients just discovering the concept. Corporations book hotels or restaurants for one-night Christmas parties or sales incentive dinners, and spring the murder unannounced. One corporation hired DMK to devise a two-act script that takes place over dinner and breakfast the next morning. The event was an ice-breaker to integrate a new 40-person research staff into the corporation. Another corporation asked for a seven-day cruise ship mystery with parts for 400 people. Instead of cocktail parties where everyone gravitates to their own cliques, the mysteries throw people together in a unique way.

DMK sees murder mysteries as just one phase of interactive entertainment. "We're developing a trade show script that requires everyone to go to each booth and exchange a business card for a piece of the puzzle," says Kenney. "Another participatory event is the scavenger hunt. Or Ben Franklin takes families on a tour of Philadelphia. When they get to the Liberty Bell, some of his friends happen to be there from other colonies and together they act out history."

In the age of the passive boob tube, interactive entertainment provides involvement. "We're a catalyst," says Kenney, "a device to get people involved."

SOURCE

Industry Association

Actors' Equity Association, 165 West 46th Street, New York, NY 10036, (212) 869-8530

Index of Businesses

About the Authors

RUSSELL ROBERTS is a full-time freelance writer with seven previously published books and over 200 short stories and articles. He resides in Bordentown, New Jersey.

The Philip Lief Group is a Princeton-based book developer that produces a wide range of books for small businesses, including 220 *Best Franchises to Buy* and *Moonlighting*. The Philip Lief Group has been singled out by the *New York Times* for its "consistent bestsellers" and by *Time* magazine for being "bottom-line think tankers."